ADVENTURE HOLIDAYS
WORLDWIDE

ADVENTURE HOLIDAYS WORLDWIDE

James Ogilvie

In Print

In Print Publishing Ltd is registered with the Publishers Licensing Society in the UK and the Copyright Clearance Center in the USA.

The right of James Ogilvie to be identified as the author of this work has been asserted by him in accordance with the Copyright, Designs and Patents Act, 1988.

British Library Cataloguing in Publication Data: A catalogue record for this book is available from the British Library.

ISBN 1 873047 36 3

Cover design by Russell Townsend
Front cover photographs, from top – Matterhorn at dawn by Conrad Dickinson; Guerba expedition truck by James Ogilvie; Sunset in Malaysia by Susan Thompson
Silhouettes by Stephen Pardue
Maps by Catherine Lawrence
Typeset by MC Typeset Ltd
Printed by Bell and Bain

First published in 1996 by
In Print Publishing Ltd, 9 Beaufort Terrace, Brighton BN2 2SU, UK.
Tel: (01273) 682836. Fax: (01273) 620958.

To J.W.O.

Foreword

Places marked *terra incognita* on the map when I was young are now included in the itineraries of many package holidays. When I first walked in the Himalayas, they were still home to over 40 million people who lived sustainable lifestyles, untainted by the devices and desires of our civilization. Today most of those ways of life are gone, their timeless societies victims of aid packages based on so-called sustainable development, often centred on adventure tourism.

Plastic litter, mountain bikes, four-wheel drive, hang-gliding, helipads, air strips, high-rise, and all the paraphernalia of the 21st century, soon follow the trail of our boot prints. Little wonder that Sir Edmund Hilary once said to me that the only thing that made him glad to be getting old was that he didn't want to live to see the day when you could get to base camp Everest by motorway. We both had to concede that tourism, now the world's number one industry, isn't going to go away and that it is the back-packers and the kayakists who are among the first to join the picket lines of green protest.

So despite the fact that there are now public toilets on the flanks of Everest, we must all continue to put our own houses in order and campaign to safeguard those areas of wilderness that are still left, for all our futures.

This book, packed full of information and good advice (I wish I were 40 years younger) is certainly a high-tech footstep in the right direction.

Take only pictures, cast only shadows, leave only ripples of understanding as you travel the world.

David Bellamy

About the author
James Ogilvie's passion for adventure travel, writing and forestry has taken him to many corners of the world, including two years living and travelling in Africa. As well as researching adventure travel for *The Economist*, he has edited a number of books, including *The 100 Greatest Holidays in the World*. Educated in Edinburgh and Oxford (Balliol College) he now lives in Northumberland with his wife Rachel, son Charles and daughter Imogen.

Contributors
Conrad Dickinson; Donald Greig; Jean Howat; Penny Grennan; Alison Stancliffe; Polly Williams.

Acknowledgments
I owe a great debt to many who, over a period of several years, helped me to turn the concept of this book into a reality. At the outset, Katie Wood helped me off down the travel writing road. From the early days, Conrad Dickinson's drive and enthusiasm were instrumental in pushing the whole project along. Latterly, Michael Popkin unwrinkled and indexed the text with considerable professionalism. Penny Grennan also proved to be an able adviser. In particular, I want to thank my publishers In Print for being clear-sighted exceptions in a uniformly myopic field.

Most of all, however, I want to thank Rachel for her patience, forebearance, support and tolerance throughout the long gestation period of *Adventure Holidays Worldwide*.

James Ogilvie

Table of contents

Foreword (by David Bellamy) vii
About the author/acknowledgments viii
Using the guide xii

Section 1: Background 1
Why go and what to expect 4
Where to go for what 8
How to go 13
Health 17
Weather, and when to go 21
Preparation for going 23
Responsible tourism 29

Section 2: Companies 36
Arctic Experience 36
Discover the World 37
Dragoman 38
Encounter Overland 39
Exodus 40
ExplorAsia 41
Explore Worldwide 42
Guerba Expeditions 43
Sherpa Expeditions 46
Super Natural Adventures 47
Trailfinders 48
Trek America 49
Wexas 50
World Expeditions 51
Worldwide Journeys and Expeditions 52

Section 3: Activities 53
Ballooning 55
Canoeing and kayaking 57
Caving 59
Climbing and mountaineering 61
Dog sledging 65
Expeditions 67
Hang-gliding 70
Mountain biking 72
Overlanding 74
Paragliding 77
River rafting 79

Riding and pony trekking 82
Safaris 84
Scuba diving 86
Ski touring 89
Tall-ship sailing 92
Trekking 95
Youth activities 98

Section 4: Countries **101**
Antarctica 101
Australia 104
Bahamas 108
Belize 113
Bhutan 116
Borneo 120
Botswana 124
Brazil 127
British Virgin Islands 130
Cameroon 132
Canada: British Columbia 135
Canada: Northwest Territories 140
Canada: The Yukon 143
Cayman Islands 147
Chile 150
China 154
Ecuador 158
The Faroe Islands 162
Fiji 165
Finland 168
The Gambia 172
Greenland 175
Iceland 178
India 182
Indonesia 187
Jamaica 191
Kenya 195
Lesotho 198
Malawi 201
Morocco 205
Namibia 208
Nepal 212
New Zealand 217
Norway 220
Papua New Guinea 224
Peru 226
Russian Federation 229
St Vincent and the Grenadines 233
South Africa 237
Svalbard 242
Tanzania 245

Thailand 249
Tibet 253
UK 256
USA: Alaska 260
US Virgin Islands 264
Venezuela 267
Vietnam 271
Zambia 273
Zimbabwe 276

Appendixes **280**
Country data 280
The Himalayan Tourist Code 290

Indexes .... ⁻**291**
Countries and what they offer 291
Activities and where to find them 294
Tour operators 296

Using the guide

Adventure Holidays Worldwide comprises four main sections. **Section 1** provides a general introduction to adventure travel, with essential information on such topics as health, preparations for going, and ecotourism. **Section 2** profiles a selection of key tour operators in the adventure travel market. **Section 3** is a chapter-by-chapter guide to 18 different activities. **Section 4** outlines recommended locations and activity highlights in over 50 countries.

The detailed **Table of Contents** provides a complete breakdown of all the chapters in the book. See **Index 1** for 'Countries and What They Offer'; **Index 2** for 'Activities and Where To Find Them'; and **Index 3** for 'Tour Operators'. **Appendix 1** provides basic facts and figures for all countries covered, while **Appendix 2** sets out the Himalayan Tourist Code.

Throughout the guide addresses and/or phone and fax numbers are supplied for all companies and organizations mentioned. At time of going to press, these have been carefully checked for accuracy – inevitably some will change over time. Similarly, prices of holidays are correct at time of going to press, but these are also subject to change, and are included primarily as indicators of the cost levels of the holidays suggested rather than as the exact amounts that will be charged. Specific holiday packages reviewed in Section 4 may change in the detail of their itineraries, and again are intended primarily to provide a practical illustration of the kinds of options that are available.

Note: The only companies in Sections 3 and 4 for which no addresses are supplied are those highlighted in Section 2, where their full contact details are provided.

Any additional or updating information is welcome. Please write to the author c/o In Print Publishing Ltd.

SECTION 1
Background

'Adventure travellers don't know where they're going next: tourists have no idea where they've been.'

Anon

That famous traveller and writer Samuel Johnson once remarked, 'The grand object of travelling is to see the shores of the Mediterranean.' In the 18th century this may have been the case, but nobody then could possibly have imagined the dramatic changes which would make today's world such a different place. The era of European Grand Tours has been swept inexorably away in a 20th century tide of Westernization, homogenization and 'coca-colanization'. Taking its place has been the philosophy of 'cheap holidays for all' and thus in the 1960s the great package holiday boom sprang forth. But this late 20th century trend towards mass tourism has brought its downside. Especially over the last two decades, the conveyor-belt mass-holiday machine has become distinctly lacklustre – even tacky, as falling trade statistics have shown. Many people have become bored with their conventional holiday, fed up with yet another two-week jaunt to some bland concrete costa or other. However, there are signs that the mass-market mould is starting to break, for a new kind of traveller is emerging. After years of mass continental travel, Western holidaymakers have gained increased confidence abroad and such confidence is playing a key part in the swing towards semi-independent travel: we've been there, done that, bought the T-shirt – now we want to experience the real thing without being chaperoned by a clipboard-clutching rep.

So today's tourists are becoming more discerning and demanding consumers. Compared with previous generations they have more leisure time, more disposable income and more awareness of the world's wild places. Television documentaries and travel programmes have fostered an interest in other countries, other environments and other cultures. With awareness and expectations thus raised, such tourists are in search of an entirely different holiday experience, an experience which captures some of the excitement of 'real' travel, but in a safe and controlled fashion,

1

sometimes alone, often with friends and increasingly as part of a small but like-minded group. Such travellers want to be challenged physically and refreshed spiritually: they want to visit untouched wildernesses and encounter diverse cultures. As never before, there is a desire for *adventure holidays worldwide*.

> 'Today's responsible travellers are keen to experience the wilderness jungle before it shrinks to become a global village. They want an exotic and active holiday with a high "feel good" factor and which carries credibility among their peers'.
>
> *Michael Palin*

So what exactly is an adventure holiday? Its definition has become somewhat blurred, as the industry has continued to evolve, but basically *an adventure holiday is one which contains an element of personal challenge through controlled risk, daring and excitement, often in a wilderness or remote area.* This kind of holiday provides a break from the humdrum of daily life, giving travellers a chance to renew their spirits, refresh their bodies and recharge their minds.

There are some problems of perception, however. For many the word 'adventure' conjures up images of people undertaking tasks of heroic dimensions, like Ranulph Fiennes or Colonel Blashford-Snell, Clare Francis or Ffyona Campbell. Mistakenly, there's a common belief that you need the digestion of a goat and the machismo of Indiana Jones before you can think about even signing up to such a trip. The overland tour is still widely associated with drug-seeking dropouts, and – worse still – there's a prevailing view that adventure equals danger and that in committing yourself to such a trip, you may be on a one-way ticket to the hereafter.

Nothing could be further from the truth. Although some early adventure companies did exist on a wing and a prayer and a battered old Landrover, those fly-by-night, cowboy outfits have long since disappeared. Taking their place today is a cadre of professional, responsible and reputable companies who are concerned about the safety of their clients' health and the security of their clients' money. Thus affiliations to – and financial bonding with – regulatory bodies such as the **Association of British Travel Agents**, the **Civil Aviation Authority** via its **Air Travel Operator's Licence Scheme (ATOL)** and the **Association of Independent Tour Operators (AITO)** are almost universal now among British adventure tour operators (see p 16).

> 'Public perception has not yet caught up with the style and standards of adventure holidays currently available.'
>
> *John Gillies, Director, Exodus*

So what does this more mature industry offer in the way of holidays to those in search of adventure? A great deal, is the short answer. Nowadays there is an ever-increasing array of off-the-shelf adventure itineraries, an almost bewildering plethora of holidays, from 'soft' trips right through to 'hard' expeditions. For example, at the soft end of the range we find such vacations as lodge-based vehicle safaris in Africa, low-altitude hut trekking in Scandinavia or balloon trips in Australia; while the hard end of the spectrum includes white-water rafting in Africa, high-altitude Himalayan tented treks and Arctic dog sledging expeditions. When describing adventure activities, it is possible to categorize them into **water-based** (for example, canoeing, kayaking, white-water rafting, tall-ship sailing, scuba diving, snorkelling and sailboarding), **snow-based** (such as winter mountaineering, dog sledging and cross-country skiing), **air-based** (like hang-gliding, parascending, parachuting and ballooning), **land-based** (such as trekking, caving and riding), and **vehicle-based** (for instance overlanding and vehicle safaris). In Section 3, eighteen adventure activities are featured, from ballooning to youth activities.

But this panoply of activities is only half of what makes up an adventure holiday: the other half of the equation is a remote and inaccessible destination. Lack of easy access and isolation from the trappings of Western civilization and culture: these are the hallmarks of an adventure destination. Despite our poor track record of destroying our environment, there are still, fortunately, remote places left in the world and in Section 4 of this book many of these are described. Every continent is covered, and over fifty different countries are selected and profiled. But it is not enough to describe the 'where' (places visited) and the 'what' (activities experienced): the 'who takes you' part of the adventure holiday is also important, so this is covered in Section 2. Each of these sections is intended to give you a feel for – and useful information about – the vast array of off-the-shelf adventure possibilities available today, to help you decide what kind of holiday suits you best.

So much for the definition. What of the experience itself – and the rewards? Fifty years ago, the only way to discover the world was to explore it. Today the world has effectively been explored, but there still remains for each of us a personal journey of self-discovery, in which we search for an answer to life's big questions. To you – the international adventurer – your trip will provide a challenging opportunity, an exciting experience, and, in the end, a sense of accomplishment. All right, so you may not be the first person ever to have set foot on a certain wilderness or the first person ever to have observed a particular species of wildlife. But each new experience will be a personal 'first' to you. Yes, it's a cliché, but your holiday *will* broaden your mind, it *will* widen your horizons, and it *will* lead you to discover something more about yourself. It *will* lead to lasting memories and – if you're lucky – it may even lead to enduring friendships. But beware! . . . a word of warning before you set off. Once bitten with the adventure travel bug, you'll be forever smitten. In the words of an adventure tour leader . . .

> ' "Is it worth it?" you ask yourself, as you step outside the tent at dawn to see the Himalayas doing passionate pink headstands all the way from Bengal to Baltoro, or as you and your group drift down the Nile till midnight below a desert full moon, and . . . what was the question?'
>
> *John Borthwick, The Adventurers Magazine*

WHY GO – AND WHAT TO EXPECT

> If you have health, a great craving for adventure, at least a moderate fortune, and can set your heart on a definite object, which old travellers do not think impracticable, then – travel by all means.
>
> *Francis Galton, 1872*

Those who decide to take an adventure holiday do so for a whole range of reasons. Many are drawn to the appeal of the *great outdoors*, emerging from their urban 'rat race' rut for a few precious weeks in the year to experience the call of the wild. Others go for *activity* – to get fit or even to lose weight – through physical challenges like hiking, mountain biking and ski-touring. For others it's the chance of seeing *wild animals* in their natural setting: an African safari or a Canadian whale watching trip for instance. Still others are drawn to the lure of *water and the sea*: navigating river rapids, crewing a tall ship or exploring sub-marine environments. And for some it's about *relationships* – one way to holiday with someone you wouldn't normally go away with alone for instance, or a way of spanning the family generation gap.

> 'Adventure travel, in our definition, is far from routine, totally unlike the usual crowded tour with visits in crowded places. Adventurers . . . are noted for their teamwork and close companionship. They often penetrate regions where few travellers have preceded them, and where they experience the luxury of stillness.'
>
> *Pat Dickerman, Adventure Travel North America*

So what sort of people actually take adventure holidays? Preconceptions can be misleading: the once-popular image of adventure travellers as young, long-haired, peripatetic paupers is utterly outdated. Although most participants today *are* aged between 20 and 45, many travellers fall outside this age range. In practice the characteristic requirement is not age *per se* but rather *attitude* – in short, a spirit of adventure and enthusiasm. Older people are often well able to cope with the rigours of these holidays. Unexpectedly perhaps, even Saga Holidays – a company which caters for the over-60s – offers a creditable array of adventure holidays for 'wrinklies', including cross-country skiing in Austria, trekking in the Himalayas and safaris in Kenya.

'The market for older people is supposed to be the most staid and boring part of the travel industry. That couldn't be more wrong. Each new year of retirees brings in customers who are more demanding than ever. They are the most sophisticated travellers in the marketplace.'

Roger de Haan, Chairman of Saga Holidays

At the opposite end of the spectrum, there are growing numbers of younger 'wannabe' adventurers; teenagers who perhaps lack the confidence or funds to participate in a trip abroad. Happily, adventures for this group can often start on home ground. For example, the **British Activity Holidays Association**, which deals with action and adventure holidays for the younger age group, reported a membership of at least 70 centres offering adventure holidays in 1995. Since the emphasis during these vacations is on individual and group reliance and the building up of self-confidence and interpersonal skills, such centres may well be providing a foundation for the next generation of international adventure holidaymakers.

So now you've decided that you want to try an international adventure holiday, or perhaps you're an experienced adventurer already. What sort of things can you expect on your trip? What are the pressures and pitfalls, and what are the opportunities and rewards?

Rather like the military adage 'expect the unexpected', an ever-present aspect of adventure holidays, especially in Third World countries, is the associated *uncertainty*. Sometimes you will not have experienced the particular physical activity beforehand; often you will not have been to the country in question before; inevitably you will not know all your fellow travellers in advance, unless perhaps you are part of a tailor-made trip. So uncertainty will always be present to some degree, and if you want to enjoy your holiday fully, it is as well to be patient, have an open mind and be prepared to accept whatever comes along.

'Adventure, for me, means having to make my own decisions and having to live with the results of those decisions. It means embarking on a project where the outcome is uncertain. It means taking a step, however tiny, into the unknown. It means being just a little frightened.'

Stephen Venables, Everest climber

By definition, an adventure holiday carries a degree of personal *risk*. As with any holiday, accidents can – and occasionally do – happen. The difference with an adventure holiday is that, first, you are more likely to get injured while white-water rafting or climbing or whatever, than while lounging on a beach. Second, when something does happen, you are going to be further from civilization, and therefore further from specialist help. Responsible tour operators (and this includes the vast majority these days) do have customer safety as their top priority. Training is provided for tour leaders, equipment is usually of high quality and many of the more remote or physically demanding trips are required to include medical experts. Some tour operators will even offer discounts to participating doctors on certain trips, if no expertise is available from within their company. Usually the experience of potential customers is matched to the rigours of the trip being offered and, wherever possible, the safety risks are minimized during the holiday itself. In the final analysis, therefore, it is important to realize that, although inherently more risky than passive vacations, adventure holidays are in reality a very safe way to travel.

It is also important to remember that many adventure holidays are by their nature 'hands-on' – you will be expected to help out with certain duties and chores such as pitching and striking camp, digging out vehicles, and so on.

'Participation is the key – the more you put into a trip, the more you will get out of it.'

Dragoman

Another common ingredient – and one which becomes increasingly present towards the 'hard' end of the adventure spectrum – is *discomfort*, sometimes even endurance. Only the most masochistic of travellers actively seeks out hardships, but if you recognize the fact that cosseted comfort is not on the holiday agenda, you will be better able to face up to the trip's demands: pitching camp in the pouring rain, going out in the midday sun, or suffering the odd bruise or ache. At the time such discomforts may seem to be at best trying, at worst major drawbacks, but in retrospect overcoming these challenges *will* prove to be confidence-building and character-strengthening experiences.

'The team is so close knit. You live together, cycle together, eat together . . . do everything together. And you get very little time to yourself. Having a sense of humour breaks that up. We all had different senses of humour but that really pulled us together. There were obviously days when someone wouldn't talk to someone else, but it always sorted itself out.'

Nick Coward, cycling expedition leader

Having a *positive attitude* to the occasional hardship is the key to enjoyment here, particularly on overlanding trips, where constant exposure to different countries and climates – not to mention petty bureaucracies – can affect even the most blasé traveller. Some of this uncertainty can be reduced by careful planning (see 'Preparation for Going', p 23), or by signing up with a reliable tour operator (see Section 2), but an element of the unknown will necessarily always be there. Central to the value beliefs of many tour operators, therefore, is the need for a *sense of humour* to carry participants through the adversities and '*mañana* syndromes' encountered along the way.

Happily, the existence of such a wide spectrum of international adventure holidays means that you can match your experience and requirements fairly well to the demands of a particular holiday. For example, if you are not especially fit, then you could opt for a soft adventure trip which does not demand too much physically – say, a vehicle-based safari. On the other hand, if you are very confident in your fitness and resilience, some of the more expeditionary types of adventures, such as an ascent of Aconcagua in Argentina (6813 m/22 348 ft), or Mera in Nepal (6400 m/21 000 ft) may be more aligned to your capabilities. Good tour operators will make a point of finding out just how well suited you are before letting you sign up to one of their adventure 'products'. For example, **Worldwide Journeys & Expeditions** grades trips on a scale from 1 – easy trekking in altitudes below 2750 m/9000 ft, to 5 – rigorous trekking involving peak ascents and roped pass/glacier crossings up to 7000 m/23 000 ft. Similarly, **Exodus** produces a leaflet entitled *Choosing a Trek* which explains their grading system (A = easy, up to E = very tough). Companies like **Dragoman, Guerba** and **Encounter Overland** have regular film or slide nights, giving an idea of what life is like on overlanding and other trips. Like Dragoman, several other companies offer a video loan facility to give potential customers a powerful visual impression (partly advertising, partly informative) of what their trips are about. Once you have whittled your choice down a bit, most tour operators will provide dossiers about the specific trips themselves. These give details about what is involved, what to expect and what to take, as well as information about such things as temperature, trail conditions, terrain steepness, and any particular fitness requirements.

> 'Never been on a walking holiday before? Two final hints: first of all, don't be over-ambitious the first time – get to know whether you enjoy it on an easier trek rather than risk putting yourself off for life. Secondly, remember that walking experience in general counts for much less than good physical condition and motivation: if you really want to get to Everest base camp, and you are fit and properly equipped, you'll get there, experienced or not.'
>
> *Exodus 1995/96 Brochure*

There are many reasons why people choose to go on adventure holidays, but when it comes down to it, these reasons are often more to do with the person as an individual, than with external factors like action, challenge, wilderness or escape. In a now-famous reply to the question 'Why did you climb Everest?', Sir Edmund Hillary remarked 'Because it's there.' But perhaps the last word should belong to Jon Carroll, a 20th century American writer, who remarked, 'I think that maybe we do not climb a mountain because it is there. We climb it because we are here.'

WHERE TO GO FOR WHAT

> 'I try to find somewhere right off the beaten track, which includes a little danger, a good pinch of the unknown and, by not planning, leaves open the element of surprise.'
>
> *Jeremy Irons*

The first decision you face as a potential adventure traveller is where in the whole wide world to go. This question is not as strange as it might seem at first sight. Thanks to long-term reductions in the real cost of travel, the world is becoming ever smaller and the choice of destinations is becoming ever greater. Adventure travel is now truly international, for no continent – not even Antarctica – is without its share of adventurers today. As I pointed out earlier, accessibility – or more correctly *inaccessibility* – is one of the distinguishing features of an adventure destination. For this reason alone, many Third World countries, especially within Central and South America, Africa and Asia, can be considered adventurous, simply by virtue of their geographic isolation, lack of infrastructure and difficult communications. On the other hand, many regions within the developed Western world – for example, parts of Scandinavia, northern USA and Canada – are also remote, isolated wildernesses, essentially adventure destinations in their own right.

> 'The world is a country which no one ever yet knew by description; one must travel through it one's self to be acquainted with it.'
>
> *J. Chesterfield, 1747*

The second choice for adventure travellers is what activity or activities to choose from the plethora on offer (see Section 3). Whether it's hiking or biking, exploring or soaring, sailing or abseiling, there are at least thirty different adventurous – that's to say physically challenging – outdoor activities offered by UK and US tour operators. For instance, you can choose from amongst the following:

- canoeing, sea kayaking;
- white-water rafting;
- tall-ship sailing, boardsailing;
- rock climbing, gorge scrambling, abseiling;
- winter mountaineering;
- walking, trekking, hiking;
- caving;
- hang-gliding, parascending, parachuting, ballooning;
- mountain biking;
- horse riding, trekking;
- scuba diving, snorkelling;
- cross-country skiing, snowboarding;
- dog sledging;
- overlanding;
- safaris (walking, horse riding, vehicle, camel, balloon);
- expeditions.

Purists may argue that overlanding trips and vehicle safaris are sedentary activities which do not deserve an 'adventure' tag. However, anyone who has been on a prolonged off-road trip will testify that the bodily demands of 'bundu-bashing' can be all-too-physical at times. Be that as it may, most adventurous activities are environmentally benign, non-polluting and sustainable, if carried out responsibly and thoughtfully (see 'Responsible Tourism', p 29).

The *destination* you eventually choose will inevitably be a compromise between the dream and the reality. Time and money (or lack of time and money) are both major factors influencing this choice. Where time is limited, it follows that the shorter the flight to your destination the longer you will have to enjoy your holiday at the other end. When thinking of adventure travels, most people imagine exotic places like the Silk Route, the Inca Trail, the Hindu Kush or the Okovango Delta. However, for British travellers there are also wild places only a short hop away, such as the Faroe Islands, Iceland, Norway, Finland and Sweden in Scandinavia, or Morocco, Gambia and Cameroon in Africa. Some companies have even extended the concept of adventure holidays to include a number of European destinations.

'Since we introduced adventure holidays in European countries we have had a tremendous take-up from the travelling public. We feel that our strength is to feature familiar destinations in a very different light. For example our trips to Sicily introduced in 1994 have been complete sellouts because we are not offering beaches but volcano climbing, bivouacing and island hopping.'

Travers Cox, Managing Director, Explore

Similarly, for American travellers, there is no shortage of adventure locations almost literally 'on the doorstep', particularly in the Pacific northwest. Caribbean diving and other water-based activities are also easily accessible from the USA and Canada. On the other hand, for both British and American travellers with more leisure time and deeper pockets, long-haul adventure destinations within Africa, Asia, the Far East, Oceana and Antarctica are becoming increasingly popular (see Section 4). Remember, however, that a shorter flight means less jet-lag and less jet-lag means more time at the other end to enjoy your adventure holiday. So if you are crossing several time zones, allow extra time at your destination to recover from the after-effects.

'If you come to a fork in the road, take it.'

Yogi Berra, 20th century American athlete

Preconceptions about where to go for a particular activity can be misleading. It is obviously not possible to conjure up much in the way of snow-based activities in the tropics, although you will find icy peaks in equatorial Africa (Mts Kilimanjaro and Kenya), New Guinea (Carstensz Glacier) and South America (Mt Cotopaxi). However, not many people realize that all sorts of opportunities exist for cross-country (or even downhill) skiing trips in such exotic places as Morocco and northern India. Similarly, Scuba diving is not confined to obvious spots like the Caribbean; parts of Australia and the Far East are becoming increasingly popular, for example. And while mountain biking is almost universally available, for a bike trip with a difference, how about Pakistan, or Kenya? Safaris, in turn, are not the sole preserve of the African continent. How about a camel safari in India or Australia, or a reindeer safari in Norway or Finland?

Continents and their activities

Although the international adventure destination scene can change rapidly, a brief overview of the main 1990s adventure destinations, along with the prospects for 21st century adventure travel, gives a useful perspective.

Northern Europe and the Arctic

Europe. Principally in demand from European Union adventure travellers limited by lack of time and/or money, European destinations tend to feature activity-based holidays which are well organized. Virtually all adventure activities are available. For true wilderness you have to go to such off-the-beaten-track places as the Faroe Islands, and parts of Eastern Europe. In particular, the Russian Commonwealth of Independent States (formerly the USSR) is slowly opening its doors to adventure travellers and is a potentially rich seam for the future.

Arctic. Several Arctic countries previously regarded as inhospitable are developing their own loyal and increasing band of devotees. In particular, the number of tour operators for Greenland, Iceland, Norway, Svalbard and Sweden is increasing steadily.

Outlook. These regions are likely to remain buoyant, especially for younger European adventure holidaymakers, where good organization is important. Demand from first-time adventurers and travellers limited by time and/or budget will continue to increase, particularly in the aftermath of the Channel Tunnel and the lifting of European Union trade restrictions.

Africa

This continent divides into those countries with a long tradition of adventure visitors, mainly because of their safari appeal, and those newly emerging destinations which offer a more diverse range of adventure activities and which are keen to benefit economically from Western tourism. Countries in the former category – for long popular with Western travellers – comprise South Africa, Kenya, Tanzania, Zimbabwe and Zambia. Later entrants include Botswana, Malawi and Namibia, while emerging countries keen to cater for adventure travellers include Cameroon, Gambia and Lesotho. Within North Africa, Morocco in particular is showing a strong increase in demand from adventure seekers. The changed political situation in South Africa is rekindling interest in adventure holidays from Europe and the USA.

Outlook. Africa is enjoying increasing popularity among adventure holidaymakers. While the demand for traditional safaris will probably remain buoyant, alternative adventure activities such as white-water rafting, watersports, trekking and more exotic safaris (walking, camel, horseback) are expected to increase in demand.

Asia

As with Africa, Asia has a number of well established adventure holiday destinations such as India, Nepal, Thailand and Pakistan. More recent ones comprise Borneo, Burma, Indonesia, Malaysia, and Sri Lanka. Among those which have emerged very recently are China (and therefore Tibet), certain Russian states (notably Siberia), Vietnam and Bhutan.

Outlook. Traditional Asian tourist destinations are expected to capitalize on the upsurge in demand for adventure holidays. Nepal and India in particular are making strenuous efforts to increase their share of this trade. There are signs that some of the more recent Asian entrants are taking steps to encourage adventure travellers, in particular Sri Lanka and China. In general, Southeast Asian countries are expected to show strong growth in the adventure sector within the next few years.

USA and Canada

Certain regions of the USA and Canada are mainstream adventure destinations. In particular, the Western states of Alaska, Washington, Oregon, California and Arizona are very popular, as are the Provinces of British Columbia, Yukon and Northwest territories.

Outlook. A continuing and buoyant demand is expected from US and Canadian citizens, while visitor numbers from Europe are expected to increase significantly for as long as transatlantic flights offer good value for money.

Central and South America

Principal adventure destinations within Latin America consist of Ecuador (especially the Galapagos), Peru, Chile, Argentina and Brazil. Other emerging markets include Belize, Bolivia, Venezuela and Mexico.

Outlook. Further increases in demand for adventure holidays within Latin American destinations are expected. Ecotourism will play an increasingly important part in attracting visitors here.

Caribbean, Indian Ocean and Atlantic Islands

Mainly countries for adventure watersports enthusiasts, the islands or archipelagoes of Antigua and Barbuda, Bahamas, Cayman Islands, Jamaica, St Vincent and Grenadines, Montserrat, St Kitts and Nevis, St Lucia and the Virgin Islands are all popular adventure destinations. Lying between India and Africa, the islands of Mauritius, Seychelles and Maldives have been popular among watersport adventure enthusiasts for some time.

Outlook. Demand from British and American travellers in particular is expected to remain steady for Caribbean adventure holidays. Active marketing by the Maldives is expected to result in increased adventure interest here.

Oceania

The main adventure destinations here are Australia, New Zealand, Fiji and Papua New Guinea.

Outlook. These countries are heavily dependent on – and therefore vulnerable to – fluctuations in long-haul air fares. Papua New Guinea is expected to emerge as a significant Oceania market in the mid-term.

Antarctica

The region has only relatively recently become involved in adventure cruise/wildlife observation holidays. Demand is specialized and for the high-budget adventurer only.

HOW TO GO

'If you want to travel cheaply you have to have either a certain amount of packaging, meaning you go on a tour and you accept to fly rather than travel by train, or else you take many more risks and you have to arrange your own travel, which is possible to do but it is slightly more dangerous and things can go horribly wrong. That's old fashioned travel but it's still the best sort.'

Michael Palin

Basically there are two ways to go on an international adventure: by organizing it yourself (as an *independent holiday*) or by letting others do the organizing for you (a *packaged holiday*). Neither is necessarily better than the other: each has its pros and cons. To decide which is better for you, you need to consider what sort of person you are. For instance, are you an extrovert or an introvert, sociable or shy, rigid or flexible in outlook? Are you assertive or compliant, fearful or fearless, comfort-loving or comfort-shunning? Answers to these questions will point to whether an organized group holiday would be best for you, or whether an independent holiday would be more suitable. Thus, sociable, compliant and rigid types will find far fewer stresses in an organized group holiday where an itinerary is at least planned (if not always adhered to). But fearless travellers who resent any structure (however loose), and who want to come and go exactly as they please, will no doubt prefer the flexibility of an independent trip.

One of the advantages of independent holidays is the ability to choose your fellow travelling companions. The importance of human relationships, group dynamics and social interactions on the trip cannot be overestimated. Adventure holiday brochures will often play up the 'wonderful things to do and see' aspects of the trip, but fail to mention the stresses and strains which arise when a small group interacts under challenging circumstances and in isolated conditions. Being cooped up in the company of the same group of people for a long period of time can bring enormous psychological pressures and these must be recognized, faced up to and talked through if the holiday is to succeed for all concerned. Of course, there is no guarantee that chosen friends will remain friends by the end of an independent trip, although the chances are higher if you have been on a similar successful holiday with them before. But friendship stakes are lower in a packaged trip, since individual expectations are correspondingly lower. You will have no preconceptions about the personalities and characters of the individuals forming the group, except that they will at least all share with you an interest in the adventure holiday itself. And who knows, you may even make lifelong friends with a like-minded fellow adventurer – it happens.

A distinction needs to be drawn between 'independent travel' in the sense of unstructured worldwide wandering (a sort of solo Hamlet globetrotting) on the one hand, and independently organized expeditions on the other. Anyone who carries out an expedition is doing it for a reason – recognizing a purpose or a challenge – and at the end is able to say 'yes, I did it' (or 'at least I tried it'). Travel with a purpose carries a responsibility, a discipline which comes from sticking to a goal and ultimately achieving it.

'I have wandered all my life, and I have also travelled; the difference between the two being this, that we wander for distraction, but we travel for fulfillment.'

Hilaire Belloc (1870–1953)

On the other hand, global backpacking, enjoyable though it may be, carries no such responsibility. Some lone-wolf globetrotters will always prefer to shun the company of other fellow-travellers, but personal safety is undoubtedly called into question when such adventurers take off into the wilderness on their lonesome. Adequate preparation is also an issue here: television travelogues by famous travellers like Michael Palin can highlight the risks and dangers of independent travel but they will often gloss over the necessary involvement of many other people – film crews, preparation teams, country-based 'fixers' and so on – in making them happen. So remember that while travelling independently means you can select your own route, timing and activities as you wish, you will need more time to prepare for the trip. (This and other aspects are covered more fully elsewhere in Section 1 – see 'Preparation for Going', p 23).

Setting apart uncertainties about your fellow travellers' personalities, being in an organized group is, for many, an ideal way to experience an adventure holiday. It may cost more than an independent trip, but it is often good value for money. It also saves you a good deal of preparation time, since all this is done for you by the holiday company. For activity-based adventure holidays which use specialized equipment such as rafts, a group holiday is usually the only practicable option. Especially when it comes to using equipment, paying for the use of a good tent and kayak works out a lot cheaper than outright purchase. Another advantage of group trips is that you are not dependent on public transport or hitching lifts. Arriving in the wilderness is one thing: knowing that your departure from it is dependent on others is quite another. Under these circumstances, the lack of a ready means of escape may become a safety issue. Packaged adventure trips also take a lot of the hassle out of travel. Experienced local ground operators and guides can often cut their way through the swath of red tape and foreign bureaucracy. They are also street-smart when it comes to where to stay and how to get about.

'Always go on group holidays with companies like Explore,

who do all the bits you never enjoyed when backpacking
(queuing, arguing and argy-bargying) but who use sweaty,
authentic, local transport rather than the temperature-
controlled tourist buses.'

Christopher Middleton, The Adventurers Magazine

One of the drawbacks of group holidays is that you are less likely
to encounter local people properly, since you are not faced with
day-to-day issues like where to eat and where to sleep. Some
overland trips can also miss out on potentially interesting encounters
simply because the schedule demands that you keep moving.

One major advantage of taking the package adventure holiday
option is *security*. When things go wrong (as they inevitably will do
at some stage or other) – for example, when the vehicle breaks
down or someone falls ill – then it is reassuring to know that the
buck stops with the group leader. Leaders take responsibility for
the group's safety and well-being, leaving you to relax and enjoy.
Against that, however, you will miss out on the buzz that an
independent traveller gets from knowing that he or she coped with
the situation and built up confidence and self-reliance during the
process.

There is also the financial security aspect of group travel. When
you book through a bonded company or industry regulator your
money is safe, in the event of the company or carrier becoming
insolvent. In the UK, there are a number of bonded schemes in
operation, such as the **Association of British Travel Agents
(ABTA)**, the **Civil Aviation Authority's ATOL** scheme and the
Association of Independent Tour Operators (AITO). Other
umbrella organizations offering benefits such as security of holiday
clients' payments include **IATA (International Air Transport Association)** and **ABTOT (the Association of Bonded Travel Organisers
Trust)**. In the USA, **TIA** (the **Travel Industry Association of
America**) and the **US National Tour Association's Consumer
Protection Plan** fulfil the same sort of function.

If an ABTA-registered tour operator goes out of business,
consumers are guaranteed a refund of their payment from the
**Association of British Travel Agents (55–57 Newman Street, Lon-
don W1P 4AH; tel: 0171 637 2444)**. The Air Travel Operator's
Licence Scheme (ATOL) is run by the Civil Aviation Authority.
All operators require an ATOL listing if they offer packaged
holidays which include a charter flight. In return for a financial
bond, operators receive an ATOL number. This bond offers
protection to consumers in the event of operator insolvency. The
address is **Air Travel Operator's Licence Scheme (ATOL, Civil
Aviation Authority, CAA House, 45–59 Kingsway, London WC2B
6TE; tel: 0171 379 7311)**. The Association of Independent Tour

Operators (AITO) has strict membership criteria which must be satisfied before new companies are allowed to join. All AITO members must adhere to a rigorous Code of Business Practice which governs their operational conduct and the safeguarding of their clients' money. The address for **AITO** is **133A St Margarets Road, Twickenham, Middlesex TW1 1RG; tel: 0181 744 9280.**

Finally, two suggestions for would-be adventure travellers on how to go. First, if you have not had much experience as an independent traveller, or if you have not visited the country concerned before, do consider at least starting out with an adventure tour operator. Use their trip to become familiar with the country's customs and culture before, if you wish, going it alone thereafter. Second, if you can afford it, think about a *tailor-made* trip. This is where you assemble a group of friends, relatives or associates and ask a tour operator to put together a bespoke trip for you. Many companies offer this service and are very happy to sort out an individual itinerary (see Section 2). Although tailor-made trips cost a little more than set-departure trips, they carry with them all the advantages of group travel but virtually none of the disadvantages.

HEALTH

'Those who die in air crashes or road accidents are usually the victims of forces beyond their control. Those who die or get ill from travel-related diseases like malaria normally have only themselves to blame.'

Frank Barrett, Guide to Real Holidays Abroad

Barrett gives a stern warning and one that should be heeded. Although the main health hazard in developing countries is in fact a serious road accident, increasing numbers of tropical adventurers have resulted in increasing cases of preventable diseases. In the West, the myth of an accessible world devoid of smallpox and cholera still persists despite evidence to the contrary and in truth one of the major difficulties for adventure travellers is getting hold of accurate information. In the UK the **Department of Health** has useful literature (phone the **Health Line – 0800 555777** and ask for Booklet T5, *Health Advice for Travellers*), but although some Post Offices stock this information, most travel agents do not. So where exactly can you go for up-to-date, detailed advice on vaccinations and health precautions?

Most people turn to their doctor for help, not realizing that while expert in the field of domestic ailments and illnesses, General Practitioners can sometimes be sketchy when it comes to esoteric tropical diseases. Similarly, travel agents, tour operators, embassies and tourist offices vary greatly in the accuracy of their information. However, help is at hand for British travellers in the form of **MASTA, Medical Advisory Service for Travellers Abroad (tel: 0891 224100)**. MASTA is a specialist organization which deals with travellers' health. It has accurate, up-to-date, comprehensive and regionally available information and advice. It will send you a written report on your vaccination and health requirements and for a small fee it will also provide you with detailed health briefs for many countries, and a health kit containing sterile syringes and needles as a precaution against AIDS. They have a network of centres throughout the UK offering health advice, including an **International Medical Centre** located in London. Linked with the MASTA database, the **British Airways Travel Clinics** are also good sources of advice on matters medical. There are branches throughout the UK (good sources of mosquito repellant not often available elsewhere, incidentally) or you can call them (**tel: 0171 831 5333**) for your nearest location. **Trailfinders** (see p 48) also has a number of travel clinics and immunization centres throughout the UK.

Auto-immune deficiency syndrome (AIDS) is a major threat to visitors and inhabitants alike, especially in parts of Europe, America, Africa and Asia. Of course if adventures of a sexual kind are what you're after then the risk of AIDS will be ever present. For example, transmission of AIDS in Thailand by prostitution is predicted to be the cause of two-thirds of deaths in that country by the end of the century. But to genuine adventurers, the dangers arise from such rare events as the need for a blood transfusion following an accident, for instance, or from other forms of medical or dental treatment involving contact with infected blood. Carrying a sterile health kit is a useful precautionary measure. Another precaution is to note your blood group and arrange with a compatible fellow traveller to receive blood from them if the worst comes to the worst.

> 'Anyone planning a "sex tour" to Thailand will save money
> by staying at home and eating rat poison.'
> *A Thai Government Spokesman, 1991*

Cholera spreads under conditions of poor sanitation and hygiene. It is most prevalent in parts of Asia, the Middle East and Africa but can break out anywhere that becomes too overcrowded and unhygienic. The vaccination does not offer 100% protection, so taking care and showing common sense with regard to what you eat and drink is a sensible approach to minimizing the risk. *Hepatitis* exists throughout the world. Hepatitis A is transmitted under conditions similar to those favourable for cholera – infected food or infected water – but you can also catch it from an infected person. Hepatitis B is transmitted by sexual contact or contaminated blood. A gamma globulin injection will give protection for up to three months, but it dwindles thereafter (a fortunate proportion of travellers are naturally resistant to hepatitis). Some travellers contracting the disease have died abroad, not so much from hepatitis as from the unhygienic conditions prevalent in some Third World hospitals.

Malaria is the worst disease hazard of all to adventure travellers visiting Africa, Asia, Central America and South America. Around 2000 British travellers contract malaria every year: of these a handful will die. Since the disease is spread by infected anopheles mosquitoes, avoiding being bitten in the first place is eminently sensible. Keep skin (especially ankles) well covered after sunset, use insect repellant, use mosquito incense coils, sleep under a net and, of course, take a course of non-resistant tablets (many treatments have become ineffective due to disease resistance). If you feel fluish after returning from a malarial area, do not rule out the possibility of having contracted the disease and see your doctor as soon as possible. **MASTA** have a telephone helpline dedicated to Malaria enquiries – **0891 224100.**

Apart from a cholera health certificate, many developing countries require documentary evidence of yellow fever and typhoid vaccinations. *Yellow fever* is spread by mosquito bites and is present in parts of Africa and South America. *Typhoid*, on the other hand, can be caught through food, water or milk and exists everywhere except New Zealand, Australia, north America and Europe. Other potential nasties include rabies, tetanus and TB. Outside the UK, *rabies* is widespread and a bite from an infected animal is fatal if not treated quickly. The golden rule is to avoid contact with animals abroad, especially cats, dogs, monkeys and bats, no matter how friendly they are: since rabies is transmitted through saliva, even a lick can be enough. If in doubt, seek medical advice immediately. *Tetanus* can be vaccinated against easily: the risks arise where medical treatment is not available. Transmitted by saliva, *tuberculosis* (TB) is unfortunately becoming more widespread.

No matter how tempting a swim might be in the tropics and parts of the subtropics, remember that *bilharzia* is commonplace. Even in moving waters free of vegetation, there is still a risk. Schistosomiasis is a painful and crippling disease and, if infection occurs, early medical treatment is essential but, happily, effective. Health-wise, there are some general rules for adventure travellers abroad. Since many diseases are spread by infected food, adopt a 'mind over platter' mentality – take care and think beforehand about what you should or should not eat and drink. Peeled fresh fruit is generally safe, while shellfish, ice cream and salads are often high-risk. Similarly, freshly cooked dishes are safer than reheated ones. Bottled water or well boiled water are *de rigueur*. Avoid tap water, ice in your drinks and home-made ice lollies (so-called 'dysentery dips'). If you do fall ill and suffer from vomitting and/or diarrhoea, avoid becoming dehydrated, especially in hot climates.

'It must be realized that going to the tropics involves accepting a calculated risk. There is no way out of this and it is foolish to turn a blind eye to the fact. That risk can be greatly minimized by taking precautions . . . but nevertheless it remains. There is no gilt-edged guarantee of health to be had simply by asking for, or following, a regime, however good.'

Preservation of Health in Warm Climates,
Ross Institute of Tropical Hygiene

An essential for intending adventure travellers is to seek advice and obtain inoculations well in advance of your trip. If you are going on a packaged adventure holiday, most tour operators will help out in providing advice. But wherever you are going, don't rely on hearsay or incomplete information from non-specialist sources. Having said that, assessing health risks is not an exact science and professional opinions can sometimes vary as to the immunizations you should have. It can be difficult to give hard-and-fast rules about what you should and should not take: if you took precautions against every known disease you'd rattle. But certain basic precautions are a must, particularly if there is a significant incidence of the disease in the place you are visiting. Taking along a first-aid kit (including sterile needles) and basic medication is sensible. Contacting MASTA early is a must. Along with comprehensive medical insurance and the right documentation to enable free or reduced rate medical treatment (if available), protecting yourself against disease is a necessity, not a choice. And finally, if you do feel unwell on returning home, seek medical advice sooner rather than later in case you have imported some undesirable alien, unawares.

WEATHER, AND WHEN TO GO

'There's a lot of bull' about the Polar regions: how high the winds are; how cold the temperatures are . . . On certain days it can be very cold, but on such occasions, it's very likely that we'll be warm and snug in our Northface tent.'

Geoff Summers, British member of
Trans-Antarctic Expedition

Most prospective travel plans are governed by cost, destination, activity and when it is convenient to go. A long way down the list of considerations is the weather. Yet this element of the holiday can make or break it, or at least contribute greatly to its success (or, if you're unprepared, its misery). Climate shock can be just as real as culture shock to international adventurers, even on short-haul trips: a flight from the UK to Spitsbergen or from southern USA to Alaska in June can transport you from summer to winter conditions in the space of only a few hours. Similarly, a winter departure from the UK to West Africa can be like stepping from freezer into the sauna: it's a shock to the system, and the system needs time to adjust to that shock. You will therefore need to balance all the other elements and expectations of your trip with the expected climatic conditions in order to enjoy the adventure to its fullest. An obvious step, though one often overlooked in the pre-departure rush and excitement, is to read up in advance about the climate of your destination. This is all the more important for independent travellers; on organized trips they inform you before-hand about what to expect, climate-wise, and what to take in the way of clothing. Remember that responsible tour operators have your health and safety as their number-one priority: an ill equip-ped member of the group can jeopardize the safety, or at the very least the enjoyment, of the rest.

It is axiomatic that there can be no guarantees about the weather, but to be forewarned is to be forearmed. If you are minimizing the amount of kit you are carrying then it is essential to ensure that you will be warm enough, dry enough and protected enough for creature comfort. Acclimatizing to your destination may take time and this needs to be accounted for when planning the length of your stay: 30° Celsius and 78% humidity take some getting used to even if you have 'been there before'. Remember, the locals manage because they're used to it – you aren't.

Climate charts, useful though they can be, seldom tell you the whole story, so it is best to compare what you have read with what you know and what others tell you. Variability in the weather can often undermine one's best efforts. For example, inconsistencies in seasonal weather patterns are probably responsible for more failed summit attempts than any other single reason. By their very nature, adventurous activities often take place in harsh environments with their associated extreme weather conditions. On the other hand, climate charts tend to state averages rather than extremes. Thus while a visit to the Cameroon rainforests and coast will call for little other than light clothes, lightweight boots and waterproof raingear, you will need a warm sleeping bag, mountain boots and thermally insulated clothing if you are going to tackle Mount Cameroon nearby. Similarly, Mounts Kenya and Kilimanjaro call for robust footwear and warm clothing, atypical of general East African needs. On the other hand, Arctic climes can surprise too: remember that much of the Arctic and Antarctic regions is desert, with annual precipitation of only 5 to 20 centimetres, most of it falling as snow when visitors are not there. High barometric pressures are commonplace during summer, causing stable, warm weather patterns – hot enough on occasions to make you strip off to all but the lightest of clothing.

> 'One of the most overlooked pieces of advice to travellers to hot countries is to wear a full covering of clothes. Shorts, T-shirt and flip-slops may be OK for Torremolinos but trans-Saharan travellers would be ill-advised to try the same style of garb in the middle of the Grand Erg.'
>
> *Carlton Reid, The Adventurers Magazine*

Look for comparisons when considering what to take. For example, London in August has a minimum temperature of 13°C and a maximum of 21°C, with humidity from 62% to 76%. However, the August temperature in Harare ranges from only 8°C up to 23°C, with humidity as low as 28% to 50%. Conclusion? You'd better take a warm jumper for those cool Zimbabwe evenings. To adventurers unused to it, humidity is one of the most significant factors influencing comfort and hence holiday enjoyment. The greater the humidity, the more uncomfortable higher temperatures become. Take note of your destination's humidity and temperature therefore, and pack accordingly. Altitude is another obvious variable when it comes to land temperatures, but sea temperatures can change too – a factor to be borne in mind if you are going on a diving trip, for instance. There is generally a 1½ month time lag between land and sea temperatures: in other words if land temperatures peak in August, the sea can take until September or October to reach its warmest.

Quite apart from health hazards caused by diseases (see

'Health', p 17) the tropics deserve a special mention when it comes to heat conditions. Travellers used to temperate conditions will need to acclimatize to tropical air temperatures which are often higher than average body temperature. High humidity places greater stress on the body in its efforts to sweat. Heat exhaustion can develop when the body's loss of water and salt is not replenished, so strenuous physical exertion associated with adventure activities will place greater demands on the body's need for water and salt.

'Prevention of heat exhaustion lies in consuming adequate quantities of fluid: in the hot season this may be 6 pints (3.4 litres) or more, daily. The most important feature of acclimatization is the development of an increased ability to sweat without undue loss of salt and of a greater ability to work in hot conditions.'

Preservation of Personal Health in Warm Climates –
Ross Institute of Tropical Hygiene

Similarly, Arctic and snowy regions carry a health warning when it comes to the sun's ultra violet rays. Thinner air at higher altitudes (if you are on a climbing trip) combined with the reflective nature of snow and ice, greatly increase the risk of sunburn, or, more seriously, sunstroke. Ultraviolet radiation increases by 100% for every 1000 m increase in altitude, while radiation reflection can increase up to 95% in snowy environments. Take cover – for your health's sake. Anti-sweat sunblock, strong sunglasses and long, loose clothing are musts in combatting today's ozone-challenged atmosphere (see 'Preparation for Going', below).

A great deal has been written about climatic differences and weather conditions in different parts of the world. This section is intended to give only the briefest of overviews for travellers to the world's main adventure regions. More detailed information about the best time(s) of year to visit particular countries can be found in Section 4 – Countries.

PREPARATION FOR GOING

'There was this guy from Liverpool, who literally just turned up on the doorstep, having phoned me up in advance and just said that he had a top secret mission. It was going to be the most earth-shattering thing – he couldn't possibly explain on the phone – that anyone had ever come up with! So he insisted on coming down to my house in Devon and, sure enough, he turned up and he had *no idea*. He had never read a single book about the polar regions, and his dream was to retrace Scott's route in the Antarctic. I had to spend nearly three hours of my time, trying to explain to this guy the *problems* that he would face in this project – I'm not saying that I was trying to put him off, but explaining, so that he simply wouldn't go and waste his life, or any more of his life, with this enterprise.'

Wally Herbert, polar explorer

In many respects, the preparations necessary for off-the-shelf adventure holidays are not so very different from more conventional holidays. Of course, you will need all the usual paraphernalia necessary for international travel: paperwork (passports, visas, currency, insurance, etc), medication (pre-travel inoculations, travel medical kit), clothing, other equipment, and so on. There are, however, some other important and special preparations which you will need to think about before embarking on your international adventure.

'Careful preparation for an expedition can make the difference between success and failure. Before I could even begin to plan my journey, I had to find out the answer to one vital question: "Can what I want to do actually be done?". "Impossible" usually means "nearly impossible" and the "nearly" is the adventure.'

Rosie Swale, Back to Cape Horn

How much you need to worry about what to take depends on where you're going, what you intend to do once there, and – most importantly – whether you're going independently or as part of an organized tour. As in the case of the 'hopeful' above who wanted to visit Antarctica, enthusiasm and vision alone are simply no substitute for efficient and effective preparation. Independent trips, particularly those tending towards the 'hard' end of the adventure spectrum, may need many weeks or months of hard planning and preparation, not to mention training. Travel in extreme environments such as mountains, rainforests, deserts and polar regions will similarly require more planning and better equipment than trips to 'softer' destinations. Such travel will also be usually more expensive. Self-contained expeditioning is outside the scope of this book, but if you are planning such a trip, a number of useful sources of advice exist in the UK, such as the **Royal Geographical Society's Expedition Advisory Service (1 Kensington Gore, London SW7 2AR; tel: 0171 581 2057)**, and the **Royal**

Scottish Geographical Society (40 George Street, Glasgow G1 1QE; tel: 0141 552 3330) and the **British Mountaineering Council (177–179 Burton Road, West Didsbury, Manchester M20 2BB; tel: 0161 445 4747)**. Another useful network for independent adventure travellers is the London-based **Globetrotters Club (BCM/Roving, London WC1N 3XX)** which exchanges information on adventurous travel and hosts presentations through regular meetings. Every two months it produces a magazine called *Globe* which provides up-to-date information on adventure destinations, tips and travel bargains. The UK's leading travel 'club' – with over 35 000 members – is **WEXAS (45–49 Brompton Road, Knightsbridge, London SW3 1DE; tel: 0171 589 3315)**. It produces a quarterly magazine called *Traveller*, and regular newsletters (see p 50). A further source of advice is the **Foreign Office Travel Advice Unit (Clive House, Petty France, London SW1H 9HD; tel: 0171 270 4129)**. They will answer specific enquiries and they issue sheets on travel and safety for a range of countries. *Wanderlust* is a bimonthly magazine produced in the UK to 'inspire the independent-minded traveller'. Articles appear about both adventure destinations and activities (**PO Box 1832, Windsor, Berkshire SL4 5YG; tel: 01753 620426**).

In the USA, the **Adventure Travel Society (6551 S Revere Parkway, #160, Englewood, CO 80111; tel: 303 649 9016)** is a trade association which addresses issues relating to ecotourism and adventure travel. It produces a regular newsletter for members and holds an annual international congress to examine adventure travel and ecotourism issues.

Given that many adventure seekers will be travelling as part of a small group (typically up to twenty people, often nearer ten) in an organized trip, one major difference which tends to separate the true adventure traveller from the casual tourist is degree of physical *fitness*. Depending on which activity or activities you are going to be doing on your holiday, it invariably pays dividends to try to achieve a level of fitness before departure which will match the trip's physical challenges. This is not to say that you cannot just turn up and expect to paddle your own canoe, stride out up that mountain, or gallop off into the sunset – often you can. But if you have made an effort beforehand to exercise those dormant muscles which are suddenly going to have demands placed upon them, it can make all the difference between holiday enjoyment and holiday endurement – and you won't need to spend the first few days restricting the rest of the group needlessly, nursing aches and strains, or, at worst, wishing you'd never come. Just a little time spent training each week for a few weeks beforehand can heighten immeasurably your appreciation of that Norwegian ski hutting trip, that Nepalese rafting experience, or that Namibian riding safari. The increasing trend towards holidays by older adventurers (Explore Worldwide's average client age is currently 39 for instance) means that being realistic about one's own level of physical fitness and matching that fitness to the trip's demands, is of paramount importance.

Apart from general fitness, another important aspect of preparation for your adventure holiday concerns personal *equipment and clothing*. Most tour operators will provide you with lists of what you need to take in the way of clothing and other supplies. Without this, most people usually make the mistake of taking far more than they actually need. A good packing tip is to look out what you think you need, then cut this down by a third or even a half.

> 'How does one pack for a walk around the world? Basically on my long journey I went up first to the Arctic and then on to South America, so I set off with loads of woollens, and the sleeping bags were heavy duty for Greenland. I just had to shed it off and send stuff home. I set off with 84 lbs of luggage, but that included bagpipes and umbrella.'
>
> *Alastair Scott, The Adventurers Magazine*

Packing for a round-the-world walk is one thing, but if you have a less ambitious itinerary and you want to take just the bare essentials, it should be possible to keep personal kit down to under 25 lb (11 kg). Above 35 lb (16 kg), any increases in weight, even small ones, can rapidly diminish your enjoyment of the holiday if you are having to carry everything yourself.

A third major difference which often distinguishes adventurers from casual tourists is their level of *awareness* about their holiday destination. By definition, many adventure trips are taken to remote destinations, frequently in Third World countries, where exposure to Western ideas, cultures and influences may be minimal, or even absent. Culture shock is what happens when the traveller is unprepared for what to expect upon his or her arrival. So time spent reading up about the natural environment and local customs of the country and the peoples you will be visiting is time never wasted. For instance, just a little homework about the wildlife you are likely to encounter on an African safari or an Arctic whale-watching trip, or about the indigenous people – whether it's a mountain trek among the Moroccan Berber villagers or a husky dog trip among the Alaskan Inuit communities – will pay dividends. Reading up about the wilderness you encounter – be it the Arctic, the desert or the tropical rainforest – or about the tribespeople – be they Tuareg, Basotho or Aborigines – will make the difference between your being an ignorant spectator and an understanding traveller; between your treating local people perhaps as mere curiosities and treating them as fellow human beings.

Cultural awareness is part and parcel of being a responsible adventure traveller (see 'Responsible Tourism', p 29) and learning something about the country you are to visit will increase your knowledge, and therefore your appreciation, of your holiday. This is never more true than when it comes to foreign languages. Taking the trouble to learn, and preferably use, even just a few words of the local language is one of the most important preparations for travel that you can make. It breaks down cultural barriers, puts people at their ease, and makes for a better chance at mutual understanding. In the UK, the **Foreign and Commonwealth Office** (address above) produces a series of leaflets entitled *Do's and Dont's* for a number of countries. These have handy tips on such things as restricted areas, where not to take photographs, dress code and so forth. Examples of these titbits of information include the fact that in Kenya it is a criminal offence to deface currency; in India you need a permit to enter the area bordering Pakistan and Darjeeling; and in Malaysia you don't mess with drugs (importers face the death penalty). The Foreign and Commonwealth Office also issues a leaflet *Get it Right Before you Go*, which includes details of the sort of things consulates can and cannot do for you.

Finally, you should not forget a few practical items which are invaluable for all adventure travellers but which are often overlooked in the pre-departure rush. Many of these are available from multi-outlet equipment suppliers such as **Nomad (0181 889 7014)**, **Blacks (0191 417 0414)**, **YHA (01784 458625)** and the **Scouts Association (01903 755352)** in the UK; the **Mountain Equipment Cooperative (130 West Broadway, Vancouver, British Columbia, V5Y 1P3; tel: 604 872 7858)** in Canada; and **Recreation Equipment Incorporated (1525 Eleventh Avenue, Seattle, WA 98122; tel: 206 323 8333)** in the USA. Some tour operators give helpful advice on those little extras: **Explore Trader (1 Frederick Street, Aldershot, Hants GU11 1LQ; tel: 01252 316016)** is a retail trading company which produces a merchandise catalogue specifically for adventure travellers.

Seasoned travellers have learned through experience to carry certain items which, to the uninitiated, may not always appear obvious. So, before heading off on your trip you might like to benefit from the wisdom of these cognoscente and consider whether you should take some of the following items (in addition to the usual paraphernalia of clothing, medical kit and other equipment):

– *Swiss army knife* (or a variant thereof). Indispensable. It is worth purchasing one of the better models, since cheap imitations can fail you just when you need them most. The real thing has 'Victorinox' stamped on the base of its large blade. Some mini-tools come equipped with pliers for those heavy-duty repairs.

– *Short-wave radio.* Excellent for keeping in touch with the world news back home, when you find that your favourite newspaper is in short supply.

– *Dental gum.* Very good for long haul flights when your teeth-cleaning routine gets overlooked and you wake up with a mouth feeling like sandpaper. Good on long-distance overland travel for the same reasons.

– *Torch.* Goes without saying, but a head torch is much better for allowing hands-free activity (like searching for the missing loo roll at a critical moment).

– *Candle.* Longer ones tend to break, so get the stubbier versions.

– *Lighter.* Matches can get wet.

– *Plugs.* (Bath and electric). Go for universal multi-fit, multi-size (and multi-voltage) types.

– *Umbrella.* Not as daft as it might seem. Apart from the obvious, it's a useful windbreak, sun shelter and snow screen. A non-conductive shaft will guard against lightning strikes.

– *Sunglasses.* Not just for the sun (make sure they are UV proof), but also useful for avoiding eye contact when you don't want to interact with that persistent bazaar trader.

– *International driving licence.* Useful as a means of identification and less valuable than a passport for security (eg against equipment hire).

– *Wedding Ring.* For women travelling alone, this can be a handy symbol to deter sexual hassle. A fake 'husband and wife' photograph may also prove useful.

– *Insect repellent.* The active ingredient in most insect repellent is DEET: the more concentrated the better. You may have your own favourite brand from among the myriad available.

– *Muslin sheet or sarong.* Light, easy to wash and easy to dry. Provides a gossamer of familiarity among foreign beds (and/or foreign bodies).

– *Disposable camera.* Often difficult to obtain in the Third World. Less tempting for thieves with light fingers than flashy conventional cameras. The waterproof varieties are excellent for adventure watersports, especially white-water rafting.

– *Ear plugs and scarf.* Strange as it may seem, these can be invaluable for those who find it difficult to sleep because of noise and/or light. Squashable foam ear plugs purchased from a chemist can effectively magic away that noisy airport terminal, that barking dog, or that snoring travelling companion. Similarly, a dark scarf wrapped round the head is wonderful for combatting Arctic summer insomnia.

– *Shemagh*. A cotton wrap-around head-covering, worn in desert regions. Useful for keeping the dust out and the sun off.
– *Neck pillow*. Great for avoiding neck cramp during those long plane, train or vehicle journeys.
– *Tooth care/repair kit*. Useful especially if you have a habit of losing fillings or dislodging bridges (for a BMA-approved kit, phone **01270 841107**).
– *Games*. Travelling games like scrabble, chess or solitaire are small and light enough to take easily and will probably never get used. But omit them and you'll wish you hadn't! Juggling balls are a great way of breaking down cultural barriers.

RESPONSIBLE TOURISM

'At the end of the trail day, ecotourism is about recognizing and empowering the metre and rhyme of innocence. When stretched over the bow of a raft, the precipice of a canyon, or simply out on a limb, the universe is reduced to that simple childlike state of pure emotion, of fun, of fear, of coloratura.'

Richard Bangs, world adventurer and partner of Mountain Travel Sobek

During recent years the growth in tourism worldwide has been staggering. In 1950, when taking a holiday usually meant a few days at Aunt Ethel's, only 25 million people were recorded as international 'tourists' (ie people using leisure time to travel abroad). By 1965, when Mediterranean package holidays became affordable for many European wage earners, annual international tourists totalled 113 million. Twenty-five years on, over a million people travelled outside their home country *every day* – an incredible 400 million international tourists each year, or sixteen times the 1950 level. This upward trend is seemingly unstoppable, for by the year 2000, tourism is predicted to be the most significant economic activity in the world, with more than 640 million tourists expected to make international trips each year. However, while tourism in general has increased at a rate of around 4% per year, tourism to remote areas has risen at a massive 30% annually. In the USA alone, more than 500 companies currently sell tours to wilderness areas. What we are witnessing is a growth phenomenon in which increasing numbers of holidaymakers are demanding an active 'get-away-from-it-all' experience – 'adventure ecotourism', if you will. But this demand can, and does, create some very real problems with its impact both on the fragile ecology of the world's wild places and impacts on the individuals and communities living there.

'Our resources are the world's quietest places, and they are just as finite as coal or iron ore or oil.'

Martin Brackensbury, Chairman,
International Federation of Tour Operators

Late twentieth century tourism has become a two-edged sword. On the one hand it can be a force for good, creating local jobs or conserving threatened ecosystems and species; on the other, it can consume and destroy whole communities, cultures and environments. All too often the twofold legacy of tourism today is cultural degradation and environmental exploitation, a good deal of it unwitting, much of it deliberate. But how has this happened and how has it been allowed to happen?

Western travellers are all guilty of wanting many things on holiday that common sense tells us must be out of step with local reality: accommodation with private beach – never mind the local inhabitants' right to public access; hot tea on arrival at the night's trekking stagepost – forget the scarcity of firewood in the mountains; taking the ultimate safari photograph – ignore the disruption to wildlife; off-piste skiing out of bounds – forget the threat of avalanches to the world below; viewing turtles on their traditional beaches – never mind disruption to their breeding patterns; collecting coral souvenirs on a diving holiday – forget the damage to life-supporting reefs . . . the list of potentially harmful effects is practically endless. And of course our impact starts even before we arrive. For example, a jumbo jet uses 16 000 litres of fuel every hour: that's 16 000 litres of non-renewable, global-warming, fossil fuel. Although adventure activities generally do not in themselves consume fossil fuels, the ever-increasing quest for remoteness among adventurous souls has led to an upsurge in long-haul flights to remote destinations. And more long-haul flights equal more consumption of non-renewable fuels.

The effects of our activities are not only environmental, however. Whenever we travel in the developing world we inevitably impinge upon different cultures, imposing our Western values, beliefs and behavioural systems on local communities, whether they want this intrusion or not. How much mutual understanding occurs through such exposure is questionable. Life as experienced by locals is generally a closed book, not necessarily because of travellers' apathy, but because neither party is equipped to communicate – literally. However likely we are to find English speakers on our journeying, a country's cultural heart will never open up to us if its language remains a secret. Furthermore, these cultural and language differences are amplified in economic terms. Even the poorest of Western travellers has far more disposable wealth than the vast majority of people he or she encounters in the developing world. For considerate tourists, this spending power carries with it a responsibility to ensure that locals are not exploited economically – even unwittingly. All too often, however, that responsibility is not recognized and the Western travellers' economic power is abused.

> 'Remember that the bargain you obtained was only possible because of the low wages paid to the maker.'
> *Christian Council of Churches Code of Ethics for Tourists*

It should not be forgotten that, being perceived as wealthy Westerners, adventure travellers can unintentionally lay themselves open to the vagaries of local or even national politics. Recent cases of independent travellers being taken hostage within certain trouble-spots underline the risks of travel within these politically sensitive countries. Responsible tourism is not just about cultural and environmental awareness; it is also about political awareness. So taking soundings before venturing into potentially volatile areas is not merely sensible: it could just save your life.

Since the Rio Earth Summit in 1992, so much has been said and written about *sustainability* that its meaning has become widely confused and misunderstood, but basically it means *meeting the needs of the present generation without compromising the ability of future generations to meet their own needs.* In simple terms, 'sustainable tourism' is about minimizing our impact, both on the environment and the peoples we encounter. John Muir, that famous Scottish/American writer, adventurer and pioneer conservationist whose efforts led to the designation of the world's first National Parks in the USA, epitomized the concept of sustainability in a famous expression, now adopted as the motto of the Sierra Club. He said, 'Take nothing but photographs: leave nothing but footprints.' In Muir's day, the footprints of hikers were few and far between: today there are enough of them to erode trails, campgrounds and even mountain tops. The ideal has thus now shifted away from leaving footprints to leaving 'nothing except shadows across the landscape' and this is a goal that adventure travellers would be wise to strive for.

> 'When I was a boy in Scotland, I was fond of everything that was wild, and all my life have been growing fonder and fonder of wild places and wild creatures.'
> *John Muir (1838–1914)*

Adventure tourism has had a mixed track record as far as environmental and cultural impacts are concerned. Some companies (including those profiled in Section 2) are exemplary, while others are at best dubious. The risks are usually much higher with adventure than with conventional tourism, since there is often a well developed infrastructure to deal with the latter, while adventure tourism usually targets undeveloped countries and fragile ecosystems.

Knowing about the issues is only part of the solution: what can you as an individual do in helping this search towards responsible tourism? As someone about to embark on an adventure holiday, you have several important choices in front of you: where to go, what to do once there, and which company to go with. The first step towards being a responsible tourist is knowing something about the effects tourists can have. Having read thus far, you know that tourism can cause problems, but you are also aware that steps are available to solve these problems, or at least lessen their effects.

Next, decide to make a positive choice in favour of travelling with a company whose principles are in line with sustainable development. Not every company will have an environmental policy or code of ethics. Even those that do can seldom control every element of their package holidays, so do not expect too much. But most people in the adventure holiday business already have an enthusiasm for their activity or their part of the world and will welcome your interest. And you can be sure that the more they see clients caring about the environment, the more they will be obliged to recognize and tackle these sustainability issues. A good yardstick by which to measure a company is the **Campaign for Environmentally Responsible Tourism (CERT) (PO Box 4246, London SE23 2QB; tel: 0181 299 6111)**. The Campaign's purpose is to encourage responsible tourism by both the travel industry and the travelling public which will benefit the long-term interests of the environment and the travel industry. CERT has produced twelve Guidelines on ways to help protect the natural world. You, the consumer, fill in a questionnaire about the operator you travelled with (the questionnaire is based on CERT's Guidelines). CERT compiles the information and, via an awards system, recognizes those companies which are particularly environmentally responsible.

What about your own needs on holiday? It is one thing to want home-from-home in a country with economic standards similar to your own, but should you make the same demands everywhere? Expecting to eat, travel and sleep as the locals do may mean a huge drop in your standard of living and most people in poor areas would not expect Western visitors to live exactly as they do, but there is a happy medium which responsible companies should work towards – and not be shy to defend. So, tailor your threshold of creature comforts to the places you are visiting and, where possible, stay in small, locally owned accommodation (unless you are camping, that is).

You may find that supporting sustainable tourism is expensive in the short term. Small group numbers, or more time on research and planning, can reduce a company's profit margins, and more than one enterprise setting out with excellent aims has collapsed because of its consequently high prices. Don't begrudge paying out a bit more if it means that the environment is less likely to suffer.

Enquire about the kind of briefing and information you will receive before you go. Some companies tour nationwide with slide shows, but, while catching one of these will give you lots of ideas, remember that such events are there first and foremost to sell holidays. Find out whether tour leaders have lived in, or are nationals of, the countries they deal with. See if they can recommend good sources of information about your holiday area or activity.

When you return, take time to consider whether you would book again with the same company. Whatever your conclusion, tell them so and say why. This feedback will help them improve things for future clients, but will also help you, when you come to make your next holiday choice – you will have a better idea of what to look for.

Also have a think about cultural issues like these:

- Were local people happy and relaxed to have you in their territory? And did a fair proportion of your tour money percolate into the places you visited? Tourism seems to work best when control is in local hands, particularly in the isolated communities often featured by adventure travel companies.
- Did the tour company treat its employees, particularly local employees, fairly? This can be difficult to assess, but a responsible operator will try to use local skills and services and suggest ways you can spend your money to good effect in the communities you are visiting.
- Was your holiday marketed responsibly? Some trips attract us with the lure of the 'exotic and strange'. Were the people you visited treated like zoo animals and was your guide happy to participate in this state of affairs? Or maybe you were promised remoteness. Was it really remote or did the flushing toilets and hot water suggest that lots of other tour operators might be coming there – creating a tourist infrastructure set apart from the local economy?
- A company can't keep complete control over its guides, but it

can provide support and training for them, and can certainly ensure that they are informed and sensitive to local tourism issues. Many US and UK adventure couriers know their 'patches' very well indeed and can interpret a place for you more satisfactorily than might a local guide – but was this true in your case? Did you learn anything new, or did you simply have your views confirmed? Would a local guide have done the job better (providing local employment into the bargain)?

When you have answered some of the above questions and embarked upon your adventure, remember that a lot of the rest is down to you. *You* have the choice to be a responsible visitor . . . or an irresponsible one. If adventure tourism is to improve its act – if it's to become more sustainable – then it needs all of its participants to help in 'thinking globally and acting locally', to try and prevent problems occurring in the first place.

If you want to know more about responsible tourism, there are a number of organizations which can help. As well as CERT (see above), there is the **Adventure Travel Society (6551 S Revere Parkway, # 160, Englewood, CO 80111; tel: 303 649 9016)**, a US-based firm established to promote, through tourism, the integration of environmentally responsible natural resource management, economic viability and the protection of social values and cultural integrity. It exists to assist regions, trade groups, states and countries with public relations, marketing and environmentally responsible management of tourism and natural resources. Each year it holds an international congress on adventure travel and ecotourism. The **Association of Independent Tour Operators (133a St Margaret's Road, Twickenham, Middlesex, TW1 1RG; tel: 0181 744 9280)** publishes a free annual directory of around 150 tour operator members. The directory provides advice on tour operators whose holidays are 'green', as well as giving 'green tips' for travellers who wish to be environmentally friendly. **Tourism Concern (Southlands College, Wimbledon Parkside, London SW19 5NN; tel: 0181 944 0464)** is a broad-based membership network which brings together British people with an active concern for tourism's impact on community and environment worldwide. It takes the view that all sectors involved in tourism – governments, industry, media, educators and holidaymakers themselves – have contributed to its negative impacts, and therefore all sectors should be involved in challenging and changing it. Tourism Concern produces a *Himalayan Tourist Code* – environmental and cultural guidelines for hikers and climbers which are an ideal checklist for the responsible traveller (see Appendix 2). At a governmental level, the **World Travel and Tourism Council (WTTC) (PO Box 6237, New York, NY 10128; tel: 212 534 0300)** is a coalition of tourism companies whose goals are to convince governments of the strategic and economic importance of travel and tourism as the world's largest industry, to promote environmentally compatible development, and to eliminate barriers to the growth of the industry. WTTC's 'Green Globe' programme is a response to the Rio Earth Summit, encouraging commitment to environmental improvement by the tourism industry. Subscribing companies commit to WTTC Environmental Guidelines and awards are presented annually to members demonstrating outstanding achievement in environmental commitment.

SECTION 2
Companies

ARCTIC EXPERIENCE

'. . . the UK's market leader in holidays to Iceland and other unspoilt areas above and below the Arctic Circle.'

Arctic Experience has been creating and operating adventure holidays in the far north for ten years. The company has one of the highest staff-to-passenger ratios in the British travel business and most of their staff have first-hand knowledge of the destinations involved (a number are Icelanders, for instance). A range of adventure activities is catered for, including hiking, camping safaris, dog-sledging, canoeing and river-rafting. Over half of the company's 20 or so 'Lure of the North' trips visit Iceland, while the remaining itineraries comprise Greenland, Spitsbergen, Frans Josef Land, Finland, Lapland, Alaska, and Canada – and even (for a price) the North Pole! For security of booking, the company is exceptionally well bonded – CAA (ATOL no 2013), ABTA, AITO and IATA (International Air Transport Association). Although some of Arctic Experience's trips are physically demanding, most are quite suitable for generalist holidaymakers. Some are especially designed for children; others for senior citizens. Three destination videos produced by the company give a flavour of *Iceland*, *Greenland*, and *Whales & Glaciers*. Holiday prices range from around £400 for a 3-night escorted tour of Iceland, to around £1400 for a 7-day Iceland rambler, to £2300 for an Arctic cruise. For the seriously wealthy, you can occasionally book a £7500 trip to the North Pole!

Arctic Experience Ltd, 29 Nork Way, Banstead, Surrey, SM7 1PB, UK. Tel: 01737 218800. Fax: 01737 362341.

DISCOVER THE WORLD

'Discover the World has become one of the market leaders, by offering well-researched and often unique wildlife experiences to a diverse range of destinations.'

In 1990, when Discover the World was established, there were not many travel companies specializing in wildlife holidays. It's a different story today, but among the growing number of ecotourism operators, Discover the World continues to be a shining and responsible example. It donates a significant proportion of its profits to conservation work. For example, over £70 000 has been raised to support the World Wide Fund for Nature, the Whale & Dolphin Conservation Society and the David Shepherd Conservation Foundation. It supports the work of the Born Free Foundation's anti-poaching efforts and is an active member of CERT (see p 32). It takes its clients' security seriously as well: Discover the World is a member not only of ABTA, but also AITO and the CAA's ATOL scheme (No 2896). The range of wildlife and wilderness holidays offered by Discover the World varies from simple weekend breaks to expeditions lasting several weeks. For example, you can choose a 2-night Gibraltar dolphin watch for around £350, including flight; or a 5-day Canary Islands trip observing and swimming with pilot whales, staying on a square rigged sailing boat for around £1000 all-inclusive; or a 17-night Galapagos wildlife adventure for £3500, including flight from London to Quito. Destinations for the company's 21-trip list include Europe, the Americas, Africa and Asia. Discover the World makes a point of keeping its groups small – 15 on average. Several of its trips are suitable for families, the minimum age being 8 (accompanied) or 15 (unaccompanied). However, most clients tend to be aged between 25 and 60. No special fitness requirements are necessary for the majority of the tours, although Discover the World's holidays are designed for people who prefer to be active and who enjoy the outdoor life, rather than lying on a beach. In addition to its UK bases, the company has an office in Holland. Arctic Experience is sister company to Discover the World.

Discover the World Ltd, 29 Nork Way, Banstead, Surrey, SM7 1PB, UK. Tel: 01737 218800. Fax: 01737 362341.

DRAGOMAN

'We are not afraid to say that we run the best overland trips and are the number 1 operator . . .'

Dragoman has been in operation since 1981, running specialized overland expeditions throughout Asia, Africa, and Latin America. Its trips, which are designed to give an overall view of the countries visited, are either 3 to 6 week journeys, or longer overland expeditions lasting from 7 to 31 weeks. The company's name derives from the local guides – or *dragomen* – who accompanied Western explorers during the 18th and 19th centuries. Financially, the Dragoman Group operates within the guarantee of a trust as laid down under the rules of the EC Directive on Package Tourism. This means that clients are protected against financial failure of Dragoman Overseas Travel Ltd. This company is one of the leaders in the overland field, with a reputation for reliability and quality. Using Mercedes 1617 overland vehicles, which carry around 20 travellers usually aged 18 to 45, average distance covered per vehicle is around 1000 km/620 miles per week in Africa and 1200 km/750 miles per week in South America. Typically, 2 or 3 days per week are designated 'non-travelling'. Accommodation is either camping or hotel/camping combination. The trips are participatory in nature and all travellers are expected to take part in camp chores. Dragoman has a strict internal environmental policy. It is involved in the 'Campaign for Environmentally Responsible Tourism' (see p 32) and is a strong supporter of Survival International, a worldwide movement to support tribal peoples. Overland prices range from £120 to £210 per week, depending on the area and the length of the journey. Dragoman has overseas agents in Australia, New Zealand, the USA, Canada, Belgium, Holland, Denmark, Germany and Switzerland. The company's 'Dragodirect' Club issues a newsletter periodically.

Dragoman, Camp Green, Kenton Road, Debenham, Suffolk IP14 6LA, UK. Tel: 01728 861133 or 0171 370 1930. Fax: 01728 861127. *Or* **Adventure Center, 1311 63rd Street, Suite 200, Emeryville, California 94608, USA. Tel: 510 654 1879. Toll-Free: 800 227 8747. Fax: 510 654 4200.**

ENCOUNTER OVERLAND

'. . . if you're serious about being there to see dawn break in the high Himalaya, about following the great wildebeeste migration of the East African plains, or about watching the condor gliding in the thermals above Machu Picchu and its forested Andean chasm, so too are we.'

One of the oldest established overland companies, 'EO', as it is fondly known by thousands, was the first to overland to Asia (1963), first to Africa (1969) and first to South America (1972). The company emphasizes the 'hands-on' nature of its holidays, and stresses the active involvement and participation of its group members in expeditioning, be it de-bogging a stuck vehicle, pitching camp, cooking meals or navigating. A typical EO group consists of around twenty expeditioners comprising five or more nationalities, aged between about 20 and 40 and with a 50/50 male to female ratio. The company's tour leaders are carefully selected and thoroughly trained. Encounter Overland uses a variety of vehicles, specially adapted by the company for rugged and testing use. In Africa this means all of the trucks are four-wheel drive, in Asia a mixture of two- and four-wheel drive and in South America they are specially adapted non-4×4. All of the trips are camping safaris, ranging in length from 2 to 31 weeks. Camping equipment is supplied (except sleeping bags). Transcontinental journeys include London to Cape Town, London to Kathmandu and Quito to Rio. Prices are very competitive, usually from around £135 per week including all meals. EO offers optional additions to overland expeditions, such as river rafting/camping trips to Nepal and South America, climbing Mt Kilimanjaro and trekking in the Himalaya. The company has offices in Switzerland, the Netherlands, Belgium, Germany, Italy, Austria, Iceland, Denmark, Norway, Sweden, Nepal (EO's local sister company is Himalayan Encounters Pvt Ltd, Kathmandu) and Hong Kong.

Encounter Overland Ltd, 267 Old Brompton Road, London SW5 9JA, UK. Tel: 0171 370 6845. Fax: 0171 244 9737.

EXODUS

'Exodus Discovery Holidays are a particular way of travelling. They involve discovering, seeing and experiencing the many different cultures and environments of the world.'

With over 20 years experience, Exodus has a proven track record in providing small group adventurous holidays. These vary in length from 1 to 26 weeks, visiting unusual and exotic destinations throughout the world. Four distinct types of holiday are offered (each with its own comprehensive brochure): *Walking Explorer* – graded, 1- to 4-week, hotel- and camping-based trips to the major mountain ranges of the world, with porterage or vehicle support, cooks and staff; *Discovery Holidays* – around 70 active and ethnic cultural tours and short safaris from 1 to 4 weeks' duration off the beaten track; *Overland Expeditions* – shorter (2-week) to longer (29-week) transcontinental trips across Africa, Asia and South America for younger and more adventurous travellers; and *Mountain Bike Adventures* – graded, short (1- to 3-week) trips fully supported by vehicles in Nepal, India, Thailand, Europe, Turkey and Morocco. Altogether, Exodus offers holidays in over 80 countries worldwide. Trips start at £340 and go up to around £2500, so there is something for everyone. The company is fully bonded with AITO and the CAA (ATOL No 2582) and it is also IATA-licensed.

Exodus, Head Office, 9 Weir Road, London SW12 0LT, UK. Tel: 0181 673 0859. Fax: 0181 673 0779. *Or* **c/o Himalayan Travel, 112 Prospect Street, Stamford, CT 06901, USA. Tel: 203 359 3711. Toll-Free: 800 225 2380. Fax: 203 359 3669.**

- brochure
- video
- other literature

prices / destinations / party nos / accom / food /
type of participants /
typical age range /
typical male v female ratio /

Companies 41

EXPLORASIA

'ExplorAsia provides the adventure and excitement of a truly exhilarating holiday set in some of the most spectacular scenery in the world.'

The fact that ExplorAsia's parent company is renowned tour operator Abercrombie & Kent emphasizes the professional approach taken by this company towards adventure holidays. ExplorAsia is a leading trekking company which has provided a specialist travel service to the Indian Subcontinent for more than 12 years. Its principal destinations are the Himalayas and Karakoram, and the company has a close association with Mountain Travel Nepal – a well known and respected Nepalese trekking agency. Another association enjoyed by the company is with Tiger Tops, who organize safaris in Nepal and India. Outside this region, ExplorAsia's destinations include the Sinai desert, the Roof of Africa (Mts Kenya and Kilimanjaro), North and South America, and the Alps. In addition to the range of holidays specified in its brochure, the company also puts together bespoke holidays and expeditions for private groups and schools. In order to match client experience with the 'hardness' of the adventure, ExplorAsia grades its treks from 2 (easy) up to 4 (strenuous and extended), and its climbs from F (easy scrambling) through PD (technically straightforward) up to AD (experienced). River rafting is also available in Nepal (via a three-day descent of the Trisuli river). Group size is kept deliberately small – around eight, on average. Accommodation is in high-quality tented camps and hotels. The company is bonded with ABTA (No 72314) and the CAA (ATOL No 2881). Its Scottish mountaineering courses cost from £330 to £380 for a week. ExplorAsia's Himalayan holidays vary in price from around £1700 for a 15-day gentle trek in the Annapurna foothills, to around £2000 for many of the more isolated treks, to over £3300 for Bhutan treks. The Nepalese expeditions such as Mera Peak, Island Peak or Parchemo, cost around £2200.

ExplorAsia, Abercrombie & Kent Travel, Sloane Square House, Holbein Place, London SW1W 8NS, UK. Tel: 0171 730 9600. Fax: 0171 730 9376.

- 3 months in 3 diff continents.

EXPLORE WORLDWIDE

'From our very first pioneering days – when our concept of small group exploratory holidays originated – we've been enthralled by the idea of adventure travel. We still are.'

The largest of all the UK adventure holiday companies, Explore Worldwide lists an impressive portfolio of more than 170 trips in over 80 countries, with such destinations as Europe, the Middle East, Africa, Asia (including Russia), North, Central and South America, and Australasia. Prices range from an affordable £400 (eight days hiking in Spain, flight from London included) to £2865 (42-day Western Australia Explorer trip). All holidays represent good value for money. The range of challenges offered – from easy, through moderate, up to major – ensures that all tastes are catered for. Since its inception in 1982, the Explore ethos has been to cater for small groups of adventure travellers (average size 16) causing as little environmental damage and cultural disturbance as possible, and using local resources and services as much as possible. Most Explore trips are led by the company's own field staff. Normally various means of transport (including foot) are used on the same trip. Explore holidays appeal to a wide variety of ages and abilities. About half of the company's customers are single, independent travellers. Explore Worldwide is a member of Green Globe (see p 35), supports the Worldwide Fund for Nature, and is AITO and CAA bonded (ATOL No 2595). Eleven Explore video cassettes are available, and these deal with some of the company's most popular holiday destinations. Explore Trader (see p 27) is a unique trading company which offers – mostly through mail order – a selection of clothing and equipment for would-be adventure travellers. The company has an impressive network of offices throughout the world, comprising Belgium, Australia, Denmark, USA, New Zealand, Switzerland, the Netherlands, Canada and Hong Kong.

Explore Worldwide Ltd, 1 Frederick Street, Aldershot, Hants GU11 1LQ, UK. Tel: 01252 319448. Fax: 01252 343170. *Or* **Adventure Center, 1311 63rd Street, Suite 200, Emeryville, California 94608, USA. Tel: 510 654 1879. Toll-Free: 800 227 8747. Fax: 510 654 4200.**

GUERBA EXPEDITIONS

'We want to show you its charm, rugged beauty and vast deserts: where Africa moves to a different beat, a world where tribal Africa is a day to day reality and where you come to expect the unexpected.'

Guerba has grown over the past sixteen years to become one of the premier African adventure specialists, taking its clients to places away from the busy commercial centres and tourist hotspots. Yet it is misleading to think of Guerba only in terms of African adventure, for the company is rapidly gaining a reputation for adventure tours – especially walking – in such places as the Himalayas, South America, the Far East and (of course) Africa. As far as their African trips are concerned, Guerba uses a fleet of Mercedes trucks, and Bedford and modern AWD 4-wheel drive trucks, specially adapted for overland conditions. These can carry up to twenty passengers and three crew. Trips range from 1- to 4-week safaris and adventure tours, to 5- to 33-week overland journeys. All corners of the continent are covered, from Morocco to South Africa. Most passengers are aged between 20 and 50: all are expected to participate in the daily routine of safari life. Guerba's walking adventure holidays – graded from 'Easy' up to 'Mountaineering' – suit a wide range of tastes, experience and ages (generally 25 to 55). Group size varies considerably but tends to average around 14, and about half the group members start out 'unattached'. Proud of their safety record, Guerba takes care of clients' financial security also, via bonding – AITO and CAA (ATOL No 2807). Since 1989, Guerba has contributed over £12 000 to the Worldwide Fund for Nature, from holiday royalties. From their *Africa in Close Up* brochure, holiday prices range from around £300 (Morocco, land-only) to £1000 for many of the fortnight African trips, to £4000 for the 29-week 'Africa all the way' overland marathon. From their *Walking and Adventure* brochure, prices range from around £400 (Mount Kenya Trek – 6 days, land only) to £2400 (Mera Peak, all-inclusive 30-day trip). The company has offices in eleven countries, including the USA.

Guerba Expeditions Ltd, 40 Station Road, Westbury, Wiltshire, BA13 3QX, UK. Tel: 01373 826611; Fax: 01373 858351. *Or* **Adventure Center, 1311 63rd St, Suite 200, Emeryville, California 94608, USA. Tel: 510 654 1879. Toll-Free: 800 227 8747. Fax: 510 654 4200.**

HIGH PLACES

'We remain small and innovative. Our trips are unpretentious, authentic and adventurous. They are designed for intelligent and discerning people who wish to retain a taste of independent travel in their holiday, and who have a regard for people and places everywhere.'

High Places began trading in 1986 and became a limited company two years later. It is run 'by outdoor people for outdoor people' and this ethos shines through in the kind of trips offered. Its groups are never more than 12 in number, and – in the case of mountaineering trips – considerably fewer. Virtually all the holidays offered are exclusive to High Places, which means that trips are personally organized and led. Most of its clients are aged 30 to 50, although a fifth are under 30 years old and a twelfth are over 60. Half the bookings are made by individuals (the other half by couples or groups) and the ratio of male to female clients is 50:50. Each year, High Places organizes a number of special trips for schools, clubs and groups of friends. Clients have financial security via CAA bonding (ATOL No 2836). The tours that High Places runs are not 'whistle-stop': tourist haunts and large hotels are avoided wherever possible. Trekking holidays are the main activity: some of these treks are even led by the company directors. High Places believes strongly in the importance of conservation and responsible travel. It follows Tourism Concern's Himalayan Tourist Code (see Appendix 2) and is unique in printing this Code in its holiday brochure. Indeed, the background information and inspiration contained in its brochure is second to none. High Places offers itineraries in Latin America, India, Sikkim, Bhutan, Pakistan, Nepal, New Zealand, Borneo, Africa, Eastern Europe, Iceland and Scotland – an impressive list for a relatively small company. Prices (which are all-inclusive) start at £240 for a 4-day winter skills course in Scotland, and go up to £2500 for such trips as the Amazon and Galapagos or Sikkim and Bhutan. Most of the trips are in the £1500 to £2000 range, however. A 5% discount is offered to travellers who have been on a High Places trip before. By offering a range of trips, clients' fitness can be evenly matched to level of challenge.

High Places Ltd, Globe Works, Penistone Road, Sheffield, S6 3AE, UK. Tel: 0114 275 7500. Fax: 0114 275 3870.

THE IMAGINATIVE TRAVELLER

'In many cases the only thing [our clients] have in common, at least to start with, is a spirit of adventure, an open mind and the desire to enjoy a holiday that offers a more fulfilling experience than just lying on a beach.'

The Imaginative Traveller holiday ingredients are 'activity, culture and fun'. The company features a great many holidays of this sort to the Middle East, the Himalayas, China, Turkey, India, South East Asia, Latin America, Australia and Europe. Examples include camel safaris in Rajasthan, white-water rafting and cycling in Nepal and trekking in Bhutan. Holidays are classified either as small escorted tours or individual trips, most itineraries lasting from one to three weeks. Clients comprise individuals, couples and small international groups, the latter varying in size from 12 up to 20. The Imaginative Traveller can also arrange bespoke tours for groups and parties. Wide ranges of budgets and abilities are catered for among the scores of holidays offered. Accommodation includes camping, hotels, palaces, castles and mountain lodges, while activities include felucca sailing, walking, riding (donkeys, camels and horses), cycling, diving, canoeing, and rafting. Resident company staff include tour leaders, qualified guides, sailors, cooks, drivers, representatives, operations managers and administration back-up. While brochure prices are quoted as land-only (ie excluding air fares), The Imaginative Traveller can help to advise on good-value air fares. The price range of trips varies from £150 for a 3-day cycling/walking and canoeing trip (in Dartmoor, UK) up to £1800 (21 days in China, including internal flights). Clients' holiday payments are deposited in a Clients' Trust Account, to ensure financial protection. The Imaginative Traveller has seven offices in Australia and four in Canada, as well as contact addresses in South Africa, Germany, Denmark, Holland, Belgium, Spain, Italy, Sweden, Switzerland, Norway, New Zealand, Malta and the USA.

The Imaginative Traveller Ltd, Head Office, 14 Barley Mow Passage, Chiswick, London W4 4PH, UK. Tel: 0181 742 3113. Fax: 0181 742 3045. *Or* c/o Himalayan Travel, 112 Prospect Street, Stamford, CT 016901, USA. Tel: 203 359 3711. Toll-Free: 800 225 2380. Fax: 203 359 3669.

SHERPA EXPEDITIONS

'We proudly claim that no-one knows the remote corners of
the world's mountain ranges quite as well as we do.'

Sherpa is the walker's company *par excellence*. Twenty years ago it
traded as Sherpa Himalayan Trekking Expeditions. As other parts
of the world were steadily added to their portfolio of walking
holidays, the name 'Sherpa Expeditions' became a more appropriate title. Now the list of destinations has swelled to the extent that
the company currently has separate brochures on the UK and
Ireland, Europe, Switzerland, Eastern Europe including Russia,
Africa and the Middle East, South America and, naturally
enough, the Himalayas. Today it arranges holidays for over 5000
customers annually. The company caters for a wide range of tastes
– gentle rambles through to strenuous peak ascents – and accommodation – hotels through to camping. Basically five different
kinds of holiday are offered: centre-based, where you make
rambling forays from one or two hotels; hotel treks, where you
stop at a different hotel each night; vehicle-supported treks, in
which you stop at pre-pitched camps; mountain expeditions,
comprising guided trips into particularly remote mountain areas
using porters or pack animals; and backpacking treks, which are
self-contained trips. Sherpa's customers are drawn from a wide age
range, from under 25 to over 60, a large proportion of them
travelling on their own. Holiday prices (which represent good
value) range from just £162 for 4 nights in Northumberland, to
£350 for a week in Europe, to just under £2000 for a 4-week
Himalayan trek. Sherpa is bonded with CAA (ATOL No 1185)
and the company has offices in the UK, the USA, New Zealand
and Holland.
   **Sherpa Expeditions, 131a Heston Road, Hounslow, Middlesex
TW5 0RD, UK. Tel: 0181 577 2717. Fax: 0181 572 9788.** *Or*
**Himalayan Travel, 112 Prospect Street, Stamford, CT 06901, USA.
Tel: 203 359 3711. Toll-Free: 800 225 2380. Fax: 203 359 3669.**

SUPER NATURAL ADVENTURES

'Unique, adventurous vacations are our speciality and we welcome travellers from around the world, providing them with wonderful lasting memories of their adventure vacation.'

Super Natural Adventures is rapidly gaining a reputation for being the premier adventure vacation broker in the Pacific Northwest, ie Alberta, British Columbia, Alaska, Yukon, Northwest Territories, Montana, Wyoming, Colorado, Utah, Idaho and Manitoba. This region offers plenty of 'world-class' adventure destinations and activities, and Super Natural Adventures acts as agent, putting adventure vacationers in touch with suppliers from the region. Its collection of destinations includes a 'difficulty rating' description for each itinerary so that trips can be matched to client expectations of (dis)comfort. Most groups are limited to a maximum of 14, although there are some smaller and a few larger ones. Most ages are catered for and several itineraries are specially designed for older adventurers and families. A few have restrictions based on weight or age of client due to legal or safety reasons. The range of activities covered includes ranch vacations, horsepacking, cycling, lodge hiking, canoeing, whale-watching, river rafting, backpacking and sea kayaking. Accommodation comprises either camping, hotel, resort or ranch. In addition, the company offers a 'Design Your Own Vacation' option which allows clients to mix and match different itineraries. Examples of shorter trips include 3-day stays in National Parks such as Jasper and Banff, in which you try a variety of adventurous activities (around $900 excluding meals) or 3-day lodge-based riding trips (around $400 excluding meals). Longer (one-week) ranch vacations cost from $700 to $1300, while horsepacking trips (lasting just under a week) are in the range $700 to $1000 (camping and ranches). Six-day cycling camping tours cost from $900 to $1500 while similar canoeing trips range from $500 to $1200. The cost of river rafting depends on the river concerned: 6 days on the Chilko–Chilcotin Rivers costs $1400, compared with 12 days on the Tatshenshini for $2500. Sea kayaking costs from $800 for 6 days up to $2600 for 10 days.

Super Natural Adventures Inc, 626 West Pender Street, Main Floor, Vancouver, British Columbia, Canada, V6B 1V9. Tel: 604 683 5101. Fax: 604 683 5129.

TRAILFINDERS

'We realized that you, the traveller, did not have the herd instinct, you wanted to choose your own itinerary to travel and explore at your own pace.'

In 1970, Trailfinders consisted of four unpaid enthusiasts with no commercial experience in the travel business. Today the team numbers over 400 looking after around a thousand people every day. Though not strictly an adventure holiday company, Trailfinders offers discount flights, especially multi-stopover and round-the-world, thus appealing more to independent adventurers than to packaged groups. Today it claims to have the widest range of flights across the globe at the lowest fares in the market. Although the company does not produce a holiday brochure of its own, it consolidates a series of itineraries through other companies' brochures, linking in with the likes of Dragoman, Encounter Overland, Exodus, Guerba, The Imaginative Traveller and Trek America. Its Travel Pass offers discounts on accommodation and tours. As well as offering discount airfares, Trailfinders provides insurance, geared particularly to the needs of active adventure travellers. At its Travel Centre, it offers an immunization centre, a visa and passport processing service, a map and travel bookshop and a library/information centre with free access to up-to-date reference material. This includes such information as timetables, newspaper cuttings of travel articles, reference guide books for most destinations worldwide, and tourist office information from around the world. Trailfinders' customers are financially secure via IATA, ABTA (No 69701) and the CAA (ATOL No 1458). The company also produces *Trailfinder*, a quarterly magazine carrying articles about off-the-beaten-track, independent trips and factual information such as climate, accommodation, visas and exchange rate for each destination covered.

Trailfinders, 42–50 Earls Court Road, London W8 6EJ, UK. Tel: 0171 938 3366 (long-haul flights). Tel: 0171 937 5400 (transatlantic and European flights). *Or* **194 Kensington High Street, London W8 7RG, UK. Tel: 0171 938 3939 (long-haul flights). Tel: 0171 938 3232 (transatlantic and European flights). Tel: 0171 938 3999 (immunization centre). Tel: 0171 938 3303 (information centre). Tel: 0171 938 3999 (map and bookshop).** *Or* **58 Deansgate, Manchester M3 2FF, UK. Tel: 0161 839 6969.** *Or* **254–284 Sauchiehall Street, Glasgow G2 3EH, UK. Tel: 0141 353 2224.** *Or* **48 Corn Street, Bristol BS1 1HQ, UK. Tel: 0117 929 9000.**

TREK AMERICA

'Get away from the "package holiday" approach and enter the world of active, exciting holidays. This is the world of Trek America, the specialists in "off the beaten path" adventures for the 18–38s.'

Trek America has operated adventure holidays throughout North America for 25 years. Its summer brochure lists trips from late March to early November, while the winter programme runs from November through March. Its 'Footloose' itineraries comprise 11 tours in North America for 'the adventure-minded traveller of any age seeking activity-filled tours at a leisurely pace.' Trek America is an ABTA bonded tour operator, and is fully licensed by the Interstate Commerce Commission in the USA, and the equivalent bodies in Canada and Mexico. Ranging from 7 days to 9 weeks, their holidays – some 45 itineraries in all – operate in the USA, Canada, Alaska, and Mexico, lasting from 7 days to 9 weeks. The general age range for customers is 18 to 38, although many travellers are aged up to 45. Average group size is limited to 13 and on each trip there are generally 5 to 8 different nationalities. Trek America specializes in outdoor activities and pursuits such as mountain biking, wilderness canoeing, white-water rafting, hiking and horse riding. Several itineraries offer a close look at the extensive network of public lands in North America: National Parks, National Forests, Provincial and State Parks, National Seashores and Monuments and Bureau of Land Management areas. Native cultures and tribal lands play an important part in Trek America's programmes: the company has a direct working relationship with the Navajo Indians for instance. Several itineraries offer overnight horseriding trips with Navajo guides in Monument Valley, which is accessible only when accompanied by members of the Navajo nation. Major archaeological sites are featured in the Southwest desert region and throughout Mexico. Trek America stresses responsible visitation, low-impact camping methods and the 'take only photos and leave only footprints (where allowed)' ethos. Prices range from around £350 to £1850 excluding flights. The company has offices in 16 countries.

Trek America, 4 Waterperry Court, Middleton Road, Banbury, Oxon OX16 8QG. Tel: 01295 256777. Fax: 01295 257399. *Or* **Premier International Corporation, dba TrekAmerica, PO Box 189, Rockaway, NJ 07866, USA. Tel: 201 983 1144. Fax: 201 983 8551.**

WEXAS

'Wexas is perhaps best known for its tradition of off-the-beaten track, adventurous itineraries and exotic travel options.'

Strictly speaking, Wexas is not so much a tour operator as a travel association, for which you pay a modest annual subscription. The company does, however, organize a large variety of adventure holidays for thousands of clients every year. Dating back 25 years, Wexas boasts an illustrious list of Honorary Presidents, both past and present. Today it offers its 35 000 members a package of benefits, including discounted scheduled air fares and round-the-world air fares; a quarterly magazine called *Traveller* (which includes articles about adventure trips taken independently to remote destinations), special insurance deals; and a *World Discoveries* catalogue listing scores of adventure holidays. These visit such places as the Far East, Australia and New Zealand, the Pacific, India, Africa, the Middle East, North America and Canada, the Caribbean, Latin America and Europe, and include Discovery Cruises. Activities on this vast range of trips include mountain and jungle trekking, sailing and riverboating, diving, rafting and safaris. Wexas is fully bonded, via IATA, ABTA (No 91989) and the CAA (ATOL No 2873). It has a wide variety of holiday prices to suit a range of budgets. For example, while a 15-day tribal trek in Thailand costs around £800, all-inclusive, a 15-day trek in Sumatra, Vietnam or Borneo costs from £1200 to £1500. African safaris start at just over £1300 (Kenya, 9 days) and go up to £2000. A 19-day trip to the Amazon and Galapagos costs £2100, all-inclusive. One feature of the Wexas portfolio is the large number and variety of 'add-on' mini-holidays which can be selected in addition to the main holiday.

Wexas International, 45–49 Brompton Road, Knightsbridge, London SW3 1DE, UK. Tel: 0171 589 0555. Fax: 0171 589 8418.

WORLD EXPEDITIONS

'. . . we strive to offer you the most fulfilling, exciting adventures available. In pursuing these goals, our primary concern is your well-being.'

One of the longer-established adventure operators around today, World Expeditions has been in existence for 20 years. Most of its clients are independently minded vacationers who recognize the benefits of travelling in small groups. Often booking more than once, they come from Europe, New Zealand, Australia and the North American continent. Quite a few clients (for example, families, scuba diving devotees, and fitness groups) ask World Expeditions to organize a customized trip for them. For more demanding trips, clients are recommended to have undergone some preparation through regular exercise. The company is bonded via the Association of Bonded Travel Organisers Trust (ABTOT No 5017). As well as its main portfolio of Himalayan treks and expeditions, World Expeditions includes the following destinations in its listings: Maldives, China, Vietnam, Thailand, Borneo, Indonesia, South America and Antarctica. It also carries a number of separate brochures including Greece, 'Off the Beaten Track', and China adventures. Its Nepal trips start at around £600, land only, for a 13-day introductory trek, going up to around £1400 for 28-day moderate-to-strenuous treks (land only) to expeditions (eg Mera Peak) at around £1800, again excluding flights. More expensive Himalayan destinations such as Bhutan and Tibet cost between £2000 and £3000, land only. World Expeditions' 7-day sailing, swimming, snorkelling safari in the Maldives costs around £500, excluding flights. Other activities include biking in China and Vietnam, 'Cultural Adventure' trips in the Far East, and Indian jungle safaris. World Expeditions has offices in Norway, Denmark, Sweden, Netherlands, Austria and Belgium.

World Expeditions, 7 North Road, Maidenhead, Berkshire, SL6 1PL, UK. Tel: 01628 74174. Fax: 01628 74312.

WORLDWIDE JOURNEYS AND EXPEDITIONS

'. . . tailored for the discerning traveller who wants to explore new environments and new cultures – or perhaps revisit places that have given pleasure previously.'

Although Worldwide Journeys and Expeditions has been in operation for only four years, its Directors have had considerably longer experience in the adventure holiday industry. One of the company's many attractions is its wide-ranging and diverse portfolio of trips worldwide. It lists over a hundred itineraries in such regions as Africa (East, Central, North and Southern), the Indian Ocean, Egypt, America (South and Central), Nepal, India, Pakistan, Bhutan, and Borneo. In addition, Worldwide Journeys and Expeditions runs a number of 'hard adventure' expeditions to the Himalayas (Rolwaling, Mera, Island Peak and Stok Kangri), Latin America (the Bolivian Altiplano, Aconcagua), and Africa (Ruwenzori). The company's treks are graded to help match clients' ability to degree of challenge. Worldwide Journeys and Expeditions stresses its expertise and track record in putting together bespoke trips for groups and individuals. Like many other adventure holiday companies, its travel philosophy is that those who travel with the company do so with 'a positive frame of mind and a sense of humour'. Its tours are sensitive to the local environment and peoples encountered, and it is an active supporter of – and financial contributor towards – many conservation foundations, including the Kasanka Trust, Save the Rhino International, The World Pheasant Association and the Himalayan Trust. Its clients are given financial security through CAA bonding (ATOL No 2778). Average group size is eight – small enough to guarantee individual attention. Tour leaders are generally hand-picked from the localities visited, which is culturally responsible and also ensures that clients receive a first-hand knowledge of the area. Worldwide Journeys and Expeditions' all-inclusive prices cover a wide spectrum, from under £1000 for the Moroccan trips, to £2000–£3000 for most of its other trips.

Worldwide Journeys and Expeditions Ltd, 8 Comeragh Road, London W14 9HP, UK. Tel: 0171 381 8638. Fax: 0171 381 0836.

SECTION 3
Activities

'While an outdoor pursuit such as mountain climbing may seem risky, even foolhardy to some, the mountaineer will often see it as a controllable and even safe activity. One of the main delights of outdoor adventure pursuits is the acceptance and control of risk.'

Go (booklet accompanying the British TV series
The Great Outdoors)

Sections 1 and 2 deal with the background to adventure holidays and profile some of the companies offering these kinds of trips. Section 4 will deal with many of the world's adventure destinations, but what about the activities involved?

In this Section some twenty mainstream adventure activities are covered, from the general (for example trekking or mountain biking) to the specific (for instance scuba diving or hang-gliding). All types of activity are profiled: land-based, water-based and air-based, while details of cost, degree of difficulty and addresses of governing body organizations are also provided. If the address and telephone/fax numbers of a tour operator are not supplied, this indicates that the company is profiled in Section 2, and you will find all the relevant details there.

People vary as to their activity interests. Some budding adventurers have a yen to try lots of different activities, while others are content to develop and hone a certain skill to personal perfection. For many it's the attraction of water that counts; some prefer to take to the skies; others need to have their feet firmly on the ground. A number want to experience the unique adventure of travelling with animals, husky dogs perhaps, or horses. Whatever your interest, the chances are it's covered here. In all, the activities profiled in this section are:

- Ballooning.
- Canoeing and kayaking.
- Caving.
- Climbing and mountaineering.
- Dog sledging.
- Expeditions.

- Hang-gliding.
- Mountain biking.
- Overlanding.
- Paragliding.
- River rafting.
- Riding and pony trekking.
- Safaris.
- Scuba diving.
- Ski touring.
- Tall-ship sailing.
- Trekking.
- Youth activities.

Get-away-from-it-all adventurers will want to head off to some distant land to turn their dream activity into reality, but it is possible to sample the delights of many adventurous sports closer to home. In the UK, apart from the multitude of individual clubs and societies devoted to specific activities, there's an umbrella club with over 5000 members called **SPICE (Special Programme of Initiative, Challenge and Excitement, 13 Thorpe Street, Old Trafford, Manchester M16 9PR; tel: 0161 872 2213)**. The club's *raison d'être* is 'excitement' although there's a social spin-off as well. Membership is open to anyone over the age of 18. In addition to organizing day or part-day activities, SPICE offers longer adventure trips to far-flung corners of the world.

BALLOONING

'I find it bizarre to be in a laundry basket suspended by a bag of hot air some 2000 feet up. But flying so slowly and quietly with 360-degree views is like looking at the Grand Canyon – your mind has never seen anything so huge.'

Russell Harris, The Great Outdoors (British TV series)

When Marie Antoinette saw the first manned hot air balloon soar majestically over the Parisian skyline she was heard to remark 'It's the sport of the Gods.' But despite its hallowed appeal, ballooning took more than two hundred years – and the introduction of propane gas burners – before finally 'taking off' in popularity. The Montgolfier brothers and other pioneering aviators of those early days used dangerous techniques to inflate their balloon 'envelopes' with hot air (ignited straw burners, for example). During the 1960s, however, a revolution in balloon design was heralded with the introduction of lightweight and powerful propane burners. Combining this technology with special gossamer nylon fabrics which were air-tight, fire-resistant and non-rip, finally allowed hot-air ballooning to come of age: a practical and safe activity for air adventure enthusiasts.

However, ballooning is not your average adventure sport. Its oft-advertised 'champagne flights' are more usually associated in people's minds with luxury, and certainly the sport is not demanding physically (unless you happen to be a member of the ground crew, lugging the basket from its landing site to the recovery vehicle). It is essentially a passive experience, unless you decide to become a pilot yourself. But although drifting with the wind in a tranquil, overwhelmingly silent (except for the whoosh of burners) and almost surreal world, is less active than piloting a paraglider or hang-glider, it still carries its own special adventure anodyne, especially in those remote parts of the world where the sport is still being pioneered.

Like other airsports, ballooning is an activity which – if you're going to take control – needs a lot of time, training and funding. To purchase a new balloon costs from £9000, although second-hand models start at about £4000. Learning to fly is also expensive: to obtain a private pilot's licence (which allows you to take solo flights but not fare-paying passengers), you need a minimum of sixteen hours in the air and a budget of up to £1500. It is this expense, more than anything else, which accounts for ballooning's exclusivity (in the UK there are fewer than 1600 certified pilots, for example). But those craving 'soft' adventure will be content with the sensation of sailing up and away in a glorified laundry basket under a beautiful bubble of colour, as a passenger rather than as a pilot.

Age is no bar to ballooning enjoyment: passengers as young as 4 and as old as 102 have flown. Usually a ballooning trip will occupy only part of a holiday rather than a full vacation in itself. Early morning or evening are the best times of the day for this activity, when breezes are at a minimum. During the middle of the day the sun's heat can create thermals which can make flights choppy. The cost of a flight varies, but around £100 is average.

Intrepid 1990s adventure pioneers are constantly dreaming up new places to balloon over. Richard Branson and Per Lindstrand's dramatic trans-Atlantic crossing in 1987 certainly captured the imagination of other 'wannabe' adventurers. Even Everest has witnessed an 'up and over' hot air balloon flight. For most people, though, something less dramatic is adventurous enough. For example, visitors to Kenya can take an early morning game-viewing flight over the Masai Mara – the ultimate aerial safari experience. Ballooning safaris in Africa are rapidly gaining in popularity, thanks to operators such as **Abercrombie and Kent Travel (Sloane Square House, Holbein Place, London SW1W 8NS; tel: 0171 730 9600)**. For flights nearer to home, see the Factfile.

FACTFILE

Organizations: in the USA, the **Balloon Federation of America (PO Box 400, Indianola, IA 51025; tel: 515 961 8809)** is a division of the National Aeronautic Association. It publishes a quarterly journal and a list of US clubs.

In the UK the **British Balloon and Airship Club (The Cottage, Old Barn Farm, Denton Road, Horton, Northamptonshire NN7 2BG)** issues a booklet listing all companies offering balloon flights in the country. The **Balloon Club of Great Britain** is located at **Montgolfier House, Fairoaks Airport, Chobham, Surrey GU24 8HU; tel: 01276 858529**.

Safety: Check that your operator is properly insured, since personal policies can sometimes be nullified during airsport participation. Balloons can be landed very gently in still conditions (below 10 mph).

Clothing: No special clothes are necessary since there is no windchill factor involved. Just dress according to the weather.

CANOEING AND KAYAKING

'As we waited for the contents of this blackened coffee pot to come to the boil, and looked out from the granite shoulders of a little island to wooded shores and the penetrating blue tossed between lake and sky, miserable hours of wind and rain might never have been. Canoeing is like that.'

Sylvie Nickels, Finnish Canoe Safari
(Traveller magazine, Summer 1988)

Although the term 'canoe' has come to be generic to all small craft, canoes and kayaks are in reality two very different things. Strictly speaking, canoes (or Canadian canoes) are the open-topped variety, often associated with North American Indians, whereas kayaks are enclosed, having a cockpit which you climb. into. Sea kayaks also have a small rudder for steering. Basically if you think of an Eskimo roll, you can in a kayak but you can't in a canoe.

Canoes mean different things to different people. Perhaps it is the still and silent passage across a deserted loch, leaving no trace of your journey behind you, canoeist in perfect harmony with the environment. Or perhaps it is the thrills and spills of rushing white water, testing your skill and strength against a river's mighty power. Whatever your persuasion, canoeing is an ideal form of adventure activity. It is accessible to all ages, it is not too expensive and it is environmentally friendly. This revolution in canoeing's popularity, be it a long trip on quiet water or a short trip on white water, has been made possible by changes in the technology of construction, from canvas and plywood to fibreglass and then to plastic.

Wherever you live, some form of canoeing will be available not far away. You can join a club and learn the basics on open water or even at the local swimming pool (an ideal venue to start practising Eskimo rolls). Independent canoe addicts will probably have their own kayak which they can take to stretches of testing water, when the flows are right. Increasingly, canoeing adventures are becoming available close to towns and cities, as more and more artificial slalom courses are constructed. But many would-be adventurers who lack experience will want to head off into the wide blue yonder to try their hand at the paddle. Adventure tour operators are alive to this need and increasing numbers are offering the chance to go coastal or sea touring in kayaks, or inland touring by Canadian canoe. Often the canoeing element will be part of a larger package which might include such things as rafting, riding and biking.

Canoeing is a safe activity as long as certain rules are followed, and as long as you can swim at least 50 metres. Buoyancy aids are a must; not the standard lifejacket type but a padded waistcoat type which does not interfere with your paddle strokes (prices £30 and upwards). Helmets (£15 plus) and paddles (£20 at least) are also essential for white-water kayakers. But if you opt for a package trip, no investment is necessary since all the gear is provided. Clothing is a different matter, however, and it is important to bear in mind that you can get cold even in summer, if you're ill-equipped. For most occasions you won't need a wetsuit, just nylon overtrousers and cagoule over a wool or fleece top and bottoms, plus trainers and a hat. Alternatively, you can invest in a special canoe jacket for between £30 and £150.

Tour operators offering canoeing trips include **Accessible Isolation (44 Downing Street, Farnham, Surrey GU9 7PH; tel: 01252 718808); Exodus Expeditions; Super Natural Adventures; Arctic Experience; Explore Worldwide**; and **Okovango Tours and Safaris (28 Bisham Gardens, London N6 6DD; tel: 0181 343 3283)**. For confident canoeists, **Arctic Experience** offers a Yukon 'paddle as you please' package in which you select from a choice of six river routes lasting from 7 to 18 days. The canoes supplied are safe and easy to handle and you can stop where and when you please, among some of Yukon's most beautiful scenery. Although briefing is provided about the routes and safety procedures, you do need to be self-reliant and have previous wilderness camping experience, since these routes traverse completely uninhabited areas. Cost for canoe rental, two people sharing, from Whitehorse to Yukon is from just over £50 to just over £100.

Other canoeing wilderness destinations include Venezuela, Ecuador, Bolivia (**Exodus** and **Explore Worldwide**). **Accessible Isolation** provides trips on over 60 Canadian rivers from the sub-Arctic to the Arctic, at prices ranging from £300 to £1500. For a sea kayaking experience, **Super Natural Adventures** offers a number of trips suitable for novice to intermediate kayakers off Vancouver Island, British Columbia. Prices range from $800 for seven days, to $2500 for ten days.

FACTFILE

Organizations: British Canoe Union (John Dudderige House, Adbolton Lane, West Bridgford, Nottingham NG2 5AS; tel: 0115 9821100). Canoe Camping Club (25 Waverley Road, South Norwood, London SE25 4HT; tel: 0181 654 1835). American Canoe Association (7432 Alban Station Boulevard, Suite B-226, Springfield, VA 22150, USA; tel: 703 451 0141).

Travel tip: When learning, check out the credentials of your instructor. He or she should be BCU-qualified or similar.

Ecotourism: The BCU has an environmental policy which states 'Wildlife and landscape are an essential part of the canoeist's pleasure for aesthetic, cultural and recreational reasons. It is in the canoeist's interest to conserve the environment.'

CAVING

For many people, the thought of descending into the bowels of the earth is claustrophobic and fearful. They imagine falling down concealed shafts into bottomless pits, being trapped under rising water or being bitten by vampires. The truth is very different, however. Once you do overcome prejudices and try caving for the first time you will discover that it holds a special kind of fascination all of its own. For many speleologists this fascination is enough to make them go underground again and again, for a whole host of reasons. Some find it is the physical challenge, others discover a scientific appeal, and for others still it is a part-time hobby. But whatever the reason, or the excuse, the compulsion for potholing remains long after the adventure is over. Perhaps it is the prospect of discovering a new cave – or even a whole new system. Each cave is different; each unique. Some are heavily adorned with stalactites and stalagmites, others are simple tunnels, still others lead into vast caverns. But underlying and unifying each caving experience is a sense of isolation from the world above, a remoteness from sunlit civilization. You can in truth be close to a human settlement or equally you can be out in the sticks, but down there in the Earth's nether regions you are in an underground adventure realm all of your own.

Caving equipment is fairly straightforward. You will need a good pair of boots, a one-piece coverall or boiler suit (or wetsuit if it's very wet), gloves, a hard hat (for headbanging speleologists) and (for reasons of safety) three sources of light. Since serious caving is a bit like upside down rock climbing, serious cavers have to carry around all the accoutrements of climbing as well (see Climbing and Mountaineering). Hardened adventurers go in for such things as exploring underground river systems, requiring a knowledge of dingy handling and sometimes even diving skills. But for first-time and novice cavers, there are plenty of less demanding underground adventure opportunities.

In the UK, the main caving areas are North Yorkshire, the Mendips in Somerset, Derbyshire and South Wales. A number of operators offer trips and courses for beginners and more experienced speleologists alike. **Edale Youth Hostel Association Activity Centre (Rowland Cote, Nether Booth, Edale, Derbyshire S30 2ZH; tel: 01433 670302)** runs trips with experienced instructors who will reveal to you a dark side of the Peak District not seen by most visitors. A weekend course costs about £80 including full board and accommodation. Other caving weekends for beginners and improvers are also organized by the YHA at **Edale and Llangollen Activity Centres** (call **01433 670302** for details). **Rock Lea Activity Centre (Station Road, Hathersage, via Sheffield Peak National Park, Derbyshire S30 1DD; tel: 01433 6503450)** runs weekend and longer caving holidays for adults throughout most of the year: cost is from £90 full board for a weekend to £200 for a week.

In the USA, details of operators offering caving trips can be obtained from the societies listed in the Factfile. The National Speleological Society will put you in touch with one of its many local chapters or 'grottos'. The American term for caving with a guide is 'spelunking' and you can avail yourself of the chance to spelunk at many locations in the USA. Some places do make special demands though, like 'nobody with a chest size larger than

44 inches' (Wyandotte Cave in Indiana) and 'no spelunking until after bat hibernation is complete' (Carter Caves State Park, Kentucky).

FACTFILE

Useful addresses: USA – **National Speleological Society, Cave Avenue, Huntsville, AL 35810; tel: 205 852 1300.** National Caves Association, 4138 Dark Hollow Road, McMinnville, TN 37110; tel: 615 668 3925. UK – the **British Cave Research Association** is located at **Holt House, Holt Lane, Lea, Matlock, Derbyshire.** The easiest way to find out about clubs is through local tourist information offices.

CLIMBING AND MOUNTAINEERING

'Great things are done when men and mountains meet;
This is not done by jostling in the street.'
William Blake (1757–1827)

The first ever mountain climb made simply 'because it's there' was recorded in 1336 by Italian poet, Francesco Petrarch. However, it was a long time before climbing mountains for sport became regarded as anything other than eccentricity or even insanity. Indeed, by the eighteenth century the fashionable thing was to regard mountains as distasteful at best or grotesque at worst. However, in 1865 that prejudice changed forever, for in July of that year, a wood engraver and climber by the name of Edward Whymper invited seven enthusiasts to join him in climbing the Matterhorn, which at that time was the greatest unconquered peak in the Alps. Arriving at the 4500 m/14 780 ft summit, Whymper recorded in his diary the simple, celebratory entry 'Hurrah!'. But disaster struck the expedition on the descent when three of the other climbing members fell 4000 ft to their deaths. This still remains one of the worst mountaineering disasters in history, and yet it has inspired a passion for climbing and mountaineering in the UK and elsewhere which continues to be as compelling as ever. The result of this enduring passion is a long and auspicious history of mountaineering feats and achievements. But although the art of mountaineering is associated with a venerable roll-call of household names, the sport is not necessarily the sole preserve of a chosen few. George Mallory, who disappeared on Everest in 1924, put it well when he remarked that the greatest danger people faced in life was in *not* taking the adventure. Many of us have our own goals and dreams, our own 'Everests', and these challenges still require the elements of dedication and personal commitment if they are to be achieved and realized.

As concepts of scaling mountains have evolved, so have associated definitions. Thus while rock-climbing can involve anything from shinnying up a moving indoor wall to scaling the monstrous 900 m/3000 ft high face of El Capitan above Yosemite's valley floor in California, mountaineering, on the other hand, involves a range of other skills and demands. These include such things as hiking long distances to base camp, camping in sub-zero conditions, map and compass navigation, and snow and ice climbing. To enjoy travelling among mountains does not necessarily mean that you have to be an expert rock climber, and conversely you can be a skilled rock climber without experiencing much in the way of mountains. For example, urban-based enthusiasts can avail themselves of indoor climbing walls which are useful for keeping skills honed and muscles toned. However, quite a number of the world's higher mountains – ie over 20 000/ft or 6100 m – can be scaled without demanding great technical skill.

The climbing world can therefore be divided into 'summit baggers' on the one hand and 'rock-face freaks' on the other. If you are looking for an outdoor technical experience in the UK or the USA, most mountainous regions have rock-climbing schools offering courses which range in length from less than a day to a week or more. In the UK the British Mountaineering Council (see Factfile) has a list of approved activity centres. To start with, your instructor 'shows you the ropes' and the holds, belaying (holding you) while you climb. Shouted instructions on your part ('ready to climb', 'climbing', 'OK' and so on) keep the instructor clear on your progress. Safety is of the utmost importance in this sport and freestyle climbing without ropes is strictly for accomplished experts only. Proper instructions, proper dress, the correct use of good equipment and adequate training ensure that safety remains paramount (your instructor should have a Mountain Instructor's Certificate and/or Membership of the Association of British Mountain Guides). Right from the start there is a great sense of satisfaction for rock-climbing adventurers, even in scrambling up a simple cliff or face: in turn that sense of satisfaction becomes a sense of achievement as seemingly impossible faces are tackled and then overcome. After that it is a question of developing and constantly refining a good, relaxed climbing style. Rock-climbing is an adventure sport which requires mental judgment as much as physical strength and agility, but these skills can be learnt, practised and perfected over time and at your own pace.

Equipment-wise what you need depends on whether you want to be a mountaineer or stick simply to rock-climbing. Especially for more testing peaks under extreme conditions, the list of kit is considerable. Jacket, salopettes and walking boots will cost upwards of £300; then there are goggles, ice axe and crampons (about £200). If it's rock-climbing you're after, then the list is shorter: special tight fitting 'grippy' rock boots (£35–£75) and a hard plastic helmet (£25–£45) for a start. Thereafter you can collect all the necessary tackle over time; ropes, harness, chalkbag, and all sorts of fancy ironmongery with names like 'nuts' and 'friends' which are used to jam into cracks to hold the belay ropes. Since organized holidays will provide all the necessary equipment, it is best to try out a taster weekend before rushing off and buying lots of kit. Many activity centres offer rock-climbing along with other mountaineering activities and skills training. In the UK, organizations such as the **Youth Hostels Assocation (8 St Stephen's Hill, St Albans, Herts, AL1 2DY; tel: 01727 845047)**, **Outward Bound Trust (PO Box 1219, Windsor, Berkshire SL4 1XR; tel: 01753 731005)**, and the **Sports Council (16 Upper Woburn Place, London WC1H 0QP; tel: 0171 388 1277)** have information about introductory courses of this type. In Scotland, **Glenmore Lodge (Aviemore, Inverness-shire PH22 1QU; tel: 01479 861276)** enjoys a justifiably proud record of running many courses in winter mountaineering, navigation skills, climbing, skiing, mountain rescue and leadership.

Certain tour operators offer rugged mountaineering expeditions. While not highly technical in nature, these trips do require a high degree of fitness and a positive mental attitude. Most require a fair input of your time (to acclimatize to high altitude) and money (to pay for peak fees and for portering supplies into remote areas). For example, **Worldwide Journeys and Expeditions** have put together a small number of 'small peak' (4600 m/15 000 ft to over 6100 m/20 000 ft) expeditions in the Himalayas, the Andes and East Africa's Ruwenzori mountains. One such summit is Island Peak (6190 m/20 305/ft) which lies only two days or so off the main Everest trail. Although considered to be one of the less difficult trekking peaks in Nepal, it does require you to be roped-up in places. Cost for the 24-day expedition is around £1900, all inclusive. Aconcagua (6813 m/22 348 ft) is not only the highest mountain in Argentina, but is also the highest peak in the Western hemisphere. For around £3000 you can attempt to climb the summit, after a period spent acclimatizing to altitude (total time 22 days). See the Worldwide Journeys and Expeditions catalogue for details.

Other operators to consider include **ExplorAsia, World Expeditions, Thin Air Expeditions (Suite 501, 223 Regent Street, London W1R 8QD; tel: 0171 495 2554)** and **Classic Nepal (33 Metro Avenue, Newton, Alfreton, Derbyshire DE55 5UF; tel: 01773 873497).**

FACTFILE

Organizations: The **British Mountaineering Council (179 Burton Road, West Didsbury, Manchester M20 2BB; tel: 0161 445 4747)** has a list of nearly 300 clubs throughout the UK. Membership confers £2 million personal liability insurance and personal accident insurance.

Clothing: For rock-climbing wear loose garments to allow for high leg and arm movements. For mountaineering consult a good outfitter or supplier.

Responsible climbing: In the UK, outdoor rock-climbing is covered by a voluntary code of ethics which aims to protect damage to vulnerable rock faces by insensitive use. The BMC can advise.

DOG SLEDGING

' "Hi! Ho!" yells the musher, and your team of huskies lurches forward through the snowy white silence across open tundra, along historic mining trails, and over icy rivers . . . Little has changed since the first great wilderness traveller passed this way. Perhaps this part of the world is a better place for having stayed the same.'

Pat Dickerman, Adventure Travel in North America

Driving your own dogs across the snow is a wonderful experience, quite different from all the other adventure activities. Fortunately, certain Arctic cultures have kept the traditions of dog mushing alive and kicking down the centuries. In Alaska, for instance, Eskimos originally used them on their seal and walrus hunting expeditions. Later, dog-drawn sledges were used to pull stores and equipment during the gold-rush years. Nowadays, skidoos have replaced dogs for most of the off-road freight haulage work, but interest in dog sledging for transporting human cargoes is still as strong as ever. In fact, thanks to high-profile activities such as the Iditarod Dogsled Race – a 1000-mile two-week marathon from Anchorage to Nome – there has been a strong revival in dogsledging in recent years. Current interest in racing husky dogs extends even to countries where winter can be somewhat hit or miss. In the UK, which has a strong following through the Siberian Husky Club (see Factfile for address), the solution for mild winters is simple: use wheeled rigs instead of sledges, and forest roads instead of snow routes!

The same commands are used to control huskies today as have been used for generations. It is a storybook myth that 'mush' is the command for faster. In fact 'hike' or 'ho' are used as signals for 'go', while 'gee' means left and 'ha' means right. After settling down, a team of huskies (usually eight or nine) will pull a laden 12-foot sledge at 5–7 mph, slow enough for a musher to run alongside the sledge for short periods. In this way distances of up to 35 miles are covered each day. Huskies are a breed apart from most dogs. They are adapted to withstand intense cold, burying themselves in their snowy beds, each covered in the morning by a soft mound of whiteness, happy enough after a night's snowfall. Driving a team of dogs across the snow can be an almost surreal experience. Often the only sounds are the muffled padding of dog paws on fresh snow and the swish of sledge runners. In North America, to encounter reindeer, moose and fox is not uncommon, while just occasionally – if you're lucky – you will catch a glimpse of wolverine, bear or lynx. Depending on where you go mushing, the dogs will be tied either in 'Nome formation' (running behind each other in pairs) or in fan formation (alongside each other). The former is necessary for places such as Lapland and parts of Yukon and Alaska, where you have to manoeuvre through trees, whereas the latter is better suited to Greenland's wide open spaces.

In the USA, there are a number of tour operators specializing in dog sledging packages. **Alaska River Adventures (1831 Kuskokwim Street, Suite 17, Anchorage, AK 99508; tel: 907 276 3418)** offers bespoke tours in Denali National Park reserve. By day you try out dog sledging or some other winter adventure: by night you sleep in a wilderness lodge warmed by a log stove under the Northern Lights. Prices are around $1000 for eight days. **Sourdough Outfitters (Box 18-AT, Bettles, AK 99726; tel: 907 692 5252)** offers training and hut-based trips from Fairbanks at the rate of $200 per day, between November and April. **Outward Bound (Route 9D, R2, Box 280, Garrison, NY 10524-9757; tel: 914 424 4000)** runs courses which teach you how to mush, navigate and survive Arctic conditions in either Minnesota or Maine, during December to March. Prices range from under $1000 for eight days to over $1500 for 22 days.

A number of UK tour operators offer hands-on dog sledging trips. With **Arctic Experience** you can opt to visit Greenland, Finland's Lapland area, or Canada's Yukon Province. For reasonably fit adventurers keen to visit Greenland, you can try either a six-night introduction or a ten-night expedition using huskies. Cost including air travel is £1200 to around £2000. Their 8-day Lapland Sledge Tour using huts, tents and hotel accommodation costs from £1200 including flights. Group size is from three to twelve. Arctic Experience's 12-day Yukon Husky Trail costs around £2000. For a hard-adventure, rugged dog sledge trip, you could try **Arcturus Expeditions (PO Box 850, Gartocharn, Alexandria, Dunbartonshire G83 8RL; tel: 01389 830204)**. They offer two 9-day 'drive your own dogs' trips in northern Norway, staying in huts. 'There may not be much incentive to wash but the expedition is very rewarding.' Prices for each are around £1600, including flights.

FACTFILE

Useful address: Siberian Husky Club of Great Britain, The Old Post Office, 3 High Street, Lamport, Northampton NN6 9HB; tel: 01604 686281.

Fitness: You do need to be reasonably fit to take part in dog sledging trips. Contrary to popular belief, the dogs don't do all the work!

EXPEDITIONS

'Explorers are travellers who change the world, they are driven by a desire to discover which transcends the urge to conquer: the pursuit of trade; the curiosity of the scientist; the zeal of the missionary; or the simple search for adventure.'

Robin Hanbury-Tenison, The Field, October 1992

What makes a journey an expedition rather than a holiday? Defining an expedition is not as easy as it might seem. From the adventure point of view, expeditions occupy the 'harder' end of the spectrum, but certain 'softer' adventure sports or activities can also be regarded as expeditions, if done in certain ways – for instance, a ballooning trip in the Himalayas or a vehicle-based safari in a remote wilderness. In essence, though, the main distinguishing features of an expedition are time (several days or weeks in duration), ruggedness (generally physically challenging), remoteness (well off the beaten track), lack of creature comforts (camping, usually), and having a purpose or goal in mind. Many people would regard expeditions as something that you do independently, as a one-off exercise, but there is a strong and rising demand for tour operators to cater for organized groups – 'instant expeditions' if you like.

In the UK, there are several philanthropic organizations and commercial operators which provide expeditionary opportunities for younger adventurers. **Endeavour Training (17A Glumangate, Chesterfield S40 1TX; tel: 01246 237201)** operates outdoor programmes for young people aged 16–24 both in the UK and, under their **John Hunt Exploration Group**, overseas. Each year, **Raleigh International** – whose most famous champion is Ffyona Campbell, the round-the-world walker – runs ten or so three-month expeditions to such remote places as Guyana, Belize, Zimbabwe and Chile. These trips are for 17 to 25 year-olds, although skilled supervisors and leaders over 25 years old are also recruited. While the purpose of these expeditions is primarily scientific research, participants themselves undoubtedly gain a great deal in personal terms. **Raleigh International** can be found at **Raleigh House, 27 Parsons Green Lane, London SW6 4HZ; tel: 0171 371 8585**. The **British Schools' Exploring Society (BSES, c/o Royal Geographical Society, 1 Kensington Gore, London SW7 2AR; tel: 0171 584 0710)** takes groups of between fifty and a hundred 16–20 year-olds to survey projects in far-flung corners of the world. Average cost for a six-week expedition place is £2000. Since its foundation, the BSES has given over 4000 youngsters a taste of adventure and a chance to do scientific and survey work, often in Arctic and sub-Arctic regions. The **Brathay Exploration Group (Brathay Hall, Ambleside, Cumbria LA22 0HP; tel: 015394 33942)** offers trips with an ecological remit to 15–25 year-olds, either in Europe or in further-flung places such as the Arctic. Cost for a five-week programme is approximately £2000. **Trekforce (134 Buckingham Palace Road, London SW1W 9SA; tel: 0171 824 8890)** sends groups of over-17s to undertake research exclusively in Indonesia, for a cost of about £2700 for six weeks. Especially for Schools, **World Challenge (Soan House, 305–315 Latimer Road, London W10 6RA; tel: 0181 961 1122)** will plan an overseas expedition for a team of pupils, once the school has come up with the idea and funding (usually about £2000 per student).

All these organizations have a scientific role and purpose, but there are other bodies in the UK which offer cultural and ecological assistance to developing countries. In a sense, these can be thought of as 'community expeditions' – where you work in teams to achieve the aim of social or environmental improvement in the recipient country. Such responsible tourist groups include **Frontier (77 Leonard Street, London EC2A 4QS; tel: 0171 613 2422)**, **Earthwatch Europe (Belsyre Court, 57 Woodstock Road, Oxford OX2 6HU; tel: 01865 311600)**, **Coral Cay Conservation (154 Clapham Park Road, London SW4 7DE; tel: 0171 498 6248)** and the **British Trust for Conservation Volunteers (36 St Mary's Street, Wallingford, Oxon OX10 0EU; tel: 01491 839766)**.

The distinction between youth exploring societies (usually charities) on the one hand, which offer the challenge of outdoor adventure or community expeditions, and commercial tour operators on the other, is becoming increasingly blurred. Among the latter are several well known companies such as **Arctic Experience**, **Exodus Expeditions**, **Explore Worldwide**, **Guerba Expeditions**, **World Expeditions** and **Worldwide Journeys and Expeditions**, as well as some smaller companies such as **Arcturus Expeditions (PO Box 850, Gartocharn, Alexandria, Dunbartonshire G83 8RL; tel: 01389 830204)**. All of these operators run packaged but challenging expeditions to remote areas of the world, sometimes involving a number of adventure activities. The number and breadth of trips is simply too great to list here: contact the above companies for detailed information.

FACTFILE

Useful addresses: The Expeditionary Advisory Centre and the **Young Explorers' Trust** (both located at the **Royal Geographical Society, 1 Kensington Gore, London SW7 2AR; tel: 0171 581 2057**) publish helpful handbooks and organize seminars dealing with all aspects of expeditions. The Royal Geographical Society itself sometimes offers seminars aimed at students planning independent expeditions.

Youth expeditions: for more information about expeditions suitable for younger people, see Youth Activities, p 98.

HANG-GLIDING

'The pilot's voice came through the helmet intercom telling me to reach past his shoulders and take hold of the control bar, and try flying. It was exciting but I wondered when I would begin to like it.'

Christina Dodwell, Travels with Pegasus

Since earliest times we have longed to free ourselves from our roots as ground-dwellers and fly, unaided, like a bird in the sky. From the dream of Daedalus and the Icarus legend to Leonardo da Vinci's designs for a human-powered aircraft, this desire eventually became reality when the first glider was constructed. But as early gliders became increasingly sophisticated, their pilots, protected by a cockpit and using mechanical devices to steer, were destined to be not quite as free as birds. It needed the invention of the first hang-glider to remove these mechanical fetters and introduce the purest form of flight known to human beings (barring attaching feathers to your body and avoiding flying close to the sun). Today you can choose from a wide variety of hang-glider designs to suit your taste and experience. A word of warning, however: once bitten by the flying bug, it's like an addiction. As the **British Hang Gliding and Paragliding Association** (BHPA) puts it . . . 'once you have flown, your life will never be the same again.'

Twenty years ago, when the earliest hang-gliders came upon the scene, it was only possible for pilots to undertake short airborne hops over sand dunes and other soft landing sites. Today, however, you can opt to buy a high-tech hang-glider capable of flying hundreds of miles and soaring thousands of feet high. Such hang-gliders are either rigid or – more usually – semi-rigid. The former are made of hard, composite materials such as glass fibre, whereas the latter have aluminium spars and battens in their wings which themselves are covered in a tight sheath of polyester cloth. Irrespective of type, hang-gliders can either be winched up on a line like a kite, before being released, or they can be aero-towed behind a microlight (powered hang-glider) and then released, or they can be launched by the simple expedient of the pilot running off a hill. The glider you choose depends on what you want to get out of the adventure sport, although now the versatility of both hang-gliders and paragliders (see p 77) is impressive. Like paragliding, hang-gliding is not an entirely risk-free activity. Indeed, if practised irresponsibly it can be positively dangerous. Most serious hang-glider accidents happen when pilots 'stall' their aircraft at low altitude and hit the ground: awkward landings on rough ground are the main cause of lesser injuries. But with a little training and experience hang-gliding is as safe as you want it to be. In the UK, all these risks and safety aspects can be learnt at one of the many BHPA centres. New students are introduced to flight in a thoroughly safe way, progressing steadily up the theory and experience curves. The BHPA operates licences for flying schools and coaching clubs to ensure that newcomers into the sport receive safe, professional training. Moreover, as well as organizing flying competitions for the more committed pilots, it publishes a monthly magazine called *Skywings*, which covers all aspects of the sport. You can purchase a used hang-glider for as little as £500, although a new state-of-the-art 'kite' will cost upwards of £2000. A new harness costs from £300, a parachute from £350 and a helmet will add £20 or more.

As far as adventure sports go, hang-gliding lies towards the hard – and expensive – end of the range. Very few operators offer tours specifically for this activity, but independent adventurers can make things even more adventurous by taking off (literally) in remoter parts of the world. Of course it goes without saying that you need to have both experience and expeditionary back-up, should things go wrong. Closer to home in the UK, centres offering hang-gliding courses and sites include **High Adventure Hang-Gliding and Paragliding Centre (Coastguard Lane, Freshwater, Isle of Wight, Bag PO40 9QX; tel: 01983 752322), Welsh Hang-Gliding Centre (Parc Brynbach, Tredegar, Gwent NP2 3AY; tel: 01495 711816)** and **Cairnwell Hang-Gliding Centre (The Dhom, Glenshee, By Blairgowrie, Perthshire PH10 7QQ; tel: 01250 885238).**

FACTFILE

Organizations: The British Hang-Gliding and Paragliding Association (The Old Schoolroom, Loughborough Road, Leicester LE4 5PJ; tel: 0116 2611322) is the UK's national governing body of the sport, with a membership of 7000. Subscription membership includes £1 million third-party liability insurance cover.

MOUNTAIN BIKING

'For my tenth birthday my parents gave me a second-hand bicycle and Pappa sent me a second-hand atlas. Already I was an enthusiastic cyclist, though I had never before owned a bicycle, and soon after my birthday I resolved to cycle to India one day.'

Dervla Murphy, Wheels Within Wheels

About fifteen years ago, somewhere in Marin County, California, a conventional bike took an evolutionary turn and thus the mountain bike was born. The world of adventure has never been the same since. Suddenly pedal power became the most versatile way of getting about since shanks's pony; *more* versatile even, since it allowed off-the-beaten-track journeys with all the advantages of walking but at a greater speed and with greater excitement. Tough and rugged, yet light enough to be carried easily, the mountain bike lets you explore the Earth's wild places while remaining part of them, not apart from them, as is the case with motorized transport. With their plentiful gears and tough tyres, mountain bikes offer freedom to roam combined with the physical challenge and mental concentration needed for dirt track manoeuvres. Whether you settle for flatter terrain, or steep mountain tracks: whether you are a fair weather biker or a mud, sweat and gears freak, the mountain bike has something to offer everyone in search of off-road adventure.

Although being fit does help when it comes to mountain biking, you do not have to be a Schwarzenegger super-hero 'spokesman' in lycra leggings to enjoy, since speed rather than distance tends to be the main cause of fatigue. Furthermore, you do not need a high degree of technical ability for most off-road biking. On average, a reasonably fit rider is able to cycle around 80–100 km a day, or about four times the distance that a walker manages. People of all ages, backgrounds and budgets are devotees of mountain biking, whether in the urban jungle or the tropical jungle. In fact it is one of the most accessible adventure activities available today.

Although a bike can vary in price from a couple of hundred pounds to a couple of thousand, as a symbol of wealth it is less extreme than a motor vehicle, so you are much less likely to alienate yourself culturally when travelling abroad among remote communities. If you do get tired on your foreign travels, then you can simply park up in a hostel or a hotel bedroom, hitch a lift from a passing truck, or load up onto a plane or ship and take the bike with you. And since bikes are a basic form of transport the world over, if you do travel independently, it is reassuring to know that most spares are readily available no matter where you go.

When you are packing for a tour, it is as well to remember the maxim 'If in doubt, leave it out.' As Saint-Exupéry put it, 'He who would travel happily must travel light.' The only really essential piece of kit you will need (apart from tools) is a helmet, so it is worth buying one before joining a tour even if you do not have a mountain bike yourself. That way, you can be sure of a snug yet comfortable fit.

It is impossible to put down all the places that offer packaged mountain bike tours worldwide – the list is simply too great and the choice increasing too rapidly. There are, however, several 'favourite' haunts offered by tour operators such as **Exodus**, **World Expeditions**, **High Places** and **Sherpa Expeditions**. These include such places as Morocco (the Atlas mountains), Venezuela (The Andes), India, and East Africa. **Karakoram Experience (32 Lake Road, Keswick, Cumbria CA12 5DQ; tel: 017687 73966)** offers 'probably the world's five dream trips': Silk Road, Across Bhutan, Leh to Manali Traverse, Lhasa to Kathmandu, and Utah's Canyonlands. Prices vary from £1500 to £2000. The usual lower age limit on packaged mountain bike trips is eighteen, but some companies, such as Exodus, will organize family trips involving younger bikers because it is such a good way for families to go on an active holiday together. Certain tours which are tailored for the less active cyclist will transport you by road to high points, letting gravity take the strain thereafter.

Finally, remember that while money can buy you the latest high-tech lightweight alloy frame, suspension system or gearing, it's *attitude* that counts. In the words of experienced expedition cyclist Nick Crane, 'Destinations are reached through the urge to make the journey rather than the colour of the bike frame.'

FACTFILE

Organizations: Cyclists' Touring Club (69 Meadrow, Godalming, Surrey GU7 3HS; tel: 01483 417217), British Cycling Federation (36 Rockingham Road, Kettering, Northamptonshire NN16 8HG; tel: 01536 412211). US Cycling Federation (1 Olympic Plaza, Colorado Springs, CO 80909; tel: 719 578 4581).

Travel tips: Avoid main roads. Correct frame size is more important than high-tech paraphernalia. Some dogs consider chasing bicyclists to be a great canine adventure: consider a pre-travel rabies vaccination if you are visiting a known rabies area. Moisture loss can be a potential hazard in hot countries so carry at least a litre of fluid with you.

Ecotourism: Mountain bikes can cause wear and tear of fragile ecosystems. Avoid unnecessary skidding and always respect walkers and horse riders.

OVERLANDING

Once upon a Victorian time there was the 'Grand Tour' – a European cultural extravaganza. Now there's the Overland Expedition, a value-for-money adventure on four wheels. Travelling by modified bus, 4-wheel drive truck, car or even public transport, the overlanding clan is becoming an increasingly common part of today's adventure travel scene. The demand for such trips is such that many reputable companies now offer intracontinental or even intercontinental tours for travellers with a thirst for adventure – over land.

You can organize an overland trip yourself, given plenty of determination, effort and time. But detailing all the preparation necessary would need a book in itself. On the other hand, if you are happy to join a team of like-minded travellers, there are a number of well established, well equipped and reliable tour operators offering many of the advantages of an independent trip (freedom, flexibility, remoteness) without some of the disadvantages (cost, specialist knowledge). Besides some of the popular overland routes which sprang up in the 1960s and 1970s, like trans-Africa Cairo to Cape, or trans-Asia Istanbul to Kathmandu, many new routes, themes and variations are now offered by tour operators, including South-east Asia, South America, West Africa and Central Asia. Typically, you travel in a group of around 20 kindred spirits in a converted Bedford (often ex-army) or Mercedes truck, on a trip lasting from eight days to eight months. Contrary to some beliefs, such tours are usually designed to be at a relaxed pace, taking in places of interest off the beaten track, rather than a mad kleptomaniac dash which tries to notch up as many different countries as possible in the shortest possible time. So rest days are often scheduled in, to allow travel-worn souls to relax and absorb the flavour of special places and festivals, or perhaps to attempt a nearby mountain peak or observe some rare flora or fauna.

Apart from the odd strategic port of call in towns, most of the overlander's time is spent travelling along remote routes and staying in quiet backwaters. This involves pitching and striking camp, usually two-person tents – a routine which quickly becomes second nature to overlanders. You will also be expected to help with the day-to-day chores of camp life; lighting fires, preparing food, washing up and so on. Although such trips do have some similarities with safaris, wildlife is not the sole *raison d'être*: passengers have a lot of contact with different ethnic groups, cultures and lifestyles during their adventure, stopping at village markets to buy fresh food and souvenirs, or simply chatting with the locals.

Africa is the continent *par excellence* for overland adventure trips. There is no shortage of experienced tour operators offering trips lasting from a few days to a few months. The London-based **Adventure Travel Centre (131–135 Earls Court Road, London SW5 9RH; tel: 0171 370 4555)** is an agency for all the main companies which include **Encounter Overland, Dragoman, Exodus Expeditions, Guerba Expeditions** and **Top Deck Travel**.

Dragoman (the name means a local guide used by 18th and 19th century explorers) uses specially-adapted Mercedes trucks. You can choose to follow in Dr Livingstone's footsteps, from Zanzibar southwards to Lake Malawi, Victoria Falls and south to Zimbabwe; or you can cross the Sahara through Mali or Niger; or you can tour the Central African region. Similarly, **Guerba Expeditions**

has a wide range of African overland trips from a regional-based 'taster' to 'Africa All the Way' – a 33-week epic. For all companies, prices range from a few hundred pounds for the shorter trips, up to about £4500 for the longest – exceptional value for an eight month trip of a lifetime.

If Asia is more to your liking, some of the above companies offer such delights as the Silk Route and the Indian Subcontinent. Alternatively, a number of different overland expeditions are also available in Central and Southern America, including one from the Caribbean to Cape Horn. Indo-China is starting to open up, while the Russian Commonwealth of Independent States looks like a promising future prospect for overland devotees.

FACTFILE

Organizations: The Adventure Travel Centre (131–135 Earls Court Road, London SW5 9RH; tel: 0171 370 4555) is an agency for all the main overland companies. The **Marco Polo Travel Advisory Service (24A Park Street, Bristol BS1 5JA; tel: 0117 9294123)** offers advice for aspiring overlanders and independent women travellers.

Travel tips: Especially for longer trips you may need to book several months in advance to allow time to obtain the necessary visas. Most trips are one-way only and you will therefore have to find the fare for the return air journey.

Ecotourism: You will make significant impacts on local cultures and the environment (camping latrines, firewood collecting, etc). Check your operator's ecotourism policies before booking and be aware of your responsibilities while travelling. See 'Responsible Tourism' (p 29).

PARAGLIDING

'As I run forward down the hill, the 250 square feet of lightweight nylon lifts from the ground behind me, inflating to form an aerofoil that rises above my head. A quick glance up to check that no lines are tangled, a few more steps and I'm airborne.'

Genevieve Leaper, Air UK Flagship Magazine, 1994

It's not a bird, it's not a plane, it's not even a hang-glider . . . paragliding is, though, an entirely new form of adventure aviation. It evolved in the 1980s from the well established sport of parascending; that is, being lifted into the air by a parachute towed by winch, vehicle or boat. Since parascending was usually conducted under well supervised conditions, it gave – and continues to give – many adventure seekers the chance to soar above the ground without prior training or experience. But parascending has its obvious limitations, such as the fact that you are fixed by a thread to the ground like some giant inverted spider, flying – yes – but yet not quite flying free.

Paragliding's different, however. Unfettered by towing machinery and the like, you have the freedom of the skies to yourself, using a combination of skill and thermal uplifts to keep aloft. Because you only need a minimum of training before you are allowed to take off, paragliding is excellent for those wanting to try an adventurous air-sport without committing lots of time and money in the process.

Unlike ballooning, in which you are a passive passenger, paragliding turns you into an active adventurer. Although paragliders cannot match up to the performance of hang-gliders, they can stay aloft in lighter winds. And though the design of a paraglider canopy is different from a hang-glider, the principles and discipline of flying are very much the same in both cases. Unlike a hang-glider, which often requires Herculean strength to be hauled uphill, a paraglider (or 'parapent' as it's called in

Continental Europe) is small and light enough (approximately 7 kg) to be carried in a rucksack. Moreover, at around £500 for a good second-hand canopy, it is also cheap. Small wonder that paragliding's popularity – like its method of takeoff – is growing in leaps and bounds: it's today's fast and inexpensive route to aviation adventure.

Most adventurers start their steps to paragliding heaven via a weekend course, which costs around £100. Apart from basic fitness (that is, the ability to walk uphill a few times) all you need is a little equipment (see below), some warm and windproof clothes, and a pair of boots with good ankle support. In the UK there are about 30 centres which teach the sport, while twice this number offer towed facilities for parascenders.

Basic paragliding is not difficult to learn. Lesson one begins with the parachute landing fall (for use in emergencies only). Paraglider pilots usually touch the ground at up to half the speed at which parachutists make contact and after a little practice you can even land without falling over. Once you are familiar with the equipment, you move on to ground control exercises, like hauling the canopy into the air and keeping it 'inflated' for as long as possible, leaning into the wind. After only two or three hours, you are ready to graduate to some elementary flights – or more accurately 50 m hops – from the lower slopes. Some paragliding schools even have tandem rigs which enable instructors to carry passengers strapped on beside them. Most adventurers will, however, want to graduate to solo flight and two to four days' tuition is all that's usually required to earn your student pilot wings. The cost of a 'fun day' at an instruction centre is around £60, while a four-day student pilot course works out at about £200. One's appetite for the open skies increases as moments of flying fear become minutes of flying freedom. Learning to be relaxed is important in the early stages; thereafter learning to be wary becomes important, since a false sense of security can catch out the blasé (reckless pilots can risk being literally carried away by strong winds).

Every adventurous activity carries with it an element of risk, and the safety records of different sports vary. Happily, paragliding has a good track record. Of the 200 000 flights made in 1991, for example, fewer than 20 resulted in serious injury. Many insurance companies view paragliding more sympathetically than other adventure airsports. Apart from being picked up by a passing hurricane, about the worst thing that can happen to you is that the soft, batonless canopy folds in mid-air under particular wind conditions (happily, reinflation occurs very quickly afterwards). Weatherwise, paragliding is an all-year-round adventure activity. Bright winter days can be every bit as good as warm summer afternoons – the less windy the weather, the better.

To purchase the safety gear (helmet and harness) will cost you around £140. A brand new paraglider will set you back around £1400 or more, but, as mentioned above, a second-hand rig costs only a third of that figure. Enthusiasts will also want to buy such items as an altimeter, charts and a reserve parachute. Although paragliding is essentially a sport for the independent adventurer, some clubs run flying holidays to other centres. Northern Spain, Morocco and the Himalayas are popular destinations. You may wish only to fix up a holiday 'taster', combining some paragliding experience with other activities. Alternatively, you may want a concentrated dose of the experience. In the UK, the **Youth Hostels Association (Trevelyan House, 8 St Stephen's Hill, St Albans, Herts AL1 2DY; tel: 01784 845047)** runs occasional taster courses on airsports. The **British Hang-Gliding and Para- gliding Association** (see Factfile) has details of your nearest centre.

FACTFILE

Organizations: The British Hang-Gliding and Paragliding Association (The Old School Room, Loughborough Road, Leicester LE4 5PJ; tel: 0116 261 1322) is the national governing body of the sport, with a membership of 7000. Subscription membership includes £1 million third-party liability insurance cover.

RIVER RAFTING

Some people call it river raft- ing; others call it river running; still others call it white-water rafting. Call it what you will, this sport amounts to real adventure on water: close en- counters of a rapid kind, as exhilarating, knuckle-whitening and physically challenging as you want. In fact, such is raft- ing's popularity today that specialist companies are setting up all over the world to cater for the increasing demand. Within Europe, Africa, Asia, America and Australasia the list of rivers operated by rafting companies is growing longer all the time.

The sport has developed to the extent that you can match your level of challenge to the grade of river, under a system where Class I equals a tranquil float and Class VI is theoretically unraftable. This grading system is worth bearing in mind before you literally take the plunge, since it is important to match your expectations with what is available (there is no point in being so petrified on your trip that you are scared off ever wanting to repeat the experience). Reliable operators can help you to decide the right sort of trip, generally starting with Class III rapids and progressing to Class IV and even V. Similarly, you can choose your length of outing from a two-hour 'taster' on the one hand, to a two-week expedition on the other. Finally, choice of raft can also affect the level of challenge.

There are basically three types of craft used for river rafting. Largest of all are the motor rigs – giant rafts with banana-shaped inflatable sides. The outboard motors on these craft make the need for paddling by their twenty or so passengers redundant. Those adventurers shunning the internal combustion engine will be more drawn to oar-powered rafts however. Here the river guide sits on a centre seat, helping to row the raft as well as steer it, while passengers provide paddle power. More adventurous still are the paddle-only rafts in which the guide – seated in the stern – steers using a paddle, while the crew again provide muscle paddle power. This need for forward momentum is important, since you have to be travelling faster than the rapids themselves in order to get through. If not, you run the risk of stopping in mid-stream (a sort of waterfall water-stall) after which there is a real danger of the raft being flipped over by a wave. It is this need to win the battle with the waves through teamwork – all pulling together – which adds a real dimension of cameraderie to the experience. But it is a mistake to imagine that you have to be big, butch and brawny before you can paddle a raft. Plenty of untrained and unfit people have done it and enjoyed it. The main thing is to put all your effort into it when the short sharp bursts of white water spring forth upon you.

Before allowing you to set out, your guide will make a point of taking you through the various safety procedures, such as what to do if you fall out of the raft. For higher classes of river these rafting safety drills include live tests during quieter stretches. The guide also carries lifelines in the unlikely event that you should become separated from the raft. Lifejackets are mandatory and for rivers of Class V (sometimes IV), helmets will also be insisted on.

In the UK there is an unfortunate and acute shortage of white-water wizardry available (put it down to land size and the ice age – British rivers just aren't big and steep enough). Some opportunities are available at a few places, however, such as the

500 m artificial slalom course at the **National Watersports Centre** at Nottingham (**Adbolton Lane, Holme Pierrepont, Nottingham NG12 2LU; tel: 0115 9821212**) or the National White Water Centre near Bala (**Frongoch, Near Bala, Gwynedd; tel: 01678 520 826**). In Scotland, the river Tay is rafted regularly by **Croft-na-Caber Watersports and Activity Centre (Kenmore, by Aberfeldy, Perthshire PH15 2HW; tel: 01887 830588)**. A three-hour trip costs around £20, including wetsuit and transport. Pacific Northwest USA and Canada are a shangri-la to the 'happily river rafter'. Details of a huge variety of rafting trips are available from **Super Natural Adventures**. You can choose from gentle Class II and III trips, right up to roller-coaster Class IV and V rivers (for real river rats, these). There are over 35 rafting companies in British Columbia alone, each carefully regulated, controlled and licensed by government officials. In fact, attention to safety makes BC perhaps the safest place to experience river rafting in the world today. Many rafting adventures are packaged here as combination holidays which include such activities as hiking, canoeing and riding. The Californian company **Mountain Travel Sobek (6240 Fairmount Avenue, El Cerrito, CA 94530; tel: 510 527 8100)** has an extensive rafting network worldwide. Their portfolio includes such places as the Grand Canyon, Peru's Colca Canyon, rivers in Brazil, Chile, Indonesia, India, Nepal, Alaska, Canada, Australia and Africa (the Zambezi below Victoria Falls offers world-class rafting adventure). Costs vary greatly, but an average price for a day trip including lunch is around $50. Also specialists in rafting the world's best white water are the operators **Adrift (Hyde Park House, Manfred Road, London SW15 2RS; tel: 0181 874 4969)**. Their portfolio includes rivers in Turkey, Mexico, Ethiopia, New Zealand, Nepal and the Zambezi. All-inclusive prices are from £800 to £1600 for 8 or 14 days.

FACTFILE

Organizations: American River Touring Association, Star Route 73, Groveland, CA 95321; tel: 209 962 7873.

Safety: You should be able to swim before thinking about tackling the more challenging rivers.

Health: In sunny climates, the main health risk is probably sunburn. Take plenty of waterproof sun lotion and wear a hat.

RIDING AND PONY TREKKING

'Remoteness and seclusion appealed to me. I felt closer to nature. Foxes, badgers, deer and all forms of wildlife proliferated where man had failed to leave his mark – and they never seemed too bothered by my small, dark nylon tent with a pony grazing peacefully beside it.'

Jane Dotchin, Journeys through England with a Pack Pony

It is surely this special sense of being part of the natural world, as well as being interdependent on an animal, which inspires travel on horseback. Coupled with speed and responsiveness, horses are without doubt the adventurer's most versatile means of transport. No exhaust fumes, no roads required, just timelessness and an immense sense of freedom. Trekking on horseback can offer even the most seasoned traveller a new dimension in exploration, for nothing can beat a brisk gallop-induced surge of adrenalin. In adventurous riding, gone are the pre-programmed responses of riding-stable ponies. Here in the wide blue yonder, horses are the intuitive, intelligent, understanding beasts they were meant to be.

Riding vacations take many forms: leisurely, taxing, packaged or entirely independent. Whichever you opt for, some previous experience in the saddle is highly advisable. Although tuition can be a part of the holiday package, some skill acquired before departure will allow you to get on with the real business of exploring. After all, you are as dependent on your mount as your mount is on you, and the quicker a mutual rapport is established, the better: nobody wants to spend the duration of their trip trying to stay on top, when there is so much else to be experienced.

Horsemanship apart, riding can be physically testing, getting to the muscles in your thighs that other adventurous activities seldom reach. So it is best to get some practice in first: traumas of the inner leg do subside, given a little time, patience and practice. And if you are worried about your natural padding, then you could always consider investing in a pair of the comically named equiknickers or comfi-rumps! Another danger zone while riding is your head: a riding hat with robust chinstrap is essential (don't assume that one will be provided). Hats start from about £30, while the beautifully coloured silk race covers will add about £10 to the cost. All British hard hats should be kitemarked and carry either the number 6473 or 4472. Guidance can be obtained from the **British Horse Society** (see Factfile), which will also provide you with details of riding school locations near you. It is possible to spend a lot of money on riding clothing, but apart from a hat the only other essential is a pair of shoes or boots with a heel to prevent your foot slipping out of the stirrup.

So what's the best destination worldwide, the ultimate home from home on the range? In fact there are many superb places to ride, and those countries with a strong riding tradition include South America, the USA, Canada, Spain, Iceland and parts of Africa (especially Lesotho). All these places have untamed and unfenced wildernesses well suited to exploration on horseback. Independent travellers will naturally make their own choices regarding destination and duration. The freedom, excitement and adventure described by Rosie Swale (*Cape Horn Revisited*) during her 14-month trip down through South America is an inspiration to any free-spirited would-be horse traveller. However, painstaking planning is essential to try to eliminate as many problems as possible before setting off, such as the purchase of steeds, registration and paperwork, and feeding supplies. Hiring local ponies which are accustomed to the conditions and climate is a good idea, as is the use of local tack. Saddles, bridles, stirrups and bits vary the world over, as do riding techniques.

Packaged trips vary from day treks from a fixed base, to post-trekking, that is moving on from place to place (often camping). One of the larger tour operators around is **J & C Voyageurs (Buckridges, Sutton Courtenay, Abingdon, Oxon OX14 4AW; tel: 01235 848747)**. Included in its portfolio are Africa and Turkey. Tours cover an average of 15 miles per day, for eight hours in the saddle. Prices, including flight from the UK, start at £700 (Turkey) and £1500 (Africa). For a trip with a difference, you could try guest ranching – staying on a ranch for a while and enjoying a range of activities in addition to riding. The USA and Canada are increasing in popularity as ranching destinations. Try contacting **Super Natural Adventures** or **Reef and Rainforest Tours (Prospect House, Jubilee Road, Totnes, Devon TQ9 5BP; tel: 01803 866965)**. Horse safaris in the Okovango Delta region of Botswana can be booked through **Okovango Tours and Safaris (28 Bisham Gardens, London N6 6DD; tel: 0181 343 3283)** from March to October for around £150 per day, excluding flight.

FACTFILE

Organizations: British Horse Society, British Equestrian Centre, Stoneleigh, Kenilworth, Warwickshire CV8 2LR; tel: 01203 696697. American Horse Shows Association, 220 East 42nd Street, Suite 409, New York, NY 10017 - 5876; tel: 212 972 2472.

Travel tip: Take insurance before going (some Horse Associations give good deals).

SAFARIS

'There is something about safari life that makes you forget all your sorrows and feel the whole time as if you had drunk half a bottle of champagne – bubbling over with heartfelt gratitude for being alive.'

Isak Dinesen (Karen Blixen)

Everyone knows the Swahili for a journey. 'Safari' – the very word conjures up images of rolling African plains teeming with wildlife, camp fires at dusk and the roaring of distant lions at night. Unfortunately, all too often the reality can be very different: clusters of designer zebra-striped minibuses crowding in on some unsuspecting big cat 'prey', a mass influx of Westerners in danger of despoiling Africa's Garden of Eden. On the other hand, if you know where to go and who to go with, you *can* expect to recapture something of the *Out of Africa* experience, the excitement and thrill of safari life as it used to be. Be warned, though; there is an addiction about safaris which leaves you with a craving for more. In the words of Beryl Markham (*West with the Night*), 'The distant roar of waking lion rolls against the stillness of the night and we listen. It is the voice of Africa bringing memories that do not exist in our minds or in our hearts – perhaps not even in our blood. It is out of time, but it is there and it spans a chasm whose other side we cannot see.'

Nowadays, the scope of safaris has widened considerably compared with the early days. You can eschew 4-wheel mobility in favour of horse, foot, steam train or even hot-air balloon. Similarly, the original concept of safaris has broadened to include continents other than Africa. For example, instead of looking for wild elephants, you can choose to ride tame ones instead, searching for tigers and other wildlife in India. Or, if you prefer, you could always try a camel-based safari in Australia's great Outback or a reindeer safari in Lapland. Of course these days you shoot your game with cameras rather than rifles, and many animal populations are a poor shadow of their former numbers, but the lure of safaris – the unforgettable call of the wild – is still the same.

The secret of a successful safari is to do your research thoroughly beforehand, looking beyond the brochure hype that promises much but may deliver little. True adventurers will not be content with a bland hotel package at a popular safari destination. They will prefer a more isolated location and a more challenging means of getting about (a camping-based walking safari perhaps) but in doing so they will treasure a memorable and rewarding experience.

Although there is no shortage of tour operators offering safari trips these days, care is needed in selecting a suitable one. At the end of the day, Africa is still *the* place to experience your safari, especially if it's your first time. Costs can vary enormously, from under £1000 for a basic camping trip, to around £1800 for an average fortnight holiday, to thousands of pounds for upmarket, bespoke extravaganzas. In general, South Africa, Zimbabwe and Kenya are cheaper than Tanzania and Botswana, while some West African countries, like Cameroon, can be quite expensive. Other good destinations in Africa include Uganda, Namibia, Malawi and Zambia.

Try to ensure that your trip has a knowledgeable guide, since she or he can make the difference between real interpretation and understanding on the one hand, and simple and passive spectating on the other. It is one thing to know what species you are seeing, but quite another having its ecology explained to you. The only equipment you will need is a good pair of binoculars – 10 × 50s are best (one pair of bins per person is essential – honeymoon couples take note!) and a suitable camera with telephoto (200 or 300 mm) lens. All too often, safari snaps are disappointing 'spot-the-animal-looking-like-a-brown-dot' affairs, so a telephoto really is important. Don't forget animal and bird identification guidebooks either. Clothing-wise, a wide-brimmed hat is useful (see Factfile).

There are too many tour operators offering safari trips to list here, but they include **Abercrombie and Kent (Sloane Square House, Holbein Place, London SW1W 8NS; tel: 0171 730 9600), Worldwide Journeys and Expeditions** and **Safari Consultants**

(Orchard House, Upper Road, Little Cornard, Suffolk CO10 0NZ; tel: 01787 228494). Other bespoke companies include **Africa Explorations (Holwell Manor Barn, Holwell, Burford, Oxon OX18 4JS; tel: 01993 822443)**, **Kumuka (40 Earl's Court Road, London W8 6EJ; tel: 0171 937 8855)** and **Africa Exclusive (Hamilton House, 66 Palmerston Road, Northampton NN1 5EX; tel: 01604 28979)**. Then there are the larger and well established, mixed-budget operators like **Encounter Overland**, **Exodus**, **Explore Worldwide**, **Guerba Expeditions**, **Mountain Travel Sobek (6240 Fairmount Avenue, El Cerrito, CA 94530; tel: 510 527 8100)**, **Discover the World** and **Wexas**.

FACTFILE

Travel tips: Wear subdued clothing. Khaki is not an affectation; it is simply the best colour to avoid distracting the wildlife, while allowing you to remain part of the background. Bring warm clothes for cool early morning game drives and for keeping night chills at bay (Africa can be surprisingly cool after dark). In general, pack lightweight long clothing made from natural fibres.

SCUBA DIVING

Divers will tell you that even today scientists know more about the dark side of the moon than they do about this planet's underwater environment. While the vast majority of the world's land mass is now mapped territory, its subsea world is still largely an unexplored, uncharted and mysterious realm. Only since 1943, when Gagnan and Cousteau designed the diving lung, has the Earth's final watery frontier started to open up to undersea adventurers. Today, diving is fast losing its exclusivity, as more and more vacationers are coming to enjoy what Cousteau once called 'the silent world'.

While the colder waters of temperate countries do offer some excellent diving, most recreational holidays are to be found in the world's warmer seas. Basically, provided you are over fourteen years old, are reasonably fit and can swim, you can start to learn how to dive. Before selecting your destination, one of the first decisions to make is whether to go shore-based or boat-based. Unless you happen to be a diving fanatic, keen to live 'above the shop' as it were, then a shore-based diving holiday is probably more suitable for you. Although you can't expect the three to five dives daily that live-aboard diving offers, a shore-based holiday is likely to be cheaper and quieter (no noises of engines and compressors). Some trips demand previous experience, which in the UK can be obtained through the **British Sub-Aqua Club**. The BSAC School offers either novice diver or sports diver qualifications. You learn the moves in a swimming pool and then go on to open water. One safety precaution is to make sure that your destination's local operator is recognized by CMAS, the world federation body which includes the British Sub-Aqua Club and **Sub Aqua Association** (SAA), and the US organizations **PADI (Professional Association of Diving Instructors)**, **SSI**, **NAUI**, and **YMCA**.

Diving equipment consists of the scuba, an acronym for Self-Contained Underwater Breathing Apparatus (basically a compressed-air cylinder with regulator) plus weights, mask, fins, snorkel tube and instruments. The complete cost of kitting out for a dive can be £1000 or more, so unless you are a diving addict, it is best to hire. Happily, most resort centres and diving schools do have equipment-hire facilities. Some items worth purchasing if you are interested in watersport adventures generally are mask, fins, snorkel and wetsuit. The latter is useful for diving in warmer waters, although very warm temperatures preclude wetsuits since these can contribute to heat exhaustion. Colder coasts will require heavy-duty wetsuits or even drysuits.

As far as destinations are concerned, the nearest exotic location to the UK is the Red Sea/Gulf of Eliat region. Although very busy in winter ('positively shoals of divers', according to one description) the diving and marine life there are nevertheless world-class. Prices for shore-based trips are reasonable, but Red Sea live-aboards can be expensive. Synonymous with diving, and handy for the USA, the Caribbean has excellent facilities, if rather over-regimented for some tastes. Site quality can vary considerably (some sites have been fished out, for example) but popular locations such as the Bahamas, Cayman Islands and Turks and Caicos Islands need to be booked well in advance of departure. In the Indian Ocean, the Maldives offer excellent diving, though strong currents can catch out the unwary. Kenya's Marine Parks are rewarding destinations for African visitors. South-east Asia is becoming more popular with divers. Thailand now offers some of the best dive sites in the world, from Cambodia in the east to Myanmar in the west to Malaysia in the south. Many locations are found fairly close to Pattaya and the island of Phuket. Popular destinations here include the Similian, Surin and Phi Phi islands off Phuket; and Ko Lan, Ko Sak and Ko Rin off Pattaya. The Philippines also have spectacular all-year-round diving opportunities, although lack of conservation scruples have caused some localized eco-disaster areas. Most diving is done from out-rigger boats called bancas, since many dive sites are a long way from shore. UK tour operators include **Wexas** and **Reef and Rainforest Tours (Prospect House, Jubilee Road, Totnes, Devon TQ9 5BP)**.

FACTFILE

Organizations: British Sub-Aqua Club (Telfords Quay, Ellesmere Port, South Wirral, Cheshire L65 4FY; tel: 0151 357 1951. Sub-Aqua Association (Bear Brand Complex, Allerton Road, Liverpool L25 7SF; tel: 0151 428 9888); Professional Association of Diving Instructors (Unit 9, The 306 Estate, Broomhill Road, Brislington, Bristol BS4 5RG; tel: 0117 9711717); United States Diving, Inc (Pan American Plaza, Suite 430, 201 South Capitol Avenue, Indianapolis, IN 46225; tel: 317 237 5252.

Travel tips: Before going take insurance, and carry a certificate of fitness to dive from your doctor and your diving qualification certificates with you. Don't fly until at least 12 hours after diving (preferably 24 hours). Diving risks are increased by dehydration, so do watch your alcohol intake.

Ecotourism: Do take heed of local laws and marine park rules. Avoid kleptomania temptations. Good marine parks have fixed moorings to minimize anchor damage to coral.

SKI TOURING

'It's when I put my skins on and walk uphill, away from the
lift lines and crowded pistes to the tranquillity of the mountains, that I get the most enjoyment from my skis.'

Steve Jones, The Adventurers Magazine

Cross-country skiing, Nordic
skiing, Langlauf: these are just
a few of the names used to
describe this activity. It is the
earliest form of skiing, dating
back over four thousand years.
If you visit Norway today you
can still see ancient rock-
carvings depicting people using
long pieces of wood and sticks,
to move and support them-
selves over snow. OK, so the
equipment may have changed a
bit since then, but the principles
are still very much the same:
travelling over undulating terrain, using human effort up the
slopes and gravity down the slopes (always assuming that a few
inches or more of snow are present). Travelling backcountry on
skis means different things to different people – forested trails,
open meadows, moorland expanses, overnight stops at huts – but
one thing is always the same: the remoteness. It is this freedom
which appeals to adventure-minded ski enthusiasts: you are making fresh but ephemeral tracks in the snowy wilderness, far from
the madding crowds that all-too-often typify the ski resorts of
downhill devotees.

One development of cross-country skiing which appeals to the
more adventurous is ski touring (sometimes called ski mountaineering or ski safariing). This consists of traversing high mountain areas, using either personal navigational skills, or the knowledge of a local guide. Ski touring has long been popular in
Scandinavian countries where many children ski before they walk,
but it is also gaining ground elsewhere in the West. The development of bindings which allows the heel to lift when moving uphill
but to lock when gliding downhill have helped this popularity – so
have developments in ski technology, where waxes or special ski
surfaces stop skis from slipping backwards when travelling uphill,

mimicking the role of the animal skins which were used in former times.

First-time cross-country skiers do not have to invest heavily in equipment, since adventure centres will hire out what you need. Some outdoor and camping shops also hire out cross-country kit for £30 and upwards per week (boots, skis and sticks). To buy the basics costs upwards of £250, which is significantly less than the cost of downhill equipment. You will also need the other essentials, such as salopettes and jacket (around £250), sunglasses, hat, and gloves. Learning basic cross-country skiing can be hard work. You need to be reasonably fit, particularly if you are attempting longer runs of 15 km and over. Once you have developed a taste for cross-country skiing (this won't take long!) you may wish to tackle the greater demands of ski-touring. Skiing off-piste carries its own safety risks and responsibilities, and ski touring should be tackled only by those with some benefits of experience (the ability to do parallel turns with confidence, for example) and fitness (tougher routes will demand that you are very fit). You will need your own backpack (60 litres or more, depending on how much kit you need) with waistband for securing the load. Especially when you're carrying a heavy backpack – giving you a high centre of gravity – falling over is easy, but picking yourself up again can be hard work!

Mountain travel carries real risks. Every year, avalanches claim the lives of many who, in most cases, ventured beyond their capabilities. Some enthusiasts carry safety equipment such as avalanche transceivers which are designed to reveal your presence under the snow if the worst comes to the worst, but the basic rule is be sensible; prevention of accidents is better than cure. In this regard, hiring an experienced mountain ski guide is one of the best precautions you can take, although it does not guarantee safety. The 1989 Klosters avalanche, which threatened the Prince of Wales's life, was not prevented by the presence of an experienced Swiss ski guide. (This incident also illustrated an interesting principle, all-too-uncommon in our litigious, blame-placing age. Prince Charles spoke afterwards about his acceptance of personal and group responsibility and refused to take legal action.)

In Europe a number of countries offer '*haute route*' ski tours or safaris: Austria (about 30 locations), France (over 17 locations), Switzerland (plenty of places), and Italy (a few places). As there is a dearth of UK operators running these trips, you will need to contact the particular national or regional tourist board of the country concerned. You will also need to be accompanied by a local guide. Advice on destinations may be sought from the **Ski Club of Great Britain (118 Eaton Square, London SW1W 9AF; tel: 0171 245 1033)** while the **Association of British Mountain Guides** (see Factfile) may also provide information about ski-touring holidays. The cost of a ski safari is approximately £80 per day, excluding flights. In the USA, **Outward Bound (Route 9D, R2, Box 280, Garrison, NY 10524-9757; tel: 914 424 4000)** carries details of courses and expeditions for ski tourers. Its courses emphasize mountain safety, first-aid and survival skills, as well as skiing techniques and equipment. With few exceptions, British ski operators either do not feature ski tours at all, or they confuse them with the less demanding cross-country skiing. Norway and Sweden are culturally and physically well equipped for the ski tourer. Details of hut-to-hut tours which you can do independently are available from the respective tourist boards (see Appendix).

FACTFILE

Organizations: The **Association of British Mountain Guides** can be contacted through the **British Mountaineering Council (179 Burton Road, West Didsbury, Manchester M20 2BB; tel: 0161 445 4747).**

Equipment: Take adhesive tape or wire and pliers for ski repairs. An unbreakable flask is a good idea, as are knife, head torch, suncream and sunglasses. Crampons, snow shovels and avalanche radios transmitting on 457 kHz, such as the Barryvox, are desirable. However, with the latter at £100 a throw to purchase, it is cheaper to rent.

Clothing: For best thermal insulation, clothing should be based around the idea of many thin layers, rather than a few thick layers.

TALL-SHIP SAILING

'I must go down to the sea again, to the lonely sea and the sky,
And all I ask is a tall ship and a star to steer her by,
And the wheel's kick and the wind's song and the white sail's shaking,
And a grey mist on the sea's face and a grey dawn breaking.'

John Masefield, from Sea-Fever

To many fortunates, the lure of real sailing means an unfettered and independent life on the ocean wave, free from the cares of a landlubbers' world. But 'wannabe' sailors lacking funds and experience are faced with a difficult and time-consuming commitment to realize that dream. Unless you happen to be in the lucky position of owning 'a hole in the ocean which you pour money into' as one definition of a yacht puts it, or unless you happen to be friendly with a yacht owner, skippering a vessel is virtually impossible without a good deal of experience, and rightly so. In the past you generally had to start off learning how to sail a small two-person dingy on an inland waterway, progressing from there to larger craft and eventually gaining a certificate in seamanship. Only then could you charter a yacht without an accompanying skipper – 'bareboat sailing' as it's called. While flotilla sailing – sailing in a group of around six yachts, shepherded by a Captain's yacht – is gaining in popularity (particularly in the Mediterranean), for many adventurers it is not quite the challenge they are looking for. So how *do* you experience a real sailing adventure without having a qualification or years of skill and experience, or both?

Fortunately, help is at hand in the form of 'tall ships meet adventure packages'. If you've ever wanted to take the helm of a square rigger, climb aloft into the rigging to set or furl sail, or experience the brisk trade winds like sailors did a hundred years ago, then this is the adventure for you. It matters not that you lack previous sailing experience – nor do you have to be some macho Bluebeard type. All you need is enthusiasm, a willingness to help in the running of the ship and the funds to volunteer, since no stowaways and press-ganged crew are welcomed on board. Only a few adventure companies offer the opportunity to live as part of the crew on a tall ship. As part of its holiday portfolio **The Natural World (57 Church Street, Twickenham TW1 3NR; tel: 0181 744 0474)** lists a number of tall ship holidays on board either the *Anna Kristina* or the *Soren Larsen*. For a few days or weeks (or even months if you have the time) you can join one of these tall ships to experience a full-blown (wind permitting) sea adventure. As a member of the crew, you are expected to take part in the running of the ship, a harder role than simply being a passenger, but one which brings its own satisfactions. Although there is no restriction on age, allowances are made for younger and older crew members when duties are assigned (going aloft is not compulsory, for instance), and of course there is also an experienced and qualified crew aboard when the going gets tough. Depending on times, winds and currents you can either opt for shorter voyages or longer open ocean crossings.

Dating from the turn of the century, but in magnificent condition, the *Anna Kristina* comes with a wonderful health warning . . . 'Potential guests should realize that she is a traditional sailing vessel, not a cabin cruiser or a cruise vessel and this is reflected in the accommodation, the creaking of the timbers and the noise of the wind in the sails.' Places aboard the *Anna Kristina* are available for sailing and whale-watching in the Canary Islands.

The *Soren Larsen* is a 30 m/100 ft tall Brigantine, originally built in 1949 in Denmark. Famous as a star of television and films, she is swift, majestic and environmentally friendly. As a non-polluting, quiet form of sea transport, she is ideal for getting close to marine life, letting passengers observe dolphins, whales and sea-birds from close at hand. Prices range from around £400 for a one-week trip departing from Tenerife in the Canaries (accommodation shared in cabins – airfare extra), to around £800 for eleven days in the Pacific (voyage-only price), to around £5400 (flight extra) for 83 days on the Pacific high seas (Panama–Easter Island–Tahiti).

For similar salty adventures closer to the UK, you could try the **Sail Training Association (2a The Hard, Portsmouth, Hampshire PO1 3PT; tel: 01705 832055)**. Members of the Association of Sea Training Organizations and the Central Council for Physical Recreation, the Sail Training Association provides adventure voyages for around 2000 people each year aboard some of the UK's largest sailing schooners. No experience is necessary for these trips (lasting from a weekend to a fortnight) and the age limits are 16 to 69 years old.

As an alternative you could try the *Lord Nelson*, a 90 tonne three-masted barque with a permanent crew of eight and a voyage crew of 40. Kitted out with all the latest equipment, the *Lord Nelson* makes trips of three to ten days off Scotland's west coast, or off the Brittany coast, prices ranging from just over £200, to £650 **(tel: 01703 631395)**. The **Astrid Trust (9 Trinity Street, Weymouth, Dorset DT4 8TW; tel: 01305 761916)** is proud owner of the 170 tonne *Astrid*, which offers voyages both for young people (17–25) and not-so-young people (up to 70). Routes include Channel Cruises (£400 – any age), Caribbean Expeditions (£3200 – 17–25 year-olds), and an occasional transatlantic voyage. Trips include seamanship instruction, diving opportunities and exploration of uninhabited islands.

In the USA, they're called 'windjammers' – two- or three-masted engineless sailing ships, built originally to carry freight cargo. A number of far-sighted US companies have bought, refurbished and converted such ships for windjamming adventurers. The **Traverse Tall Ship Company (13390 West Bay Shore Drive, Traverse City, MI 49684; tel: 616 941 2000)** offers 3- or 6-day windjamming voyages on Lakes Michigan and Huron aboard the 114 ft *Manitou* at a cost of $400–800. **Windjammer Barefoot Cruises (1759 Bay Road, Miami Beach, FL 33139; tel: 305 672 6453)** has been running windjamming adventures in the Caribbean for 40 years. They have a fleet of tall ships which cruise the British Virgin Islands or the West Indies, on one- or two-week trips, at a cost of between $700 and $1700.

FACTFILE

Organizations: Royal Yachting Association, RYSA House, Romsey Road, Eastleigh, Hants SO5 4YA; tel: 01703 629962. The RYA runs sailing courses throughout the year. **United States Sailing Association, PO Box 209, Newport, Rhode Island 02840; tel: 401 849 5200**.

Travel tips: You'll be provided with buoyancy aids when you join the ship. Training in the procedures and equipment is also given.

TREKKING

'The Himalaya may not have quaked at the sound of our trudging boots and we certainly didn't set any new speed trekking records. But Sarah and I scaled great personal heights. No, we had no mother–daughter deep meaningfuls – we were too preoccupied with serious matters (like the merits of moleskin versus animal wool on the sore bits). But every day when our guide said "We go there today," my heart would sink as I peered into the mauve distance of far-off hills. Yet every evening we hugged our mugs of chai and said "We made it!". After that, I know all things are possible.'

Bridget Fraser, 'Conquering My Everest',
The Adventurers Magazine

Walking, hiking, rambling, trekking – call it what you will – human ambulation is by far the most popular of all leisure pursuits, despite techno-wizard equipment manufacturers attempting to push the latest fashionable and expensive gear for other activities. It is also the purest and most natural way of seeing a place, for by walking through a landscape you become part of it – at one with it – experiencing the place with each of your five senses. Put your boots on, sling on a day pack, and you're ready for a gentle jaunt into the wide blue yonder. Or strap on a backpack containing the accoutrements of a camping trip and you're on course for a more serious expedition.

Whatever the reason, whether it's a growing awareness of the importance of fitness or simply a need to escape the city smog, there has been a strong upsurge recently in the numbers of people rediscovering the simple pleasures of a walking trip. Certainly, as far as health is concerned, walking is one of the most effective and greenest ways of keeping fit. For urban escapologists seeking a walk on the wild side, there are plenty of tour operators offering trips to just about every wilderness destination imaginable (and a few you never thought of). On Planet Earth, star treks for mountain-loving humans include the Rockies, the Andes (especially the Inca Trail), the Himalayas and certain African peaks like Toubkal, Kenya and Kilimanjaro.

If you have not done much in the way of lengthy trekking before, then it is sensible to escape to the hills in your own country with someone experienced in the ways of walking before stepping out on a serious trip abroad. However, most operators take clients' experience and ability into account by offering a wide spectrum of walking holidays and grading the trips within their brochures accordingly (see 'Why Go – And What to Expect', p 4). One of the great advantages of an organized trip is that you do not have to worry about carrying a heavy rucksack; mules, donkeys, local porters or Sherpas will take the strain for you, and sometimes vehicles will do the transporting of kit from one overnight stop to the next. Another advantage is that guides accompany you, so getting lost is something you don't have to worry about. Once you have been on some accompanied trips, however, you may want to try your hand at an independent journey: in fact, for many people the packaged approach has acted as a springboard to a world of independent adventures.

Being relatively fit is only half of the equation for ensuring walking enjoyment: suitable clothing is the other. Well-fitting boots priced at £30 and upwards are essential (don't leave breaking them in until your trip itself; that is a certain recipe for blisters). You will also need weatherproof gear to match the climate you are trekking in (see 'Weather, and When to Go', p 21). Mountaineering outfitters and equipment suppliers are able to advise you on your likely needs.

If you are looking for a walk on the wild side, then you should treat some of the likely-sounding destinations with caution if you do not want to re-encounter the madding crowd while on holiday. For example, just forty years ago, when Nepal was closed to foreigners, only a handful of intrepid Western adventure seekers explored the Himalayas there, ignoring the access restrictions; but now you can find more than 200 trekking agencies in Kathmandu alone. In fact, Nepal plans to increase its annual visitor intake from the current 300 000 up to a staggering one million by the end of the century, cashing in on the fact that trekking accounts for a quarter of the country's foreign exchange earnings. In this way, the golden goose of Nepalese adventure is in danger of being visited to death. All is not global gloom, however. There are also many examples of countries taking a responsible approach to controlling visitor numbers and impacts – Bhutan is just one – and visitors themselves can make the difference through their own actions (see 'Responsible Tourism', p 29).

Broadly speaking, walking holidays can be divided into hillwalking or mountain trekking on the one hand (generally involving hut-to-hut tours) and less demanding rambling trips on the other (involving lower-altitude walking and more comfortable accommodation). Some operators offer camping trips, which incline more towards the hard end of the adventure spectrum. Since it's the most popular of all the adventure activities, trekking is offered by a large number of tour operators, including **Exodus, Explore Worldwide, High Places, Arctic Experience, Mountain Travel Sobek (6240 Fairmount Avenue, El Cerrito, CA 94530; tel: 510 527 8100), Sherpa Expeditions, Guerba, Worldwide Journeys and Expeditions, Himalayan Kingdoms (20 The Mall, Clifton, Bristol BS8 4DR; tel: 0117 923 7163), Ramblers Holidays (Box 43, Welwyn Garden AL8 6PQ; tel: 01707 331133) and ExplorAsia.**

Sherpa is a company dedicated to walking holidays. Their trips are graded from A (can be enjoyed by anyone who leads a reasonably active life) to D (needs stamina, fitness and familiarity with mountain walking). Sherpa offers brochures for the Himalayas, Europe, Britain and Ireland, Switzerland, Africa and the Middle East, South America and Eastern Europe.

FACTFILE

Travel tips: Exodus produces a useful leaflet, *Choosing a Trek and the Exodus Trek Grading System.*

Ecotourism: Tourism Concern's Himalayan Tourist Code is a useful checklist for trekkers who want to protect the natural environment and cultures of the places they visit in this area (see Appendix 2).

YOUTH ACTIVITIES

We live for the most part in an urban-based society, where, for many young people, adventure consists of playing the latest interactive computer game – or worse. For these people, exposure to adventurous outdoor activities is often sadly lacking. Opportunities to break out from studies and experience life in the great outdoors are usually available only during vacation times through school or university clubs. While some admirable self-development programmes do exist, such as the Duke of Edinburgh's Award Scheme in the UK, many younger people need the reassurance of a packaged experience, specifically tailored to introduce them to the excitement of outdoor adventure as a prelude perhaps to independent adventuring. Fortunately, this need has been recognized and met through the rise of multi-activity centres, especially throughout the UK. These have developed and refined a variety of holidays offering the sorts of outdoor challenges so often otherwise lacking, for people as young as six and upwards.

Understandably, the main requirement at such places is participant safety. Sadly, as recently as 1993, four young students on an 'organized' canoeing trip were drowned off the south coast of England near Lyme Regis. Since then many centres have looked very closely at their safety procedures, but the problem still exists of a lack of statutory regulation in the UK. In theory, anyone can open an adventure holiday centre, and this is reflected in a range of safety consciousness amongst operators. There are hundreds of such centres in the UK. A few are excellent, many are good, but a number leave something to be desired. This places a responsibility on those adults who send young people away on such holidays to check out their credentials in advance. Although there are no specific government regulations applying to these centres, there are, however, voluntary guidelines. One way through the safety maze is to book through the **British Activity Holidays Association (22 Green Lane, Hersham, Walton-on-Thames, Surrey SK12 5HD;**

tel: 01932 252994). BAHA lists approximately 70 operators running over 200 centres, all of which have agreed to operate under voluntary guidelines via a laid down Code of Practice for Outdoor Adventure Activity Providers.

For parents or guardians of younger kids, the idea of a youth activity holiday can be tinged with guilt, when they send little Johnny or Jane off for a holiday 'on his or her own'. But such vacations are far from a kind of glorified kennel for the young: invariably they give the potential for enjoyment and personal development, an opportunity to mix with people of the same age, and a chance to try out new sports and activities.

So what sort of activities are offered at these adventure centres? The answer is, just about anything, depending on the child's age. From soft sojourns like an afternoon's gentle fell-walking, to harder trips lasting several days, you can find virtually the whole range of adventure if you look hard enough. One of the best known adventure holiday organizations is the **Outward Bound Trust (PO Box 1219, Windsor, Berkshire SL4 1XR; tel: 01753 731005)** which runs year-round outdoor activity courses for 14 to 24 year-olds at forty-odd centres throughout the world. **Endeavour Training (17A Glumangate, Chesterfield, S40 1TX; tel: 01246 237201)** provides outdoor programmes for 16 to 24 year-olds, particularly those from disadvantaged backgrounds. Many of their courses are in the UK, although they have an overseas branch, the **John Hunt Exploration Group**, which provides a limited number of places attached to expeditions further afield. The **Youth Hostel Association (Trevelyan House, 8 St Stephens Hill, St Albans, Herts AL1 2DY; tel: 01727 845047)** draws on its hostel network and sixty years of experience to run youth action courses of varying duration and cost (you do not have to be a YHA member, incidentally).

One of the largest commercial youth activity adventure organizations in the UK is **PGL Adventure (Alton Court, Ponyard Lane, Ross-on-wye, Herefordshire HR9 5NR; tel: 01989 764211)**. PGL organizes holidays for a range of ages, from 18 year-olds to as young as 6 year-olds, with a choice of over 75 different activities in 21 centres in the UK and abroad. Each year, throughout Britain alone, it caters for around 13 000 young people at its camps. Prices range from a day camp (£20) to a full week in the UK (£300) or overseas (£1500). **Action Holidays (Jumps Road, Todmorden, Lancashire OL14 8HJ; tel: 01706 814554)** arranges holidays for around 2000 young people (5 to 15 year-olds) each summer. Options include watersports, horse riding and rock climbing, prices ranging from about £130 to £260 per week.

In the USA, many adventure operators are geared up to dealing with the needs of younger people. US teenage programmes focus on such activities as backpacking, rock climbing, canoeing, caving and survival skills. One of the most popular operators is **Trek-America (PO Box 189, Rockaway, NJ 07866; tel: 201 983 1144)** which offers two- to nine-week soft adventure trips camping and exploring in North America. Weekly prices start at around $600. **Inner Quest (Rt 1, Box 271-C, Purcelville, Virginia 22132; tel: 703 478 1078)** offers challenging outdoor adventure trips for around 8000 10 to 16 year-olds each year. The emphasis is on personal growth, development and outdoor skills, trips costing from $600 to $1000. If it's 'achieving exciting things, in exciting places, with exciting people' that you want, then **Castle Rock Ranch (412 County Road 6NS, Cody, WY 82414; tel: 307 587 2076)** is for you. Horse trekking, rock climbing and rafting are just a few of the options, which range, according to activities covered, from $2000 to around $5000, for three-week trips.

FACTFILE

Safety: If in any doubt about the safety-worthiness of the operator concerned, ask to see evidence of affiliation to BAHA or governing bodies of the particular sports covered. You might also care to check out the centre's or operator's insurance cover, staffing ratios, and first-aid cover.

Further information: The **Sports Council Information Centre, 16 Upper Woburn Place, London WC1H 0QP** has information about many of the individual sports and activities offered for younger people in the UK. For the USA, contact **Outward Bound, Route 9D, R2, Box 280, Garrison, NY 10524-9757; tel: 914 424 4000**.

Expeditions: Harder youth adventure is available via a number of organizations offering packaged expeditions (see Expeditions, p 67).

SECTION 4
Countries

NB: Throughout this section, if the address and telephone/fax numbers of a tour operator are not supplied, this indicates that the company is profiled in Section 2, and you will find all the relevant details there.

ANTARCTICA – A WORLD APART

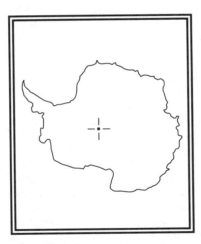

Antarctica is the ultimate adventure destination, an indescribably beautiful – almost surreal – desert, forever frozen in the savage grip of permanent winter. This is a world apart; the last great wilderness on Earth, larger than the whole of Europe. It is also the only land mass on this planet in which homo sapiens is – and will always be – an unnatural visitor. There are no permanent human populations here, only a few scientists existing for short periods in temporary bases, and a handful of seasonal tourists. Antarctica's exclusivity is not really surprising: after all it is not the sort of place where you simply turn up, expecting a warm welcome and a cheerful blazing log fire. One has only to read the extraordinary tales of endurance by household-name explorers – people like Shackleton, Captain Scott and Ranulph Fiennes – to realize the ultimate and sometimes fatal inhospitality of this stark and barren land. Usual summer temperatures of −20°C to −35°C *inside* tents make daily living a constant battle against the cold. Paradoxically, the other difficulty facing

Antarctica's occasional visitors is lack of water. For this continent is in reality a vast frozen desert, where dehydration is a very real and constant threat.

The wilderness of this 'world apart' seems eternal and invincible, and yet Antarctica is subject to an uneasy truce of twelve nations, each with varying degrees of claims to ownership. Jostling together on a human rookery on King George Island, several of these nations (some with a token military presence) maintain a toehold on the continent, ever mindful of Antarctica's rich mineral deposits and its long-term (there's a 50 year ban on mining) potential commercial possibilities.

Antarctica's fertile seas attract a wealth of marine life, the immense biomass of krill supporting a food web of fish, seabirds and whales. The topography of the continent is dramatic: sweeping bays, compact coves, rock-strewn coastlines and black volcanic craters contrasting with the huge white masses of icebergs. The 'White Continent' is not the monotonous landscape that many suppose it to be: under the sun's rays it is an awesomely varied spectacle, glistening with every colour imaginable, reflecting sparkles of sunshine which fill the whole sky with light.

Most tourist visitors arrive on one of the handful of cruise ships which set out from Rio de Janiero or Tierra del Fuego each summer. These trips are for the seriously wealthy only – each passenger pays several thousand pounds for the privilege. You also need plenty of disposable time, as well as disposable cash, since the usual length of passage is about a month. But for these lucky few, the rewards are unforgettable: gazing on unparalleled scenery and encountering wildlife not conditioned to fearing people. Visiting cruise ships pass many landmarks made famous in the annals of exploration. In 1915, it was from one of these, Elephant Island, that Shackleton and his small team of adventurers made one of the most extraordinary journeys ever undertaken, crossing 800 miles of the wildest seas in the world in little more than a glorified rowing boat. Arriving in South Georgia, he was eventually able to raise the alarm and find a way of successfully rescuing the rest of his crew who were stranded back on Deception Island. Shackleton would not have dreamt of today's cruise ships which invade the remoteness of Antarctica's shores. After crossing the notoriously unwelcoming stretch of water known as Drake's Passage, these ships hug the Antarctic coastline, occasionally allowing passengers a photo-opportunity on land. Donning heavy duty weatherproof gear, and putting ashore in zodiac inflatables, visitors can see such memorable sights as emperor penguin rookeries, elephant seal colonies, wandering albatrosses, and an occasional abandoned research hut. Albeit briefly, such excursions touch the wilderness. And yet despite the extraordinary isolation and wildness of the place on which they set foot, these passengers are in reality glorified trippers – passive spectators rather than adventurers in the proper sense of the word. Their forms of transport are luxurious floating hotels, fitted out with all mod cons and serving up cordon bleu cuisine. Physical challenges are minimal or non-existent. As yet, alternative options are thin on the ground.

For those inclined to an Antarctic cruise, **Abercrombie and Kent** (see ExplorAsia, p 41) runs trips on the *MV Explorer* – one of the few ships built specifically for polar waters. She has been venturing south to the White Continent for some 25 years and her shallow draft and zodiac landing craft allow easy access to the wild shoreline. The Explorer has room for 96 passengers and the price of a cruise is £4000 per person. **Arcturus Expeditions (PO Box 850, Gartocharn, Alexandria, Dunbartonshire G83 8RL; tel: 01389 830204)** offers cruises in five ships, ranging from 87 m up to 100 m in length. Operating under safety and environmental guidelines drawn up by the International Association of Antarctica Tour Operators, these ships make voyages of between 15 and 33 days. As with most other operators, Arcturus's ships visit the sub-Antarctic Islands – South Orkney, South Georgia and the Falkland Islands. Their 19-day '**Footsteps of the Explorers**' trip aims 'to retrace the routes of Shackleton, Bruce, Nordenskjold and others and visit places they spent winters at the turn of the century.' Prices vary according to length of passage and cabin, ranging from £4600 up to over £9000, all-inclusive.

If you would rather not take a cruise, but still have plentiful funds to finance a very different sort of trip, then it is possible to fly to the 'world apart' on a rather nail-biting DC6 flight. Operating out of Punta Arenas in Chile, **Adventure Network International (c/o Quark Expeditions, Post Road, Darien, CT 06820; tel: 203 656 0499)** is the alternative. This is the company which enabled Michael Palin to complete his Pole to Pole epic journey and which flew Ranulph Fiennes and Mike Stroud to the start of their unsupported continental crossing. For an all-inclusive $11 000, Adventure Network International will transport you to their summer base and ice landing strip in the Patriot Hills, nestled within the Ellesmere Mountains. An extra $7000 will secure a visit to an emperor penguin colony while an extra $9000 will get you to the south pole itself (weather permitting). Seriously rich adventurers can climb Mount Vinson (16067 ft/4899 m) – highest peak in the continent – for about $25 000. Part of the reason for this expense is Adventure Network International's responsible approach to the ecological importance of Antarctica: all waste products (of human as well as other origin) are flown out of their Patriot Hills base. When you add up the costs of flying literally everything in and out, not to mention waiting for weather 'windows' and the odd aborted flight, you begin to realize why Antarctica is the preserve only for adventurers with plenty of funds.

FACTFILE

Organizations: The **British Antarctic Survey (High Cross, Madingley Road, Cambridge CB3 0ET; tel: 01223 61188)** has an ongoing programme of research.

Cruises: The season for cruises is November to February.

Climate: The weather changes suddenly and without warning. All tour operators give provisos in their terms and conditions that what you see is entirely dependent on the vagaries of weather and ice conditions. Discovery of an ozone 'hole' in 1987 focused world attention on the continent's importance with respect to global warming.

AUSTRALIA – WONDERFUL LAND OF OZ

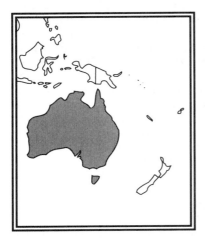

When entering Australia you encounter a mirror of strangeness, of English-speaking otherness. Everything may look similar, yet is in fact stunningly different. It is a land of stark beauty and even starker contrasts. There are endless beaches, rainforests teeming with wildlife and deserts which seem to go on forever. Australia offers everything the adventure traveller could ever want.

To many people the Outback epitomizes Australia: it is not so much an area as a state of mind – a feeling for a land that can never be tamed. Although it cannot push the world away it will remain one of the last frontiers. To the Aborigines, the outback is a world shrouded in 'The

2 week Australia outback tour   2 weeks Bahamas
2 weeks sydney   3 weeks Bhutan £2400
2 weeks perth ✓
2 weeks Darwin
2 weeks Great Barrier Reef

Australia   105

Dreaming' – spirits of their ancestors who 40 000 years ago arrived in this great land. The best time to tour the Outback is during the cool winter months between May and October. In South Australia the gateway to the Outback is through the **Flinders Range National Park** with its striking granite peaks and colourful cliffs. There is a two-day trek around Wilpena Pound, a huge natural amphitheatre; or you could try the one-day climb to St Mary's Peak. At 'The Red Centre' in Northern Territory you can explore the **Uluru National Park** which contains Ayers Rock, one of the world's greatest natural wonders. Sacred to the Aboriginal people, it is noted for its spectacular colour changes at sunrise and sunset. There are walking tracks around the base and up to the top of the rock. **Australian Pacific Tours (tel: 01 879 1424)** offers outback safaris from 10 to 28 days. **Australian Explorer Tours (tel: 03 820 0700)** also offers tours in the remote areas of Northern Territory and Western Australia.

Kakadu National Park in Northern Territory is a magnificent 12 600 sq km wilderness, listed as a World Heritage Site. There is a host of bush walking options including the spectacular **Arnhem Land Escarpment**. Here you will have the best chance to see some superb Aboriginal rock art as well as a great variety of wildlife, including buffalo and giant crocodiles. **Willis's Walkabouts (tel: 089 85 2134)** operates 14–22 day walkabouts deep into the heart of the Kakadu wilderness. Another good bushwalking area in the north is **Katherine Gorge National Park** with its rugged scenery and startling variety of plantlife. Here there are trails ranging from one hour to five days. It is also possible to **canoe** the Katherine river for a distance of some 170 km/105 miles. To hire a canoe try **Kooaburra Canoe Hire (tel: 097 723 604)**.

For a combination of adventure and a cultural experience you could head north to the Cobourg Peninsula where **Seven Spirit Bay** and **Gurig National Park** contain a unique wilderness habitat with a resident community of naturalists, fishermen and craftspeople. Here you can explore the area by boat, mountain bike or on foot. Contact **Seven Spirit Wilderness Pty (tel: 089 816 844)**.

Western Australia is aptly called the 'Golden West'; it is the nation's biggest state and indeed everything about it is big. In the far north is the *Kimberly Wilderness Area*, a magnificent region of rugged mountains, huge rivers and inland plateaux. Within this region lies the imposing **Purnululu National Park**, a huge massif of giant beehive-like mounds, gorges and palm-fringed rockpools. The Park is very remote with few facilities and walkers must carry in all food and water. The area is really accessible only during the dry winter season, when the rivers die down to trickling streams. **Willis's Walkabouts (tel: 089 273 966)** operates scheduled walking tours in this Park.

On the state's southern coast is the **Nuyts Wilderness Area**. This is a walker's paradise, with karri and jarrah forests, an abundance of wildflowers and wide ocean beaches. There is a two-day walk following a well defined track. Some spectacular rough walking can be had in the **Stirling Range** in the south and also, further north, in the **Kalbarri National Park** which is famous for its spring wildflowers.

In New South Wales, to the west of Sydney, lie the beautiful and dramatic **Blue Mountains**. They are formed by a high sandstone plateau dissected by deep forested gorges, plunging waterfalls and sheer cliffs. There is a wide range of walking trails along the ridges and through the valleys. Another popular bushwalking haunt is in the **Warrumbungles**, a small but spectacular group of volcanic peaks to the north of Sydney. There are also countless other walks up and down the length of the **Great Dividing Range**, which straddles Australia's east coast. **Trailfinders (tel: 0171 938 3366)** offers a wide range of tours throughout Australia.

Another way to explore Australia is on horseback. In the spectacular high country of Victoria there is a range of day and weekend trails, following original bridle trails blazed through the bush more than a century ago by cattlemen and gold miners. Contact **Bluff and Beyond Trail Rides (tel: 057 75 2212)**.

Victoria is also one of Australia's most popular canoeing areas encompassing mountain white water, still lakes, gentle rivers and excellent sea kayaking. The **Mitta Mitta** river offers great rapids as well as beautiful river scenery. **Bogong Jacks's (tel: 057 27 3382) Great Divide Bush Explorer** includes two days canoeing in the upper **King Valley** and **Mt Cobbler** region of the Great Dividing Range.

If you are a lover of forests you should head for **Daintree National Park** in the far north of **Queensland**. Reputed to be the oldest forest on earth, it is also a mountainous region of stunning vistas and sea views. Crystal-clear streams swarming with fish and turtles cascade past great tree ferns, epiphytes and lianas. **Trailfinders (UK tel: 0171 938 3366)** offers a range of tours including a stay at the Bloomfield Wilderness Lodge.

North of Brisbane, **Fraser Island** is a walker's paradise with tall rainforests, huge sand dunes and beautiful lakes. There is a three-day circuit of the island. **Lamington National Park** in the Macpherson Range has a good network of tracks through forests, high waterfalls and gorges. Not to be missed in Queensland is the spectacular **Carnarvon Gorge**.

Those in search of watery pursuits need go no further than the **Great Barrier Reef**. Like emeralds in a sapphire sea the islands stretch down the Queensland coast and shelter Australia's best cruising waters. The **Cumberland** and **Whitsunday** Groups are home to Australia's largest fleet of bareboat and fully crewed charter yachts. The best time to cruise is during the dry, sunny months from June to September. Most charter companies are based at Shute Harbour and Airlie Beach or Hamilton Island Resort in the Whitsunday Passage. One such is **Cumberland Charter Yachts (tel: 079 467 500)**. You could also try **Whitsunday Rent a Yacht (tel: 079 469 232)**.

The **Great Barrier Reef Marine Park** contains an iridescent wonderland of coral and fish, a nirvana for divers and snorkellers alike. For scuba divers and snorkellers there are specialist one-day boat trips leaving from Cairns, as well as daily trips to **Lizard Island** which is surrounded by the coral reef. Further south, **Heron Island** also provides superb snorkelling. Underwater operators include **Cairns Dive Centre (tel: 070 51 0294)**.

One of the best ways to explore Queensland's islands is in a sea kayak. **World Expeditions (tel: 02 264 3366)** runs a seven-day **Hinchinbrook Island** and **Coral Sea** adventure which allows paddlers to explore rainforests, golden beaches and to see turtles, dolphins and manta rays.

For Australians life is a beach, from bustling Bondi to the secluded strands of the north. There are tremendous surfing opportunities throughout the country and particularly on the 40 km/25 mile long **Gold Coast** in Queensland and in New South Wales at **Narabeen**, **Manly** and **Cronulla**.

If possible don't leave Australia without a visit to **Tasmania**, which is still an unspoilt wilderness of soaring mountains, forests and rushing rivers. There are tremendous hiking opportunities in the **South West National Park**. On **Franklin** river you can have a spectacular 11-day white-water rafting trip. Contact **Tasmania Expeditions (tel: 003 34 3477)**.

It is difficult to suggest an adventure tour in Australia: there is such a variety of places to see and things to do. However, **Explore** offers a number of adventure holidays throughout Australia. Their '**Reef and Rainforest**' trip consists of a 17-day wilderness and island cruise. Travelling by 4-wheel drive vehicle north of Cairns, you explore Daintree Rainforest and Lakefield National Park. Passing through vast uninhabited areas of bush you camp out in the wild outdoors, next to waterfalls or dry creek beds. Reaching Australia's northern tip, you take a boat across the Torres Strait to Thursday Island. Boarding a catamaran cruise boat, you spend three days exploring the sheltered Albany Coast, glimpsing wilderness inaccessible by road. Total cost of the trip is £2200, including return flight from London.

FACTFILE

Climate: The north is tropical, with a monsoon from January to March, while the south is subtropical to temperate. Rainfall is distributed throughout the year but varies from area to area.

Conservation: Bushfire is a major risk. Check for local regulations and restrictions. Portable stoves are environmentally responsible.

BAHAMAS – OUT ISLAND ADVENTURES

'Even the singing of the birds is such that a man could never wish to leave this place.'

Christopher Columbus

Many people think of the Bahamas as Nassau, Paradise Island and Cable Beach – a Caribbean playground of hotels, cabarets, and casinos. The truth is that the Bahamas is a lot more than tourist traps and glitz. It is a collection of no fewer than 700 islands and cays (most of them uninhabited), an archipelago which stretches some 250 000 square kilometres between Florida and Cuba. Diving in the Bahamas is world-class, its climate is superb year-round, and its seas are warm and inviting. It is easy to reach from the USA and from the UK. English is the official language and it is not as expensive to visit as many other Caribbean destinations. The beauty of the Bahamas to adventurers is that you can easily escape from the more popular spots to havens of peace, solitude and wildness. Small wonder then, that the Bahamas' Out Islands are rapidly becoming alluring destinations for watersport adventurers of all kinds.

Of the 700 islands in this Caribbean archipelago, only about 30 are inhabited. Most of the others remain largely unknown, overlooked by tourists and sightseers, but each of these 'Out Islands', as they are called, form Gardens of Eden in miniature. With names like Abaco, Andros, the Exumas, Crooked Island, Eleuthera, Cat Island, Long Island, Berry Islands, Harbour Island and Bimini, these places all offer spectacular wilderness and watersport prospects, though each is different in its own way. Keen to preserve these remote areas from the ravages of mass tourism, the Bahamas government has developed a protection strategy which allows only appropriate, small-scale development and activity in what are referred to as 'eco-sensitive' island areas. Eight of the Bahamas' twelve National Parks are found on these Out Islands, several of which are important for breeding birds and turtles.

Known as the 'sailing capital of the world', **Abaco**, with its designated reserves – **Pelican Cay Land and Sea National Park** and **Fowl Cay Land and Sea Preserve** – has enticed divers and snorkellers for years. Within these areas you can find coral reef gardens resplendent with purple seafans and corals such as Elkhorns and Brain Corals. The reef system here forms winding tunnels and caverns which are home to countless Silverside minnows, the minnows' predators, and their predators in turn (Spiral cavern at Walker's Cay has a resident population of some 25 sharks, for example.)

With its miles of shallow flats, **Andros** is known as the 'bonefish capital of the world'. Its main diving area is centred on **Small Hope Bay Lodge** in Fresh Creek, where divers' and snorkellers' needs are fully catered for. Off the coast diving opportunities abound – reefs, wrecks, drop-offs and blue holes – while further out stretches the Great Barrier Reef, second largest in the Western hemisphere. This reef has an incredible 1800 m/6000 ft drop down to the 'Tongue of the Ocean' trench. But over-curious divers should be cautious off Andros: legends abound of the magical red-eyed, three-fingered, three-toed elf-like creature called a Chick Charney. According to Indian folklore, this creature can cause great mischief if disturbed.

Strung out along the eastern edge of the Great Bahama Bank, the chain of **Berry Islands** offers its share of diving treasures: underwater rock formations, shipwrecks and reefs. **Bimini** – Ernest Hemingway's 'Island in the Stream' – has been a favourite with divers for decades. Only 20 minutes from Miami by seaplane, Bimini's abundant and varied marine life forms a strong attraction for the ecologically aware. Experienced divers can 'drop in' from the Bimini Barge to visit the resident green moray and stingrays. As an alternative marine adventure, you can discover an undersea world near Bimini which some people claim is actually the lost continent of Atlantis. And if you ever tire of watery pursuits, there is always the island itself, with its 'wild hog' trails winding among the natural vegetation. Despite being one of the ten largest islands in the Bahamas, **Cat Island** maintains a strong sense of privacy thanks to its unspoilt white sandy beaches and pine forest seclusion. Christened after a British sea Captain by the name of Catt, the island has a lush interior of verdant forests and rolling hills. These hills include the highest point in the Bahamas, **Mount Alvernia** (a heady 63 m/ 206 ft above Caribbean sea level) which has impressive 365° views. This spot appealed to a hermit called Father Jerome, who some fifty years ago carved an ornate replica of an Italian monastery out of the limestone there. On one exquisitely detailed tile in a stone wall reads the evocation 'Thank you Lord for the Moon and the Stars'. Alone on the mountain, with celestial displays of shooting stars like fireworks in the warm Caribbean night, this place must sometimes have seemed like heaven-on-earth for Jerome.

Crooked Island is often referred to as 'The Fragrant Isle' because of its sweet scent of herbs and flowers. The waters surrounding Crooked Island are crystal clear, revealing coral reefs which slope gently from 1.5 to 12 m/5 to 40 ft before plunging down sharply 600 fathoms to Crooked Island Passage. Virtually unexplored, these 72 km/45 miles of barrier reef are home to a visual extravaganza of tropical fish. The lyrical sounding island of **Eleuthera** is also a popular haunt of watersports enthusiasts. Surfers can 'catch the waves' here, while divers can explore the underwater pinnacles at Cove Eleuthera – feeding grounds for much of the area's marine life. One of the most challenging dives here is a 5-knot drift at Current Cut, home to spotted eagle rays and horse-eye jacks. Equally lyrical in name, the **Exumas** form a collection of 365 islands – one for every day of the year. The **Exuma National Land and Sea Park** has a great variety of marine life. Eco-dive operators will guide you around this extraordinary submarine ecosystem and help to interpret it for you.

For shipwreck enthusiasts, Devil's Backbone – a shallow reef area off **Harbour Island** – contains dozens of wrecks, including, of all unexpected things, a locomotive. Not far away (Harbour Island is only two square miles in extent) lies '**The Plateau**' – an area well-known for its marine life. **Long Island** is a place of contrasts, with its turbulent rocky headlands and calm white beaches. It lives up to its name, being about 100 km/60 miles long but rarely more than 5 km/3 miles scross. Here is a place of rugged headlands falling steeply into the sea, fertile grazing lands, rolling hills and surf-washed sandy beaches. The Long Island Regatta is held every May. Underwater, the **Long Island Blue Hole** is just one of many adventurous dives on offer here. Bottlenose dolphins and turtles are often seen, while the Bahamas shark-feeding dive, which originated here 15 years ago, still continues. Half a mile off the Cape Santa Maria Beach lies the 'Ship's Graveyard' with (among other wrecks) the steel freighter Comerbach still sitting upright in 30 m/100 ft of water.

The **Family Islands** stretch across a huge expanse of crystal Caribbean Sea. Ideal for vacation escape artists they are secluded though not isolated, being served by the national carrier Bahamasair.

The costs of diving in the Bahamas vary considerably, from about $350 for three days diving and accommodation, upwards. Accommodation of all types is available, and there is usually no difficulty in finding places which hire out dive equipment (nor is it difficult to find diving instructors). Christopher Columbus, the first European visitor to this region, pronounced the Bahamas 'very green and fertile and the air very balmy'. Certainly the climate here is very benign: thanks to a combination of the Gulf Stream and balmy south-eastern trade winds, temperatures rarely fall below 16°C or rise above 32°C. Occasional rainfalls occur during the summer, but these are usually brief and always refreshing.

Local diving operators include **Romora Bay Dive Shop** (Harbour Island and North Eleuthera), **PO Box 146, Harbour Island, tel: 809 333 2323**; **Chub Cay Undersea Adventures** (Barry Islands), **tel: 809 325 1490**; **Bimini Undersea Adventures, tel: 809 347 3089**; **Cat Island Sea Club, tel: 305 474 4821**; **Exuma Fantasea, tel: 809 336 3483**; **South Eleuthera Divers, tel: 809 334 4083**; and **Stella Maris Diving** (Long Island), **tel: 809 336 2106**.

On Grand Bahama, **East End Adventures (PO Box F-44322, Freeport; tel: 809 352 6222)** offers all-day eco-conscious safaris to the Lucayan National Park and cays off the western end of the island. **UNEXSO (Underwater Explorers Society, PO Box F-42433, Freeport; tel: 809 373 1244)** offers basic and advanced diving instruction, diving with dolphins, diving with sharks and night dives.

For the adventure of a lifetime, you could try the '**Swimming with Dolphins**' programme operated by **Discover the World**. This is a unique opportunity to swim with spotted dolphins, which live off the coast of the Bahamas and seem to enjoy human companionship. The area chosen for the encounter has clear and shallow waters (5.5–9 m/18–30 ft deep). On day 1 of the trip you fly to Miami and transfer to Fort Lauderdale, where you board the research vessel – a 21 m/70 ft steel-hulled schooner. Early morning on day 2 the group (6–10 in number) sets sail for West End, a small port on Grand Bahama. After clearing customs, there is a chance to go swimming or snorkelling here. The next five days are spent with the dolphins (weather permitting). You do not go searching for them: you drop anchor and let them find you. Each encounter is different. If there are only a few present, a limited number of your group will be allowed in the water, but if there are plenty, then everyone can get in. On day 8 the vessel sails back to Freeport on Grand Bahama in time to take the flights back to Miami and onward. No diving skills are needed for this adventure, although you do need to be a reasonably strong swimmer and some previous experience with mask and snorkel (even if in a pool) is essential. Accommodation is in small 2- or 4-berth cabins, departures are in December, June, July and August and the cost, including scheduled flights from London to Miami, is around £1700.

FACTFILE

Diving: Sea temperatures generally reach the high 20s in summer and are in the mid-20s in winter.

Transport: Island-hopping is easy using regular scheduled flights by Bahamasair. Mailboats are slower but more fun (you share deck-space with farm animals and pineapples).

Responsible tourism: The Ministry of Tourism offers an excellent and unique programme called 'People-to-People' which aims to foster communication, exchange ideas and advance international friendship. If you write to the **Ministry of Tourism, People-to-People Programme, PO Box N-3701, Market Plaza, Bay Street, Nassau (tel: 809 322 7500)** about a month before arriving in the country, your interests can be matched with those of Bahamaians on the Ministry's database. You will then be introduced to the local people concerned who will show you an angle of the Bahamas not normally experienced by tourists. **Camping** is not permitted on any of the islands of the Bahamas.

BELIZE – REEF AND RAINFOREST REFUGE

'Perhaps the charm comes from the sense of the temporary,
of the precarious, of living on the edge of destruction.'

Graham Greene, Getting to Know the General

Although only a tenth of the size of the UK (some 23 000 square kilometres/9000 square miles) Belize has a kaleidoscope of topography, from its coast – with numerous islands, coastal cays and the second largest barrier reef in the world – to its lush and tropical interior. Along with its neighbouring Central American countries, Mexico and Guatemala, Belize has many remains from the Mayan civilization which waxed and waned from 2000 BC to 1000 AD. Today, the country's population is relatively small – only 8 people per square kilometre – and tourism is still in its infancy. In 1993, for instance, there were only 200 000 holiday visitors, but the numbers are increasing steadily. With a strong emphasis on ecologically and culturally responsible tourism, Belize can expect to avoid the problems of mass tourism experienced elsewhere. If this can be achieved, the outlook here for adventure holidays in the 21st century will indeed be rosy.

Underwater attractions are one of the country's biggest magnets for adventurers, for the whole coastline is studded with rewarding diving spots. There are three atolls, more than 70 hard corals, 430 species of reef fish and of course the world's second largest barrier reef (after Australia's). Belize City is the main hub for seabound excursions, for this is where the live-aboard dive vessels depart from. Belize's three coral atolls can be visited via day dive excursions from Belize city but most trips are longer, using live-aboard dive vessels. Near Dangriga, along the central coast, the ocean is studded with hundreds of small cays. There are a number of small resorts which shuttle you out to the barrier reef for shallow and deep dives in coral gardens and grottoes. **South Water Cay** is regarded as the most idyllic inhabited caye in the country, its **Marine Wildlife Refuge** at the southern end being the location for International Zoological Expeditions. Breaking on the shallow reef, the Caribbean Sea forms a shimmering line of surf, while inside the coral crest myriads of coral formations slope down gently to depths of 40 feet or so. Cutting the reef are deeper fissures and canyons which wind down to deeper waters. Around **Laughing Bird Cay** and **Little Water Cay** there are wonderful diving sites among the shallow reefs and 'sea gardens'.

Belize has a number of offshore cays popular with divers. These include **Ambergris Cay** in the north and, to its south, **Cay Caulker**. The **Hol Chan Marine Reserve** diving area, which is easily accessible from both places, has an abundance of shallow water corals and gorgonians. A rewarding diving experience here is to drop down into one of the deeper canyons which intersect the shallower reefs and gradually swim along to the drop-off, an almost mystical experience in the morning light. One of the best dive sites in the country is **Big Cay Bokel**, at the southern point of the Turnereffe Islands, and one of these trips is the spectacular and exhilarating Elbow Reef. Although dives are often prevented here by strong currents, when conditions are calm you can see an astonishing variety of smaller fish, together with their predators, and larger creatures such as sharks, grouper and the huge manatee, some of which weigh up to 680 kg/1500 lb and grow to over 4 m/14 ft. These gentle creatures are often found feeding in the grassy flat mangrove areas around the Turnereffe Islands. Other good diving spots are **Blackbird Cay**, home to Oceanic Society Expeditions which researches bottlenose dolphins, and Lighthouse and Glover's Reefs. Lighthouse Reef is close to Belize's first National Reserve, **Half Moon Cay** which is home to the endangered red-footed boobies and rare sea turtles. An extraordinary phenomenon here is the Blue Hole, 100 m/350 ft wide and 120 m/400 ft deep, which was once dry, as evidenced by stalactites, but became submerged after the ice age. The diving around Half Moon is spectacular, with huge southern stingrays and eagle rays for company and visibility in excess of 60 m/200 ft.

Turning to the interior of Belize, getting about by road can be tricky. However, the country boasts an extensive network of trails for off-road hiking, mountain biking or riding, which are designed for all ages and abilities of adventurers. These trails are found in the National Parks and Resorts and on private land. Some of these routes lead you through tropical rainforest, while others take you to other natural attractions such as waterfalls, caves and rivers, or archaeological ruins dating from the Mayan civilization. Experienced bush guides are available to accompany you on more challenging trips, identifying and interpreting the vegetation which you pass through. One memorable trail is the route crossing

Mountain Pine Ridge Reserve, leading to the **Rio Frio Cave**. Sightings of parrots, land crabs, bats, tarantulas and black orchids (to name but a very few species) are practically guaranteed. The **Hidden Valley Falls** are a spectacular attraction, water cascading over a thousand-foot drop into the jungle below. Ecotourism is big in Belize, as it should be, thanks to the efforts of such organizations as the Belize Ecotourism Association, which promotes only those 'green' operators who subscribe to an ecotourism code of ethics. Trips to wilderness areas have to be led by experienced, well trained responsible naturalists and guides. For all its attractions, Belize has yet to become a mecca for tourists and, fortunately for adventure visitors, it is just possible that it may never become so.

Local adventure and ecotourism operators include **Island Adventures (PO Box 83, San Pedro, Ambergris Cay, tel: 501 2 62488), Ian Anderson's Adventurous Belize (PO Box 332, Belize City; tel: 501 2 33903),** and **Belize Diving Service (PO Box 667, Belize City; tel: 501 2 22143)**. US and UK tour operators offering trips to the country include **International Expeditions, Inc (One Environs Park, Helena, AL 35080; tel: 205 428 1700)** and **Explore Worldwide**.

For an introduction to the country, **Explore** offers a 15- or 20-day '**Discover Belize**' trip, billed as 'a total Belize Experience which includes exotic wildlife, jungle rivers, idyllic cays, tropical forests and the archaeological wonders of the Maya civilization.' From Belize City, the trip visits the Temple of the Sun at Altun Ha, continuing to the marshy lagoons and wetlands of Crooked Tree Bird Sanctuary. From there you explore the ancient ruins of Lamanai, which is accessed by jungle river and along rough approach trails through dense rainforest. Three days are spent exploring the great Mayan ceremonial centre at Xunantunich, as well as the forest reserve of Mountain Pine Ridge and the 300 m/1000 ft water-shaft at Hidden Valley Falls. In this region you learn something of the native herbal and medicinal plants as you walk the jungle trails. Driving along the Hummingbird Highway to Hopkins fishing village on the Caribbean, you visit Coxcome Jaguar Reserve and spend a day trail walking in the mahogany forest – home of the big cats. Then, turning north, you take a launch through the Manatee Lagoon, where lucky travellers will catch a glimpse of the giant 'seacows', to the tropical island of Cay Caulker, an idyllic spot for underwater exploration. A five-day extension on the island of Cay Caulker is ideally suited to snorkel and dive enthusiasts. Accommodation on this trip is in lodges and resthouses: group size is 12–16. The total cost for the 15-day adventure is around £1400 from London, while the 5-day extension costs only around an extra £100.

FACTFILE

Ecotourism: The following guidelines are issued to holiday visitors to Belize: stay on the trail; do not remove plants or corals; maintain a minimum distance of 20 ft from wildlife; pack out trash and litter; don't buy threatened animal or plant products/souvenirs.

Climate: Subtropical with a brisk prevailing wind from the Caribbean sea. High annual temperatures and humidity. Monsoon season is June to September.

BHUTAN – KINGDOM OF THE THUNDER DRAGONS

'Bhutan after all is a Himalayan kingdom where people live a rural life in small villages in remote valleys. Their Buddhist culture and their isolation from a turbulent world seem to have preserved a natural, innocent happiness that King Jigme Singye Wangchuck has every right to protect.'

Steven Barry

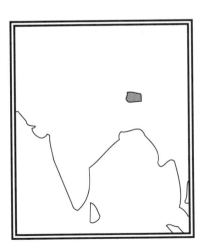

Of all Himalayan countries, Bhutan is still the most mysterious and least visited. Unlike Nepal, its neighbouring tourist 'honeypot', Bhutan has preserved its past, presenting a rare insight into an isolated kingdom where time has stood still. Travellers in search of adventure are bound to experience something of the mystery and majesty of this colourful and deeply religious country called by its people 'Druk Yul' – meaning Kingdom of the Thunder Dragons.

Determined to preserve Bhutan's priceless and timeless culture and traditions, King Jigme Singye Wangchuck is allowing his country's doors to be opened only gradually to the modern world. 'Gross domestic happiness' is his declared aim rather than gross domestic product, and strictures banning 'destructive influences' like television, or rules on wearing traditional national dress, are strictly enforced. Western tourists were allowed to enter Bhutan only as late as 1974. Currently, the number of tourists totals a mere 2500 each year and there is an upper ceiling of 5000 set for the end of the century. Forget independent adventuring here: the Bhutan Tourism Cooperative actively discourages low-budget visitors travelling on their own. You must either join an organized group or make up your own party of six or more travellers in order to qualify for entry. Furthermore, in an effort to protect the sanctity of Bhutan's places of worship, nearly all monasteries, temples and shrines were closed to foreign tourist groups in 1988. But despite all these official restrictions and high costs, the rewards for adventurous souls visiting this unique and mystical 'Kingdom of the Thunder Dragons' are immeasurable.

Bhutan's small oval landmass – only 320 km/200 miles east–west and 160 km/100 miles north–south – is hemmed in by China and India, while its northern boundary with Tibet consists of mighty and still largely unclimbed Himalayan peaks. There is a recently constructed road running east–west, which, though often blocked by avalanches and monsoon rockfalls, provides the main means of travel in this country of deep gorges, forested hillsides and snowclad peaks. The eight or so north–south rivers which cross Bhutan's main roadway offer the only other means of communication in this inaccessible wilderness. Receiving much heavier rain than the rest of the Himalayas, Bhutan's vegetation is extremely lush. More than half of its land surface is covered by forests – a great contrast to Nepal – while over two million acres are set aside as National Nature Reserves and wildlife sanctuaries.

'Druk Yul' started life as late as the 17th century, when a number of independently administered centres were formed in the country. These still exist today, each centre with its own monastery or fortress (*dzong*). The latter form the very core of Bhutanese life, representing authority, religion, law and order to its pre-industrial population of around a million. Invariably built in strategic locations, these imposing *dzongs*, with their huge sheer white walls, seem to cling impossibly to steep sided gorges, dominating the natural landscapes over which they exert their influence. Buddhism dominates Bhutanese society. There are many temples, both large and small, scattered throughout the country, while prayer flags, giant prayer wheels and isolated *chortens* (cairns) provide constant reminders of Bhutanese religious fervour.

The kingdom is divided into three regions: west, central and east, all of which are linked by the single mountain road. This road starts in the southwest at **Phuntsholing**, the traditional point of entry, finishing in the east near the isolated town of **Sakten**. The extreme western region is prohibited to foreigners and, like its Nepalese and Tibetan counterparts, is largely unexplored. **Paro**, the only airport, is the usual entry-point for visitors flying in from Kathmandu or Delhi. Predictably, a huge *dzong* dominates the valley here, forming the starting point for a trek up to **Mt Chomalhari** (7316 m/23 997 ft). From here you wind up the steep forested trail to Taksong Monastery, perched precariously on an impossibly steep rockface, one of Bhutan's oldest and most imposing places of worship. As the trail winds upwards you begin to enter the abode of mountain dwellers and yak herders. If you are lucky enough, you will be invited to enter the smoky confines of their tents and offered a traditional cup of salty tasting butter tea or a pungent chunk of white yak cheese. Passing beneath the shadow of Mt Chomaihari which the British explorer F. Spencer Chapman attempted (unsuccessfully) to climb in the 1930s, you enter the village of **Laya** (3887 m/12 750 ft) where the local women wear their hair long and free, unlike the short cropped style seen in the rest of the country.

Laya forms a gateway to the largely unexplored remote region of **Lunana**, which has only recently been opened to visitors. The first Westerner to visit this remote region was a botanist, Frank Ludlaw, in 1949. Access to Lunana is gained via the lung-busting but spectacular **Gonhu La Pass** (5232 m/17 160 ft) where Bhutan's highest mountain, **Gangkar Punsom** (7552 m/24 770 ft) can be seen. Legends about the mountains abound, like the notorious *Dredmo* or abominable snowman, although you are more likely to see *bhural* (blue sheep), eagles and vultures than yeti. After trekking back down the heavily forested valley of Mocho you can enjoy the relaxing hot sulphur springs at Gasa.

As you leave western Bhutan heading towards the central region of **Bumthang**, you cross the **Pele La**, a 3000 m/9800 ft high grassy plateau in the middle of the Black Mountain range. Just over the pass lies a strategically placed regional *chorten*, its eyes staring out to the four points of the compass. As you continue through this spectacular scenery of gorges and tree covered valleys the mighty Torgsa *dzong* comes into view. This huge and domineering structure affirms the authority and mystery that once emanated from this traditional seat of power. Now home to the Royal Family, it acts as an effective gateway for east–west communications. East of the Torgsa *dzong* lie the pastoral valleys of Bumthang, land of stories and legends. The most notable legend concerns a place known as Kuje Lhakhang, where the Guru Padmasambhaua meditated so long that his body left an impression in the solid rock. The road continues to rise as it travels eastwards and eventually crosses the highest point, **Thumsing La**, at 3780 m/

12 400 ft, before descending into eastern Tibet.
One of the principal operators in Bhutan is **Karakoram Experience (32 Lake Road, Keswick, Cumbria CA12 5DQ; tel: 01768 773966)** which offers a variety of trips and treks, including a strenuous expedition which takes in two peaks over 5300 m/ 17 400 ft (price on request). Other operators include **Explore**, whose 22-day '**Land of the Dragon**' tour includes wildlife viewing, an overland journey and several days' trekking, at a cost of £2400. **Exodus** offers 19 days' trekking for £2500, all-inclusive.

Bhutan offers some of the finest walking in the Himalayas and one of the more up-market companies offering treks here is **Worldwide Journeys & Expeditions**. Their 17-day '**Bumthang and Gangtey Treks**' comprise two short treks in the beautiful valleys of central Bhutan. The journey begins at Paro, with a visit to Taktsang, the 'Tigers Nest' monastery, perched high on its 600 m/ 2000 ft cliff face. Continuing from Thimphu to Gangtey, site of another monastery, this is where you start the trek proper. The first trek, which lasts three days, takes you through forests of rhododendron, magnolia and juniper, across two undemanding passes with excellent views. A night is spent at the monastery in Gogona, situated in an isolated valley. The second trek follows a circuitous route from the Bumthang Valley across the 3800 m/ 12 500 ft Phephela Pass to the Thang Valley, a beautifully scenic walk. Some nights are spent camping but most are spent in lodges or hotels. Trips are usually made in May and October and the cost, including airfare, amounts to around £3000.

FACTFILE

When to go: September to October or mid-March to early June are best.

Travel tips: If you show respect you may be able to visit occasionally isolated temples despite the ban. Respect Bhutan's desire not to move too quickly into the 20th century. Do not attempt to Westernize locals and do not buy antiques for export.

Other information: All tours are expensive due to the government's desire to raise foreign currency.

BORNEO – JUNGLE SANCTUARIES

'But there was no doubt about the view disclosed through the gap: the ground fell away to the east; we looked out across the jungle-covered hills rolling to the horizon. We stood at the heart of Borneo . . .'

Redmond O'Hanlon, Into the Heart of Borneo

Divided between Indonesia, Malaysia and the independent state of Brunei, Borneo combines in one land mass all the ingredients for a perfect adventure – whatever type of holiday you're looking for. The world's third largest island (after Greenland and New Guinea), Borneo encompasses great variations of culture and language. Equally varied is its scenery, much of which is unspoilt, and its wildlife (some species do not occur elsewhere in the world). While there is popular tourism in some parts of the island, elsewhere there are vast tracts of inaccessible rainforest, innumerable misty mountain peaks, and entire networks of rivers and tributaries which, even today, are comparatively unknown to all but the locals who inhabit them.

On the northwest coast of the island is **Brunei**, which is something of an anomaly. This small, oil-rich place, comprising only 5765 sq km/2225 sq miles – roughly a quarter of the size of Wales) is one of the world's wealthiest countries. Governed by the British for almost 100 years until independence in 1984, even now it has a population density of only 40 people per square kilometre, and, despite inevitable industrialization following the discovery of oil, has not lost sight of its ancient traditions and beliefs. Brunei's landscape is mainly equatorial jungle infiltrated by rivers, which form the principal means of transport in less accessible areas. Outside the capital of Bandar Seri Begawan, a number of village settlements can be found clustering around estuaries. In several places, notably in Temburont district and at Rampayoh in Belait district, there are still excellent examples of traditional longhouses, which are the main form of dwelling-place for the local inhabitants. Also of note is the **Water-village** within the capital itself, said to constitute the largest collection of stilt habitations in the world.

When the British Protectorate of North Borneo was dissolved, Brunei became an enclave, bounded to the north by the South China Sea, and surrounded on all landward sides by **Sarawak**, which divides Brunei into two separate parts. Along with neighbouring **Sabah** on the northern tip of Borneo, Sarawak forms the area of East Malaysia, 645 km/400 miles to the west across the South China Sea. Sarawak and Sabah are both ideal adventure travel destinations, either in themselves or combined with exploration of the rest of Borneo. Sarawak, the larger state, consists of swampy coastal plains, with rivers penetrating far into the mountainous jungle of the interior. Sabah, known as 'The Land Below the Winds' since it is out of reach of the typhoons which batter the Philippines, is very similar to Sarawak, having a narrow coastal plain leading up to a mountainous interior. This is the site of **Kinabalu National Park**, home of **Mount Kinabalu**, which, at 4101 m/13 455 ft, is the highest in Malaysia and one of the highest in South-east Asia. The Park itself covers 767 sq km/296 sq miles of tropical rainforest, some of which is criss-crossed by marked trails, and there are also hot springs at Poring on Kinabalu's southern edge. Despite Mount Kinabalu's height, the ascent is less arduous than might be supposed and there is vehicular access for part of the way up. Nonetheless, the climb demands a good level of fitness and you should allow two days or more for the experience. This area also offers good opportunities for more experienced climbers and mountaineers as well. Kinabalu National Park is home to over 500 species of birds and over 800 varieties of orchid, and it is worth taking time to appreciate them. This is equally true of the fauna and flora throughout the rest of Sabah, for much of its indigenous flora in particular is very rare. Sadly, time may be short for some of the rarer species, for Sabah, and indeed Malaysia as a whole, relies heavily on exports of timber from the state's rainforests to generate foreign exchange.

In contrast to Sabah's National Parks is the beach resort of Tanjung Ara, which lies just outside the capital of Kota Kinabalu. Offshore there are several uninhabited islands, two of which, Pulau Mamutik and Pulau Sulug, form **Tunku Abdul Rahman Park**. Here, as on Borneo's northern coast, however, development is taking place, and the idyll is slowly being eroded.

Tucked away in the northeastern corner of Sabah is Sandakan, the old capital of Borneo, which is now a timber shipping port. There are two reasons for making the 400 km/250 mile trip here from Kota Kinabalu: one is to visit the **Gomantong Caves**, where birds' nests are collected for the eponymous Chinese soup, the other is to spend time at the **Sepilok Orang Utan Rehabilitation Centre**. This remarkable institution was set up to help reintegrate orphaned and captive orang-utans into the wild. These 'wild men of Borneo', as they are known, are also victims of forest and habitat destruction, and their numbers have been decreasing for several years. The Rehabilitation Centre is playing its part, however. Its programme has gained the support of the Malaysian government, which has introduced strict laws about orang-utan conservation. Visitors can spend a day, or longer, here, watching these gentle giants in their natural environment.

Arguably the greatest attraction of Borneo for adventure travellers – and certainly the most challenging – is the southern three-quarters of the island, which belongs to Indonesia (see p 187). Although **Kalimantan** forms one of the five main islands of Indonesia, it is nowhere near as developed as the rest of that country's holiday destinations. This is an area for more intrepid travellers. The landscape ranges from swampland and mangrove forests in South Kalimantan to the highlands and the Muller and Schwaner mountain ranges. At 156 610 sq km/60 450 sq miles, **Central Kalimantan** is the largest of Kalimantan's four provinces. The people here are known collectively as 'Dyak', and fall into around 200 different tribes, predominantly of Chinese and Malay origin. Facilities are few, rivers form the main transport routes, and little English is spoken. Fauna and flora include rare proboscis monkeys which are found on Borneo alone, and the magnificent, and equally rare, black orchid. In **East Kalimantan**, at one time a favourite haunt of Joseph Conrad, there are good opportunities to see bearded wild pigs, freshwater river dolphins, pythons and barking deer. The Makaham river which flows through this province is a suitable starting point for expeditions upstream to Dayak villages, ideally between September and December, just before the start of the rains (which last from November to May). Although the Makaham is usually navigable all year, high water at certain times can lead to travellers having to walk through parts of the jungle, carrying their canoes. Central Kalimantan offers further possibilities for seeing orang-utans in their natural habitat, at the **Camp Leakey Station**. A network of trails leads through the 3500 ha/8650 acre reserve, which can also be toured by boat or, for the more adventurous, swamp wading. Otters, crocodiles, monitor lizards and gibbons are some of the animals which inhabit this area, while the abundant birdlife here includes herons, flycatchers and kingfishers.

The most remote and inaccessible part of Kalimantan – and, indeed, of Borneo – is **West Kalimantan**, a 146 760 sq km/56 650 sq mile swampy area of isolated river villages and uncharted waterways. Visitors are few and far between, and it is usual to travel in Borneo with an organized group. Life here is dominated by the 1100 km/680 mile Kapuas river, Indonesia's longest, which offers the only viable transport route into the interior and which stretches up the border with Sarawak in the centre of Borneo. Trips start from the estuary on Borneo's southwest coast near Pontianak, the island's largest city. Due to its average annual rainfall of 320 cm/126 inches, Pontianak is known as the 'Floating Town' and because it is situated right on the equator, the place is hot and humid all year round. You can travel 900 km/560 miles up the Kapuas as far as Putusibau or, if transport is available, for another 200 km/125 miles beyond. The choice thereafter is to undertake an arduous overland trek, or to turn around and come back again.

Several tour operators include Borneo on their listings of adventure and eco-tours. **Worldwide Journeys and Expeditions** offer three trips – '**Sabah Wildlife Safari**', '**Highlights of Borneo**' and '**Borneo Adventure**', lasting from 14 to 20 days and costing between £1600 and £2100. Billed as 'the ultimate jungle experience', their Borneo Adventure includes longboat trips, longhouse accommodation, swimming in jungle streams, exploring the rainforest, visiting the orang-utan sanctuary, white-water rafting and climbing Mount Kinabalu, all for £2100, including flights. A 25-day east-to-west island crossing is offered by **Encounter Overland**, while **Explore** offers a 16-day '**Borneo Adventure**' and a 6-day '**Headhunters' Trek**', the latter involving an ascent of Mt Kinabalu, all-inclusive price around £1200. Other operators to consider are **Guerba** (3 trips) and **The Imaginative Traveller** (5 trips, including a staggering 58-day adventure, price £2400, excluding flights).

For an illustration of just how much can be crammed into 16 days, **The Imaginative Traveller's 'Best of Borneo'** is a good example. After arriving in Kota Kinabalu, you spend three days making an assault on Mt Kinabalu. A night is spent on the mountain at a resthouse, whence you make an early morning walk to catch the dawn breaking from the summit. The view is spectacular, with the jungles of Borneo in one direction and the South China Sea in the other. After the climb, you return to Kota Kinabalu for some well deserved sleep. On day 5, you take an early morning flight and board a fishing boat to Turtle Island, where giant turtles come ashore in the evening to lay their eggs. On returning, you visit the orang-utan reserve at Sepilok, before flying to Miri. A light aircraft takes you to Gunung Mulu National Park on day 7 to witness magnificent rainforests and sights such as Clearwater Cave – which contains Asia's longest underground river and Deer Cave, home to millions of bats. After overnighting in Sibu, you travel by small motorized canoe to meet the Iban people in longhouses rarely visited by Westerners. The night is spent in Kuching, after which you take a boat to Bako National park for some excellent walking and beaches (days 13 to 15). On day 16 you return to Kuching for the conclusion of the adventure. Maximum group size is 12 and the cost, excluding international air fares but including domestic flights, is approximately £1000.

FACTFILE

Conventions: Hospitality is always lavish and warm, but do respect social conventions and customs, such as the removal of footwear before entering certain buildings.

Climate: Tropical without extremely high temperatures. Main rainy season is November to February in the east, and August in the west, but it can rain at any time, so take rainproof gear. Lightweight cotton or linen clothing is best for lower altitudes.

BOTSWANA – SEA OF LAND, LAND OF WATER

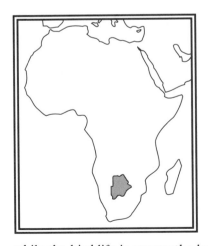

Time moves slowly in Botswana. If you are looking for a wilderness experience with a distinctive pioneering flavour then this is the place to be: some of Botswana's more developed neighbours have lost these qualities in the name of 'progress'. Undoubtedly Botswana's greatest asset is its fauna: impressively, almost a quarter of the country is designated for wildlife conservation. Some of southern Africa's largest game herds congregate in unfenced reserves here, while the bird life is among the best anywhere in southern Africa.

Botswana is a landlocked country of unrivalled contrasts and endless horizons. The vast and virtually waterless Kalahari desert

– made popular by the writings of Laurens van der Post – covers two-thirds of the country's land surface. Yet the **Okavango**, the world's largest inland delta, covers an area as large as Northern Ireland. This contrast of land and water is one of the delights of a Botswana adventure holiday, for no visit is complete until you experience the lure of both desert and delta. Combine Botswana's large wildlife population with its very sparse human population – under two people per square kilometre – and you have the perfect recipe for an unforgettable African wilderness adventure.

Travelling around a country the size of France, one of the problems confronting visitors here is how to devote sufficient time to experience all of its attractions. Foremost among the highlights is the **Okavango Delta**. This is Africa's 'last Eden' – the heart of Botswana's life-support system. Rain which falls on the Angolan highlands 950 km/600 miles away, swells the Okavango river, finally reaching the Delta some six months later, fortuitously just as Botswana's dry winter season is under way. As the Delta level rises, channels form and spread, providing a life-sustaining source of water for the abundant surrounding wildlife. By far the best way to experience Okavango's beauty and tranquillity is to be punted gently along in almost complete silence in a *makoro* or dug-out canoe. The chance of a close encounter of the hippo kind adds a certain spice to this experience.

The **Moremi Reserve**, a thousand square miles of pristine wildlife sanctuary, extends into the Delta and includes Chief's Island – only reachable by air or boat. Moremi is regarded as the first example in which an African people, in this case the Batawana, set aside part of their land expressly to be protected forever. The Reserve displays a wide variety of habitats: swamps, floodplains, reedbeds, mopane woodland and savanna. It is one of the most beautiful corners of Africa, with an extraordinary range and quantity of species too numerous to list here.

Also among the finest game reserves in Africa is **Chobe National Park** which borders Moremi Wildlife Reserve. Stretching along the Chobe River and taking in most of Botswana's northern boundary, Chobe National Park is well known for its enormous elephant population (which numbers many thousands): you can usually see several hundred in one day. Bird life is also abundant on the flood plains and along the banks of the river.

If you have time on your Botswana holiday after seeing all this, try to visit the salt pans of **Makgadikgadi** and **Nxai** – difficult to pronounce and not particularly easy to reach either. For much of the year these pans are expanses of bare salt stretching as far as the eye can see, but after the summer rains, huge herds of wildebeest, zebra and gemsbok congregate here. Definitely for the more adventurous, these pans can be reached only by four-wheel drive vehicles and there is no permanent accommodation – only seasonal tented camps.

The remoteness of Botswana's wilderness makes certain demands on you. Rough terrain safari vehicles are essential for visiting the game reserves and, if sleeping under canvas or even under the stars appeals, plenty of camps offer basic accommodation, right down to those consisting only of an ablution block. This remoteness factor will probably point you towards choosing a packaged safari in Botswana, unless you are a determinedly independent traveller. **Abercrombie & Kent (Sloane Square House, Holbein Place, London SW1W 8NS; tel: 0171 730 9600)** lists a range of high-quality driving and flying safaris, with prices ranging from £2000 upwards.

A good example of a Botswana trip can be found in **Guerba**'s 15-day '**Botswana Adventure**'. The safari starts in Harare, capital of Zimbabwe, where a short flight takes you to Victoria Falls. After a couple of days acclimatization, you head off by four-wheel drive vehicle to Chobe National Park in Botswana, where you are likely to see elephants and many other animals. Crossing the Linyanti River on day 6, you enter the Caprivi strip, a long neck of land belonging to Namibia. You are now on the edge of the Kalahari Desert and its famous Bushmen inhabitants. You will meet small groups of Bushmen close to the Tsolido Hills, and see some of the region's many rock paintings, which depict the hunter–gatherer lifestyle still practised today by these people. South of Tsolido lies the Okavango Delta. Three days are spent here travelling by *makoro* canoe and short foot safaris, before the adventure ends at Maun. The cost of this trip is around £1500 from London, or £800 from Harare. Group size is from 7–22 and accommodation is hotel (one night) and camping.

FACTFILE

When to go: May to July is the best time for the Okavango. The rainy season lasts from December to March.

Travel tips: The Botswana Division of tourism provides a publication called *Where to Stay in Botswana*, which gives details of prices and facilities. For a copy write to **Tourism Development Unit, Ministry of Commerce and Industry, Private Bag 0047, Gaborone**.

Other information: If you plan to spend a good deal of time in southern Africa, consider buying a vehicle and selling it when you leave. Cost for something in good working order is around £2500.

BRAZIL – AMAZING AMAZON

'The first impression which I received when I had recovered my breath was the extraordinary view over the country which we traversed. The whole Brazilian plain seemed to lie beneath us, extending away and away until it ended in dim blue mists upon the farthest sky-line. In the foreground was the long slope, strewn with rocks and dotted with tree ferns; farther off in the middle distance, looking over the saddleback hill, I could just see the yellow and green mass of bamboos through which we had passed; and then, gradually, the vegetation increased until it formed the huge forest which extended as far as the eyes could reach, and for a good two thousand miles beyond.'

Sir Arthur Conan Doyle, The Lost World

Brazil makes up nearly half the total area of South America, with a land mass greater than all the European countries combined, or greater than the USA. It borders every other country in the subcontinent save Chile and Ecuador, while on its eastern edge stretches a 7400 km/4600 mile coastline blessed with some of the world's most beautiful beaches. However, despite its huge size, Brazil is not as topographically varied as you might expect. Most of its territory is less than 200 m/650 ft above sea level, consisting of low plains, elevated plateaux and extensive basins. Its climate ranges from tropical in the north, through subtropical for most of the country, to temperate in the south. Geographically, Brazil can be divided into five regions: southeast, north, northeast, central–west and south.

Most visitors to the country arrive in the southeast, at Rio de Janeiro. Once you have had your fill of the Copacabana sand, sun and sea, however, you may want to head off to explore the wilderness of Brazil's interior. If you are looking for a Robinson Crusoe experience, it is worth heading south to the so-called 'Green Coast' with its deserted beaches and clear waters – perfect for diving and other watersports. You can arrange a tour of the hundreds of small islands by boat. Just over 160 km/100 miles from Rio, close to the São Paulo highway, lies the **Itatiaia National Park**, a 10 500 ha/26 000 acre area of dense forests and mountains. Nearby lie the **Algulhas Negras** and **Prateleiras Mountains**, excellent places for camping and climbing.

Nature dominates in the north of Brazil. This region is almost entirely covered by the **Amazon**, whose rivers and rainforests amount to a huge 40% of Brazil's territory. One-fifth of all the world's fresh water is in the Amazon basin: here also are half of the world's 20 longest rivers, including the mighty Amazon which is over 6400 km/4000 miles from source to mouth. Destruction of the rainforest in some parts of Brazil has focused world attention on the importance of the unique Amazonian ecosystem. Here, 1800 bird species and 250 mammal species live in a seemingly infinite variation of plants and trees. Reckoned by some to account for production of half the world's oxygen supply, the Amazon is often referred to as the 'green lungs' of the planet. Aquatic plant life here is abundant, perhaps the best-known plants being *Victoria regia* – giant water lilies – whose leaves sometimes reach over two metres (6.5 ft). For travellers here, waterways are, not surprisingly, the main transport routes.

Those in search of adventure in central-west Brazil will be drawn to the **Panatal**, which, like the Amazon rainforest, is one of the last major untouched wildlife reserves on the planet. Protected by law, it consists of a huge vegetated lowland plain, almost the size of former West Germany. During the rainy season, January to June, the place is a riot of colours and an explosion of scents from blooming flowers. The Panatal also includes many rivers and crystal-clear lakes. Birds are abundant, and among the rarer species of animal you may be fortunate enough to encounter jaguars, peccaries, bobcats, wild boars and alligators. You can stay at ranch houses, the best time to visit being July to December. The Panatal's 1627 km/1011 mile **Araguaia** river contends for the title of the waterway with the greatest variety of fish in the world.

Northeast Brazil is sometimes called the 'Golden Coast', its 3500 km/2175 mile coastline boasting warm waters, clear sky and sunshine the year round. Watersports and sailing tours are offered from many of the coastal settlements. Some 40 minutes by ferryboat from the town of Salvador lies **Itaparica Island**, with its deserted beaches, palm trees and clear waters.

Brazil's south region is the only part of the country where the seasons are clearly defined. Wooded mountains and grassy plains dominate, but the most famous natural landmark is the **Iguassu Falls**, situated on the border of Brazil, Paraguay and Argentina. These are the largest falls in the world: the sound of the torrential force of water plunging earthwards can be heard from miles away. Like its African sister, the Victoria Falls, spray forms in great clouds, often carrying rainbows up to the sky. For a closer look, you can take a boat trip through the 'Devil's Pass' below. Much further south and east lies the **Aparados si Serra National Park**: its Itaimbezinho Canyon is a good spot for camping.

One of several overlanding companies offering trips which include Brazil is **Encounter Overland**. Their 9-week '**Amazon & Andes**' trip starts at Rio, meanders through the Amazon region and continues through Venezuela, Columbia and Ecuador. Passing through Cuiaba, the provincial capital of the Matto Grosso, the expedition truck heads west to the Panatal. Continuing north through the forest to Porto Velho, you board a riverboat to head up the Rio Madeira, sleeping on deck in hammocks. At Manaus the oily black waters of the Rio Negro fuse in an 8 km/5 mile wide band with the Amazon. Several ferry crossings are needed for the next leg of the journey, to Boa Vista. Climbing the Amazon Basin, the truck eventually leaves Brazil, entering Venezuela. Around half of the 9 weeks is spent in Brazil. Accommodation is camping, with the odd hotel.

FACTFILE

Camping: The **Camping Club of Brazil** has 43 sites in 13 states.

Climate: Varies from arid in the winter to tropical in the northern jungle and eastern beaches. Temperate in the south.

Travel tip: All water should be regarded as potentially contaminated – drink bottled water.

BRITISH VIRGIN ISLANDS – NATURE'S LITTLE SECRETS

'The appearance of the island when I came on deck next morning was altogether changed . . . Grey-coloured woods covered a large part of the surface. This even tint was indeed broken up by streaks of yellow sandbreak in the lower lands, and by many tall trees of the pine family, out-topping the others . . . The hills ran up clear above the vegetation in spires of naked rock.'

Robert Louis Stevenson, Treasure Island

Just 80 km/50 miles east of Puerto Rico, but light years away in lifestyle to most Western travellers, lie the sixty-odd islands, islets and cays known as the British Virgin Islands, or BVI. Apart from one, all these islands are volcanic in origin, so unlike many of the other Caribbean archipelagos with a flatter terrain, the BVI have a more rugged, private feel to them. Their jagged peaks and vestiges of tropical forests frame miles of beautiful sandy beaches and secluded anchorages: ideal island adventure territory. The first visitors to the BVI were Arawak and Carib Indians, followed in turn by early British, Dutch, French and Spanish explorers and freebooters. In 1585 – en route to conquering Hispaniola – Sir Francis Drake sailed his fleet through the Atlantic–to–Caribbean waterway now named after him (historians say he did it on a personal whim, rather than for any reasons of strategy). During the 17th century these islands became a notorious hideout for pirates, but now they are strictly a hideaway for vacationers. Ballooning adventurer and business entrepreneur Richard Branson found his own slice of paradise when he acquired Necker, one of these islands, and it is easy to see why he did. The superb climate and clear waters nurturing the British Virgin Islands provide some of the best sailing conditions available, while the spectacular undersea world offers excellent diving opportunities. You won't find casinos, late-night discos and fancy floor shows here – and you won't miss them either.

A good introduction to the flora of the islands can be gained from a visit to the four-acre J.R. O'Neal Botanic Garden, on **Tortola** – the main island. To see something of the once-ubiquitous forest which adorned these islands, you can visit **Sage Mountain National Park**. Although not strictly a rainforest in the true sense (Tortola receives less than 100 inches/254 cm of rain per year) the ecosystem here displays many rainforest characteristics, such as hanging vines, large elephant ears and other philodendrons, as well as tall mahogany, cedars and manilkara trees. At 523 m/ 1716 ft **Mount Sage** is the country's highest point. If you want a good overview (literally) of the island you can visit the Park and hike one of its nature trails such as the Rainforest Trail or the Mahogany Forest Trail. Landlubber adventurers will also be drawn to the trails of **Virgin Gorda** island, with its 107 ha/265 acre **National Park** stretching from the 305 m/1000 ft contour up to the island's highest point (418 m/1370 ft). Virgin Gorda has one other National Park – Little Fort, a small wildlife sanctuary – as well as an extraordinary labyrinth of passageways and grottoes formed by giant shore boulders at a place called **The Baths** (good for snorkelling, or exploring the labyrinthine passageways on foot).

Anegada (population 150) is the only coral island in the BVI. In contrast to the other islands here, it is so low down (highest point 8.53 m/28 ft) that if you arrive by boat, you can hardly see the place. For diving enthusiasts this area is reckoned to have more wrecks (over 200 at the last count) and extensive reefs, than any other island in the Caribbean. Other islands to explore include **Green Cay** (encircled by almost unbroken beach – a perfect 'desert island'); **Ginger Island** (uninhabited – for adventurous explorers only); **Cooper Island** (good for snorkelling); **Guana Island** (a wildlife refuge with ten times the variety of species found elsewhere on similar-sized islands); and **Norman Island** (believed to be the setting for Robert Louis Stevenson's *Treasure Island*). Off Norman Island lie The Indians, a collection of tall and imposing rock formations. Beneath these, a series of marine canyons, grottoes and coral formations make this place a popular spot for divers.

A large number of UK tour operators offer BVI packages, including **Simply Caribbean (3 Victoria Avenue, Harrogate, HG1 1EQ; tel: 01423 526887)**, **Caribtours (161 Fulham Road, London SW3 6SN; tel; 0171 581 3517)**, and **British Virgin Island Holidays (11–13 Hockerill Street, Bishops Stortford, Herts CM23 2DH; tel: 01279 656111)**. Once there, you can book diving tours through one of several local operators, including **Dive BVI** at Leverick Bay **(tel: 809 495 7328)** or Peter Island **(tel: 809 494 2561)**, **Kilbride's Underwater Tours** at Virgin Gorda **(tel: 809 495 5513)**, or **Underwater Safaris** at Cooper Island **(tel: 809 494 3235)**. Horse riding is available on Tortola (**tel: 809 494 2262, or 809 494 4442**), while windsurfing instruction from certified tutors is available from **Boardsailing BVI (809 495 2447, or 809 495 7376)**.

FACTFILE

Accommodation: Costs from about $50 per person upwards. There is a variety of places to stay, many charmingly rustic.

Permits: A cruising permit is required for all cruising in the BVI.

Transport: Bicycles must be registered at the Traffic Licensing Office in Road Town.

CAMEROON – SEAT OF THE GODS

'A reserve isn't a zoo: animals are at home and there's nothing between you and them. If you take our advice, we shall help you, for it would be a pity that they attack you. Please follow your guide and leave your tracker to him. When drawing near and coming into contact with animals, everybody must keep silent completely. We assure you of exciting moments.'

Tourist Guidebook

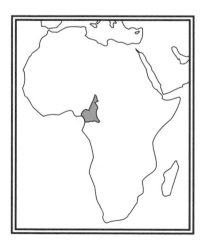

Cameroon lies at the hinge point between East and West Africa, a melange of cultures (208 ethnic groups at the last count) and ecosystems, ranging from dry northern savanna grasslands to wet coastal rainforests. Because of its unique geographical location, Cameroon has some of the richest and most varied fauna in the African continent. Its six National Parks encompass a very wide range of habitats and wildlife. Add to its safari potential and rainforest importance the lure of Mount Cameroon and the lunar landscape of Kapsiki, and you have what André Gide described as 'one of the most beautiful landscapes in the world'.

Cameroon is a country more for travellers than for tourists. You have to be prepared for anything to happen . . . and for nothing to happen, since the game of 'waiting for officialdom' is almost a national pastime here. The country's climatic idiosyncracies can be more than a little trying too, like the 365-day precipitation of some coastal areas, where annual rainfall is measured in metres. Being patient – and a little street-wise in the weird and wonderful ways of Africa – helps travellers to appreciate a country not well geared to the demands of bewildered Western holidaymakers. But rewards for the intrepid and the adventurous can be both memorable and enriching.

Principal attraction for climbers is **Mount Cameroon**, a 4070 m/ 13 360 ft high volcano, the highest peak in West Africa. Two people are credited with having 'discovered' Mount Cameroon: a Carthaginian called Hannon in the fifth century and the Portuguese navigator Fernando Po'o in 1472. The former was moved to describe it as 'God's Chariot', the latter as 'The Seat of the Gods'. Every January this deified landmark sees an international pilgrimage of a secular kind – a trial of strength unparalleled elsewhere in Africa. Hundreds of runners gather in the nearby village of Buea to compete in the Guinness Cameroon mountain race, trying to break the current record of only a few hours up and down the mountain. Buea is also a stopover for many of the Trans-African overland trips which travel south towards Nairobi. Although the climb of Mount Cameroon can be done within a long and tiring day, it is much more enjoyable to take two, staying overnight in one of the mountain's three huts. You will need a guide (there is no shortage in Buea) as well as reasonable hiking boots and a good sense of balance (the mountain's steep volcanic clinker has an unnerving knack of tripping you up and biting back when you fall). Packing warm clothes may seem ridiculous when you are sweating through the lower forested slopes, but you will be glad you did at the mountain's freezing summit.

Cameroon's rainforests are legendary. Places like the **Mount Cameroon and Korup Reserves** have achieved international recognition lately, as world attention has focused increasingly on alarming rates of tropical deforestation and the need to conserve this particular habitat. Walking through these ecosystems is like stepping through the looking glass into an Alice-like wonderland which becomes curiouser and curiouser the more you venture within. More than half of all African bird species and a quarter of the continent's primates have their home here. Altogether some 3000 types of animal are known to inhabit this high-rise sauna, but the actual figure is probably nearer 10 000, as more and more species are discovered. This part of Africa's forest belt is probably sixty million years old, and during that time some fantastical ecological relationships have developed. Like the barteria tree and one of Cameroon's many species of ants. The barteria tree has evolved hollow branches, which act as a vast internal network of ant passages and tunnels. In return, these same ants defend the tree against all threats and intruders by emerging en masse and in countless numbers. To strike through a barteria branch with a panga (or cutlass as they're called in Cameroon) is to experience instant insect gang mugging.

Contrasting with these steamy coastal rainforests, northern Cameroon is a savanna landscape, with open vistas, moonscape scenery and a more benign climate. Near **Kapsiki**, a clutch of improbably sheer-sided mountains emerge in a parody of Paramount Picture branding, offering spectacular rock climbing opportunities for the more experienced. Most northern of Cameroon's six National Parks is **Waza**, designated in 1968. During the dry season (November to May), a wide variety of antelope and their predators are to be found here, as well as elephants, giraffes, hippos and hyenas. In the wet season, prepare to be disappointed, since the wildlife is no longer dependent on waterholes and can (and does) disperse widely. Further south lies **Benoue** National Park. About the same size as Waza (175 000 ha/432 400 acres) it is not so seasonally dependent for game viewing, and camping is also available. Other National Parks are **Boubandjidah** (haunt of rhinos and Derby eland – Africa's finest and largest antelope); **Kalamaloue** (good for elephants); **Faro** (Cameroon's largest National Park) and **Mozogo Gokoro** (smallest park, principally of botanical interest).

Cameroon is not frequented by US and UK adventure tour operators, principally because the demand is relatively low. However, the picture could change as those more familiar with North, East and southern Africa start to look for an adventurous West African destination. Overland companies such as **Encounter Overland**, **Dragoman** and **Guerba** which use the West African route usually spend a few days in Cameroon.

For example, Guerba's '**West Africa Special**', which consists of a 12-week overland trip from Dakar in Senegal to Douala in Cameroon, spends several days in the country. Crossing into Cameroon from Nigeria, you experience a dramatic change in scenery from flat undulating topography to the dramatic volcanic plugs of the Kapsiki region. Your visit to Waza National Park may reveal elephant, giraffe, antelopes and good birdlife. After travelling through Cameroon's colourful interior you spend two days on the coast at Kribi, relaxing prior to finishing at Douala. The cost of this 12-week overland adventure works out at approximately

£2000 when joining at Dakar. Trips run March to June and November to January, according to demand.

FACTFILE

When to go: Best months are November to May. Rainy season is June to October, depending on your whereabouts in the country.

How to go: Cheapest carrier is Aeroflot via Moscow, but it's a long trip. Cameroon Airlines flies once a week, and Swiss Air is an alternative. Flights are obtainable either to Douala or Yaounde.

Travelling: Bush taxis are cheap but can be life-threatening. Car rental is very expensive.

Rainforests: The World Wide Fund for Nature has a centre at the Korup Project and local guides can be arranged inexpensively. Enquiries to **WWF, Panda House, Weyside Park, Catteshall Lane, Godalming, Surrey GU7 1XR, UK.**

CANADA: BRITISH COLUMBIA – SUPER NATURAL ADVENTURES

In the whole of Canada's great outdoors, there is nothing that can compare to British Columbia: not only is it the country's most scenic province, it is undoubtedly one of the northern hemisphere's classic adventure holiday locations. Most of BC's terrain is mountainous – the Rocky Mountains or 'Great Divide' running the length of the province – and two-thirds of the land is clothed with beautiful, mainly evergreen, forests. It has a wonderful coastline, a plethora of lakes, many exciting rivers, and a climate which enables both winter and summer activities. Adventurers come from all over the world to experience the leading edge of outdoor active life, be it hiking, climbing, skiing, scuba diving, river rafting or riding. There are more National Parks, Provincial Parks and other protected areas than you can flap a map at. In summary, with plenty to offer independent travellers and packaged vacationers, solo travellers and family groups, this is the ideal destination to get a real feel for what adventure holidays are all about.

As a way of getting close to British Columbia's scenery, you simply can't beat kayaking or canoeing, whether on sea, lake or river. Among the best places for lake canoeing is **Bowron Lake Provincial Park**, in the Cariboo Chilcotin region of the province. A 10-day, 117 km/73 mile wilderness circuit takes you through a chain of lakes, connecting rivers and easy portages (where you carry the canoe). In **Wells Gray Provincial Park**, the Clearwater-Azure water tour is delightful: 120 km/75 miles of wilderness and wildlife, including moose, deer, caribou, wolves and bears (contact **Wells Gray Ranch, RR1, Box 1764, Clearwater, BC, Canada V0E 1N0; tel: 604 674 2792**). On the border of **Valhalla Provincial Park** lies **Slocan Lake**, a good place to make shorter trips and where you can camp or picnic on the lake's sandy shores. Other inland waters good for canoeing and kayaking include **Lake Okanagan** in interior BC, and the **Blackwater River** in Cariboo country. Off-the-beaten-track adventures in northwest BC include the **Nanika** and **Swan Lake** chains plus the **Bulkley**, **Morice** and **Kispiox** rivers, or the remote **Spatsizi**, **Stikine** and **Dease** rivers.

The coast of Vancouver Island offers magnificent opportunities for **ocean kayaking**. Off the east coast lie the **Gulf Islands**, with their sheltered beaches, winding roads and superb vistas. You can take a trip to suit yourself, from just an afternoon, to as many days as you wish. If you venture further north into **Discovery Passage** and **Johnstone Strait**, you may see orcas, or other species of whales. The wilder west coast offers such attractions as **Hot Springs Cove** (which lives up to its name), **Cape Scott Provincial Park** and the **Broken Group Islands**. North of Vancouver Island, the **Queen Charlotte Islands** offer wild and remote coastal kayaking, with visible evidence of former Haida Indian Settlements, and plentiful wildlife.

The mountainous terrain of British Columbia forms ideal conditions for white-water river kayaking and canoeing, ranging from testing Class III challenges for canoeists, to wicked Class V challenges for kayakers. These same rivers are also a paradise for white-water rafting addicts, whether on a shorter (two hours) or a longer (two weeks) trip. Popular spots within reach of Vancouver are the **Chilliwack**, **Thompson** and **Fraser** rivers and the **Kootenay** and **Kicking Horse** rivers. Also accessible from Vancouver, the **Chilko** river has one of the steepest drops in North America, while its cousin – the **Chilcotin** – is tamer, but with more evident wildlife.

Longer expeditions take place in BC's northern rivers. A ten-day trip down the **Skeena** river is a wonderful experience which combines spells of tranquil water with bursts of exciting white water. The fact that the **Stikine** river is only accessible by trail makes for an almost pioneering adventure experience. But what is often described as 'the most scenic mountain wilderness trip in the world' is the classic **Tatshenshini–Alsek** rivers adventure, which takes you from northern BC into Alaska's Glacier Bay National Park. For rafting wilderness adventures, one of the main BC operators is **Hyak (Suite 204, 1975 Maple Street, Vancouver, BC, Canada V6J 3S9; tel: 604 734 8622)**.

Riding adventures are a legacy of former times here, when flesh-and-blood horsepower was the only way of going long distances overland. Today you can still get a taste of the old days by staying at a guest ranch or alternatively going on a camping trail ride. Guest ranches are a good way for the whole family to take an adventure vacation, since conditions can be as soft or as hard as you want them to be. Horses or ponies are available from as short a time as an hour to as long as a few days. The local wrangler will provide instruction, matching a mount to your ability, before taking you out into the BC backwoods. At the other end of the spectrum are more demanding trail rides or packtrips. Here, you overnight under canvas, in teepees or sometimes in cabins, your group tackling a trail of maybe a hundred miles or more. Pack-horses sometimes accompany these trips if they're self-contained affairs. One of the best parts of the province for saddling up on a horsepowered adventure is the **Cariboo Chilcotin**, near the Rainbow Range in Tweedsmuir Provincial Park. In the eastern part of the Cariboo, numerous cattle ranches entertain guests of all ages. The **Cariboo Mountains**, bordering Wells Gray and Bowron Lake Provincial Parks, comprise good guest ranch/riding territory. **Crystal Waters Guest Ranch** near Little Fort is everything you could want it to be (**Box 100, Dept RR, Bridge Lake, BC, Canada V0K 1EO; tel: 604 593 4252**). Other excellent areas for riding adventures are the **Spatsizi Plateau Wilderness** and **Mount Edziza Provincial Park**, both situated in the north of BC. In the Rockies, good horsey spots are the **Top of the World Provincial Park** (elevations here exceed 1800 m/5900 ft) and **Mount Robson Provincial Park**, where a trail crosses the Continental Divide through the heart of the mountains. Other ranges in which to try horse trips are the **Okanagen/Similkameen** region and the **Cascade Mountains**, including **Manning** and **Cathedral Provincial Parks**.

Most Canadians are attuned to life in the wilds, even if it is just a short walk in the forest. But while many locals are outdoor freaks, their wilderness is plentiful enough for all to enjoy, without any crowding whatsoever. The number and range of trekking and mountaineering experiences in British Columbia are simply too great to list here: it is possible only to pick out a few spots. The **Rockies** have a plethora of parks with trails a-plenty, such as **Mount Robson**, **Hamber** and **Assiniboine Provincial Parks**. Parallel to the Rocky Mountains lie the **Selkirks**, **Purcells** and **Monashees**. Less well known than their neighbouring ranges, these areas offer some spectacular hiking opportunities. One testing trek is the **Alexander Mackenzie Heritage Trail**, named after the explorer who crossed Canada in 1793. The trail itself stretches for 250 km/ 155 miles across the Chilcotin Plateau from the Fraser River to Tweedsmuir Provincial Park. Another testing hiking route is the **West Coast Trail**, established originally as a life-saving route for shipwrecked sailors. Stretching up the west coast of Vancouver Island for 77 km/48 miles, it is a classic walking adventure. Located just north of Vancouver, the **Coast Range Mountain Trail** stretches 320 km/200 miles, but it is best to take a guide here. Other favourite hiking spots are **Strathcona Provincial Park** on Vancouver Island, **Stone Mountain Provincial Park** in the north of the Province, **South Moresby National Park** on the Queen Charlotte Islands, **Spatzisi Plateau Wilderness Provincial Park** and the **Stein River Valley**. BC's largest Park – **Tweedsmuir Provincial Park** – is excellent for backpacking.

As you might expect, mountain biking is popular in BC and the province is ideal for independent trips on two wheels. Group tours (about a dozen people per group is commonplace) are also available, most trips covering approximately 64 km/40 miles each day. These trips are accompanied by a guide who helps interpret the places through which you pass and the wildlife you encounter. Excellent cycling routes are to be found on **Vancouver Island**, the **Rockies**, the **Gulf Islands** and the **Kootenays**.

Apart from the usual outdoor activities, BC has some unexpected and original adventures, such as **Campbell River Snorkel Tours**. Here you can spend a morning or longer swimming among the thousands of migrating salmon and other fish in Campbell River, on Vancouver Island. All the necessary kit (wetsuit, snorkel, flippers) and transport is provided for you. Contact **760B Island Highway, PO Box 62, Campbell River, BC 9W 4Z9; tel: 604 286 0030**. Other more conventional underwater trips are available in the form of scuba diving off the east and west coasts of Vancouver Island. The west coast in particular has dozens of wrecks (well deserving of its name 'Graveyard of the Pacific'). For art-loving diving adventurers, how about a trip to **Saltery Bay** on BC's Sunshine Coast? Here you will discover a bronze statue of a mermaid submerged in 18 m/60 ft of water – one of only three underwater statue sites in the world!

Caving opportunities are plentiful in the province. All 2000 or so caves are 'wild'; that is, they have no walkways – helmets and head torches are thus required. Cave systems to consider include **Upana, Little Hunstan Lake, Horne Lake, Paradise Lost, Artlish River** and the intriguingly named **Black Hole.**

Further details of adventures and adventure companies are available from the Tourist Board (see Appendix 1). There are a large number of local tour operators, such as **KA-NA-TA Wilderness Adventures (RR1, Box 1766, Clearwater, BC, V0E 1N0, Canada; tel: 604 674 2774).** In the UK, **Accessible Isolation Holidays (44 Downing Street, Farnham, Surrey GU9 7PH; tel: 01252 718808)** features a plethora of shorter adventure trips in their 'Journeys of Discovery' portfolio.

Without doubt, the major source of information about all types of adventure holidays – and the umbrella organization for local companies – is **Super Natural Adventures.** Lack of space makes it impossible to give more of a flavour of the great range of adventure holidays this company features, but as an example of a backpacking trip, their '**West Coast Trail**' is hard to beat. This 10-day trip (or its harder 8-day adventure variation – the '**Wilder West Coast Trail**') takes you along the 77 km/48-mile trail which stretches along the southwestern coast of Vancouver Island. Seven of the ten days are spent actually hiking the trail, reckoned by many to be one of the top ten hiking trails in the world. Certainly, it is the trip of a lifetime, during which you experience sandy beaches, blowholes, caverns and caves, petroglyphs, whales, sealions, eagles and the oldest and largest Douglas Fir known in Canada. Professional guides lead you in small groups (maximum size eight) and accommodation consists of camping. You will need to be in good physical condition, since parts of the trail are demanding, but (especially on the 10-day trip) the pace is fairly easy. The price from Vancouver, which includes transfer flights to Victoria, food and equipment (you will need to take sleeping bag and hiking boots) is about $850.

FACTFILE

Tourist alert: In the summer, the Royal Canadian Mounted Police and news media cooperate in a 'Tourist Alert' programme which is designed to communicate urgent messages to visitors.

Travel Infocentres: Located at over 140 communities throughout the province, these centres provide helpful information about activities and accommodation. Look for the Travel Infocentre signs.

CANADA: NORTHWEST TERRITORIES – NORTHERN MAGNETIC WILDERNESS

'There was a strong smell of pine, and subtle wood fragrances filled the air, reminding him of his old life of freedom before the days of his bondage. . . . There was something calling to him out there in the open.'

Jack London, White Fang

The Northwest Territories are quintessential wilderness: one of the Earth's great undiscovered adventure regions. Occupying a staggering third of Canada's land surface and having one of the world's longest ocean coastlines, this area also boasts a waterfall twice the size of Niagara (Wilberforce Falls) and a river 500 km/300 miles longer than the Rhine (the Mackenzie). But despite an area the size of India and a population (65 000) small enough to fit comfortably into a large stadium, the Northwest Territories are not isolated from the rest of the world. Currently, some thirty scheduled and chartered air carriers operate services there from a number of Canadian cities.

Visitors to this superb outdoor playground can choose from an exhaustive list of adventure activities: canoeing, kayaking, river rafting, hiking, biking and dog sledging, to name but a few. Geographically and scenically, the area boasts an impressive roll-call of rugged coastlines, huge icebergs, rolling tundra, boreal forest and magnificent mountain ranges. Settlers here are a mix of Inuit, Dene and Metis ethnic groups whose ancestors roamed this land for centuries before the arrival of European explorers and traders. The Northwest Territories have the unique distinction of containing both the geographic north pole and the magnetic north pole. But it's the heady combination of scenery, landscape, people and wildlife which together make this place a special one for adventurers the world over: in short, a 'northern magnetic wilderness'.

Adventure travel in Northwest Territories (NWT) dates back to the days of early explorers, trappers, gold prospectors and

Mounted Police. Today, although 'hard' expeditionary travel is beyond the means of most people, there is still an exciting array of 'softer' (but still rigorous) holiday packages available. Official protection of the land is afforded by no fewer than five National Parks (there are several more proposed). These are **Aulavik National Park** (tundra habitat on the Thomsen river in the western Arctic); **Nahanni National Park Reserve** (a corridor of wilderness along the south Nahanni River); **Auyuittuq and Ellesmere Island National Park Reserves** (Arctic ecosystems); and **Wood Buffalo National Park** (on the Alberta Border, the only NWT Park accessible by road and home to the world's largest herd of wild bison). The Northwest Territories also have a large number of Territorial Parks including **Twin Falls Gorge** located along the Mackenzie highway near Enterprise (which offers a series of hiking trails); **Katannilik** on Baffin Island (good for dog sledging, cross-country skiing, hiking and canoeing); and **Blackstone** (a staging post for trips into the Nahanni National Park).

For river adventures, the waters of the Northwest Territories are among the finest anywhere in the North American continent. Its rivers vary from tumultuous torrents racing through mountain gorges to milder meanders drifting through taiga ('land of little sticks'), lush moose pastures and tundra flats. Forming part of the mighty Mackenzie watershed, **Slave** river used to be the main freight route into this great northern land. Along its 2000 km/1200 mile length, portaging was only ever necessary in one place, the 'Rapids of the Drowned' in the lower Slave. Today, freight cargoes have given way to human cargoes, for the Slave is a fine rafting and canoeing river, and has abundant associated wildlife. Even more popular is the **South Nahanni** river – one of Canada's premier canoeing and rafting rivers. The lower reaches of this watercourse flow through Nahanni National Park, with its superb canyon scenery: many companies offer trips here. Mountain River, which is renowned for its white water, drops an average of 4 m per km/20 ft per mile. This demanding challenge is not for novices however, and paddlers should be well equipped and well prepared. Another challenging river is the **Hood**, with a 4 km/2.5 mile portage around the world's highest waterfall north of the Arctic circle (Wilberforce Falls). For river adventures, there are a number of local operators offering packages such as guiding services, air pick-up at the trip's end, use of rafts or canoes, accommodation and meals. These include **Adventure Canada (Missigssauga, ON; tel: 800 363 7566); Canada's Canoe Adventures (Hyde Park, ON; tel: 519 641 1261); Canoe Arctic Inc (Fort Smith, NWT; tel: 403 872 2308); Nahanni Wilderness Adventures Ltd (Didsbury, AB; tel: 403 637 3843); Subarctic Wilderness Adventures Ltd (Fort Smith, NWT; tel: 403 872 2467) and Whitewolf**

Adventure Expeditions Ltd (Port Coquitlam, BC; tel: 604 944 5500). Sea kayaking is growing in popularity and more and more operators are offering trips in NWT, especially in the **Nunavut** region. Kayaking amidst the ice floes or up the Baffin fiords is an unforgettable experience. Local companies offering trips here include **Eclipse Sound Outfitting Ltd (Pond Inlet, NWT; tel: 819 899 8870); Niglasuk Co, Ltd (Arctic Bay, NWT; tel: 819 439 9949);** and **Qullikkut Guides (Clyde River, NWT; tel: 819 924 6268).** For land adventures, hiking and camping opportunities are limitless. These are usually offered by adventure tour companies in areas with a high proportion of Alpine or Arctic tundra (few long trails exist in the boreal forest). One of the popular longer hikes is the **Canol Heritage Trail.** This follows the route of the old Canol Road and pipeline which was built during the second world war to carry oil over the Mackenzie Mountains to Whitehorse. Not to be treated lightly, this trail includes some demanding river crossings. Elsewhere, the **Mackenzie Mountains** offer world-class backpacking and climbing opportunities. In the Baffin region of the Territories, an extensive system of hiking trails is being developed in the wide-open tundra of **Katannilik Park.** Associated shelter huts make longer hikes possible here. In **Auyuittuq National Park** on Baffin Island there are some superb hiking trails, also with associated shelter huts. Companies which can help with drop-off/collection services, equipment hire and guide services include **Country Walkers Inc (Waterbury, VT, USA; tel: 802 244 1387); High Arctic International Explorer Services Ltd (Resolute Bay, NWT; tel: 819 252 3875);** and **Northwinds Arctic Adventures (Iqaluit, NWT; tel: 819 979 0551).**

Snow-based trips are also plentiful in Northwest Territories. Locals talk about 'snow season' trips rather than 'winter' trips, since snows can occur here as late as May! But these same snows are a ticket to adventure freedom, enabling unhindered travel over frozen rivers and lakes. Whether this is by dog team or cross-country skis, the opportunities are limitless. There are 'groomed' cross-country ski trails as well as ski touring expeditions, and you can even learn to 'mush' a team of huskys. Most local companies will kit you out with the necessary clothing and equipment as well. Companies offering snow-based trips include **Adventure Northwest Ltd (Yellowknife, NWT; tel: 403 920 2196); Purlaavik Outfitting (Iquauit, NWT; tel: 819 979 6074); Northwinds Arctic Adventures (Iqaluit, NWT; tel: 819 979 0551);** and **Arctic Nature Tours Ltd, (Box 1530, Inuvik, NWT; tel: 403 979 3300).**

There is another, rather unlikely adventure sport available in NWT – scuba diving! Enthusiasts can experience diving 'north of sixty' on **Great Slave Lake, Prelude Lake** and a number of other spots, both fresh and salt water. For more details about equipment hire, instruction and certification contact **Diventure Sports (Yellowknife, NWT; tel: 403 669 9222)** or **Niglasuk Co Ltd (Arctic Bay, NWT; tel: 819 439 9949)**.

UK operators offering adventures in NWT include **Arctic Experience** and **Arcturus Expeditions (PO Box 850, Gartocharn, Alexandria, Dunbartonshire G83 8RL; tel: 01389 830204)**.

FACTFILE

Camping: The private and government campgrounds urge 'no trace camping', partly to discourage bears.

Permafrost: Most of the hotels in Arctic communities are on water delivery services because of the permafrost. Conservation of water is therefore encouraged.

Driving: Carry good spare tyre, jack, insect repellant, flares, good first-aid kit, shovel, blankets, food, matches, candles, sleeping bag and extra clothing.

CANADA: THE YUKON
LAST GREAT WILDERNESS

Conjuring up romantic images of snowy wilderness, hardy Klondike gold prospectors and pioneering settlers, the Yukon of today is unquestionably a first-class adventure destination. The poet Robert Service wrote of it, 'There is a land – oh it beckons and beckons, and I want to go back and I will': and it's true, Yukon's unique mystery exerts a powerful, indescribable attraction to those who would travel there.

Situated between Alaska (see p 260) and the Northwest Territories (see p 140), the Yukon encompasses a great variety of landscapes: Alpine meadows, mountains, Arctic tundra, enormous glacial ice fields, fertile river valleys, forests and lakes – a half million square kilometre Shangri-la for adventure travellers. Hardly any people live there, and of its meagre 30 000 population as many as two-thirds live in the capital, Whitehorse. As a consequence, the backwoods inhabitants beyond the main settlements are rugged survivors, imbued with that pioneering spirit which was such an essential quality for the early settlers here. The other consequence of Yukon's boundless wilderness is an abundance of wildlife: beavers, foxes, bison, wolves, bears, moose, dall and store sheep, mountain goats, and, of course, the world-famous megaherds of caribou. Over 200 species of birds are also found in the Yukon, including trumpeter swans, peregrine falcons and bald and golden eagles. In a world in which wilderness areas are eroding and disappearing rapidly, it is encouraging that the Yukon remains a pristine fastness, particularly those designated areas such as **Kluane** and **Ivvavik National Parks**. Given all these adventure attributes, it is gratifying that the place boasts a wide variety of affordable guiding services, wilderness camps and active excursions. River rafting, canoeing, hiking, riding, skiing, dog mushing, mountain climbing and wildlife viewing – the Yukon has it all.

To re-live a little of the 1898 Klondike gold rush experience, you could enter the Yukon via the **Chilkoot Trail**. Starting in Dyea, Alaska, this three-day, 53 km/33 mile hike to Lake Bennet has the remains of the Klondike stampede littered here and there along the route – picks, shovels, wagon-wheels, boots and pot-bellied stoves. What takes only a few days today used to take those early 'gold-fever hopefuls' as long as three months, as they lugged their ton of supplies over the Chilkoot Pass, before building rafts and boats to ferry themselves down the Yukon river to Dawson City.

Kluane National Park has some of the best hiking opportunities in the world. You can choose between the marked trails, of which there are a goodly number, or go 'freestyle'. Ideal places for the latter option are the meadows and glacial viewpoints of the **Donjek Valley**, with superb views of the **Donjek Glacier**, an 11 km/7 mile wide sweep of crevasses, moraines, rock and ice. Alternatively, you could enlist the services of an 'outfitter' (or guide) and enjoy an excursion on horseback for a day, a week or longer. Sure-footed horses will carry you up through forests high into Alpine meadows and over mountain passes; in the evening you cook over a traditional camp fire and at night you sleep under canvas.

The **Dempster Highway** – the only road in Canada which crosses the Arctic circle – is every cycle tourers' dream. It winds its way north and east for 740 km/460 miles from Dawson City over the Arctic tundra to Inuvik in the North West Territories, the most northerly driveable point on the continent. The environment en route is wild: here is a land where the sun shines for a whole season, not just for a day: you may even have to wait half an hour for a herd of caribou to cross the road! Because of its lack of glaciation and its weathering by wind and water, all the topography here in the east is suited for cycling. The mountains are gently rounded, the stunted treeline-trees may be hundreds of years old and the flowers may take decades to bloom. This is the land of the Invit peoples who still maintain the traditions of their ancestors, enabling them to survive an often harsh life in the world of the far north. The monolithic granite formations of the **Tombstone Range** and the beautiful backdrop of the **Ogilvie Mountains** make magnificent locations for hiking and backpacking. For part of its route, the Dempster Highway follows the ill-fated Lost Patrol dog sledge expedition, during which a group of brave pioneering Royal Mounted Police lost their lives to blizzards and starvation. The dog sledging tradition is upheld strongly in Yukon and winter races and competitions are held throughout February and March. The most famous of these races is the **Yukon Quest**, Canada's answer to the Alaskan Iditerarod. The Yukon Quest is a demanding event which takes its competitors a thousand miles, from Fairbanks in Alaska to Whitehorse in Yukon. Dog sledging is a popular winter activity in Yukon, but more popular still is ski touring, travelling from one hut to the next. Many outfitters in the **Kluane National Park** offer such trips, which last up to eight days.

The Yukon offers world-class climbing and expeditioning opportunities. In western Yukon, the **St Elias Mountains** rival the Himalayas in size and stature, offering a remote and exciting destination for serious expeditions. Besides incredible peaks, the St Elias Mountains contain the largest non-polar icefield in the world and as a consequence snow and ice climbing routes abound. There are 15 summits over 4000 m/3000 ft, including Canada's highest peak, **Mount Logan** (5959 m/19 551 ft). For rock climbers, the 'Cirque of the Unclimbable' area near Watson Lake comprises a famous suite of challenging routes.

No trip to the Yukon would be complete without taking to the water, like the early explorers and adventurers. Yukon rivers are unique in as much as you can canoe in all the mountain stretches. A ten-day trip from Whitehorse to Dawson City through the Five Finger rapids, follows the route of the early gold prospectors after they had negotiated the Chilkoot Pass. The most popular rivers include the **Bonnet Plume, Snake, Wind, Pelly, Macmillan Peel, Alsek, Firth** and **Tatshenshini**. Varying from one day to two weeks or more, these watery trips by raft, canoe or kayak can be memorable experiences. Encountering a grizzly clawing salmon from a clear stream or listening to wolves howling at the northern lights are memories which will linger long after the trip is over.

Locally, there are many tour operators offering adventure trips, for example **Arctic Nature Tours Ltd (Box 1530, Inuvik, NT, Canada XOE OTO; tel: 403 979 3300); Arctic Edge Ltd (Box 4850, Whitehorse, Yukon, Canada Y1A 4N6; tel: 403 633 5470)** and **Yukon Mountain and River Expeditions Ltd (Box 5405, Whitehorse, Yukon, Canada YTY1A 4Z2; tel: 403 668 2513)**. In the UK, **Arctic Experience** offers a 10-day 'Husky Sledge Trail', where you drive your own dog team through backcountry Yukon, staying in cabins and lodges. All-inclusive price is £1900 and departures are from November to March. **TrekAmerica** run a 26-day Klondike trip through western Canada, including a list of optional activities, for around £1100 including ferry trips but excluding flights.

One of the best companies to offer trips within Yukon is **Super Natural Adventures**. For the adventure of a lifetime you could take their 12-day **Tatshenshini River** trip. This begins in Whitehorse where you stay overnight in an hotel. The next day the group (maximum size 18) transfers by van to Dalton Post, an old fur-trading outpost and store on the way to the Klondike goldfields. The St Elias Mountain range becomes an ever-present backdrop and all traces of civilization are left behind as you take to the river. After some exciting white water, the river breaks out into a broad forested valley. Here you actually leave Yukon and enter British Columbia. The wildlife in this area is particularly rich, with a strong likelihood of seeing bear, moose, mountain goats and mountain sheep. As you continue downstream, the scenery changes dramatically with mountains and glaciers towering above the valley. Midway through the trip, the Tatshenshini joins the Alsek River and from here the rafts float into Alaska's Glacier Bay National Park. The adventure ends in the tiny fishing community of Dry Bay, where the rafts are unloaded and you return to Whitehorse via a charter flight. Necessarily, camping is the main form of accommodation. The total cost for this trip is just under CAN$3000, which includes accommodation and meals, but not international flights.

FACTFILE

Winter activities: Snow can continue up to May in the St Elias Mountains and can start again in September in the far north.

Rafting: Seek local advice before rafting down unknown rivers.

Information: There are six Information Centres in Yukon; at Watson Lake, Carcross, Whitehorse, Haines Junction, Beaver Creek and Dawson City.

CAYMAN ISLANDS – MARINE PARADISE

'When asked the usual "What did you do on your holiday?" I can now say: "I stroked the velvet-soft underbellies of 4ft-wide stingrays; came face to face with Sweet Lips the 200 pound jewfish and Snaggle Tooth the barracuda; inspected barrel sponges as large as Greek olive urns; and met Crazy Eddy the Moray eel . . ." '

David Wickers, travel writer

Nestling within the warm waters of the British Caribbean, the Cayman Islands are a Mecca for divers; an offshore wildlife haven as well as an offshore tax haven. To swim with glittering shoals of tarpon and to dive among sunken wrecks and enchanted coral gardens are all part of the adventure experience here. According to underwater guru Jacques Cousteau, the Caymans are one of the best areas for diving in the world – a real marine paradise, in truth.

When Christopher Columbus discovered America in 1493 it was actually the Cayman Islands which he first encountered. Now a British Crown Colony, the Caymans consist of three islands: **Grand Cayman** (at 196 sq km/76 sq miles the most developed; **Cayman Brac** (39 sq km/15 sq miles and relatively undeveloped); and **Little Cayman** (an isolated retreat slightly smaller than Cayman Brac). This small archipelago – more accurately the tips of giant submerged islands – lies nearly 800 km/500 miles south of Miami and 290 km/180 miles west of Jamaica. Caressed by the gentle Caribbean trade winds, the islands are encircled by beautiful coral reefs, life support systems to an extraordinary abundance of underwater flora and fauna. The water is warm, calm and sheltered, while underneath the surface visibility extends to an incredible 60 m/200 ft. Just offshore you can take a shallow scuba dive of up to 15 m/50 ft), while further out the water plunges to incredible depths of 1500 m/5000 ft or more. Diving at usual depths of around 30 m/100 ft is not only an exhilarating experience, but a safe one too, since over thirty accredited professional operators and more than seventy dive boats are available to take underwater adventure seekers to and from their diving destinations. If you have time, you can also take a course in diving instruction and become certified in the Caymans. This instruction includes familiarization with the local laws protecting the ecology of the Cayman Islands Marine Parks.

Tarpon Alley, a long and narrow underwater canyon, is just one of Grand Cayman's many diving highlights. This is home to giant shoals of tarpon fish whose almost solid walls of silver part as if by magic when you swim through them. In the shallow dive spot dubbed **Stingray City** you can weave in and out of the flapping (and friendly) forms of countless eponymous fish. There are also rare and beautiful black coral gardens, swaying seaplumes and seafans to marvel at, and man-made wonders too, in the form of over 250 eerie ship carcasses, many worth exploring. Here also are extraordinary barrel sponges – just one among a huge variety of sponges unrivalled elsewhere in the Caribbean. The renowned **Cayman Wall** – a sheer drop of coral reef that disappears into a blue abyss called the **Cayman Trench** – is the largest hole in the Caribbean, as deep as Everest is high. For a unique underwater experience not available elsewhere, you can try the **Atlantis submarine**. Based in George Town harbour, the Atlantis takes up to 28 voyagers 'through the final frontier of inner space' to depths of up to 45 m/150 ft. Its hour-long trips are an excellent way to introduce young explorers (four years old and over) to the extraordinary world of the submarine. Night dives are also available, revealing many nocturnal species usually hidden to daytime divers. Cost per trip is around US$70. Serious underwater adventure addicts can take a ride on one of **Research Submersible Ltd**'s three-man Perry submarines which travel to depths of 225 m/750 ft, off the spectacular Cayman Wall.

If you are unable to dive, this need not stop you learning and thereby starting to discover something of the adventure that underwater Cayman has to offer. It's the perfect place to learn scuba diving, with several centres specializing in courses for beginners. For instance, **Red Sail Sports**, based on the beach by the Hyatt Regency Hotel, offers a one-day introductory course for around US$100 and a fully certified open-water course (which takes four days and includes classroom and swimming pool tuition) for around US$500. Generally you need to be in good health, to be able to swim at least 200 m/650 ft and tread water for ten minutes. Dive centres are also often able to arrange night dives and the hire of more specialized equipment such as underwater video cameras.

As well as undersea adventures, there are opportunities all over the Caymans for other watersports: not surprisingly, since watery pursuits are the islands' top attraction. You can skim the sea's surface on a hobie cat, windsurfer or waterskis, or you can rise above it all on a parasail. Unlike some other Caribbean islands, the Caymans are not renowned for their inland beauty, but Seven Mile Beach (the name slightly overestimates the length of this stretch of sand, but not by much) is, however, one of the most beautiful coastlines in all of the Caribbean. This is turtle territory, and you can wade out to sea and practise feeding them, as a prelude to feeding more testing species – stingrays, for instance. Distance here is not a problem: although Grand Cayman is the largest of the islands, it is still small enough for you to breeze comfortably around in a day or so. Originally inhabited by a collection of misfits and outcasts – like shipwrecked seamen, pirates and a steady stream of deserters from Oliver Cromwell's army – today, the islands' inhabitants are as warm, friendly and welcoming as you could wish for. Driving is on the left hand side of the road, and in this and other ways the British influence is still very much in evidence (English is the spoken language).

There are several local dive and other activity operators, including **Cayman Diving Lodge (tel: 800 852 3483)**; **Red Sail Sports (tel: 800 255 6425)**; and **Treasure Island Divers (tel: 800 872 7552)**. Other tour operators listing the Cayman Islands include **Divers World (26 Temple Fortune Parade, London NW11 0QS; tel: 0181 458 5115)**; **Regal Diving (22 High Street, Sutton Ely, Cambridgeshire CB6 2RB; tel: 01353 778096)**; and **Dive & Sail (Nastfield Cottage, The Green, Frampton on Severn, Gloucestershire; tel: 01452 740919)**. Prices start from around £1000 for a week's diving, all-inclusive.

FACTFILE

When to go: With average temperature 77°F, a trip can be planned anytime. Prices can rise by a third or more during the winter season.

Diving safety: Use only certified dive instructors and ask to see their internationally recognized qualifications (eg PADI, NAUI, BSAC, NASDS or similar). You are not permitted to fly until at least 12 hours after diving.

Marine regulations: Scuba divers may not use spearfishing equipment, nor take, injure or destroy any fish. Divers and snorkellers must use a flag attached to a buoy when outside safe swimming areas.

continued

FACTFILE continued

Habitat preservation: There are strict ecotourist regulations, including confiscation of your boat if you drop anchor on to coral. Cayman Islands tourist literature states, 'Our coral reefs, shells, fish and sea fans are our national treasures. Please resist the temptation to take them out of the country with you. Our people, as well as future visitors like yourself, enjoy seeing them on our shores and in our waters!'

CHILE – ATACAMA TO ANTARCTICA

'Getting into another world isn't so easy nowadays. So, although my adventures with Alfonso [a horse] lasted only a week, it seemed to me a remarkable length of time to have gone without seeing a road or a house, hearing any mechanical sounds, carrying money or drinking water other than straight from rivers. On three of those bright spring days under Chillan volcano last November, we travelled without meeting a soul – through pastures, past orchards in full flower, under snow-capped peaks where condors soared and into valleys you could pass straight by unless you knew which stream to follow . . . We were in the Chilean Andes.'

Mark Ottoway, Sunday Times, 8 April 1990

Though no more than 185 km/ 115 miles at its widest point, Chile stretches an incredible 4180 km/2600 miles from north to south, which, as you might expect, gives rise to huge variations in climate and scenery. Apart from being the longest country in the world, Chile can boast a roll-call of many other distinctions, such as the Atacama – the world's most arid desert; the Andes – mountain backbone of the continent; Chungara – the world's highest lake; some extraordinary and unique islands in the Pacific Ocean; and Patagonia – the remote, inhospitable and majestic gateway to the Antarctic. Chile has masses of wilderness (altogether there are thirty National Parks) and all of these scenic contrasts and wilderness areas combine to make the place an adventurer's paradise. There are limitless possibilities for trekking, mountaineering, rafting and mountain biking, not forgetting Chile's ubiquitous horses and the country's reputation, made famous by the writings of such travellers as Rosie Swale, A.F. Tschiffely and Mark Ottoway, as a rider's expedition ground, *par excellence*.

The country divides into three regions; Northern, Central and Islands, and Southern. Within the **Northern Region**, starting at Arica near Chile's northern boundary with Peru, stretches the **Atacama**, the world's driest desert. You can experience a little of desert life by taking a trip to the hot springs of Mamina or the oasis of Pica Valley. At 4000 m/13 000 ft above sea level, the **High Plateau** of North Chile is a place of great beauty. Here you can discover the emerald green waters of **Chungara**, the world's highest lake, habitat of flamingoes and other wild birds which have adapted to life at high altitude. Chungara Lake is part of the **Lauca National Park**, now designated a World Biosphere Reserve. This Reserve is home to around 1500 endangered vicunas, as well as llamas and alpacas. In the heart of the Atacama salt flats lies the **Valley of the Moon**, a vast expanse of desert, devoid of any animal or plant life. Also memorable are the **El Tatio Geysers**, huge pillars of steam, some reaching as high as 10 m/30 ft into the air. The origin of the nearby mysterious geoglyphs – giant figures painted onto the sides of the hills – remain unexplained even to this day. Though normally associated with Peru, the '**Inca Trail**' passes through northern Chile; hiking adventures here and elsewhere within the Northern Region can be rewarding. Further into the desert in Copiapo is the world's highest active volcano, the **Ojos del Salado** (6893 m/22 622 ft). Although a non-technical climb, its high altitude can catch out the unwary, so it is recommended that you acclimatize before attempting the ascent.

More temperate and hospitable than the north, the **Central Region** is a pastoral and mountainous area where snow-covered Andean peaks provide a wonderful backdrop to cultivated fields beneath. Opportunities for climbing and mountaineering are abundant here, not to mention horseback expeditions. **Aconcagua** (6958 m/22 830 ft) – highest mountain in the Western hemisphere – is the jewel in the Andean crown. Although situated in Argentina, Aconcagua is accessed from Chile. Again, the climb is not technical, but many adventurers are foiled by poor weather or the effects of altitude. Few people know that Chile is the best country in the Southern hemisphere for skiing. From Santiago you can visit the downhill ski resorts of **Portillo**, **Farellones** and **Valle Nevado**, although lovers of wilderness will be more inclined to head off-piste on cross-country trips. As well as riding, trekking and climbing, rafting is gaining popularity in Chile. Only 45 minutes from Santiago, the **Maipo** river rapids are a short, two-hour trip. Other rafting rivers, generally of Grade 3 challenge, include the **Trancura**, **Fuy**, **Bueno**, **Petrohue**, **Cisnes** and **Baker**. Most famous of all Chile's rivers is the Grade 5 river **Bio Bio**, 600 km/370 miles from Santiago, considered by afficionados to be one of the world's greatest white-water experiences. Unfortunately, this river experience is under immediate threat of being lost forever to a multi-dam hydroelectric scheme.

Some 650 km/400 miles west of Valparaiso lie the **Juan Fernandez Islands**, accessible by boat or plane from mainland Chile. This place was the original inspiration for **Robinson Crusoe** for it was here, in 1704, that one Alexander Selkirk was shipwrecked, his only possessions a Bible, a gun, a pound of gunpowder, an axe, a lump of tobacco and some clothes. The story of his four years and four months struggle for survival led Defoe to write his well known best seller. Today, the archipelago is a National Park, boasting an incredible variety of flora and fauna. Another group of islands – six times as far from mainland Chile as the Juan Fernandez Islands – is home to one of the world's great achaeological enigmas. Known to its original inhabitants as 'The Navel of the World' but today more prosaically called **Easter Island**, the place is shrouded in mystery. Just how its Moai – huge stone figures carved with silica axes, some weighing 50 tonnes, some more than 10 m/30 ft high – came into being, remains a mystery even to this day. Local inhabitants still believe that the Moai possess eternal powers. Other sites on the island include the crater of the volcano **Rano Kao** and the caves of **Puna Pau** volcano. You can hike there or hire horses – a good way to get around this 160 sq km/60 sq mile island. There are regular 5-hour flights from Santiago to Easter Island, en route to Tahiti.

The **Southern Region** of Chile is full of virgin landscapes: glaciers, ice floes, volcanoes, mountains, lakes, rivers, beaches, islands and ancient forests. In the east are found the **Petrohue Falls** and river, popular with kayakers and white-water rafters alike, while **Laguna de Laja** is an area of impressive waterfalls. The winding Southern Highway or Carretera Austral stretches 100 km/ 680 miles south from Puerto Montt, passing through landscapes which offer endless scope for adventurous activities. If you try sailing in the Aisen region, negotiating the many channels and islands there, you reach the **San Rafael Lagoon**, a small but astonishingly beautiful gateway to the Pacific Ocean, complete with 30 000 year-old glacier. Inveterate adventurers will want to continue to Chile's southernmost tip, including **Punta Arenas** and

Tierra del Fuego. The settlement of Punta Arenas is a starting point for exploring the fascinating **Magellan Channels** and you can hire boats here. Beyond Cape Horn lies the infamous Drake's passage and in the distance, Earth's final frontier – the Antarctic.

Chile is a popular adventure destination and many companies offer trips there, including **Mountain Travel Sobek, 6240 Fairmount Avenue, El Cerrito, CA 94530, tel: 510 527 8100** (rafting, hiking and climbing); **High Places** (trekking in the Patagonian Andes); **Exodus** (low-altitude Patagonian trekking); and **Explore** (Andean Lakes and Wilderness). Depending on length of trip and degree of remoteness, prices (including flight) start at around £1800 and go up to around £2500. An attempt at Aconcagua costs around £3000 (**Worldwide Journeys & Expeditions**).

Journey Latin America (14–16 Devonshire Road, London W4 2HD; tel: 0181 747 8315) offers a 16-day 'Volcanoes, Deserts and Glaciers' tour of Chile. The trip starts at Santiago, where you spend a day settling in. By day three you visit Lacuna National Park (where you are likely to glimpse alpaca, llama and vicuna) and the high-altitude Lake Chungara. On day 4 you take a morning flight to Antofagasta, continuing by bus through the desert to Calama and San Pedro de Atacama. Days 5 to 7 are spent in the desert, visiting Moon Valley and pre-Inca remains, as well as the vast salt flats of the Andean foothills. After returning by 'plane to Santiago, you fly to Puerto Montt, en route to Punta Arenas, some 1600 km/1000 miles to the south. From the latter you take a minibus to Torres del Paine National Park, with its sheer rock faces, glaciers and mountain lakes. Four days are spent here, camping and exploring. On day 16 you return to Puerto Natales, thence to Puerto Arenas and Santiago for the end of the adventure. Group size is up to 20, departures are during February, May, July, November and December, and the cost is from £1600 to £1900 including domestic and international (London–Santiago) flights. Various local expenses and taxes should also be allowed for – in the region of £400.

FACTFILE

Climate: Varies from hot and arid in the north to very cold, wet and stormy in the extreme south. Central Chile has a Mediterranean climate with a wet season (May to August). Altitude has a marked effect on temperature in Chile.

Air travel: The main domestic airlines offer multiple-flight tickets for getting around the country. These have to be bought before you visit Chile and reservations made well in advance.

CHINA – SILK ROAD SPLENDOUR

'These mountains are so lofty that it is a hard day's work, from morning till evening, to get to the top of them. On getting up, you find an extensive plain, with great abundance of grass and trees, and copious springs of pure water running down through rocks and ravines. In those brooks are found trout and many other fish of dainty kinds; and the air in those regions is so pure, and the residence there so healthful, that when the men who dwell below in the towns, and in the valleys and plains, find themselves attacked by any kind of fever or other ailment that may hap, they lose no time in going to the hills; and after abiding there two or three days, they quite recover their health through the excellence of that air.'

Marco Polo (1254–1324)

China is vast: a huge polyglot collection of over 50 nationalities comprising a quarter of the world's population. More like a continent than a country, China stretches a staggering 5000 km/ 3100 miles from east to west, and has a host of neighbouring countries: Mongolia and the Russian Commonwealth of Independent States (p 229) to the north, North Korea to the east, Vietnam (p 271), Laos, India (p 182), Bhutan (p 116) and Nepal (p 212) in the south, and Pakistan and Afghanistan in the west. Altogether the country contains 23 provinces, 5 autonomous regions and 3 municipalities. But despite China's huge population, only a tenth of its land surface is suitable for agriculture and, just as in Marco Polo's time, there are many wild and uninhabited regions awaiting the adventurous.

Almost a third of the country comprises mountains, not only the Himalayas but also the **Altai Mountains** in the north, the **Tianshan Mountains** in the northwest and the **Kunlun Mountains** in northern Tibet. Lying on the border with Tibet is the most famous of all China's peaks – **Mount Everest** (8848 m/29 198 ft) or as they prefer to call it in China, 'Mount Qomoolangma'. Tibet itself, one of China's autonomous regions, is well known as the 'Roof of the World' and is the subject of a separate section elsewhere in this book (p 252). Five mountains were declared sacred in the reign of the Han dynasty emperor Wu Di (156–187 BC): Mount Taishen (the holiest of all); the Western Sacred Mountain, Mount Huashan; the Southern Sacred Mountain, Mount Hengshan; the Northern Sacred Mountain, again called Mount Hengshan; and the Middle Sacred mountain, Mount Songshan. But as well as its high points, China contains one of the world's lowest areas – the **Turpan** basin in Xinjiang. Lying 155 m/508 ft below sea level, this basin is the lowest place on earth after the Dead Sea. In addition to some extensive arid areas such as the **Takla Makan** desert, China is criss-crossed with over 1500 rivers, including the **Yangtze** and **Yellow** rivers. This great variation in topography and associated climate has led to an abundance of wildlife – over 30 000 species at the last count, including several endangered ones. Some hundred species of wild plants and animals are under protection, including panda, golden monkey, white dolphin, crested ibis, red-crowned crane, and Yangtze alligator.

China has the oldest continuous civilization in the world, with a recorded history stretching back some 4000 years. But its recent history has shown troubled moments, most notably in 1989 when a group of students and workers occupied Tiananmen Square in Central Beijing, demanding political reform. The square was cleared by the Chinese authorities with great loss of life and diplomatic relations with the West became more strained. Although the political and economic reforms that have affected other Communist countries, notably those of the former Eastern Bloc, have not been so evident in China, international relations have improved somewhat in the years since Tiananmen and tourism is now growing rapidly. Like its neighbouring Russia, China offers a potential goldmine of opportunities for adventure travellers. Such visitors, though currently small in number, are poised to grow dramatically, as China continues to welcome Westerners.

Because they are so huge, the distances in China demand that visitors spend much of their time travelling in order to get a flavour of the country's extraordinary diversity. The state travel agency, **Luxingshe** (CITS), tends to organize most of the tours in China. While it is possible to travel independently, it is very difficult. However, more and more specialist operators are running packaged adventure trips off the beaten track and this is a highly recommended approach to seeing China for all but the most determinedly independent of travellers. A good deal of tourism in China is geared to cities, particularly Beijing in the northeast or

Hangzhou and Shanghai in the east and indisputably there is much to marvel at in terms of sights: temples, buildings, parks and museums. But once city life has lost its lustre, restless adventurers will want to head for the peace and quiet of the hills, glimpsing something of the country's array of natural attractions. However, one man-made attraction outside the cities which should not be missed is the **Great Wall**, one of the wonders of the world and said to be the only man-made structure visible from the moon. Some 2600 years old, it stretches 5400 km/3375 miles from Shannaiguan Pass in the east, to Jiayuguan Pass in the west.

Other attractions outside the cities are too numerous to list here, but a few deserve mention, like the beautiful **Lake of Heaven** near Urumqi in Northwest Provinces. Here a beautiful turquoise-coloured lake nestles amidst the Tianshan range of mountains. You can go riding with the local kasaks among this spectacular scenery. In the same area **Turfan** has the reputation of being China's hottest place, the second lowest point on Earth after the Dead Sea. Nearby, the **Flaming Mountains** give an appearance of being on fire under certain light conditions. In the Southern Provinces lies **Hainan Island**, a tropical paradise on the south coast of Guangdong Province, with unspoilt beaches, palm groves, fresh seafood and coconuts. In northeast China lies what Chinese emperors called 'the geomantic place for prosperity' – **Changbai Mountain**. A 3 km/1.8 mile climb from its base to its summit takes you through the temperate zone to an Arctic realm. Winter mountaineering and cross-country skiing, or summer hiking are popular activities here. Contact **Heilongjiang Provincial Tourism Bureau (124 Dazhi Road, Nangang District, Harbin, Heilongjiang Province, People's Republic of China; tel: Harbin 31441)**.

Perhaps the greatest attraction to China adventure travellers is the ancient and mysterious **Silk Road** – one of the earliest east–west trading routes, stretching from Xian, once the capital of China, westwards across the heart of Central Asia to Afghanistan. With huge mountain ranges and deserts to cross, the Silk Route was a formidable undertaking to traders and explorers like Marco Polo. In fact, only comparatively recently has it been possible to traverse this region without extreme difficulty. Silk Road explorer trips are offered by a number of adventure tour operators, including **Exodus** (25 days, £2400 all-inclusive); **Explore** (25 days, £2200, all-inclusive); **Encounter Overland** (36 days, Beijing to Islamabad); and **China Adventures (c/o Sundowners International, 267 Old Brompton Road, London SW5 9JA; tel: 0171 370 6845)**, the latter offering a 25-day Beijing to Urumqi soft adventure trip for £2800.

For a soft adventure in China at a leisurely pace, you could try **World Expeditions' 'China Bicycle Ride'**. This 22-day trip includes

13 days of cycling – the natural way to get about the country. From Hong Kong you travel by steamer up the Pearl River into China. The cycling part of the adventure takes you on an exploration of Guangdong Province, where you stop at small villages and experience a side of the country missed by many tourists. Accommodation is in local hotels and the food is also local. The pace of cycling in the group is not frenzied: there is plenty of time to stop and take in the local sights and sounds. If you've had enough of pedalling, there is always a back-up minibus to pick up any stragglers. By day 16 you take the evening train to Beijing where three days are spent in and around the city. Departures are throughout the year and the all-inclusive cost for joining in Hong Kong is $1598.

FACTFILE

Social conventions: Although their reputation for inscrutability is largely unjustified, the Chinese do not usually volunteer information and it is advisable to ask questions if you are unsure of anything. Don't be offended if you're followed by crowds, especially in remoter areas: Western visitors are rare, inevitably attracting curiosity. In greeting, handshaking may suffice, but sometimes you will be applauded, in which case it is polite to clap back. Good manners dictate that you arrive a little early for any special invitation.

Climate: Its vast size gives rise to a diversity of climates. In the northeast, summers are hot and dry, winters very cold. The central region has high rainfall, hot summers and cold winters, while the southeast has high rainfall, semi-tropical summers and cool winters.

Clothes: Respect cultural mores and avoid wearing revealing clothing if inappropriate.

ECUADOR – FOUR WORLDS TO DISCOVER

'Señor, we understand perfectly, that in an affair like yours, it is necessary to dissemble – a little; and you, doubtless, do quite right to say you intend to ascend Chimborazo – a thing that everybody knows is perfectly impossible. We know very well what is your object! You wish to discover the treasures which are buried in Chimborazo . . .'

Edward Whymper, 1892

Straddling the equator, Ecuador, the smallest Andean country in South America, contains four amazing and contrasting 'worlds': Amazonian rainforest, Andean sierra, Pacific coastline and the Galapagos Islands. Although little more than the length of Great Britain, Ecuador has a vast variety of tropical rainforests, mountains, gorges, beaches and highland plains. When combined with its good communications links, this makes Ecuador the perfect South American destination for adventure travellers who wish to explore a wide variety of back-country landscapes in a short time.

From the rarefied atmosphere of the capital, Quito (2700 m/ 9000 ft) it is only half an hour's flying time to the rich and humid basin of the **Amazon**. Budget-conscious travellers may opt for the excitement of a twelve-hour bumpy bus trip, risking the prospect of washed out dirt roads, especially during August. Once there, you will find that the River Nopo and its associated tributaries are the only 'highways' in this jungle region called **Oriente**: dug-out canoes laden with people and supplies ply these rivers throughout the year. River adventures in the Oriente vary from day trips in motorized dug-out canoes to longer expeditions in unpowered craft. Here you can view the rich bird life and try to identify hummingbirds, toucans and macaws from among the 1000 or more species that have been recorded in the upper Amazon basin.

Most adventure vacationers visiting the jungle decide to stay either in a tented camp or rustic jungle accommodation such as La

Sela Lodge or Satcha Lodge. After awakening to what sounds like a whole orchestra of bird sounds, you can experience a full day's hiking and/or canoeing in the Amazon basin, led by a Quinchua Indian guide. You see rare and exotic birds and tropical plants, and learn about their medicinal uses. Climbing up 45 m/150 ft on to man-made platforms overlooking dense and unbroken rainforest canopy, you have a chance of hearing the unmistakable shriek of howler monkeys, or catching a rare glimpse of the primaeval sloth. Afterwards, in camp, you can spend the rest of the day either fishing or enjoying a refreshing swim in a nearby lake (pirhanhas permitting!).

After returning to Quito, most travellers head south down Ecuador's central valley. In 1802 this valley was aptly named 'The Avenue of the Volcanoes' by Alexandre von Humbolt, and today if you travel down the Pan-Am highway on a clear day you'll see many glacier-mantled volcanoes. Such lofty summits as these are becoming a popular magnet for experienced high-altitude climbers, their long access and well placed mountain huts making it perfectly possible to achieve two or three ascents in a fortnight. After a few days of acclimatization in and around Quito, a typical itinerary for climbers starts at the colourful town of **Banos**, with its natural thermal springs. This town lies beneath **Tingurahua**, a 5200 m/17 000 ft snow-covered volcano. Once acclimatized, you can attempt to bag the highest active volcano in the world – **Mount Cotopaxi** (5898 m/19 347 ft). Your midnight start is compensated for by magnificent views at dawn over the Amazon Basin. The main jewel in Ecuador's glittering crown of summits is the mighty **Chimborazo**, at 6310 m/20 696 ft the country's highest peak. First climbed by Edward Whymper in 1880, it is in fact the furthest point from the Earth's centre, due to the world's equatorial bulge.

For adventurers less fanatic about summits, Ecuador offers numerous trekking opportunities, both in the mountains and at lower level. More popular treks include the ancient **Inca Trail** from Guasuntos to Ingapica, which follows an ancient Inca road network. **Ingapica** is a remote and important site, with remarkable mortar-less stone building constructions in a fine stage of preservation. A trip worth combining with a visit to these Inca ruins is the railway journey from **Alusia** where a hair-raising series of switchbacks negotiates the steep descent over the '**Devil's Nose**' towards the heat and humidity of the coast. North of Quito, trekking suitable for beginners is available around the **Otavald** countryside, where the average altitude lies between 2000 and 4000 m/6500 and 13 000 ft. Local staff with mules and horses can assist in the carrying of luggage. Traditional rural villages and varied vegetation zones make this a culturally and ecologically rich experience. A visit to the traditional Indian market held every Saturday in

Otavalo is a must. This colourful and bustling gathering dates back to pre-Inca times and, as well as traditional crafts and weaving, it provides a forum for the purchase of Ecuador's national dish – the guinea pig!

More experienced trekkers may wish to tackle the rough cross-country trail from **El Quinche** (4100 m/13 448 ft) in the Andes, all the way to **El Chaco** (1200 m/3936 ft) in the Amazon lowlands. With few traces of human habitation along the way, there may be a chance of seeing the rare mountain tapir or the Andean speckled bear. Many of Ecuador's cross-country trails can also be explored by horse or mountain bike: numerous agencies in Quito offer such programmes.

No trip to Ecuador is complete without a visit to the enchanted islands of the **Galapagos**. This volcanically formed archipelago 1000 km/622 miles west of Ecuador's Pacific coast is one of the world's most famous natural treasures. Comprising over thirteen major islands, this setting was Charles Darwin's natural labora-tory, inspiring him to write the *Origin of Species* following his visit here in 1835. Although the Galapagos's scenery is barren and volcanic it has a certain haunting beauty. When the first seafarers arrived in 1535 they found some of the strangest and most wonderful wildlife imaginable: birds that could no longer fly, seagoing iguanas and dragon-like lizards from prehistoric times, as well as giant tortoises – or *galapagos* in Spanish. Amazingly, virtually every island in the Galapagos was found to have its own indigenous species. But best of all, they found that the animals of the islands were completely unafraid of people – and this is still the case today.

Your Galapagos trip will vary enormously depending on the type of cruise you select. You may choose a 90-berth passenger ship with all the shipboard amenities going, or you may opt for one of a variety of smaller yachts. Generally the routine is to sleep aboard and enjoy one or two guided shore visits each day, together with opportunities to swim or snorkel. The very playful sealions will perform underwater acrobatics and most snorkellers will see penguins, tropical fish, a variety of rays and – if you're lucky – sharks. More ardent underwater enthusiasts can arrange trips on fully equipped dive boats with qualified diving guides.

UK operators that offer trips to Ecuador include **Himalayan Kingdoms**, **Explore**, **High Places**, **Journey Latin America (14–16 Devonshire Road, London W4 2HD; tel: 0181 747 8315)** and **Galapagos Adventure Tours (29 Palace View, Bromley, Kent BR1 3EJ; tel: 0181 460 8107)**. Several well established agencies based in Quito offer a variety of adventurous activities. These include **Angermeyer** and **Metropolitan Touring**.

Guerba offers a 15-day '**Enchanted Ecuador**' adventure for approximately £800, excluding international flights. In groups of around 6 to 12, you travel by 4-wheel drive vehicle from Quito, passing through the Amazon jungle to Pimpilalla, where you join the local Indian community in their daily life. Days 4 and 5 are spent in Banos, with optional hiking or riding excursions into the surrounding hills. Day 6 is spent travelling to Ambato – the largest purely indigenous market in Ecuador – and thence to Riobamba for the night. The next day you continue through some of the country's finest scenery to Cuenca. On day 8 you head out into the hills to visit the largest Inca ruin in the country. Days 9 to 11 are spent in Alandaluz, a privately owned ecological centre in Guayas. Accommodation here is bamboo huts on the beach. From here you can explore the Machalilla National Park, the islands of Salango and El Ahorcado, and Cantalapiedra Ecological Reserve. You then return by air to Quito, spending the last two days winding down at Otavalo, with its colourful markets. Most accommodation on the trip consists of small guesthouses, jungle cabanas, monasteries or farms. For an extra £800 you can bolt on **Guerba's Voyage Galapagos** trip, visiting 8 to 10 islands within this extraordinary archipelago.

FACTFILE

When to go: This depends on what you want to do. There is no perfect time of year to see everything. Best months for climbing are December–January and April–May, while the wettest months are June–August. Climate is generally unpredictable!

Travel tips: Best views on 'Devil's Nose' railway ride from Alusia are from the carriage roof. Local bus travel is cheap, easy and frequent (hitch-hikers are expected to pay). For a more adventurous trip to the Galapagos, choose from among the smaller boats.

Information: The UK-based **South American Explorers Club** has a wealth of detailed information on Ecuador. Write to them at **41 Nortoft Road, Chalfont St Peter, Bucks SL9 0LA**.

THE FAROE ISLANDS —
THE WINDY EDGE OF NOTHING

'The boat herself no longer pitched nor rolled in her normal
style. At the same moment, the cloud base rose another thirty
or forty feet, and we saw them: thousands upon thousands of
seabirds pouring out from the cliffs of Mykinos; gulls, guillemots, razorbills, fulmars, gannets, puffins, skuas and terns.
They came in droves, in squadron after squadron, wheeling
and turning, and swooping and dipping down toward the
queer limpy contorted sea. I was awed. If there was any place
which fitted the idea of paradise of birds, this was it. "It's
fantastic!" I shouted to George above the roar of the wind.'

Tim Severin, The Brendan Voyage

Like hardy little flowers, the
Faroe Islands (Sheep Islands)
rise mysteriously and magically
from their surrounding ocean
fastness, pounded relentlessly
and continuously by the powerful North Atlantic surf. Their
close association with the sea
and seafaring goes back over
many generations. The early Ir-
ish monks who discovered these
islands were later driven out by
Norse Vikings, and for many
centuries afterwards the Faroes
maintained historic links with
both Norway and Denmark.
Home rule was established only as recently as 1948 and indeed
until the 20th century these islands were largely isolated from the
outside world. This isolation led in turn to the development of a
unique culture, influenced greatly by the surrounding sea and by
Nordic folklore. The Faroese language is Nordic, similar to
Icelandic, although English is widely understood. Today, nowhere
else in northern Europe possesses such a rugged maritime setting
coupled with an unspoilt culture which still offers genuine hospitality, and, on occasions, real friendship. In short, the Faroes offer an
unparalleled adventure destination for lovers of wild island landscapes, a country 'on the windy edge of nothing', as Eric Linklater
described it in the late 1940s.

Lying approximately 600 km/370 miles west of Norway and
300 km/190 miles northwest of Scotland, the Faroe archipelago

consists of some 18 rocky islands covering an area of around 1300 sq km/500 sq miles. Countless millenia have eroded and shaped this once volcanic landscape into a series of terraces and shelves that serve as footpaths for the islands' 70 000-odd resident sheep, and nesting sites for their millions of seabirds. Centuries of exposure and sheep grazing have resulted in a complete absence of tree cover, yet this stark landscape has a haunting fascination which lingers long in the memories of visitors.

Despite the islands' near-Polar latitude, their climate is surprisingly temperate thanks to the Gulf Stream (summers average 11°C, while winters are a mild 4.5°C). Vast tracts of surrounding ocean ensure an abundance of rain (official statistics record 280 days per year!) so be prepared for the worst. Sudden changes in weather are a fact of life here and references are often made to 'local' conditions where parts of an island separated by only 10 minutes walking can vary from sweltering heat to mist-shrouded cold. Such coastal mists are very common, especially in late summer and autumn, while in winter a memorable experience for visitors is to witness the spectacle of the *aurora borealis*, or northern lights. The tiny population – only 47 000, scattered throughout all 18 islands – is linked by an impressive array of communications, including ferries, roadways, helicopters and island causeways. Most of the archipelago can thus be reached fairly easily.

The largest island, **Stremoy**, houses nearly half the entire Faroe population, most inhabiting **Torshavn**, one of the world's smallest capital cities. In the north of the island lies **Saksun**, an ancient and traditional village of typical Faroese farmhouses lying at the head of a cove. This can be entered only by small boats at high tide due to the presence of huge sandbanks. On the west coast lie the enormous **Vestmanna** bird cliffs: steep and isolated rockfaces hewn with grottos and ledges, overlooking a complex of offshore skerries and needles. Accessible only by small boats, these cliffs are a birdwatcher's paradise, housing legions of guillemots, kittiwakes, razorbills, petrels and ubiquitous puffins. In this vicinity, ancient footpaths lead through deep valleys and up steep mountain slopes to give superb views of natural, sea-hewn landscapes.

Eysturoy, the second largest island, offers a multitude of natural attractions for walkers. The old and traditional northerly village of **Gjogy** lies at the head of a deep gorge which provides its natural harbour and from which its name derives. Until recently this harbour and track, marked by cairn arrows through the rocky hills behind, were Gjogy's only links with the outside world. Not far to the northwest lies the beautiful valley of **Ambadalur** with its magnificent views of **Bugvion**, the highest sea stack in the Faroe Islands. The east coast village of Oyndarfjorour is the home of another of the Faroes' natural wonders, the so-called **rinkusteinor** or shifting shore boulders that for centuries have been rocked and rolled by the tremendous forces of the waves and currents. Majestic natural surroundings and splendid opportunities for hiking and walking make **Eidi** a magnet for adventurers. Eidiskoun cliffs rise dramatically and vertically out of the North Atlantic to a height of 354 m/1160 ft, providing excellent views out to the rock stack of **Risin of Kellingin** (giant and witch). Legend records that the giant and witch were immortalized in stone by the sun's rays as they tried to tow away the Faroe Islands towards Iceland. Equally impressive views await fit hikers who take a guided trip up the island's highest mountain, **Slaettarantindur**.

To the west lie the tiny islands of **Vagar** and **Mykinus**, the former containing the Faroes' only international airport. Vagar also boasts a magnificent waterfall – **Bospalapossur** – which tumbles into **Sorvagsvatn**, the Faroes' largest freshwater lake. On its west coast lies **Gasadular**, a remote and stunningly beautiful valley only readily accessible by helicopter. **Mykinus**, an unforgettable and isolated rocky outpost with only 25 inhabitants, is also one of the hardest places to reach in the Faroe Islands. It can sometimes take days of waiting for the weather to clear sufficiently to enable boats or helicopters to cross the narrow channel. Mykinus has the only gannet colony on the islands, reached by crossing an exciting narrow suspension bridge which spans the 35 m/115 ft wide gorge to the islet of **Mykinusholmur**.

In many ways the most southern island – **Suduroy** – is different from the rest of the Faroe archipelago. At 470 m/1542 ft high, **Beinisvorom** is an impressive peak and yet it is one of the most accessible vantage points on these islands. Even the least fit walker can enjoy visiting this area to observe the teeming birdlife on its mighty sea cliffs. In northwest Suduroy the rockstack of **Asmundarstakkur** emerges from the sea, its sheer face (87 m/285 ft) climbable, but only with difficulty. The **Nordoyar**, six remote northwesterly islands, offer fine terrain for fell walking, with their numerous footpaths. **Fugloy** (bird island) lives up to its name, while **Suinoy** (pig island) offers easily climbed peaks with magnificent views. On the northwest part of **Vidoy** lies **Cao Enniborg**, at 750 m/2460 ft the highest sea cape in the world.

The Faroes are principally for independent travellers. They are a good destination on which to 'cut your teeth' and see what adventure preparation and planning are all about. Once there, however, you will have no difficulty in finding the numerous local operators who offer a range of adventurous activities, including boat trips to the sea cliffs, mountain hikes along traditional stone 'cairn trails' and combined bike and sailing trips. Such operators are almost all based in the capital, **Torshavn**.

FACTFILE

When to go: May to August are the best months, weatherwise. The ferry from the UK takes 22 hours from Aberdeen or 14 hours from Lerwick. Flight time from Glasgow Airport is 2 hours.

Travel tips: Local weather forecasts are broadcast daily in English at 8.05 am.

Beware the sudden appearance of thick fog when hiking: take a map and compass.

It is forbidden to leave paths marked by cairns.

If you are biking, it is sensible to check your brakes regularly. Bikes are welcome on the public buses (blue). Some of the islands' tunnels are quite long and car exhausts can be a problem. Bikes can be rented from Torshavn.

Camping is allowed only by permission of landowners or at designated camping places.

Tourist Board: Faeroese Islands Tourist Board, PO Box 368, FR – 100, Torshavn; tel: 12277.

FIJI – SOUTH SEA PARADISE

'Isles of the Southern Seas': the very words conjure up images of romance, discovery and adventure. In Fiji there is tremendous scope for adventurous activities which will quickly take you far beyond the bounds of a tropical beach. Fiji consists of 322 islands: the two largest are **Viti Levu** and **Vanua Levi**, both extinct volcanoes rising abruptly from the sea. As well as endless, idyllic, tropical beaches, Fiji has some of the world's safest rainforest, stunning waterfalls, and a coastline brimming with colourful, coral reefs. As if these were not enough, the Fijians themselves have a well deserved reputation for tremendous hospitality and friendliness.

The opportunities for trekking are superb: you can walk through upland grasslands and thick forests and then cool off in mountain streams. As you pass through highland villages you are liable to be greeted and treated as an honoured guest by the entire village. There is the rugged three-day **Trans-Viti Levu Trek** from the Cross-Island Highway to the Navua River at **Namuamua**, which leads up and down jungle river valleys through the rainforest. (Because of the many river crossings this trip is not possible during the rainy season.) Another exhilarating hike is the **Sigatoka River Trek** from the forestry station of Nadarivatu to Korolevu. If your taste is for mountains you could try the four-day **Mt Victoria Trek** up the country's highest peak to 1322 m/4339 ft. This trek finishes off with a bamboo raft trip down the **Naqelewai**. If you wish to visit an island village it is advisable to make the arrangements through a tour company to ensure that you don't offend local custom. **New Frontiers (tel: 679 722755)** offers a range of organized treks.

Not surprisingly there is also enormous scope for all kinds of watersports. Surfing enthusiasts should head for **Namotu** and **Cloudbreak** at **Tavarua Island**. There are great windsurfing opportunities too, particularly in the **Pacific Harbour** area, now rated as one of the best locations in the world.

The coral reefs around Fiji are a diver's paradise. You don't even need to be an expert to enjoy the coral reefs; it is possible on some beaches to walk along the reef at low tide. With a mask you can see even more of this stunning underwater world of coral canyons teeming with colourful fish. For serious diving, some of the best places are around the **Mamanuca Islands**, **Beqa**, **Savusavu** and **Taveuni**. The **Great White Wall** at Taveuni is a unique diving experience as you plunge 30 m/100 ft through a gorgonian-lined tunnel to a vertical tapestry of vibrantly coloured soft coral. This is for experienced divers only. There is a good network of dive operators offering guided boat dives, training and equipment rental. On Taveuni you could try **Dive Taveuni (tel: 880 441)**; on Beqa try **Beqa Divers Fiji (tel: 361 088)**. Water conditions are best from May to October, during the cool season.

For those in search of adventure above the waves there is ample opportunity to charter a yacht from **Suva**, **Taveuni** or the northern **Lau Islands**. For further information you should contact **Rosie The Travel Service (tel: 679 722755)**.

The Natural World (57 Church Street, Twickenham TW1 3NR; tel: 0181 744 0474) offers three Fijian trips to Yasawa, Toberua and Nukubati islands. Each trip consists of a three-day soft adventure in which you can choose from diving, snorkelling, rainforest excursions or caving. Prices, excluding flight, are around £400 for each of the three island itineraries. **Explore** offers a Fiji one-week '**Sailtrek Stopover**', available in conjunction with its New Zealand tours (you fly to Fiji from Christchurch). From Nadi, on Viti Levu – the largest Fijian island – you sail with a small group (minimum size only two people) on board a square rigger tall ship (the Ra-Marama) to the Yasawa islands. These smaller Fijian islands have beautifully clear waters and limestome rock formations. Two days are spent seatrekking around Yasawa and Waya islands, Vomo reef and Beachcomber island. From the island camps here you can snorkel and 'chill out' and you're sure to be given a warm welcome by local villagers, perhaps taking part in a kava ceremony – a drink with soothing effects! Day 6 is spent walking in the Nasori highlands to the traditional village of Toko, where you spend the penultimate day, before flying back home. The cost for this adventure is around £400 as a supplement to the **Explore** New Zealand trips.

You don't need to be an energetic adventurer on Fiji, as there are so many idyllic islands fringed with deserted beaches and dotted with palm trees where you can snorkel, fish for your supper and enjoy the solitude. Such unspoiled islands include **Toberua**, **Motoriki**, **Ovalau** and **Kadavu**. There are several small camping resorts catering expressly for those travellers who want to do their own thing and enjoy a *Robinson Crusoe* experience.

FACTFILE

Climate: The climate is tropical with a dry season from May to October and the rainy season from December to April.

Dress: It is considered impolite for women to wear shorts in the city streets or villages. Skirts or 'sulas' are advised.

FINLAND – LAND OF GREEN GOLD

'. . . we had races in sledges, drawn by reindeer over the smooth grass; and amused ourselves by riding upon the backs of these animals; being always outstripped by the Lapps, who were as much delighted with our awkwardness as we were with the strange gestures and manners of this very singular people.'

Edward Daniel Clarke (1769–1822)

Finland is supremely unspoilt: no crowds, no litter, no traffic fumes. Although a third larger than the UK, the country has fewer than a hundred towns (never mind cities). With a population density of only sixteen people per square kilometre (compared with 238 in the UK) it is an empty land of lakes, tundra, and forests. The latter give rise to Finland's name 'land of green gold', for as much as two-thirds of the country is clothed in beautiful evergreen pine and spruce forests, more than any other European country. Forestry harvesting operations are becoming more noticeable, but with 25 National Parks scattered throughout the country, getting away from the mark of human hands is not a problem at all. North of the Arctic Circle lies the wilderness of Lapland and here you are down to fewer than two people per square kilometre. Culturally, the Finns are attuned to adventure. With an enthusiasm for keeping fit, with wilderness literally on the doorstep, and with limitless fresh air (meaning *fresh* air) small wonder that they are keen on the outdoors, retreating to their lakeside cabins during the summer and donning their skis in the winter. This is a marvellous part of Europe for all sorts of adventures, accommodation is plentiful (for example there are over 350 camping sites) and yet, surprisingly, it is not particularly well known or visited by British tour groups despite its proximity (2½ hours by air).

In adventure terms, the country can be divided into Lakeland, Forestland and Lapland. To the Finns, **lakes** are symbolic of the sanctity and beauty of their environment. Most of the country's 180 000 or so lakes are situated between the coastal area and the eastern frontier. They form a veritable labyrinth, with myriads of islands, headlands and bays. And in summer they are surprisingly warm, thanks to the shallow depths which heat up quickly and stay hot under the midnight sun. Many of the lake systems are joined up in some way or other – a legacy of their former importance as communication routes, but now they are useful discovery routes for tourists and travellers alike.

Most of Finland's **forests** are found in the southern and coastal regions, like **Karelia**. The highest point in this region – the **Koli Heights**, which overlook Lake Pieleinen in northern Karelia – are a mere 347 m/1138 ft high, illustrating the fact that Finland is not mountainous in the way that some other Scandinavian countries are. **Kainuu**, the region around **Lake Oulujarvi**, is wild and beautiful, with huge forests, lakes and rapids, while the **Voukatti** region is renowned for its cross-country skiing.

Lapland north of the Arctic Circle is known as 'Europe's Last Wilderness' and it is indeed a wonderful place for adventures. Occupying 100 000 sq km/39 000 sq miles, the region has vast uninhabited stretches of tundra, low fell birch scrub (few conifers grow here) and marshlands. To protect this countryside, several National Parks have been created – over half a million hectares in all. Although Finnish Lapland occupies the Arctic zone, it differs greatly from typical Arctic conditions. Because of the Gulf Stream's benign effects, Finland's climate is much milder than that of, say, Siberia, Alaska or Greenland, all of which are at the same latitude. In summer, its dry atmosphere is both refreshing and invigorating. Temperatures in July and August reach as high as 35°C, but mosquitoes can be aggressive then, so don't forget to dress accordingly and take the repellant. The other uncharacteristic thing about Lapland is that it is inhabited all year round, by nomadic humans as well as nomadic reindeer (there are around 200 000 in each case). Reindeer form an important part of Lapp culture: many of the 4500 true Lapps in the area herd their own reindeer, and during the winter months there are reindeer round-ups and special reindeer-driving competitions. Extensive camping facilities are found within the region, or if you prefer more solid accommodation, rudimentary log cabins are dotted about for use by visitors.

In eastern Lapland, **Suomutunturi**, which lies on the Arctic Circle, is a well known winter sports centre, as are **Pyhatunturi**, **Luostotunturi** and the **Saariselka Fells**. Also in eastern Lapland, the **Lemmenjoki National Park** has marked routes for hikers. In western Lapland the ground is higher and the vegetation correspondingly sparser. The ranges of **Yllastunturi**, **Olostunturi** and

Pallastunturi have centres for snow sports in winter, and good hiking opportunities in summer. Lapland's position north of the Arctic Circle means constant daylight in summer and the Northern Lights in winter. Autumn comes early to Lapland and it is then, during late August and September, that the place is at its best: midgeless, fresh yet sunny, and exquisitely beautiful.

Summer activities are limitless. Hiking is ever-popular, the best months being June, August and September (avoid the July mosquitoes, at least in Lapland). With so much forest about, you have to be careful about lighting fires, so portable stoves are recommended as a substitute. Unlocked fell huts along many of the trails are available for anyone to use, while for the locked huts, keys are obtainable in advance from local tourist centres. Predictably, sailing and boardsailing are popular activities in Finland. With navigable distances of up to 300 km/186 miles, the chain of lakes at **Saimaa** is a popular area for watersports, but a good deal of pleasure can be had from the smaller lakes and lake systems. Canoeing possibilities are endless, from the coastal waters dotted with thousands of islands, to rivers flowing down to the sea, to the lakes of the Great Saimaa region, to the rivers in the wilds of eastern and northern Finland. Since the country is relatively flat, cycling is a popular way of travelling. You can hire bikes, and there are a number of recommended tours and routes, most of which follow old country roads in the main, although more major road stretches are included. If you take these routes you can stay in Youth Hostels, camp sites or guest houses. All the camp sites are close to water and most are well equipped. The camping season starts in late May and ends in September, although some sites stay open all the year round. For the independent adventure traveller in Finland this is a wonderful way of seeing the country.

As for winter sports, 'Finns are born with skis on' the saying goes and opportunities for cross-country skiing during the season are too numerous to detail here. There are marked trails all around the country, heading out from settlements over the low and gently-sloping fells. Ski tours cover daily distances of 25–45 km/15–30 miles over an eight-hour day and tours are available both for novices and for experienced skiiers. Some tours visit Lapp villages and stay overnight with the local people. One adventure almost unique to Finland is a reindeer safari, in which the strongest beasts of the herd are selected, trained and harnessed to pull visitors gently along in a sleigh. These safaris last anything from a day up to a week. You can even sit a reindeer driving test – successful candidates are given a reindeer driver's licence!

Waymark Holidays (44 Windsor Road, Slough SL1 2EJ, tel: 01753 516477) offers 7 and 10 night cross-country, chalet-based skiing trips at Akaslompolo in Lapland, 200 km/125 miles north of the Arctic Circle. These are Grade 2 and 3 trips, available from November to April for around £1000. One local operator offering a wide range of adventure trips (dog sledging, ski touring, canoeing, rafting, even reindeer safaris) is **Lapland Travel Ltd (Maakuntakatu 10, SF-96100 Rovaniemi; tel: 60 16052)**.

Ramblers Holidays (PO Box 43, Welwyn Garden, Hertfordshire AL8 6PQ; tel: 01707 331133) offers a two-week half-board **Finland and St Petersburg** soft adventure. The trip starts in Helsinki from where you take the train across southern Finland to Joensuu and continue by road to Koli in North Karelia. You stay here for four nights, giving you a chance to explore the park and the lake. Travelling south by road from Koli to Savonlinna, you enter the heart of Finnish Lakeland. Again you stay for four nights, which gives you the chance to go walking, canoeing or relaxing. Continuing south by road you travel to Kouvola from where you join the train to St Petersburg. After spending another four nights here, you fly back to London. Departures are in June, July and August and the tour charge is just under £1000. Accommodation is in unpretentious hotels.

FACTFILE

Sailing: Further information is available from the **Finnish Yachting Association, Radiokatu 20, 00240 Helsinki; tel: 9 0 1581**.

Canoeing: Further information is available from the **Finnish Canoe Association, Radiokatu 20, 00240 Helsinki; tel: 9 0 158 2363**.

Language: Almost all Finns speak English; most speak it very well indeed.

THE GAMBIA –
SMILE ON THE FACE OF WEST AFRICA

'Twelve months had passed, and with the big rains ended once again, The Gambia's season for travellers had begun.'
Alex Haley, Roots

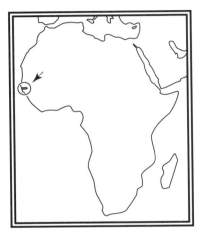

Small but perfectly formed, The Gambia is one of Africa's tiniest countries, a 480 km/300-mile ribbon of river bounded by strips of mangrove, tropical forest and bamboo. Never more than 24 km/15 miles from each bank, the country's border is entirely surrounded by Senegal, save for a 64 km/40 mile coastline strip. Early in the 19th century, Mungo Park, the great British explorer, set out from a place called **Karantba Tenda** in the west of The Gambia to trace the source of the Niger. Since then the country has shared a long association with Britain, which includes its reputation as the oldest English-speaking Commonwealth country in West Africa. It has enjoyed a high degree of stability since independence in 1970, and is the only former British West Africa territory not to have experienced a successful military coup. Now, despite recent political uncertainties, it is generally regarded as the most stable country in West Africa, if not in the whole continent.

From small beginnings in 1965, tourism has grown steadily. The country's pleasant equatorial climate (70–80°F in winter, 80–90°F in summer) and flat terrain make it a location primarily for visitors in search of soft adventure. When you combine its affordability (half the price of the Caribbean), its proximity to Europe, virtually guaranteed sunshine and abundant birdlife, you can see why The Gambia makes an ideal winter destination for a less strenuous adventure holiday for UK travellers (from 0° to 70° in under six hours from Britain). Coastal activities are plentiful, from surfing to windsurfing. Its beaches are long and wide, soft and sandy, while the sea is like vintage champagne, foamed by the force of great Atlantic rollers.

If you are unfamiliar with the African continent then The

Gambia is an ideal place on which to cut your teeth as an independent traveller. By shunning 'touristy' activities and experiencing the 'real' Gambia, you soon come to know and love the adventurous magic of the place: uncertain driving on equally uncertain roads with no direction signs; early morning beach trips to watch the 'pirogue' boats bringing in their catch; learning to live with erratic electricity and water supplies; absence of TV (The Gambia has no broadcasting stations); no delivery of UK newspapers or magazines; the list goes on and on . . .

A good way to start to experience the real Gambia is by travelling through the country itself. Taking public transport (bush taxis or buses) is an excellent way to break out from the coast's cosseted comfort to bushwhack into the interior – a dusty plain with baobabs, silk cotton trees, figs and acacia thorn. Squeezing into a crowded minibus and heading up country can be an adventure in itself, never mind reaching your destination. But if you would rather be left to your own devices, then pedal power is the environmentally friendly solution to getting about. And if you get tired of cycling, a number of local tour operators offer adventurous trips off the trammelled track. Their open-topped Landrovers can take you into less accessible parts of the country to see village life: the construction of buildings or the preparation of food.

If water transport up the **river Gambia** (West Africa's longest river, also considered to be a sign of fertility) is more appealing, you can take a two-day cruise upstream in a small boat under sail (wind permitting). There is a good chance of seeing dolphins in the estuary, as well as superb bird life, and there is also the opportunity of a refreshing swim in the river (crocodiles permitting!). With its numerous creeks, or *bolongs*, the whole river system provides an ideal habitat for The Gambia's rich bounty of bird life. Of around a thousand species known to occur in the West African continent, nearly 600 have been recorded here. Its plethora of exotic species with equally exotic names, such as the Green Crested Touraco or the Long Crested Helmet Shrike, makes this country a great destination both for the experienced birdwatcher and the amateur.

Only twelve miles from the capital, Banjul, lies **Abuko**, The Gambia's principal wildlife area. Neither a zoo nor a game reserve, it is a tiny jungle in the middle of a savanna, whose small size (100 hectares/250 acres) belies the rich flora and fauna present. In 1977, the President of The Gambia, Sir Kairaba Jawara, solemnly declared, 'My Government pledges its untiring efforts to conserve for now and posterity as wide a spectrum as possible of our remaining fauna and flora.' The so-called 'Banjul Declaration' appears to have been honoured since then: indeed,

David Attenborough himself described this area as 'a living jewel in the sun'. Certainly, its roll-call of reptiles, animals and birds (over 200 species are found here) is a haven for the wildlife enthusiast. Try taking a leisurely hike through the leafy pathways to absorb the spirit of the place.

About 160 km/100 miles east of Banjul by road or river lies the peaceful **Tendamba Camp**, not tented but with traditional huts. Campfires are lit each night and sometimes locals perform African music and dance. Other wildlife attractions include **Baboon Islands National Park**, another newly created wildlife sanctuary.

One of the best operators offering trips to The Gambia is called, simply, **The Gambia Experience (Kingfisher House, Rownhams Lane, North Baddesley, Hampshire SO52 9LP; tel: 01703 730888)**. This company caters for all tastes, from backpackers to hotel holidays to new villages at prices ranging from around £500 for 7 days including return flights from the UK, board and lodging, to around £1000 for 14 days. Tailor-made packages are available for specific itineraries, including adventure cruises, birdwatching trips, or Landrover adventures. **The Gambia Expedition Co Ltd, Box 378, Serre Kunda, The Gambia**, offers a selection of well planned, adventurous excursions, from short trips up to two days or longer. Another Gambia-based company, **Crocodile Safaris (tel: 96068** – despite utilities often malfunctioning, The Gambia's phone system is surprisingly reliable), offers birdwatching and safari trips, with knowledgeable local guides at reasonable costs.

FACTFILE

When to go: All year round. Avoiding the British and American winter can be a good idea.

Travel tips: Seek advice on the various inoculations and anti-malarial measures.

GREENLAND – WORLD'S LARGEST ISLAND

At rejse er at leve ('To travel is to live')
Greenland saying

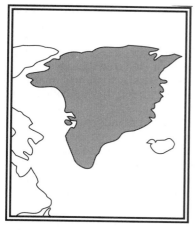

If you count Australia as a continent, Greenland is the world's largest island. Few places in the northern hemisphere can match its awe-inspiring grandeur, its timeless scenery and its unspoilt wilderness. It is a place of superlative proportions: thirteen times the size of the British Isles, yet with only a thousandth of the population. When it's light here, you can gaze in wonder at the world's second largest icecap (Antarctica has the largest) but summers are short and the silent, frozen winter world reigns without interruption for much of the year.

Unlike the Scandinavian Arctic region, which is warmed by the Gulf Stream, here there is no benign current to influence the weather. In fact the coastal waters are cooled by the icy Greenland current and the air is cooled by the inland icecap which is up to three kilometres thick in places. The coastal margin surrounding the icecap is rugged and mountainous, some 39 500 km/24 500 miles long and deeply indented. In fact the world's largest fjord, **Scoresby Sound**, is here. Greenland's highest mountains, **Gunnbjorns Fjeld** and **Mount Forel** (both on the east coast), rise to around 3400 m/11 100 ft and 3200 m/10 500 ft respectively. In western Greenland, the highest peak is the 2000 m/6500 ft **Mount Atter**.

Though still in the grip of the Ice Age, in general the climate is very variable. Most precipitation falls as snow on the coastal fringes and winters can be severe, particularly in the north. But summers can feel surprisingly warm as well, for although temperatures range between only 5°C and 10°C, the dry atmosphere and the sun's rays and reflections from the ice are powerful, causing sunburn if you are not careful. How cold you feel depends on what kind of adventure you're up to: if it's trekking or ski-touring then your exertions will tend to heat you up, whereas if it's dog-sledging, the rushing air and less active mode of travel will tend to cool you down (dog-sledging trips in spring can experience temperatures as low as −27°C, sometimes lower). Often, the visibility is very good and on a good day the clear Arctic air makes for spectacular views of as far as 200 km/77 miles or more.

Although effectively under Danish rule since the 14th century, Greenland has recently become a semi-independent nation, known as 'Kalaalit Nunaat' – the Land of the People. In all, there are around 60 000 people living in Greenland, mostly on the west coast, consisting mainly of Inuit groups with some Europeans (principally Danes). **Nuuk** is the country's capital and largest settlement, with a population of 12 000. The Greenland language is fascinatingly unlike any other – for a single Greenland word can sometimes express what would take a whole sentence in other languages. No roads exist, most transport being by sea, skidoo or air (helicopters and Dash-7 aircraft).

The best time to embark on a Greenland adventure is from mid-June through to the end of August, although dog sledging trips are best taken during March to May. Dog-sledging is a way of life for many of Greenland's permanent east coast residents, and many opportunities exist for the adventure visitor to try his or her hand at driving a team. Although best done in spring, dog sledging can be done all the year round, for example on Disko Island. Sledges are not identical throughout the country, but vary according to where you are. In the southern part of the country, snows clear during the summer months, making hiking and backpacking possible. Although there are no official campsites, there are cabins and sheep crofts available for accommodation (or you can pitch camp almost anywhere except sheep-farmers' fields). Guides are available to show you the best routes. Whale-watching trips set off from the south, too. Many different species inhabit the rich feeding areas around Greenland, including fin-whales, minke whales, blue whales, humpback whales, narwhal, beluga, sperm and pilot. During an all-day trip it is not unusual to see three or four different species. As you might expect, ski touring opportunities are plentiful, though you have to be self-contained and trips need to be well-planned and preferably accompanied by a guide.

Unless you are an experienced adventurer, it is better that you stick with a company, travelling with the experts. As the Greenland tourist information rightly states, 'Greenland's parliament has openly expressed that romantic amateurs are not welcome to go on expeditions. Rescue operations cost the Greenland society and the Danish Government far too much.' **Arctic Experience** offers a number of trips to Greenland, including a 6- or 10-night Husky Sledge Adventure (inclusive prices £1200 to £2300). **Arcturus Expeditions (PO Box 850, Gartocharn, Alexandria, Dunbar-**

tonshire G83 8RL; tel: 01389 830204) runs a number of trips to Greenland. Their unique, 23-day '**Peary Land Expedition**' in northern Greenland costs around £4700 (maximum group size 8), but there are more affordable camping/hiking trips to **Mesters Vig** in the northeast (18 days, £2000) and **Qaanaaq** in the northwest (18 days, £2500). They run a skiing expedition to northeast Greenland (18 days, £2100) and a sea kayaking trip to the eastern Fjords (17 days, £2000).

Between June and September, **Aurora Expeditions (13 Horsely Wood Cottages, Horsley, Northumberland NE15 0NR; tel: 01661 853814)** run 17-day self-contained trips to the remote **Angmagssalik Region** of southeastern Greenland ('one of the least spoilt and most beautiful areas in the world'). These are adventurous backpacking treks in which you carry equipment and provisions. All-inclusive cost is around £2000. On day 1 you fly from Heathrow to Keflavik (Iceland) and overnight in Reykjavik. Day 2 sees you flying to Kulusuk, overnighting in a guesthouse. From here you start the real adventure, travelling by boat to the head of Tasilaq Fjord and walking two or three miles to Camp One. The next two days are spent walking 10 miles a day up Tasiaq valley and over to Sermilik fjord. Days 6 to 8 involve coastal walking to Iliverna valley. The longest walk is on day 9 (13 miles) to the head of Ikasaulaq Fjord. Days 10 and 11 involve walking to camp nine at the settlement of Tiniteqilaq. On the afternoon of day 12 you take a boat down through Sermilik fjord, passing icebergs, to Pupik, on the west coast of Angmagssalik Island. The next two days are spent walking across the island to the settlement of Angmagssalik itself. After a day unwinding here, you transfer by boat to Kulusuk and finally back to the UK via Iceland. Group size is from 8 to 15. You will need a sleeping bag, suitable footwear, weatherproof clothing and rucksack. Aurora provides the tents and other camping equipment.

FACTFILE

Delays: Unpredictable weather can cause delays and interruptions to transport services to and from the country. If travelling independently, you should take sufficient funds to meet this eventuality.

Dog sledges: The dogs may look cute, but they're not pets. Pat them at your peril. In Greenland's snow-way code, dog sledges have right of way.

Photography: As with all Arctic photography, use skylight or UV filters and a lens hood, and take plenty of film.

ICELAND – LAND OF ICE AND FIRE

'I saw deep valleys meeting one another in all directions, precipices dug out like wells, lakes appearing as ponds, and rivers as streams. On my right was a succession of innumerable glaciers and a forest of peaks, some of which were crested with faint smoke-wreaths. The undulations of this infinite series of mountains, with their foamlike patches of snow, reminded me of the surface of a stormy sea.'

Jules Verne, Journey to the Centre of the Earth

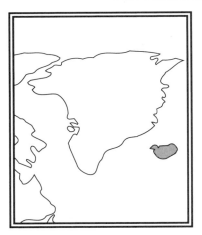

To call Iceland a 'land of ice' is only half the story: fire is the other element which characterizes this extraordinary Arctic land. It is a young country, still in the process of being formed. A tenth of its land mass is made up of lava and there are at least 200 volcanoes, of which more than 30 have erupted at some time during the last 1100 years. This geothermal activity in turn has led to the creation of geysers and hot springs: indeed, one of Iceland's claims to fame is its boast of more hot springs than any other country in the world. And yet, side by side with this land of fire, is an abundance of frozen water, mostly found in the south. Glaciers cover almost an eighth of the land surface and these massive icecaps are the largest outside Antarctica and Greenland. In places, deeply-crevassed glaciers sweep down from these ice features, sometimes reaching sea level. This combination of ice and fire makes for plenty of rivers, but with their swift currents and waterfalls, none is regarded as generally navigable. Taken together, it is this extraordinary contrast of elements and their associated landscapes which gives rise to plentiful adventure opportunities within the country.

Thanks to the Gulf Stream, Iceland's climate is surprisingly benign: coolish in summer but often mild in winter. Average temperatures in summer are 11°C to 15°C in the lowlands, while winter temperatures are not as cold as those of, for instance, New York or Vienna. The best months of the year for summer travelling are mid-June to early September, the midnight sun making 24-hour days throughout June and July. Much of the country has a rugged, at times even bleak, appearance: only a quarter of its land surface has continuous plant cover and only 1% is forested. But during the short Arctic spring and summer there is a frenzied activity of growth, with Arctic and Alpine flowers thriving in seemingly barren landscapes. Winter also gives rise to snow-based adventures, so the country is adventure-friendly throughout the whole year.

The area can be divided into a number of regions: the Western Peninsula, the Western Fjords, the North, the Interior, the East, the South and the Southwest. The varied landscapes and geological formations of **Western Iceland** make this area of particular interest to hikers and riders (Icelandic ponies are renowned for being hardy and footsure) while **Snaefellsnes Glacier**, towering over the area, provides plentiful adventures of an icy kind. One of the first parts of Iceland to be colonized (by Celts and Scandinavians), this region is often mentioned in the historic 'Sagas'. Just to the north lie the rugged and precipitous **Western Fjords**, with their steep cliffs and deep fjords. It's a roughhewn and remote landscape, this; of particular interest to walkers, where often the next farm is some days' hike away. Largest of all the precipices in this region is **Latrabjarg**, 30 km/19 miles long, 444 m/1457 ft high and less than 300 km/186 miles from Greenland: the most westerly point in Europe. You can take an organized walking/wildlife tour from the main settlement, Isafjorour, with good chances of seeing Arctic foxes, seals, eider ducks and a host of other birds.

Paradoxically, the **North** has higher temperatures in midsummer than the south and yet its climate also shows more extremes. This usually means more snow in the winter and thus ideal conditions for ski enthusiasts. The coastal scenery of this part of Iceland comprises broad fjords separated by towering mountains. In early summer you can sometimes see ice floes and icebergs which have drifted southwest from Greenland. Though rare, reports of polar bear passengers on these bergs are not unknown. Here is the young Iceland: volcanoes, earth tremors, hot springs and mud pools are plentiful in this geologist's (and vulcanologist's) paradise. This is also ideal horse country, and pony trekking opportunities are plentiful. You can take a trip from as short as one hour to as long as seven days or more. Many farms offer accommodation for independent travellers in this region.

A real magnet-pull to Iceland's adventure seekers is the **Interior**, for here the remoteness and solitude of this uninhabited part of the island are at their most pronounced. The terrain is rugged, even desolate, tracks are often rough, and rivers are unbridged. Independent trips into the Interior have to be well planned and it's best to seek the services of an experienced local guide before hiking, skiing or generally venturing forth here. Just north of the Myrdalsjokull glacier are the hot springs of **Landmannalaugar**, where you can camp or sleep in one of the mountain huts. Trips can be made to see the stone arch over the waterfall at **Eldgja** – the world's largest volcanic fissure – or to see the world's largest lava desert at **Odaoahraun**. Even in the summer you can go skiing in the Interior, at the **Kerlingarfjoll mountains**.

Eastern Iceland is an area of mountains and deep fjords but little volcanic activity. Today, many visitors arrive here from the Shetland Islands or the Faroes and indeed this is the part of Iceland nearest Norway, where settlers first landed from Scandinavia and Ireland in the 9th century. **Skaftafell National Park** is found here, as is Iceland's highest mountain, **Oraefajokull**, a volcano which towers over its surrounding mantle of glacier.

Ice and fire are omnipresent in **South** Iceland; glaciers, lava fields, hot springs and black volcanic sands attracting adventure travellers here. Horse-based adventures are also plentiful in the south and a good starting point for treks is the settlement of **Laugarvatn**. Gullfoss waterfall on the **Hvita river** is an impressive sight, as is **Mount Hekla**, one of the world's most infamous volcanoes, which has erupted three times during the recent past. One sight not to be missed is the vast glacier of **Vatnajokull** which covers an area larger than all the other glaciers in Europe put together. There are camping opportunities in **Skaftafell National Park**, with access to hiking trails, all with the impressive backdrop of Vatnajokull glacier. The **Myrdal** area has further good hiking and pony trekking opportunities, while nearby **Myrdalsjokull** glacier offers hiking and skiing trips. This southern part of Iceland is also the site of the Althing, Iceland's ancient parliament. **Southwest** Iceland has a rugged, moonscape feel about it, with its huge lava fields and complete absence of trees, rivers and valleys. There is plenty of volcanic activity here, though, with a large number of steam-spouting fissures.

Many tour operators include Iceland within their lists. **Arctic Experience** is one of the best, offering no fewer than 14 tours, ranging from a weekend break at £400 to '**Wild Iceland**' (11 nights, up to £1300) to the '**Great Iceland Odyssey**' (14 nights, up to £2100). Arctic Experience's '**Iceland Odyssey**' (14 nights, £1800) focuses on walking in the country's most spectacular areas, while a range of other action tours is also available. Associated with Arctic Experience, **David Oswin Expeditions (Millgarth, Kirklinton, Carlisle, Cumbria CA6 6DW; tel: 01228 75518)** offers a 12-day walking adventure, price £1100, while **Dick Phillips (Whitehall House, Nenthead, Alston, Cumbria CA9 3PS; tel: 01434 381440)** organizes 2- to 3-week walking tours ('we still have parties who walk for ten days without seeing another person') in the south or northwest, for around £700. For horse-based trips, a well known local operator is **Saga Hestar (Saga Horses) (Nordurgardi 10, 860 Hvolsvelli, Iceland; tel: 354 8 78138)**.

Arctic Experience's '**Ice and Fire Exploration Trek**' is a backpacking expedition 'for those who are not deterred by prolonged physical challenge'. This trip makes high demands on participants (usually much fewer than 15), both physically and psychologically. The terrain is rugged and unmarked by footpaths for practically the whole trek; there are numerous glacial rivers to ford and a testing glacier to cross. So wild and remote is the route that during the 10-day expedition you are unlikely to encounter any other walkers. But the rewards are high indeed and the scenery is unrivalled. On day 1 you fly to Keflavik, transfer to Reykjavik and overnight in a guesthouse. A drive on day 2 takes you to Eldgja, a huge volcanic fissure, where the trek proper starts. On day 3 you follow the fissure inland towards the icecap. An ascent of the Fogrufjoll ridge and crossing of the powerful Skafta river takes place on day 4. After camping by Skafta glacier you trek to the Laki Craters, scene of the cataclysmic 1783 eruptions. A roped river crossing is necessary on day 6 prior to camping at Raudholar (Red Hills). One more major river crossing – the Djupa river – is required on day 7. The next day includes some superb views over the icecap to Iceland's highest summit. Two nights camping at Nupsa Valley are followed by a hike in the Nupsa Canyons. On day 10 you climb Sulutindar, camping at Graenalon, a large glacial lake. Day 11 is spent crossing the icecap just above Skeidarajokull, with impressive views of the outwash plains below, before camping in Nordurdalur at the edge of Skaftafell National Park. Day 12 involves local exploration and bathing in hot springs, whilst the following two days involve returning to Reykjavik and then home. This adventure of a lifetime costs only around £1200, all-inclusive, although you will need certain camping equipment and clothing.

FACTFILE

Arrival: Virtually all visitors arrive either by air from Europe or North America at Keflavik International Airport near Reykjavik, or by ferry from Europe at Seydisfjordur in the East.

Climate: This is notoriously unpredictable: as they say, 'Iceland doesn't have a climate – only weather.' Be prepared for a variety of conditions. The Northern Lights are often visible as early as September.

INDIA – ADVENTURE ROMANCE

'The land of dreams and romance. A country that all desire to see, and having once seen, by even a glimpse, would not give that glimpse for the shows of all the rest of the globe combined.'

Mark Twain

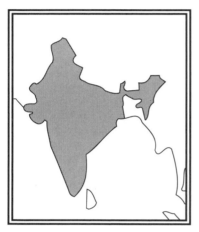

Kipling once remarked, 'Some people say that there is no romance in India. Those people are wrong. Our lives hold quite as much romance as is good for us. Sometimes more.' Those travelling in India quickly discover the special romantic attraction that the country exerts, an attraction woven from many strands: the country's long and rich history, its diverse cultures and religions, its spellbinding landscapes and scenery and its magnificent wildlife. The country's beauty is especially rich and varied, from dramatic Himalayan peaks to dusty Rajasthani deserts. And although most adventure travellers are drawn to Himalayan trekking trips, plenty of other activities are there to be experienced, like white-water rafting, wildlife safaris, airsports, mountaineering and coastal watersports. For a winter adventure with a difference, you can even try skiing in the Himalayas. All these things and more add to the compelling allure of 'Indian romance'.

Most adventure travellers in India start with some form of trekking holiday. In many ways, India is an ideal destination for this activity, with its mist-wreathed Western Ghats, the blue tranquillity of its Nilgiri Hills and its spectacular northern and eastern Himalayas. The latter stretch 3500 km/2200 miles along India's northern and eastern frontiers, the world's highest mountain range. Occupying a fair slice of their range is **Jammu and Kashmir** – the most northerly of India's 25 provinces. This is a 'trekker's mecca' – a memorable place of snowy peaks, evergreen forests, flower meadows, wild orchards and clear streams. Srinagar, the capital, is the starting point for many of these treks, notably to the **Zabarwan and Shankaracharya Hills**, while two other popular trekking stations are found at Pahlagam and Gulmarg. Srinagar is also the roadhead for trips into the arid plateau of **Ladakh**. This area has some of the largest glaciers in the world outside the polar regions. Its divisional capital, Leh – which lies on the fabled **Silk Route** – is a gathering place for many independent and group trips to this region.

Immediately south of Jammu and Kashmir lies the small province of **Himachal Pradesh**. Its landscapes vary from raging torrents and barren rocky valleys in the north, to gentler orchard groves in the south. Starting from Manali, you can trek to Bara Shigri glacier or over the Baralacha to Leh. Or you could start at Kullu, in the centre of the province, traversing paddy fields and heading up to the snowy peaks nearby (particularly spectacular are the views from the Rohtang Pass). Legacies of the days of the British Empire are found in a clutch of hill stations where officers and their wives would escape the hot and dusty summers down on the Indian plains. These hill stations include Dalhousie (treks to the glacial lake of Khajjiar are rewarding) and Simla (a base for treks into Kullu Valley via the Jalori Pass).

Southeast of Himachal Pradesh, in the province of **Uttar Pradesh**, lies a region known as the **Uttarakhand**. Set high up in the **Garhwal** area of the Himalayas, this area abounds in legends of the Indian gods. Of interest to visiting adventurers is its reputation as the source of many of India's great northern rivers, most notably the Ganges. Mussoorie, another British summer hill-station, is a good base for treks into the Gangotri and Yamounotri valleys, while Rishikesh, situated just north of the sacred city of Hardwar, is the base for treks to Badrinath, via the arrestingly beautiful **Valley of Flowers** (at its best in August). Another trekking magnet in Uttar Pradesh is the region of **Kumaon**. The town of Almora is an ideal base for treks into the region's pine and rhododendron forests, while Nanital, another hill-station, is a charming starting point for shorter treks among the region's orchards and forests. With magnificent views of the central Himalayas, Ranikhet is a good base for treks to **Kausani** which has a view so legendary that it was reputed to have inspired Mahatma Gandhi in his writings.

Wedged between Nepal on the west and Bhutan on the east lies the tiny area of **Sikkim** and **Darjeeling**. This region, dominated by the five summits of the mighty Kanchenjunga, is also a place of gentler hills, valleys, lakes and streams, offering wonderful opportunities for casual and serious trekkers alike. Darjeeling – once home to Everest climber Tenzing Norgay and now home to the **Himalayan Mountaineering Institute** – is also the starting point for low and high altitude treks. From here, good destinations include

Tiger Hill (breathtaking views of the Himalayas), and surrounding peaks (Phalut, Sandakphu, Singalia and Tanglu).

Although most people have heard of the Himalayas, fewer know about the **Western Ghats** – a mountain range running perpendicular to their sister Himalayas. The Western Ghats stretch a third of the length of the country, northwards from the southernmost tip of India. Not so imposing as their more famous Asian counterparts, the Western Ghats are, however, beautiful in their own right – lush, thickly forested and intimate. The hill station of Mahabaleshwar in the north of the range (Maharashtra province) is an ideal base for trekkers, as are Lonavala, Khandala, Matheran and Bhor Ghat.

Worlds apart from the Himalayas lie the **Nilgiri** range: friendlier and gentler terrain altogether. With its easier trekking conditions and climate, this area (sometimes called the 'Blue Mountains' because of their lilac hue) is a good introduction for first-time trekkers in India. Nilgiris has three main trekking centres: Kotagiri, Ootacamund (treks to Wenlock Downs, Kalahatti Falls and Munumali Game Sanctuary) and Coonor (treks to Drogg's Peak and Lamb's Rock).

Trekking is not the only adventure activity for which India is well known. White-water rafting is becoming increasingly popular. The most popular waters for river running are, in **Jammu and Kashmir**, the Zanskar (grade III); Indus (II–III); Chenab (IV–V); and Lidder (III–IV); in **Himachal Pradesh**, the Beas (III–IV) and Sutlej (IV–V); in **Uttar Pradesh**, the Ganga (III–IV); Bhagirathi (IV); Alaknanda (III–IV); Tons (IV–V); and Sarda (III–IV); and in **Sikkim**, the Teesta (IV) and Rangit (III–IV). (For an explanation of grading, see p 80.) Rafting options vary from half-day scenic runs for amateurs on low waters, to six-day challenging rafting expeditions. These expeditions are organized by well trained professional Indian teams and the country is justly proud of its reputation as the 'rafting capital of the east'.

In addition to trekking and rafting, India has plenty of other adventure opportunities. From small beginnings, skiing is becoming more widespread in parts of the Himalayas: for instance **Gulmarg** is a good place for cross-country skiing and ski mountaineering. Riding is a popular activity, especially around the hill-station region of northern India. Adventure airsports such as hang-gliding, paragliding and ballooning are all available. Formed in 1970, the **Balloon Club of India** is located at New Delhi's Safdarjung and has a thriving membership. Hang-gliding is a relatively new activity in India but there are already clubs in several areas. Noteworthy spots for this activity are the Srinagar Valley in **Jammu and Kashmir**, Billing, Kangra, Dharamsala, Shimla and Kasuli in **Himachal Pradesh**; and the Nilgiri Hills in

Tamil Nadu. If underwater activities are more to your liking, the **Andaman Islands** in the Bay of Bengal, have a good reputation for Scuba diving. Or for an adventure with a difference, how about a camel train safari in **Thar Desert?** Camel safari options vary from 4 to 15 days, the best areas being in the heart of the Thar, around Jodhpur, Jaisalmer and Bikaner. Some of these trips take you well away from civilization and you'll find yourself camping under the stars and living very simply. Shorter, one- or two-day 'Taster' camel safaris are also available. Rock climbing is an almost year-round activity in India. Opportunities are too widespread to list here, but some highlights to mention are the 3600–4300 m/12 000–14 000 ft rock needles of Manikaran and the impressive mountain ranges across Rohtang Pass. For mountaineering proper, permission must be obtained from the **Indian Mountaineering Federation** (see Factfile).

Another of India's major adventure attractions is its plethora of wildlife sanctuaries, which harbour over 1200 species of birds and over 350 species of mammals (including the very endangered rhino, Asiatic lion, Asiatic elephant and tiger).

One of the most comprehensive Indian adventure portfolios available is offered by **Mysteries of India** (motto – 'for the independent traveller'), trading as **Pleasureseekers Ltd (92 The Green, Southall, Middlesex UB2 4BG; tel: 0181 574 2727).** They list a variety of mountain trekking, desert walking, camel safari, wildlife safari and river rafting trips, varying in price from a few hundred pounds up to around £1500.

High Places offers several adventure trips in India. For example, their **South India** trip consists of an 18-day varied journey through the Kerala region, hiking, biking and boating. After flying to Bombay on day 1, you fly to the spice capital of India – Cochin – a town surrounded by numerous islands and peninsulas. After acclimatizing here on day 3, you spend some days hiking amongst the tea estates in the Cardamom Hills and, if you're lucky, you might be rewarded by the spectacle of wild elephants. The hike includes an ascent of Ainimundi, the highest peak in southern India at 2694 m/8836 ft. Travelling south, you stay at the Periyar wildlife reserve, where tiger, elephant, bison, deer, fish eagles and many kingfishers all have their homes. Back towards the coast you take a colourful two-day boat ride (days 9 and 10) through the palm-fringed backwaters and lagoons around Kerala. After two days of cultural awareness around Ashram, you pick up your bikes (normal Indian bikes) and spend around 5 hours each day for two days pedalling along the flat lanes around this region. Friendly encounters with the locals are plentiful. Finally, you reach what High Places regards as the best beaches in India, to mellow out, or indulge in a little watersports activities. On day 17 you return to

Bombay and the adventure ends with your return flight on day 18. Accommodation is in comfortable hotels, guest houses and rest houses. The total cost is around £1600 and departures are from November to February. If harder adventure is more in your line, ask to see High Places' more physically challenging Indian trips.

FACTFILE

Climate: Varies greatly depending on where you are. In general, the rainy season lasts from June to August. Trekking is usually best from April to June and from September to November.

Trekking: There is no system of issuing trekking permits, but certain Restricted and Protected Areas are out-of-bounds unless you have the correct documentation (contact the Government of India Tourist Office before departure, or local Tourist Offices once you arrive).

Mountaineering: The Indian Mountaineering Foundation can be contacted at **Anand Niketan, Beneto Juarez Road, New Delhi 110 021**.

Ecotourism: Tourism Concern (see p 34) issues a Himalayan Tourist Code highlighting cultural and environmental responsibilities (see Appendix 2). In summary, the latter reads 'Limit deforestation – make no open fires; remove litter – burn or bury paper; keep local water clean – avoid using pollutants; plants should be left to flourish in their natural environment; help your guides and porters to follow conservation measures.'

INDONESIA – ARCHIPELAGO OF THE GODS

'The massive bulk of the cone seemed interminable: two steps up, one step back in the soft ash. An imminent dawn gradually awoke with the deepest violet. I stood on the highest point in Java, and the island emerged from the night and stretched out under the first rays. The Indian Ocean lay to the south, volcanic pinnacles piercing the ethereal cloud below. And Semeru was just one of the many to be climbed.'

Julian Ross, 'Volcanic Cycle', The Adventurers Magazine

Stretching along the equator, between the Australian and Asian continental mainlands, lies Indonesia. This country is the world's largest archipelago, a fascinating collection of more than 17 000 islands, adding up to over two million square kilometres/770 000 square miles. The cultures, colours and vitality of these islands are compelling, as are their landscapes. On some of them there is a very high population density, while others are deserted. The names of the Indonesian islands – names like Java, Sumatra, Sulawesi, Irian Jaya, Bali and Lombok – have a magical evocation all of their own, luring adventure travellers of all kinds to this extraordinary stretch of the globe.

Java contains 75% of Indonesia's population, most of whom live in Jakarta, the capital. This is the main arrival point for adventure travellers, although before heading off the beaten track, you should try not to miss **Borobodur**, probably the largest Buddhist sanctuary in the world, with its five kilometres of relief carvings. In the east of Java, **Mount Bromo** is still very active and you can make a trek by horse to the edge of its crater from Surabaya nearby. **Mount Semeru** (3676 m/12 057 ft) is just one of several challenging climbs for independent adventure travellers in Java.

Often called 'Orchid Island', **Sulawesi** is a place of high volcanic mountains, misty valleys, plentiful lakes and sandy beaches. Offshore, there are some superb and still-untouched coral-fringed islets, among the least visited in Indonesia, while **Bunaken Island** is a good place for snorkelling and scuba diving, with a spectacular drop-off. **Bantimurung Nature Reserve** lies in the south, home to countless exotic tropical butterflies. As with the rest of Indonesia, this place lies on an area of volcanic activity and there are numerous geysers and hot springs, including Karumengan, Lahendong, Kinilow and Leilem. National Parks and nature reserves on Sulawesi include **Tangkoko Batuangus** (grassland hills and valleys, home to black apes) and **Dumoga Bone** (dense forest with a rich flora). **Goa Mampu** is a legendary cave, with fantastical stalactites and rock formations, as well as a large resident bat population.

Sumatra is Indonesia's second-largest island, an equatorial adventure-land with volcanoes (in the Bukit Barasin range of mountains) hot springs, sandy beaches and lush jungle, much of it inaccessible. Several nature reserves have been established here to protect Sumatra's rare and sometimes unique flora and fauna. Organized safaris are available at **Mount Loeser Reserve** (a sanctuary for orang-utans), **Bengkulu** and **Gedung Wani**, enabling visitors to see such species as tigers, elephants, tapirs, orang-utans and rhinos. Most famous of Sumatra's many lakes is **Toba**, 852 sq km/329 square miles in extent, once a volcano but now a flooded crater with an inhabited island called Samosir, at its centre. Reached by a half-hour boat ride, Samosir has rest houses for wanderers who want to stay for a while. Located in Sumatra's wilderness interior south of Mount Loeser, **Bohorok** is a good place for adventures, with its tropical habitats and rugged terrain. In the west of Sumatra lies a beautiful spectacle – **Ngarai Sianok**, a canyon 150 m/490 ft high, its thin winding river surrounded on both sides by a lush green valley. Among the tropical greenery of the **Anai Valley Nature Reserve** runs the crystal water of the river Anai, with an impressive waterfall 40 m/130 ft high. For watersports, **Lake Sinkarak**, longest in Sumatra, has much to offer. Its surrounding area is good for hiking and camping, as is the **Solok–Diatas–Dibawah** lakes region, with its cool mountain air and beautiful landscapes. Cave enthusiasts will be attracted to the coolness of the **Ngalau Indah Caves**, home to thousands of resident bats. Off the coast of Sumatra, the group of four **Mentawai Islands** is a Nature Reserve, with untouched forests and rare monkeys and other animals not found anywhere else.

The area of **Eastern Indonesia** – made up of almost 14 000 islands – contains limitless opportunities for adventure travellers. Its **Moluccan** or **Maluku Archipelago** comprises around a thousand islands, mostly deserted. Those that are inhabited are so isolated from each other that they have developed unique languages and culture. With its reputation as a source of nutmeg, **Banda Island**, in the middle of the Banda Sea, is often regarded as the original 'Spice Island'. The other sub-region of Eastern Indonesia is the remote **Nusa Tengarra Archipelago**. Here, Timor Island is currently out-of-bounds for tourists because of political factional fighting, but north of Timor lies a remote string of more peaceful but fairly inaccessible islands such as **Solor, Lembata, Adonara, Alor, Wetar** and **Pantar**. Rarely visited by tourists, there are many old fortresses on these islands, whence seafarers used to make whaling trips. Elsewhere here, the island peoples of **Roti, Ndau** and **Sawu** have changed little since prehistoric times. 'Tropical paradise' islands abound in this area; for example the **Terawangen Islands, Lucipara, Kangean, Tenggaya, Bone Rate** and **Tukang Besi**. The extraordinary western part of the island of New Guinea, **Irian Jaya**, is one of the last great unexplored areas of the world. Even today, visiting ships are often greeted with flotillas of warriors in war canoes. A magnet-pull to serious adventurers, Irian Jaya visitors must, however, first obtain a special permit from the State Police Headquarters in Jakarta.

Bali and Lombok are the main islands of Eastern Indonesia. Just a short ferry ride east of Java lies **Bali**, 'Landscape of the Gods', with its volcanic mountains, lakes, rivers, and bays with white sandy beaches. Although densely populated, Bali possesses some adventure hideaways that tempt the active traveller. Stretching east–west across the island is a volcanic chain of mountains, dominated by the 3170 m/10 400 ft peak of **Gunung Agung** – the 'Holy Mountain'. Ten hectares of nutmeg trees comprising the sacred monkey forest reserve at **Sangeh** are, as expected, home to a variety of exotic primates. Batur Mountain and Lake are areas of volcanic activity. The caldera of **Batur** is impressive: 11 km/7 miles across and 18 m/60 ft deep. **Goa Lawah** is a bat cave, guarded by a temple believed to date back nine centuries. Off the west coast of Bali, the little island of **Menjangan** has beautiful coral reefs and a wealth of tropical fish. **Lombok** – its name means 'chilli pepper' – is an unspoilt island only fifteen minutes flight from Bali. Though small, Lombok possesses one of the highest volcanoes in the Indonesian archipelago. **Mount Rindjani** (3745 m/12 290 ft) lies in the north part of Lombok, the area of most interest to adventure travellers. Here is a region of thick forest, superb views and glorious beaches, some of white sand and others of black, volcanic sand. At the coastal area of **Pamenang** you can hire a boat and go snorkelling or scuba diving in the clear tropical waters.

The Imaginative Traveller offers several small group adventure tours to Indonesia, from 15 days ('**Bali by Bike**', £550; '**Krakatoa, Rhinos and Elephants**', £600) to 30 days ('**Islands of Adventure**', £1000). Their exploratory adventure trips to Sulawesi, Irian Jaya and Kalimantan cover some wild country. **World Expeditions** offers three Indonesian soft adventure trips costing from about £800 for 14 days to £1500 for 27 days, excluding air fares.

Mountain Travel Sobek (6240 Fairmount Avenue, El Cerrito, CA 94530; tel: 510 527 8100) offers a number of rafting and other trips, while local operators **Santa Bali Tours and Travel (Hotel Bali Beach Arcade, Sanur, Bali, Indonesia; tel: 287628)** offers a variety of short adventure tours, including trekking and biking.

Explore offers a number of Indonesian adventure holidays including a 19-day seatrek. One of their trips, the 15-day '**Tribal Sumatra**', includes rainforests, volcanoes and visits to lake tribes. After flying to the island's capital, Medan, and visiting the orang-utan reserve at Bohorok, the group (15–20) is driven to the mountain town of Brastagi (1300 m/4300 ft). There then follows a 3- to 4-hour hike to the top of Mt Sibayak. Days 6 to 8 are spent tucked away on Samosir Island, in the middle of Lake Toba (800 m/2625 ft), visiting the Toba Batak tribe, with their communal losmens – 'horned' roofed houses with sweeping gables. This place is excellent for walking trips as well. Crossing the equator on your way to Bukittinggi, you pass through a profusion of tropical flora and fauna. Here you can go canyon walking (Ngarai canyon) or trekking to tribal villages. The group is then driven to the remote area around Lake Maninjau. Hiking to Lawang Crater is on offer here. On day 13 the group is driven to Padang before flying to Jakarta for the international flight home. Accommodation is bed and breakfast (10 nights) and guesthouse (2 nights). The price for this adventure is approximately £1200, to and from London, and trips run throughout the year.

FACTFILE

Climate: Tropical, varying from place to place. The driest weather is from June to September while the western monsoon brings the main rains between December and March. Cooler temperatures occur at higher altitudes and rainstorms can happen at any time of the year.

Conventions: The country has 250 languages and dialects. Social courtesies tend to be fairly formal.

JAMAICA – LAND OF WOOD AND WATER

'This is Jamaica now – an Isle
Where I have found a hallowed place,
Walked in the footsteps of the stars,
And gazed on Beauty face to face.
                    Stella Mead

Christopher Columbus declared Jamaica 'the fairest island that eyes have ever seen' and it's true, the leafy gullies, soaring mountains and golden beaches of this quintessentially Caribbean island are very beautiful indeed. Now admittedly, Columbus was given to lavishing praise on practically every island he passed, but Jamaica really does have a lot more to offer than the reefers and rum which many assume to be the mainstay of life here. Of course, if all you are looking for is a week of laid-back partying, then undoubtedly it could be arranged, but that would be to miss the richness of the island's centre, quite comfortably aloof from the more commercialized resorts. It is primarily Jamaica's size which makes this possible. Where other smaller Caribbean islands suffer from the proximity of the idyllic and the commercial, the 11 424 sq km/4411 square miles of Jamaica allow both to flourish independently and give the adventurous traveller scope to leave the cocktail bar behind and discover the real people, the real paradise.

The third largest of the Greater Antilles, Jamaica is part of a huge submerged mountain range. Above sea level, the country is dominated by the towering peaks of **John Crow** and **Blue Mountains**. Like a spine, these mountains run the length of the island, the land around them subsiding into lush rainforest gullies, immensely fertile coffee plantations in the north and east and thick mangrove swamps in the southwest. The coast is fringed with golden beaches, but since many of these are privately owned it is worth seeking out the quieter public beaches at **Long Bay** and **Port Maria**. This is the Jamaica of the indigenous Arawak Indians, long since driven out of the island which they called 'Xaymaca' ('land of wood and water') and it is this Jamaica which the adventure traveller should aim to explore when disembarking at Kingston. The capital itself is not only an excellent pit stop for provisions, but, having been extensively damaged in 1988 by Hurricane Gilbert, is also a living testimony to the resilience of the Jamaican people.

Those in search of Jamaica as a 'land of water' will find a multitude of different adventurous pursuits on offer. Watersports are available on many of the public beaches, though it is well worth shopping around for suitable deals. Although possible all round the island, the best windsurfing and waterskiing is on the north shore between Falmouth and Montego Bay, where **Burwood** and **Trelawny Beaches** offer stretches of turquoise waves and gentle winds. The dozens of little bays and immense variation in Jamaica's coastline make it perfect for day and half-day sailing trips, and – for the more dedicated sailor – longer distances (even a circumnavigation). So, depending on your needs, you can choose between short cruises which leave from, among other places, Ocho Rios, Port Antonio and Montego Bay, or the independence of a yacht charter, where the freedom of the waves and winds is all yours. An anchorage not to miss, if the latter appeals, is that metaphor for paradise – **The Blue Lagoon** – which is situated in the northeast. While it may not be the actual lagoon where Brooke Shields was to be seen gambolling in a loincloth, it offers (particularly early in the morning) that sense of romantic isolation which many travellers to this part of the world would seek. Other great anchorages are in **Negril**, off the seven-mile beach of white sand; and at Treasure Beach in the south, near the famous Lover's Leap cliff where a plantation owner's daughter and her slave lover took their lives in a romantic tryst.

For the adventurer not content to remain above water, there is a lot of excellent scuba diving around the Jamaican coast, where a ring of offshore reefs supports a great diversity of marine life. While many of these reefs were once in rather poor condition, they are now, for the most part, protected, and the damaged corals are gradually repairing themselves. Jamaica's dive operators are willing to take both experienced divers and newcomers to these preserved coral garden refuges.

Jamaica's watery paradise continues, perhaps at its most untouched, inland. Here rivers tumble from the mountain tops, sometimes vanishing underground to emerge in a pool, like at Jupiter, near Ginger House, south of Port Antonio; sometimes cascading dramatically in rapids like Reach Falls, inland from Manchioneal; or further from the crowds at Maggotty and the Black River Gorge, not far from Apple Valley. Not to be missed, despite regular flurries of tourists, are **Dunn's River Falls** at Ocho Rios, where a sequence of waterfalls drops 180 m/600 ft into the Caribbean ocean itself. For more challenging watery pursuits, a range of rafting opportunities is available, from a stately cruise on a bamboo raft up the **Rio Grande** near Port Antonio, to more difficult rafting on the aptly named **White River**. The Arawaks at this point would remind us that Xaymaca is not only a land of water but also a land of wood. Certainly exploration of the forests and the mountains is rewarding. Here thrive some 3000 varieties of flowering plants and 250 species of birds. Expeditions on foot or on horseback can be as ambitious or as sedate as you choose, but do always take local advice on routes and don't leave for the mountains unprepared for a drop in temperature or for rainfall. The 2257 m/7402 ft) **Blue Mountain** peak presents a formidable climb from Mavis Bank, but on a clear day after dawn you can sometimes catch a glimpse of Cuba. The descent through virgin rainforest and orchid scattered woodland is equally memorable. There are two somewhat basic huts on the peak itself for climbers wishing to spend the night. Slightly less taxing but no less stunning trails can be found beyond Newcastle in Holywell National Park and at Hardwar Gap. Over in the west is the virtually uninhabited **Cockpit Country**, a strange and rocky area riddled with caves and originally occupied by the second tribe to claim Jamaica as its own, the Maroons. This part of the island houses the **Windsor Caves**, full of bats and underground rivers and accessible only to experienced cavers. The mass exodus of bats from the caves at sunset is a remarkable spectacle.

Because Jamaica has such a wealth of inspiration for the adventure traveller, planning your time carefully is perhaps more important here than for other Caribbean destinations. Seeing and doing everything on one visit alone is impossible. While Jamaica (again unlike some of its more exclusive neighbours) can be discovered on a lower budget, there are quite a number of good tailor-made packages for the sailor and diver from around £1000–£1500, depending on season. Contact **Caribbean Connection (Concorde House, Forest Street, Chester CH1 1QR; tel: 01244 329556)** and **Simply Caribbean (3 Victoria Avenue, Harrogate HG1 1EQ; tel: 01423 526887)**. It is important to work out carefully the location of your base, in order to ensure relatively easy access to the parts of the island at the top of your priority list. If your budget is smaller or if you are keen to explore Jamaica under your own steam, there is a good selection of more reasonable accommodation all over the island, a list of which is available from the Jamaican Tourist Board. Activities can be organized either through your hotel or direct from the organizations themselves. **Jamaican Yacht Charters (tel: 952 2578)** offers crewed vessels, cruises and independent charters. Dive operators (PADI registered) include **Seaworld Resorts** in Montego Bay (**tel: 953 2180**), **Dolphin Divers** (**tel: 957 4481**) in Negril and **Sea and Dive Jamaica** (**tel: 974 5762**) in Ocho Rios. **Rafter's Rest** in Ocho Rios will give you details of rafting on the Rio Grande (**tel: 993 2778**). Horse riding can be organized from most hotels in the main towns. Hikers would be well advised to contact **SENSE Adventures** (**PO Box 216, Kingston; tel: 927 2097**), **Jamaican Alternative Tourism Camping and Hiking Association** at the same address or the **Forestry Department** (**tel: 924 2667**) which organizes and advises on trekking and rafting expeditions.

Explore offers a 16-day soft adventure in Jamaica – its '**Fairest Isle**' trip. After arriving at Montego Bay you transfer to Runaway Bay – your base for expeditions into Cockpit Country. The undulating limestone hills of this region were a traditional stronghold of the Maroons or runaway slaves. You drive into the backroads that criss-cross this region and visit a huge underground cavern. On day 3 you drive to Black River, one of Jamaica's oldest towns, and take a boat trip to see varied birdlife and crocodiles. After a tour of Kingston on day 7, the group (around 12–16) heads high into the Blue Mountains where a hike is made to the remote Cinchona Gardens (5500 ft). A winding banana road takes you across the country's hinterland to Port Antonio, where you take a river trip on bamboo rafts through dense rainforest. On day 14 you drive along the coast via Dunns River Falls, to Runaway Bay. Finally days 15 and 16 are spent returning to London. Accommodation on this trip is bed and breakfast (11 nights) and full board at hostels (3 nights). You must be reasonably fit to get the most out of the walks, but the hike to Cinchona is optional. All-inclusive cost for the adventure is around £1400.

FACTFILE

Climate: It's a fairly uniform 20–30°C all year round, but do be prepared for the occasional burst of rain.

Currency: The official currency is the Jamaican dollar and rules on trading are very strict. However, do take care with prices, as they are often quoted in US dollars which have a different value.

Travel tips: Car hire can be expensive (over $300 a day) and should be booked in advance.

Although people are given to panic-mongering about safety on Jamaica's streets and you should be prepared for people trying to sell you anything and everything, observe usual urban caution and you should have no problems.

KENYA – LAND OF SAFARI

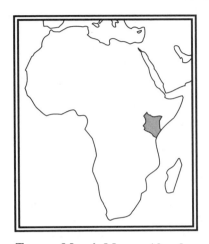

Someone once christened Kenya 'A land of infinite contrasts: the whole of Africa in one country.' After all, where else can you find glacial ice, a sandy coastline, arid deserts, sweeping savannas, dense rainforests, a rift valley, large lakes – even an inland sea? But perhaps the best description you can apply to Kenya is 'land of safari'. More than a tenth of Kenya is set aside expressly for the protection of wildlife: some 40 National Parks and Reserves including household names like **Tsavo**, **Masai Mara**, **Aberdares**, **Amboseli** and **Mount Kenya**. These are vast tracts of wilderness devoted to the preservation of flora and fauna – undoubtedly Kenya's greatest attraction for holiday adventure seekers.

Once only the province of a wealthy sporting élite, safaris are nowadays much more affordable, though to camera-shooters rather than rifle-shooters. The whole spectrum of these trips has broadened considerably in Africa, and nowhere more so than in Kenya. UK and locally based operators are now offering everything from expeditionary-type walking or riding safaris (camels as well as horses!) to less energetic steam-train safaris, light aircraft safaris, or even, for some people, the ultimate: hot air balloon safaris. But to most holidaymakers on mainstream packaged adventure, a safari means a vehicle-based trip.

There is, however, a penalty to the ever-increasing pressures that Kenya's visitors exert on the environment. In some cases a rather too commercialized approach to tourism has led to certain reserves appearing overcrowded at times. After all, it only takes the presence of a few other safari groups on the horizon – or closer – to tame one's sense of wilderness, and on occasions this dividing line is crossed. For true adventure travellers, therefore, it is best to avoid the cheapest budget 'on the beaten track' safaris if you want to experience the wilderness as well as the wildlife. Choosing from among the operators listed in Section 2 will help get you far from the madding, thrill-seeking crowd.

Nowhere in Africa is wildlife more plentiful than the **Masai Mara**, with its huge concentrations of antelope, gazelle and carnivores, including the indigenous black-maned lions. The smaller but equally fascinating **Amboseli National Park** lies in the shadow of Mount Kilimanjaro. At one time Amboseli was a favourite safari hideout and retreat for writers such as Ernest Hemingway and Robert Ruark.

If it's mountains you're after, then Africa's second highest peak – **Mount Kenya** – will tempt you away from the game reserves. Two hours' drive from Nairobi takes you to the starting point of your three-day guided trek up this 5200 m/17 000 ft marvel, with its own Twin Peaks – Batian and Nelion. Mount Kenya's equatorial slopes display an extraordinary flora, ranging from the tropical to the Arctic – a delight for botanists and non-botanists alike. To avoid altitude sickness, two nights are spent on the approach route before the ascent of the third highest peak, Point Lenana. You should be reasonably fit (many people experience altitude effects) and you will need warm clothes and hiking boots.

What better after a strenuous climb than to head for Kenya's coast with its 550 km/340 mile stretch of unspoilt white sandy beach lapped by the warm waters of the Indian Ocean and safeguarded by coral reefs? There are now four **Marine Parks** – the first to be established on the African continent (in 1968). Snorkelling and scuba diving are available in many locations and windsurfing is popular all along the coast.

Kenya is as 'user-friendly' for the independent traveller as it is for packaged adventure visitors, but if this is your first time visiting East Africa it is as well for you to go on an organized tour. This will avoid the worries of finding accommodation, and more particularly transport into the National Parks, some of which demand four-wheel drive (and thus expensive) vehicles. There are more tour operators offering trips to Kenya than you can shake a shambok at. Some combine trips to Tanzania and many combine coastal holidays with wildlife safaris. Other 'bolt-on' additions include catering for those keen to climb Mount Kenya, or to see **Lake Turkana** (formerly Lake Rudolf) – home to 20 000 crocodiles and the giant Nile perch. One particular local company committed to the care and preservation of Kenya's natural environment and wildlife is **Let's Go Travel (PO Box 60342, Nairobi; tel: Nairobi 340331/213033)**, corporate members of the East African Wildlife Society and contributors to Kenyan conservation projects. Their $300 three-day **Masai Mara** adventure camping trip includes short hiking trips. Alternatively, Let's Go Travel offers bicycle-based camping safaris ($550, six days) or horseback safaris ($2500, eight days). For $100 per person per day they will design a camping safari to suit your needs, so long as there are four or more of you. Price includes transport, driver/guide, camping and Park fees, plus accommodation and meals.

Another company committed to responsible adventure tourism is **Guerba Expeditions**, which offers a number of Kenya and East African trips. Their £1200, 22-day '**Kenya Safari and Coast**' tour includes flights, camping in Masai Mara, Amboseli, Samburu and Tsavo, guided bird walk at Lake Baringo and snorkelling in the Indian Ocean. Guerba supports World Wildlife Fund and Action Aid, a charity concerned with helping the peoples of less developed countries. **Wexas International** offers small group diving courses from £200. Beginners can go on a 'fun dive', while more experienced divers can take an advanced course or escape on a dhow-based marine safari.

For a memorable hiking safari, **High Places** offers a '**Kenya Wild and High**' 18-day trip for an all-inclusive price of about £1900. On day 1 you fly to Nairobi and the adventure starts with a short drive down into the Great Rift Valley to a camp overlooking the plains. Here you relax for a couple of days, observing the wildlife and adjusting to the pace of life. Days 4 through 7 are spent walking through the Loita Hills, in Masai territory, following little-used trails and using local warriors as guides. On days 8 and 9 you go wildlife viewing in the Masai Mara National Reserve, before a seven-day trip on Mt Kenya, involving a complete traverse of the massif. The trek starts on the foothills of the northwestern side, climbing gradually through forest and up into open moorland. It culminates in a stiff scramble by starlight up to Point Leana in time to watch the African dawn from your vantage point at almost 5000 m/16 400 ft. Finally you turn back towards civilization: Nairobi on day 17 and the return flight home on day 18. Accommodation throughout is camping (except in Nairobi) and a reasonable level of fitness is required. Departure in July.

FACTFILE

When to go: April to June and November are rainy months, less suitable for camping, climbing and camel safaris but also less popular with tourists. Scuba diving season runs from September to April.

Travel tips: Best times for game viewing are early morning and late afternoon. Respect the local culture, for example when it comes to taking photographs.

Other information: Cholera, yellow fever, typhoid and malaria precautions are essential. Swimming in lakes and rivers is definitely not recommended due to the risk of bilharzia.

LESOTHO – MAGIC MOUNTAIN KINGDOM

'Except along the fringes of civilization, the ox-wagon has vanished into oblivion and with it have gone the camp fire and the night under the stars. To the fortunate few alone the upland trail remains; the voices of the mountain, the clatter of rhythmic hoofs, the neighing of a foal in panic. For yet a while the echo will linger. The spell of Africa is the nostalgic evocation of evanescent beauty; the swan song of a dying day.'

R.C. Germond, Chronicles of Basotholand

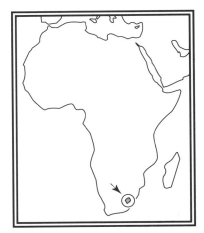

Alps of Africa, Kingdom in the Sky, Roof of Africa, Magic Mountain Kingdom: these are just a few of the many apt names given to Lesotho, a majestic, mountainous monarchy nestling in the heart of southern Africa. But this extraordinary country is much, much more than just these things alone, as increasing numbers of adventure travellers are discovering for themselves. One of only three states in the world completely surrounded by a single country – in this case South Africa – Lesotho (or Basotholand as it was formerly known) was annexed by Britain in 1868, finally gaining independence, though remaining part of the British Commonwealth, as the Kingdom of Lesotho in 1966.

Lesotho is true expedition country: the quintessential African mountain fastness. Its range upon range of spectacular peaks have their genesis in the country's northern foothills, progressively gathering height southwards until finally plunging dramatically down the sheer cliffs of the Drakensbergs, into Natal (see South Africa, p 237). Lesotho's high altitude gives it the distinction of being the only country in the world whose lowest point is more than 1370 m/4500 ft above sea level. Since it also gives rise to snowfall in the highlands during winter (May to July) you can even try your hand at a bit of cross-country skiing if you take the necessary equipment. Although these peaks cannot compare in stature with those of other continents, Lesotho's **Thabana Ntlenyana** is the highest mountain (3841 m/12 606 ft) in the sub-continent. Unlike other African countries featured in this book, very little game is found in Lesotho, but there are plenty of bird species, including Africa's answer to the condor, the six-foot wingspanned Lammergeyer or Bearded Vulture. Some of the country's other attractions include a wonderful climate (over 300 days of sunshine a year), a healthy environment (no malaria or bilharzia), and memorable adventurous attractions away from the hubbub and hurly burly of Western life.

Principal among these attractions are riding trips. Lesotho's association with ponies goes back over many generations, trekking being one of the country's most well established – yet most exciting – activities (see Riding, p 82). Without any previous riding experience you can head off into the hills in an organized party from one of the trekking centres, to spend a few hours, or a few days and nights, on a bare mountain (trees are a scarce commodity in Lesotho). The lack of fences, the plethora of ponies, and the numerous tracks connecting equally numerous villages, combine to make Lesotho an unmatched African destination for those eager for horse riding adventures. This lack of tall vegetation also gives travellers superb panoramic vistas over the immensity of Lesotho's magic mountain scenery. Away from the larger settlements, village hospitality is a byword, strategically placed white flags fluttering from makeshift poles indicating where the numerous 'Joala' rondavels (beer huts) are located.

Apart from mountain ranges, one of the first things that strikes you when you look at a map of Lesotho is its size (it is only about the extent of Belgium). But this hides the fact that it can take a long time to get from A to B over the difficult terrain. Apart from a sprinkling of tarred roads, generally on the lower lying ground, there are few good transport links, and this isolation increases the attraction of Lesotho to adventurous hikers. Independent travellers can easily enjoy the freedom of the mountains, following the many trails which lead from one village to another. Experienced hikers have been known to chalk up many 'African Munroes' – mountains over 3000 m/9800 ft – in Lesotho's high 'Maluti' ranges. Warm autumn days from February to April are perfect for short hiking trips or longer expeditions. Everywhere you go there is always a friendly greeting *Khotso!* ('Peace!') and when you become footsore and weary, you can simply paddle or swim in the nearest mountain stream, or shower under one of the many waterfalls. The most spectacular of all of Lesotho's many waterfalls is at Semonkong, in the central massif. At 192 m/630 ft tall, the **Maletsunyane Falls** comprises the highest single-drop waterfall in southern Africa.

Lying in a remote corner of the south east, **Sehlabatebe National Park** (meaning 'Plateau of the Shield') is often referred to as the 'Dreamland of Lesotho'. Its outstanding scenery and weirdly shaped sandstone rocks, eroded over the years by the wind, impart a profound sense of history: these mountains are 50 million years older than the Alps, fossilized dinosaur tracks within the region dating back some 200 million years! An unexpected bonus at Sehlabatebe is the presence of a fine lodge, almost a mansion in fact, which offers a civilized base from which to explore its wild and magnificent surroundings.

A must for all adventure seekers is the **Outward Bound Centre** near Pitseng in northern Lesotho. Like all OB Centres, its aims include exposing participants to self-discovery through physical and mental challenges which help equip them to meet the demands of the modern, changing world. Courses here range from five days to over two weeks, and the Centre caters for people from all walks of life aged 16 and over. Challenging activities such as hiking, canoeing, rock-climbing, abseiling and group tasks are designed to encourage team building and leadership development. Don't pass it by: out of the 35 or so OB locations worldwide this one has to be scenically near the top of the list.

Basotho Adventures (PO Makhakhe 922, Lesotho; tel: 09266 785336) organizes tours into the interior by pony, four-wheel-drive vehicle, charter aircraft or on foot. These trips last from three days to a week and can be tailored to suit your time and your pocket. Malealea Lodge is a wonderful place to base yourself for hiking or riding trips. Contact the Lodge at **PO Makhakhe, 922 Lesotho**, or alternatively **PO Box 119, Wepener, 9944, Republic of South Africa; tel: 09266 785 336 or 051 473200**.

Few British-based operators offer trips to Lesotho (at the moment it is more a destination for the independent traveller) although **Exodus** lists an enticing 14-day trekking adventure. This '**Kingdom of the Sky**' itinerary departs London on day 1, arriving Johannesburg and transferring to Lesotho on day 2. The adventure proper starts on day 3 in the Valley of Paradise from where you set off through small valleys and narrow gorges, into the Maloti mountains. Porterage on the trek ensures that you are not burdened by a heavy pack. After visiting several waterfalls en route, the final destination is the Maletsunyane Falls, a journey which takes eight days. The trip finishes at a beautiful mountain lodge, where, for two days, there's the chance to explore the area nearby either on foot or by Basotho pony. Accommodation includes 4 nights lodge-based and 7 nights in village houses or rondavels. The group size is from 8 to a maximum of 16 and the all-inclusive cost is approximately £1500.

FACTFILE

When to go: All year round. May to July for possible snow-based trips. There's no jet lag for European visitors due to the similar time zone.

Travel tips: Drive carefully. Lack of fencing can create livestock hazards. Inform the Chief if you are stopping or camping at a village. He (or more likely she) will be helpful. Don't take photos of Basotho without their permission.

MALAWI – WOODED WILDERNESS

'I have never known such stillness. The only sound was the sound of one's blood murmuring like a far sea in one's ears; and that serene land and its beauty, and the level golden sunlight seemed to have established such a close, delicate, tender communion with us that the murmur in my ears seemed also like a sound from without; it was like a breathing of the grasses, a rustle of the last shower of daylight, or the swish of the silk of evening across the purple slopes.'

Sir Laurens van der Post, Venture to the Interior

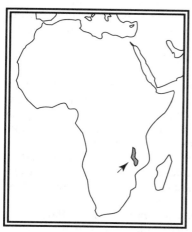

Asked to think of Africa, many people conjure up images of wide-open savannas dotted with thorn acacia, supporting vast herds of plains game – in short, the sort of scenery typical of Karen von Blixen's writings. Malawi is different. It's not a large country – only half the size of the UK in fact – but this landlocked sliver of the African continent offers much to attract and reward adventure travellers. A particular feature, and a memory that remains with travellers long after leaving, is its abundance and variety of **woodlands**. These forest ecosystems vary from indigenous baobabs and borassus palms in the lowlands, to rare cedar and evergreen montane forest at higher altitudes. Much of this forested land is encompassed by National Parks and, happily, the more dangerous (to hikers) forms of wildlife such as lion and elephant are absent in many of these areas. When you combine Malawi's moderate climate (which rarely dips below 20°C) with its spectacular scenery, wildlife and healthy environment, you have the perfect recipe for a more unusual and unforgettable African adventure holiday.

One of the main attractions of Malawi is its eponymous natural lake, the third largest in Africa (after lakes Victoria and Tanganyika). **Lake Malawi** lies at the extreme southern end of the Rift Valley. It has the great advantages of being free from both bilharzia and crocodiles, making it a paradise for devotees of adventure watersports. Chief among these are snorkelling, scuba diving, sailing and windsurfing. **Lake Malawi National Park** was the first in the world to give protection to marine life. Ecologically, the lake supports more kinds of fish than any other in the world: some of its 500 or so species are found here and nowhere else in fact. In turn, the lake's fish populations support a wealth of bird life, including fish eagles, black eagles and several species of kingfisher. Many overland trips stop off at lake Malawi en route from Nairobi to South Africa, for a welcome chance to wash off the dust from their travels. This is a great opportunity to indulge in a water-based safari in the Lake Malawi National Park, either in modern craft (canoes, inflatables or cruisers) or – for the more adventurous – traditional dhows. For a few days you can take a break from the open road, snorkel among tropical fish, catch the afternoon breeze on a sailboard, and then pitch camp on one of the Lake's twelve islands. What better way to cook your catch of fish than on camp fire under the Southern Cross, beside the shores of what Livingstone once described as the 'Lake of Stars'?

No fewer than five National Parks border Lake Malawi. Chief among them is **Nyika National Park** in the north, one of Africa's richest orchid habitats. This Park occupies most of the Nyika plateau – that 'serene land and its beauty' about which Laurens van der Post wrote so evocatively. Its chowo forest is excellent for day walkers and serious hikers alike. You can choose from a one day to a six day wilderness hiking safari, staying in self-contained chalets, log cabins or under canvas. You must be accompanied by a local guide, however. The best time for exploring this wilderness is May to November. July and August can bring frosty nights, while rains fall between December and April.

If it's elephants you're after, then **Kasungu National Park** is the place to visit. Lying about 110 km/70 miles north of the capital, Lilongwe, its miombo woodland supports high concentrations of *Loxodonta africana* – the African elephant – as well as large herds of buffalo, antelope and zebra. Rondavel huts offer basic accommodation, while the best time to visit is from May to December. Smallest of the five National Parks, **Lengwe** offers some rare prizes to the safari addict, most notably in the forms of its elusive blue monkey and Nyala antelope. With its deciduous woodland and thicket vegetation, Lengwe contains a number of game viewing hides, a rest camp and nature trails.

Liwonde is one of Malawi's most fascinating National Parks. With its diversity of habitats, including riverine swamps, mopane woodland and grassland, the dominating feature of this area is the Shire River. This is the haunt of hippo, mud turtles, crocodiles and swampland birds. You can experience accompanied walking safaris here but the season is short (August to October) since many of the roads become impassable due to heavy rainfalls outside this period.

A must for committed backpackers and climbers is **Mount Mulanje Forest Reserve**. At approximately 3000 m/9800 ft, Mulanje is the highest peak in Central Africa, dominating its surrounding plains and dense, forested ravines. Here, rock climbers can tackle the considerable challenge of Africa's largest sheer face. The Department of Forestry maintains a number of basic huts close to the mountain, but you will need to bring your own camping equipment and supplies. Climbers can contact the **Mountain Club of Malawi (PO Box 240, Blantyre)** and arrange to join an organized hike, in which case the Club equipment in the huts is available for use. Local porters can also be hired by arrangement. One note of caution: the weather on Mulanje can change without warning and the 'chiperone' mist can reduce visibility to almost nothing for days at a time, so take this into account when embarking on your mountain trip.

High Places offers high trekking on the plateaux of Mulanje and Nyika, sticking where possible to ridges and escarpments for some astonishing mountain views. As well as a few days at Lake Malawi, this 21-day tour includes a 7-day trek around Mulanje, staying in huts each night. Departure is in mid September, accommodation is in cottages, huts and tents and the cost is £1700 including flights.

As an example of an in-depth holiday in Malawi, **Explore** offers a 19-day lodge/camping adventure entitled '**Unspoilt Eden**'. You fly to Lilongwe on day 1, spending the next day acclimatizing in the capital. On day 3 you travel by expedition vehicle to Luwawa Forest Reserve, continuing on day 4 to Nyika Plateau where you follow wilderness trails at altitudes of around 2600 m/8500 ft. After a game drive in Nyika on day 5, you are driven to Vwaza Reserve on day 6 for more game viewing. On day 7 your vehicle descends the steep escarpment, taking you to Nkata Bay on Lake Malawi. Here you spend a relaxing day at Chintheche beach. On day 9 you are driven to Salima and thence on day 10 to Liwonde National Park, on the eastern bank of the Shire River, for game drives and walks. The next three days are spent tackling Mt Mulange. The group hikes to a hut at around 1800 m/6000 ft and then you decide whether you want to continue to the 'Island in the Sky' at nearly 3050 m/10 000 ft. Finally, on day 16 you are driven to Cape Maclear, spending the next day here windsurfing, snorkelling or boating to a nearby island. On day 18 you return to Lilongwe and on day 19 you return home. Accommodation on this holiday consists of 7 nights resthouses/chalets, 8 nights camping and mountain hut. Mode of travel is Safari Landrover and on foot and there are 1 or 2 vehicles in the group taking from 6 to 8 adventurers. The cost for this trip is approximately £1200 from London, with departures throughout the year.

FACTFILE

When to go: The dry seaon lasts from May to October. Temperatures range from 20–27°C.

Travel tips: Culturally, travellers should conform to local dress standards. Avoid taking photos close to official locations. Take plenty of food if you stay on the islands in Lake Malawi since food availability can be limited. Lake weather can be unpredictable.

Watersports: Scuba diving courses are offered from lakeshore hotels. Beginners' courses take a day: more advanced courses last a week. Make sure that instructors are NAUI qualified.

Health tips: Malaria here is particularly resistant to certain types of drugs.

MOROCCO – HIGH ATLAS AND BEYOND

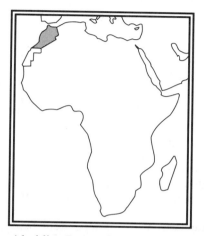

Morocco has always been a country for travellers – a place of history where traders from Europe, Africa and Arabia combined and fused together in an extraordinary array of contrasting cultures. Although globalization and Westernization have made their impact upon these ancient trade routes, a sense of history, tradition and, above all, remoteness, still remains today. It is true that many visitors to Morocco are searching for a fantasy – a Hollywood Casablanca or a Disney Aladdin. But for adventure travellers, the real Morocco lies away from the bars and the kasbahs. The real Morocco is to be found in the High Atlas . . . and beyond.

Morocco's train system ends at Marrakesh. You are literally at the end of the line here – and at the beginning of your adventure. Beyond the towering, rose-coloured minaret of Koutobia, which has dominated the city's skyline for eight centuries, rise the unforgettable **High Atlas**, with their unlikely winter dusting of snow. This 640 km/400 mile chain, with ten peaks over 4000 m/ 13 000 ft high was known to the Phoenicians and Greeks as the abode of the legendary giant Atlas, who supported the world on his shoulders. It's a huge area, separating the Mediterranean lowlands of northern Morocco from the desert wastes of the Sahara. For independent travellers to these mountains, the only way on from Marrakesh is to take your life in your hands and, for a few dirhams, experience a 'share taxi' up to the mountains. Prepare to redefine the word 'full' when applied to a car, as you become wedged solidly between increasing numbers of children, old ladies, herdsmen and livestock. Don't look too closely at the precipitous, unprotected slopes which fall away beneath you at every hairpin bend and maybe even give thanks when you arrive safely at your journey's end.

Oukaimeden is 43 km/27 miles south of Marrakesh. Leaving behind the hot and dusty souks of the city, you enter a new rarified world of freshness and coolness, where the sun shines for over 300 days every year. Here is Morocco's foremost winter sports playground. For, unlikely as it may seem, this is one of Africa's select few skiing areas – and the best of Morocco's three resorts. In fact Oukaimeden's ski-lifts are among the world's highest, taking skiers from 2500 up to 3300 m (8200–10 800 ft) and giving excellent views over Marrakesh and the northern plains. Oukaimeden is not for beginners, however: the skiing can be technical, with icy conditions and steep slopes. Nor is it possible to rely on consistent snow, unfortunately. The best time of the year is December to April, but the snow can be sparse, which is bad news, or too abundant, which is worse since the road to the lifts can be frustratingly cut off. This will not deter cross-country ski enthusiasts however, since the Atlas slopes provide some superb expeditionary skiing. Do bear in mind, though, that this is a remote area: facilities are few and such ski trips will need to be self-contained. Outside the main Atlas massif, the best areas for cross-country expeditionary skiing are **Mount Tidiquin** in the Ketama District and **Djebel Bou Volane** in the Middle Atlas. Downhill facilities are offered at **Djebel Habra**, **Djebel Hebri**, **Ifrane** and **Azrou**, in the Middle Atlas.

For off-the-beaten-track summer adventure, independent trips into the High Atlas can be arranged with the local authorities. Although mountain bikes are becoming increasingly available for hire, the best way to experience 'Atlas magic' is on foot. Life can be made easier for hikers by hiring (for a reasonable charge) mules and their drivers, while trips can be tailored to last from one to several days. These mountains offer endless hiking possibilities: discovering Berber villages, crossing high plateaux, encountering the occasional cave with its prehistoric wall-etchings or forging up deeply incised valleys. Apart from camping, there are three types of permanent accommodation: mountain 'inns'; staying with families in their homes; and hut refuges. Lovers of mountains will inevitably be seduced by Morocco's highest peak – **Jbel Toubkal** – all of 4165 m/13 661 ft high. Starting point for the trek is Asni, some 29 miles south of Marrakesh. The hike to Mt Toubkal's summit lasts three or four days. Take a warm sleeping bag or blankets since even in summer it can be cold at night.

If you have time, a trip to **Todra Gorge** in '*Le Grand Sud*' – as Moroccans call this area – is a memorable experience. Situated near Tinerhir, the Gorge itself is a vast fault in a high plateau, comparable with Colorado's Grand Canyon. As you pass higher up the river the fords become deeper and deeper, while the sky becomes a mere slit at the top of dark, forbidding rock walls. Rivers flowing through some of these mountain gorges are starting to become used for water-based adventure trips. Morocco might not seem the obvious place for white-water rafting or kayaking, but with over 300 km/185 miles of rapid waters available, this activity is gaining in popularity all the time.

When you enter Morocco's mountain habitats, a degree of caution is needed. Aspects of Morocco's mountain ecology have already begun to suffer through unsympathetic treatment by visitors. This environment *is* a fragile one and can be damaged easily through thoughtless actions by users. Moreover, respect by visitors of Morocco's proud and ancient peoples is of the utmost importance. To help increase awareness of these issues, the Moroccan Ministry of Tourism has issued five simple guidelines for seekers of adventure in the mountains (see Factfile).

Sherpa Expeditions offers a number of trekking trips to Morocco. These self-contained affairs include teams of mules and drivers which carry tents and other equipment, leaving you to carry only a day pack. Their 15-day '**Jbel Toubkal**' trip involves 10 days of trekking and includes an ascent of the summit as well as climbs of less well-known peaks. Cost varies from £600 to £700. **Exodus** has a '**Moroccan Sahara**' trip comprising of 15 days winter exploration of the Anti-Atlas and Sahara, including the Todra Gorge, at a cost of £500–£600. **Worldwide Journeys & Expeditions** offers a 9-day '**Mount Toubkal Trek**' for £800 and a 13-day '**High Atlas Trek**' for around £1000; both trips are all-inclusive.

As an example of a comprehensive adventure holiday, **Exodus** offers '**Highlights of Morocco**' which provides a 15-day exploration of the mountains, deserts, souks and cities of central and southern Morocco. After arriving in Marrakesh on day 1 you set off on day 2 to Morocco's biggest waterfalls, the Cascades d'Ouzoud, where you can swim in the forest pools nearby. The group then travels into the green hills and lakes of the Middle Atlas on day 3, visiting the imperial city of Meknes and the Roman ruins of Volubilis on day 4. A tour of Fez on day 5 is followed by a trip by road to the eastern reaches of the Atlas on day 6. On the next day you experience the rock formations of the Ziz Gorge and the desert's edge, camping by the sand dunes of Erg Chebbi. Day 8 sees you following the Dades Valley with its kasbahs and palmeries to Todra Gorge, where the next day is spent exploring this impressive geological feature. On day 10 you follow the 'Kasbah Road' west towards Ouarzazate and head towards the Atlas Range. Driving into the High Atlas the next day, you walk the last hour to the friendly Berber village of Arroumd. More exploring of the mountains on foot takes place on day 12, and on day 13 you are driven back to Marrakesh. The next day involves a guided tour of the palaces, souks and tombs of this city before you fly back home on day 15. Accommodation comprises 3 nights in a tourist-class hotel, 2 nights in village houses and 9 nights camping. Travel is by expedition vehicle and group size is between 6 and 20. Price is around £550 including flight from London and departures take place between May and September.

FACTFILE

Information: The Ministry of Tourism has a **Mountain Information Centre** giving annually updated details of GTAM (Grand Crossing of the Moroccan Atlas). This practical information includes lists of guides, agencies, accommodation and transport and is available from the **Moroccan Tourist Board**.

Mountain rules: as issued by the Ministry of Tourism –
● Show respect for the cultural heritage and dignity of the local people.
● Do not abuse Moroccan hospitality.
● Always dress in a way that does not cause offence.
● Do not photograph people without first obtaining consent.
● Burn combustible rubbish and place non-combustibles in a proper place.

NAMIBIA – AFRICA'S GEM

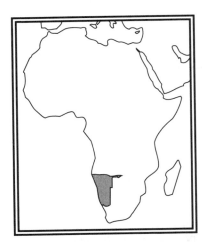

Formerly known as South West Africa in the days when it was administered by South Africa, Namibia offers today's adventure traveller a country of spectacular natural beauty, abundant wildlife and clear, unpolluted skies. Stay away if agoraphobia bothers you, but for lovers of space, silence and solitude the magic of Namibia will bewitch and beckon long after you've left the country.

Think of Namibia and you probably imagine a desolate coastline, diamonds galore, and, above all, desert. Certainly the country contains – and is in fact enclosed by – vast tracts of arid land. To the east lies the Kalahari (see Botswana, p 124) while to the west stretches the 1300 km/800 mile Namib desert and its rainless coastline. 'Namibia' is a Hottentot word which means 'great plains' and it is this wild, wide-open wilderness which creates such a lasting impression on visitors. The striking landscapes become apparent even before you touch down, with sand dunes, rocks and hills constantly changing colour, shadow and texture when viewed from your aircraft window. But to be appreciated fully, these dunes and rocky plains should be seen from ground level. Ancient rock strata, largely unshrouded by vegetation, are absorbing to geologists and non-geologists alike, while unusual prehistoric plant species – well adapted to Namibia's arid conditions – have to be seen to be believed.

The inhospitable nature of Namibia has helped to preserve its wilderness: imagine a country four times the size of Britain but with fewer than 1.2 million inhabitants and you begin to see why it is so empty. Intrepid German missionaries first opened up the interior for settlement during the mid-19th century, finding a diversity of tribes, races and cultures, such as the pastoral Himba and Wambo and the Stone Age hunter/gatherer Bushmen. Even as late as 1960, the coast and its hinterland were largely unpenetrated by humans, but today, now declared independent, Namibia is opening its doors wider and wider to international adventure tourists. Its dry climate gives the place a major advantage over many other African countries, since tropical diseases are virtually unknown here.

The main areas of interest to adventure travellers are the Northern, Southern and Namib regions, although there are attractions in the Central region as well. For example, safari fundi can gain a good introduction to Namibia's wildlife by visiting **Daan Viljoen Game Park**, only 24 km/15 miles from Windhoek, Namibia's capital. Since there are no large carnivores here, you can explore the Park on foot. Travelling northwest from the capital you encounter the **Spitzkoppe**, dubbed the 'Matterhorn of South West'. Rising 1800 m/6000 ft from the Namib plain, this ancient volcanic area has recently revealed many rock paintings and implements on its precipitous granite slopes. Some 112 km/70 miles further on lies the majestic massif of the Brandberg, visible from vast distances. Its principal peak – the **Kønigstein** (2579 m/ 8460 ft) – is the highest in the country. Often clothed in a veil of mist, it has attracted and challenged climbers and explorers for decades.

Mountains and gorges are also to be found in the **Southern region**. The 1580 m/5182 ft extinct volcano of Brukkaros looms darkly over an inhospitable sun-scorched plain, its bare sides devoid of any vegetation. But for those prepared to make the hot climb, its 1800 m/6000 ft wide crater rim is a remarkable sight. A short journey away stands the lone rock sentinel called in Nama 'Mukurob' ('finger of God'), a knarled column of eroded stone which points to the sky. But chief among adventure attractions of the Southern region is **Fish River Canyon**, one of Africa's natural wonders, a gigantic ravine 160 km/100 miles long, up to 27 km/17 miles wide and in places almost 600 m/2000 ft deep. Over several milennia, Fish River's erosive power has gouged a mighty canyon second only in size to America's Grand Canyon. A 100 km/60 mile hiking trail winds along the bed of the ravine, taking up to four days to complete. Before setting off you have to get a permit from the Department of Tourism (see Factfile for address), and since the trail is strenuous you have to produce a medical certificate of fitness. Groups must number at least three. When you reach the end of the trail at Ai-Ais, hot springs offer the chance to soak your weary limbs in outside pools or indoor baths. Accommodation varies here from basic to up-market.

In the **Southwest region** lies the **Namib**, at 23 300 sq km/9000 square miles Namibia's largest and most unusual wildlife reserve. Among its many ecosystems are granite mountains, gypsum and quartz plains, towering sand dunes, an estuarine lagoon and a canyon rich in wildlife. You can camp at various points in the Park. The Namib is one of the oldest deserts on earth, and some of the highest sand dunes in the world (300 m/1000 ft) are to be found here. It exists because the cold Antarctic Benguela current flows close to the shore, resisting evaporation and also capturing any moisture blown towards the land from mid-ocean. Herds of mountain zebra, gemsbok and springbok roam these plains, while the extraordinary Welwitschia plant is to be found here. Among the world's oldest and strangest flora, these 'living fossils' produce only two leaves, up to nine feet long, their sole source of moisture being fog or dew. In the south of this region lies a huge dried up pan called **Sossusvlei**. Occasionally it becomes flooded by the Tsauchab river, and then, sparkling like a jewel amid a dry sea of dunes, this oasis attracts antelope, ostriches and a myriad of birds.

For adventurers in search of complete wilderness, the **Skeleton Coast Park** should not be missed. In Afrikaans they call it *Seekus van die dood* – 'Sea Coast of the Dead' – because of the many wrecks (beached whales as well as ships) which litter its treacherous coast. Stretching several hundred miles southwards from Angola, its combination of crashing Atlantic breakers, wind-contoured dunes, canyons, jagged mountains and unexpected waterholes create the bizarre feeling that you are on another planet. But despite its desolation, this Skeleton Coast is a place of rare beauty, supporting a surprising variety of desert animals. Although the southern section of this Park is accessible to travellers, a permit is needed from the Directorate, Nature

Conservation and Recreation (see Factfile). Tented accommodation is available at two small fishing resorts, Torra Bay and Terrence Bay. The only practical access to the northern section is via a fly-in safari, available throughout the year from Windhoek. From the base camp at Sarusas, four-wheel drive vehicles can take you to such places as Rocky Point, Cape Frio and the Hoarusib Canyon.

Chief among wildlife attractions in Namibia (and indeed in southern Africa) is the **Etosha National Park** in the **Northern region**. Covering an area greater than Israel, this mighty game park supports colossal numbers of carnivores, antelope and birds. Once an inland lake the size of Holland, its pan now comprises a gigantic shallow depression inhabited mostly by mirages and dust devils. In exceptional years rain fills this depression, its shallow water attracting enormous numbers of waterfowl, while game animals are drawn to forty mineral-rich perennial springs on the pan's edges. To add to Etosha's sometimes eerie atmosphere, a dense stand of *Moringa ovafolia* (a tree confined to Namibia) exists southwest of the pan, uniquely on a plain (it usually prefers rocky slopes). The thicket's name? . . . The Haunted Forest. Some 325 species of bird have been recorded within the Park, one of the most colourful being Namibia's national emblem, the crimson breasted shrike. Lions are common here, along with the shyer cheetah and leopard. Countless numbers of antelope, including springbok, kudu and duiker inhabit Etosha, while elephants, giraffes and rhino abound. Accommodation for visitors is available in three camps, but the Park is closed during the rainy season (November to mid-March).

Many operators include Namibia on their itineraries, including **Exodus** and **Explore**. For off-the-shelf holidays to the country, **Worldwide Journeys and Expeditions** offers a number of different trips, including fully supported Landrover safaris, from £1500 for a 15-day 'Highlights Safari', to £2900 for a 15-day 'Wilderness and Wildlife' trip.

Worldwide Journeys and Expeditions also offers 'Namibian Explorer', a participatory camping safari, designed to show you as much of the country as possible within 17 days. Arriving from your international flight on day 2, you spend the third day acclimatizing in Windhoek itself, staying at a pension. On day 4 you are driven to Etosha Game Park, where you spend three days game viewing and camping. On day 7 you are driven to the mountainous region of Damaraland where you are taken on guided walks in the Etendeke Mountains and shown rock paintings at Twyfelfontein. You continue south to Swakopmund on day 9, stopping en route at Cape Cross seal colony. Again, as with most of the other stops on this trip, camping is the form of accommodation here. On day 11 you drive to Namib Naukluft National Park, camping overnight and exploring the Sossusvlei dunes on day 12. Fish River Canyon is your destination for days 13 and 14, with local excursions being taken in the vicinity. You then return to Windhoek via Hardap Dam, finally departing from Namibia on day 17. Departures for the Namibian Explorer are from July to October and the cost (including airfare) is approximately £1900.

FACTFILE

When to go: April to October is best. November to March can be very hot.

Travel tips: Take plenty of drinking water on the long-distance drives. Game Park reservations should be made through **Directorate, Nature Conservation and Recreation, Resorts Reservations, Private Bag 13267, Windhoek 9000.** Permits available from **Department of Tourism, Private bag 13297, Windhoek 9000.**

Other information: Tap water is relatively safe but is usually chlorinated.

NEPAL – ROOF OF THE WORLD

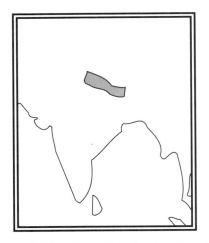

Although Nepal is the highest country in the world, it is also one of the smallest, not much bigger than the state of Florida, or England and Wales combined. Dubbed 'The Roof of the World', its northern frontier with Tibet is formed by the great Himalayan massif; the youngest and highest mountain range on earth. Nepal contains no fewer than eight of the world's fourteen highest peaks, all over 8000 m/26 000 ft: Everest, Kanchenjunga, Annapurna, Lhotse, Dhaulagiri, Manaslu, Makalu, and Cho Oyu. Despite its tiny size, Nepal exhibits an enormous variation in topography, with altitudes ranging from just 70 m/

230 ft to the summit of Mount Everest at 8848 m/29 039 ft. This incredible variation results in an equally diverse climate, which ranges from tropical through temperate to Arctic. Isolated from the rest of the world for most of human history, this landlocked 'forbidden kingdom' was shrouded in mystery until it first opened its doors in 1949 to a few intrepid explorers. Climbers like Shipton, Tilman and Hertzog paved the way for others to follow so that today the number of foreign visitors is around 250 000 per year – either too many, or too few, depending on who you listen to. Nepal is a feudal kingdom whose life and customs are still firmly rooted in the Middle Ages. Its remote mountain villages are inhabited by hospitable communities whose way of life has remained largely unchanged for centuries. To appreciate its mountain grandeur, you have to leave the towns behind and walk to the foot of the peaks themselves. In doing so, you pass through tropical forests and across bleak mountain deserts, through deep lush valleys and over windswept passes. Visiting Nepal is more than an ordinary adventure: it's an experience in which you become embroiled in a different culture whose every aspect of life is determined by religious significance. Hinduism exists alongside Buddism – the very foundation of life for the mountain people. Particularly during the autumn trekking months, adventure travellers become quickly attuned to the many festivals and religious activities which are such a feature of this fascinating country.

As the major city and entry point into Nepal, Kathmandu provides an ideal springboard for adventurers. When you've had your fill of the capital's temples, shrines, bazaars and crazy driving, claustrophobia will demand that you break out into the real, remote Nepal. As the country lacks any modern infrastructure of roads and railroads, travellers tend to use internal flights operated by Royal Nepal Airlines using short take off and landing aircraft. These flights are, at best, somewhat exciting, when you combine the vagaries of Nepal's weather, the ruralness of its runways and the horizontally challenged nature of its topography. On balance, though, flying here is less gruelling than taking buses or lorries with their dubious mechanical track-record. Given the precipitous nature of Nepal's roads and hairpin bends, evidence of road accidents is not hard to find.

The country is divided into a series of regions which display distinctive differences. Generally the part of Nepal west of the Kali Gandaki river is not too often visited by trekkers: facilities are few and distances are great. A notable exception is the trip to **Rara Lake National Park**, one of the world's remotest game sanctuaries, which was established by the King of Nepal in 1975. It is about 3000 m/10 000 ft high here and lakeside snow lingers as late as

May or June. Further west and north towards Simikot lie little known valleys accessible only on foot and primarily used by Tibetans trading along traditional border routes. The lifting of restrictions in 1989 enabled trekkers to pass through the high valleys of the **Dolpo region**. This largely ignored area has remarkable windswept scenery which stretches far away to the arid plateau of Tibet. Here, even the most travelled Westerner is disturbed by the sight of a Sharman (spirit-possessed holy man) becoming seized by an inner spirit, as viewed from a yak tent, far from civilization . . .

Eastern Nepal is equally remote. The area around **Kangchen-junga** is still partially restricted, with only about 500 organized trekkers a year allowed in. A trail leads up from the rice and tea growing lowlands to the high glaciers of the world's third highest mountain. Twin Otter aircraft fly regularly to Tumingtar – capital of the remote **Arun valley**, where you can descend through tropical forests on the banks of the huge Arun River towards Namche Bazaar, the main village of the Khumbu region. This traditional trade route crosses high forested ridges, connecting culturally distinctive villages. These are home to the world-renowned Sherpas, long recognized for their altitude tolerance and mountaineering skill. These 'Tigers of the Snow' have assisted numerous expeditions and gained worldwide recognition, particularly when Sherpa Tensing stood at the top of Everest with Hillary in 1953. The Solo-Khumbu's main attractions are its majestic mountains and isolated monasteries. Most visitors to this region have as their goal Everest base camp. Although fewer than 12 000 tourists visit this area every year, the detritus of Western visitors has been, and continues to be, a pollution problem.

Far more popular for adventurers and trekkers is the region north of the very accessible town of Pokhara. Just 40 minutes flight (eight hours by bus) from Kathmandu you can be up into the foothills of the **Annapurna Himalayas** where a five-day trek takes you to the fabled **Annapurna Sanctuary**. A ten-day trip takes in a huge diversity of landscapes, ranging from cultivated terraced slopes to steamy rhododendron forests to arid desert-like wildernesses similar to the Tibetan Plateau. The colourful Gurung villages and ever present influence of ex-Ghurka soldiers make this diverse region one of the most spectacular in Nepal. Between Dhalagiri and Annapurna lies **Kali-Gandiki**, one of the deepest gorges in the world. Together with the Thorung pass (5416 m/ 17 764 ft) this is more than enough of a challenge for moderately fit trekkers embarking on the 22-day Annapurna trek.

Contrasting with the northern mountainous region is **Terai region** in the south, a rich and fertile plain. The highlight of a visit to Terai is a jungle safari in the **Royal Chitwan National Park**.

Established in 1973 as a wildlife sanctuary, the Park houses numerous wild animals including the famous royal Bengal tiger, the one-horned rhinocerous, wild boar, sloth bear, four species of deer and more than four hundred species of birds. Dugout canoes are used to cross the Naryani river (dangling figures in its crocodile infested waters is not recommended). Elephants prove to be by far the most convenient form of transport as well as the safest: trained mahouts can force the elephants to trumpet loudly enough to force the prehistoric bulk of a charging rhino to back down.

The last ten years have seen the emergence of river rafting as a major adventure activity. Nepal has so many dramatic mountain rivers that it is hardly surprising that rafting has become such a popular pursuit. There are numerous exciting runs, mainly on the **Sun Kosi, Trisuli, Kali** and **Gandaki rivers**. In particular, the Sun Kosi is rated as one of the world's top ten rafting rivers. Evocative place names such as 'Pinball' and 'Ladies Delight' conjure up excitement, but the remains of crushed buses and broken bridges are potent reminders of the dangers of such rivers. Rafting is an ideal accompaniment to a mountain trek. Arriving at one of the tented camps in the Chitwan National Park, with its open fires and 'jungle magic' is a memorable experience.

For those visiting Nepal for the second or third time, more experienced trekkers can extend their challenge to one of the 18 or so 'trekking peaks'. This description is a misnomer, since all of the peaks are over 5000 m/16 400 ft high and require some technical Alpine experience. At 6654 m/21 825 ft, **Mera Peak** in the Khumbu Himal is the highest of the so-called trekking peaks.

Mountain biking is also gaining in popularity. You can take a valley trip around Kathmandu or an organized trip around Royal Chitwan National Park. It is also supposedly possible to ride 70% of the **Langtang trek**, but for the remaining 30% be prepared to carry the bike. In trekking there are basically four options financially, which from least to most expensive comprise: going on your own; organizing your own porters; getting a trekking company in Kathmandu to organize everything; or going on an ex UK package.

Himalayan Kingdoms (20 The Mall, Clifton, Bristol BS8 4DR; tel: 0117 923 7163) offers Lake Rakka from £1800 (ex UK) and a more adventurous trekking peak (Mera Peak) from £2150. **Thin Air Expeditions (Suite 501, 223 Regent Street, London W1R 8QD; tel: 0171 495 2554)** has some excellent adventure trips including 'Everest – Highest Trek in the World', a 31-day extensive trek which treks to nearly 5500 m/18 000 ft on Everest's north face. **World Expeditions** offers several Nepal trips, priced from £600 (13 days, basic trekking) to £2000 (24 days, high peak expedition), both excluding air fare. Kathmandu-based **Temple Tigers** (contact

Tourist Board) has its own jungle lodge in the Royal Chitwan National Park and can also organize rafting and trekking.

Classic Nepal (33 Metro Avenue, Newton, Derbyshire DE55 5UF; tel: 01773 873497) offers a 20-day '**Discover Nepal**' trip which is designed to introduce you to trekking, rafting and wildlife safaris. It costs approximately £1700, all-inclusive. On day 1 you depart London Gatwick with Royal Nepal Airlines, arriving in Kathmandu on day 2 and transferring to your hotel. After acclimatizing in Kathmandu for a day, you fly to Pokhara, camping overnight. Day 5 sees the start of a seven-day trek in the Annapurna foothills, taking in lush forests and small farming villages. This is undemanding trekking (maximum altitude, 2250 m/7400 ft) and there are memorable views of the Annapurnas and other famous peaks. The trek ends on day 11 in Pokhara with spectacular views of the Himalayas. On day 11 you are driven to the Trisuli river for the start of a two-day rafting trip which combines rapids and white water with calmer, more peaceful stretches. The rafts bring you to the Royal Chitwan National Park where you stay at Chitwan Jungle Lodge. Here, accompanied by guides, you spend two days experiencing a variety of adventures including jungle walks and elephant safaris. On day 16 you are driven to Everest Panorama Resort in Daman with its sweeping views of eight peaks over 8000 m/26 250 ft in altitude. Day 17 is spent returning to Kathmandu and during the next two days there is a range of optional tours in and around the capital. Finally, you return to London on day 20. Departures are from March to April and October to January. Trekking time averages 4 to 6 hours a day and you are only expected to carry a day pack, Sherpas performing the heavier carrying duties. Group size varies from 8 to 15.

FACTFILE

When to go: October and November (clear skies), March/April (rhododendrons at best). Avoid June/July (monsoon).

Travel tips: Carry small denominations for purchases while trekking; do not encourage begging for money; add iodine to water (or boil); keep currency receipts; Kathmandu has a plethora of second-hand bookshops which stock books, maps and guides.

NEW ZEALAND – LAND OF THE LONG WHITE CLOUD

'New Zealand is probably the most beautiful place on earth.'
James Mitchener, Return to Paradise

When the Maori settlers first sighted New Zealand in the eighth century the 100-mile long islands appeared cloaked in cloud. They christened it 'Aotearoa', Land of the Long White Cloud. However, this name should not conjure up an image of grey misty days: while North Island has a subtropical climate, the weather in South Island, though cooler, is still sunny and there is the added bonus of snow in winter. New Zealand must be the perfect Antipodean adventure destination. Though only the size of the British Isles, it contains endless white beaches, jagged mountain peaks, lush, unspoiled native forests, geysers, lakes and deep, brooding fiords. Whether it's hiking through spectacular mountain landscapes, rafting through towering gorges, or sailing round the beautiful coastline, an adventure holiday in New Zealand will be an unforgettable experience.

Wilderness is New Zealand's untamed heritage and perhaps the most dramatic scenery is to be found in the mountainous south west of South Island. In **Fiordland National Park** and **Mount Aspiring National Park** are some of the world's most spectacular walks. One of the most famous is the **Milford Track**, a six-day hike crossing the scenic McKinnon Pass and the three thundering leaps of Sutherland Falls. There are also the high Alpine **Routeburn Track**, a three-day walk which hugs the tops of the magnificent Hollyford Valley, and the **Greenstone Valley** walk, a mellow riverbank track along an ancient Maori trail. In short, there are trails to suit every level of fitness, from gentle one-day hikes to strenuous ten-day expeditions. They can be undertaken as guided trips or independently. Most of the trails have plenty of huts along the way, thus reducing the amount of equipment you have to carry. **Venturetreks (tel: 09 799 855)** offers a wide range of organized walking treks through this area, costing anything up to

NZ$1000. **Greenstone Valley Walk (tel: 0294 29572)** offers a guided walk through the Greenstone Valley and a six-day combination with the Routeburn Track from NZ$370 to $850). **Mountain Recreation (tel: 02943 7330)** offers treks in Mount Aspiring region. Not to be missed by the committed climber is **Mount Cook National Park** in South Island. At over 3700 m/12 140 ft Mount Cook is the highest peak in New Zealand and, incidentally, training ground for Sir Edmund Hillary. It is renowned for its difficult weather conditions and loose rock, so it is essential to take a guide for the ascent. One of the companies providing climbing guides is **Alpine Guides (Mount Cook; tel: 05621 834)**.

New Zealand's rivers offer adrenalin-packed action for rafting enthusiasts. Of the North Island rivers the **Rangitikei**, the **Motu** and the **Rangitaiki** have a rugged, natural beauty and wild, white water. In South Island you should head for the **Landsborough**, one of the steepest rivers rafted in the country. Starting from Mount Cook National Park it passes through imposing glaciers and miles of untouched native forest. Rafting companies offering trips can be contacted through the **New Zealand Tourist Office** (see Appendix 1).

For a more gentle, though equally enjoyable, river adventure you could try a canoeing trip on the **Whanganui river** in North Island. Rich in native forest and birdlife, the Whanganui National Park provides a magical setting as you drift gently downstream through steep papa cliffs and majestic Rata trees. Several canoe operators organize canoe trips, including **Canoe Safaris (PO Box 5065, Mt Maugani)**, and **Venturetreks (tel: 09 799 855)**.

Further north the maritime reserves of the **Bay of Islands**, **Hauraki Gulf** and **The Bay of Plenty** offer excellent sailing opportunities. Yacht charters are widely available and you can either 'bareboat', skippering the boat yourself, or take a skippered charter. It's a tremendous way to explore the beautiful coastline and some of the smaller islands which are abundant in birdlife. Charter companies include **Bay of Islands Yacht Charter (tel: 0887 78545)** and **Rainbow Yacht Charters (PO Box 8327, Symonds Street, Auckland; tel: 09 378 0719)**.

With its endless coastline, New Zealand boasts some superb beaches which are still uncommercialized, wild places with sparklingly clean water. For the more remote beaches you can head north to **Doubtless Bay** and to the northernmost tip of **Cape Reinga**, a place of spiritual significance to the Maoris who believe it to be the departure place for their spirits. New Zealand has enormous scope for surfing and windsurfing, whether your taste is for wild west coast action or for the more peaceful conditions on the east. There are some splendid surf beaches around Whangarei at **Ruaraka** and **Ocean Beach** as well as on the east of the

Coromandel Peninsula. Some of the finest seascapes in the country are to be found on the East Cape between Opotiki and Gisborne. If you are an enthusiast for adventure underwater you will find that New Zealand is a diver's paradise. Good diving spots can be reached from the coastline, particularly in **Northland**, but the best diving in the country is to be had off a boat on one of the many islands around the coast of Northland. The clear waters around the **Poor Knights Islands** offer spectacular viewing of a huge variety of colourful reef fish. Off **Cavalli Island** you can explore the wreck of the Rainbow Warrior, flagship of the Greenpeace fleet. Contact the **New Zealand Underwater Association (PO Box 875, Auckland 1)** for information on dive charter boats.

Not only is New Zealand a land of mountain and water but also of forest and volcano. **Urewera National Park** is the largest unbroken tract of native forest in North Island in an area of rugged mountains, ravines and lakes. Further south at **Tongariro National Park** you enter a landscape of glacial moraines and volcanic vents. At Ketetahi the hot springs, boiling mud and geysers are unforgettable. **Te Reuhawi Safaris (tel: 073 65131)** offer five- and seven-day treks through the Urewera National Park (NZ$500–700).

If you want to sign up to a packaged adventure tour of New Zealand's North and South Islands **Explore** offers a number of options. Its '**Nature's Restless Islands**' package consists of thirty-two days of 'caves, mountains, fiords and glaciers'. This trip, which includes hiking, canoeing, glacier walking and an optional dolphin swim, costs around £3000 all-inclusive. Shorter Explore options feature either North Island or South Island adventures.

Mountain Travel Sobek's (6240 Fairmount Avenue, El Cerrito, CA 94530; tel: 510 527 8100) 'Exploring New Zealand' trip offers an 18-day soft adventure which includes plenty of easy-to-moderate day hikes within a variety of scenically impressive areas, using comfortable accommodation. Days 1 to 3 involve your flight to Auckland and acclimatization in North Island. On day 4 there is a morning drive to Rotorua, followed by a hike in the Whakarewarewa Thermal area, with its steaming lakes and soaring geysers. More thermal activity is witnessed on the following day with exploration of Waimangu volcanic valley and Huka Falls. You then continue to Tongariro National Park where day 6 is spent on a full hike. After a stop in Wellington, the group takes a ferry across Cook Strait on day 8 for the second part of the holiday, which starts in Nelson Lakes National Park. Day 9 is spent hiking here, then it's on to Cape Foulwind for further hiking on day 10. After continuing to Greymouth, day 11 involves a visit to Hokitika, then a hike on Fox Glacier, where you don hobnail boots and follow your Kiwi guides through a labyrinth of ice caves.

Day 12 involves a hike around Lake Matheson, day 13 a morning walk and day 14 is free in Queenstown. Another morning walk on day 15 is followed by a drive to Twizel, and then its off to Mt Cook National Park for a full day's hike. After that it's a drive to Peel Forest for a short hike before continuing to Christchurch on day 17. On day 18 you fly home. The cost of this adventure holiday is around $3000, excluding airfares.

FACTFILE

Climate: The warmest months are December, January and February, and the coldest June, July and August, but the climate is fairly mild throughout the year.

Travel tips: Self-drive campervans are an ideal way of exploring the country and getting off the beaten track (price is about £50 per day, low season, for a two-berth vehicle). For the more energetic there are also great cycling opportunities, either independently or as part of a group.

NORWAY – MOUNTAIN MADNESS; FJORD FEVER

Once visited, wild Norway is never forgotten: it haunts you like a scene from one of Ibsen's plays. The country can be described as the land of fjords and mountains, and its an addiction to the landscapes – a kind of fjord fever or a mountain madness – which makes people long to return again and again to experience the country's delights. Adventure activities abound here, the more popular ones being hiking, skiing, river rafting, pony trekking and canoeing, but for 'headbanger adventurers' there are some more off-the-wall activities – like scuba diving north of the Arctic Circle, for instance! Climate-wise, it's a healthy country, summer lasting from May to September and winter sports taking place from December to late April. The Gulf Stream's influence helps to make June, July and August unexpectedly warm. Situated close to northern Europe, Norway's main airports are less than a two-hour flight away. The country is larger than the UK and yet its population numbers only 4.3 million, so travellers can be assured of abundant space, solitude and silence.

The main areas of interest to adventurers are the Western Fjords and North Norway. The **Western Fjords** consist of 2400 km/1500 miles of spectacular, deeply indented coastline. Some of these fjords are only 100 m/328 ft wide in places, with vertical cliffs rising over 1000 m/3280 ft on either side. Sognefjord is the longest of these inlets, running for a distance of 200 km/124 miles into interior Norway. Other spectacular fjords include Hardanger, Nord, Romsdal, Ryfylke and Sunn. Travelling from valley to valley is possible via the efficient ferry services. The Hurtigruten Company runs 'The world's most beautiful voyage': 11 days along the fjord coast, calling at 34 ports and including an excursion to the North Cape Plateau. Prices including air or sea connections from the UK vary from £1500 to £2800 (contact **Norwegian Coastal Voyages, NSR Travel, 21–24 Cockspur Street, London SW1Y 5DA; tel: 0171 930 6666**). For travellers arriving either by ferry or air, fjord Norway can be accessed easily via a number of cities such as Stavanger and Bergen.

North Norway consists of majestic mountains, rolling moorland, sheltered fjords and countless islands. It offers much to hikers, riders and canoeists in summer, while winter ski-touring is also popular. The Reisdalen region has some extraordinary primaeval pine forests, cliffs and waterfalls. Geographically, North Norway is where mainland Europe borders the Arctic Ocean and every year many people arrive here to make the 1900 km/1200 mile pilgrimage up from Oslo to the North Cape – Europe's most northerly point.

The Norwegian people are 'born to ski'. Norway was the birthplace of telemark skiing and it was the Norwegians who turned skiing into a modern sport. They established its basic technique, invented ski waxing, the modern binding and the laminated ski. For ski-touring and cross-country ski enthusiasts, the country is a delight, with more than 60 000 km/37 000 miles of tracks and routes throughout the country, many centres opening as early as December and January. Although daylight is shorter than further south at this time of the year, a full day's skiing can be enjoyed from 10 am to 4 pm. By March and April, daylight hours are in step with the rest of Europe. Average temperatures are similar to those of the Alps and whether it's warm or cold, the crisp, dry air is always exhilarating. All the major resorts offer plenty of cross-country skiing trails, as well as equipment hire and accommodation. These resorts include Gola, Voss, Trysil, Oppdal, Hemsedal, Geilo, Lillehammer, Gausdal, Dombas, Roros, Beitostolen and Sjusjoen.

One area of special note to adventure-seekers is **Hardangervidda** in the heart of Southern Norway. This is Europe's largest mountain plateau, a 10 000 sq km/3900 square mile wilderness which is home to thousands of wild reindeer. A third of the area consists of Norway's largest National Park. This is the only place in the world where species belonging to a western, coastal climate and those thriving in an eastern, inland climate are found in the same area together. The Hardangervidda scenery is varied, with dramatic valleys, glaciers and waterfalls in the east and gentler slopes in the west. Seamed throughout the region are a variety of trails, once vital communication links from east to west but now ideal for hiking in summer and skiing in winter.

Managed by the Norwegian Touring Association, these trails are well maintained. Some of the routes are demanding in nature, while others are suitable for families with younger children. For longer trips there are several huts positioned strategically for use by hikers and skiers. These offer modest accommodation – there's no luxury – but all the essentials are there: a bed for the night, wood burning stoves and food supplies. Though some of these cabins are staffed, a few are not and it is a refreshing illustration of Norwegian honesty that the system is not abused. Nights in the staffed huts can be booked in advance at reasonable rates by contacting the **Norwegian Touring Association** or **DNT (Den Norske Turistforening, PO Box 1963 Vika, 0125 Oslo 1)**.

Hardanger jokulen – the mighty glacier 1870 m/6140 ft above sea level is an icy magnet to climbers and walkers. Be warned, however: never head out there without an experienced guide; the crevasses can be a lethal trap for the inexperienced. Guides can be contacted through DNT or via local tourist offices. Hardangervidda is easily accessible from Route 7 – the main Oslo to Bergen road, or at Finse, a high-altitude station on the Bergen–Oslo railway. Accessing the area from Eidfjord not only gives you easy access to the plateau, but allows you to see some of the best fjord scenery in Norway.

For adventure trips to Norway, you could consider **Waymark Holidays (44 Windsor Road, Slough SL1 2EJ; tel: 01753 516477)**, which offers several cross-country skiing and ski touring itineraries, ranging in price from around £600 to £900 per week. Some of these tours require previous experience. You can go dog sledging in Norway's Arctic region with **Arcturus Expeditions (PO Box 850, Gartocharn, Alexandria, Dunbartonshire, G83 8RL; tel: 01389 830204)**. Cost for a 9-day 'drive your own dogs' trip is from £1700 to £2000.

As an example of a small group Norwegian adventure holiday, **Waymark** offers a two-week moderate-to-demanding trip in July entitled **'Sundat & the Vidda'**. From Rjukan, 200 km west of Oslo, a road climbs up to the small settlement of Skinnarbu, whence you take a boat 10 km up the lake to Sundat Farmhouse, home of Philip and Maiken Yatman, leaders of this holiday. The first week is spent at Sundat, walking in birch-clad hills and mountains behind the farm but also crossing the lake to walk in Skinndalen, a valley on the western side where elk, reindeer, the rarer lynx and wolverine, and a variety of birdlife are found. The second week is spent backpacking on the Hardangervidda, staying in huts, some of which are privately owned while others are owned by the Norwegian Touring Club (DNT). First you take the boat up the Mosvann Lake to Mogen at the northern end, where you continue by foot on to Lagaros, then west to Bessa, southwest to Litlos (2 nights), south to Hellevasbu and finishing at Haukeliseter before returning by taxi and boat for a final night at Sundat. You will need to take a rucksack large enough to carry supplies for six nights on tour. Accommodation in the huts and at Sundat is in single-sex multi-bunk rooms. Some of the huts are self-service, while others are wardened. The price of the trip, about £800, is based on reductions allowed for Alpine Club members: non-members pay a higher rate, so it may be worthwhile joining. Waymark can provide more details.

FACTFILE

Climate: The Gulf Stream confers a moderate climate on coastal areas. Inland temperatures are more extreme, with hot summers and cold winters.

Transport: Nordturist rail tickets (also called Scanrail cards) allow 21 days' unlimited travel in certain Scandinavian countries, and reduced ferry crossing costs as well.

Accommodation: Offsite camping is allowed in uninhabited areas (not lay-bys), but fires are not allowed in forested areas between 15 April and 15 September. There are over 1000 authorized camp sites in Norway.

PAPUA NEW GUINEA – LAND OF MOUNTAIN AND FOREST

'I looked around at the dripping moss-covered forest, at the jagged rocks of black and white limestone and I realised that we could rely only upon ourselves in this place so far removed from the outside world where a cry is only to the wilderness.'

Jack Hides, travel writer

Consisting of over 600 islands, Papua New Guinea is one of the last true wilderness areas of the world. It is an unconquered frontier, where you can discover the magic of an unspoiled paradise of rugged mountains, fast flowing rivers, volcanoes and thermal pools. Much of the island is covered with a blanket of various shades of green from the dark green of the tropical rainforest to the lighter shades of mist and mountain forest. Set against this tapestry of green are brilliant flashes of colour: birds of paradise, rhododendrons and orchids. Papua New Guinea is renowned not only for its startling profusion of plant and animal life but also for the astonishing diversity of its people: there are over a thousand tribes on the island speaking about 700 distinct languages; some are pockets of people just emerging from the Stone Age.

Papua New Guinea is not for the faint-hearted: roads are scarce in the mountainous hinterland and the only two ways to travel in most parts of the country are by air or on foot. There are a number of walking tracks, one of the best known being the 90 km/56 mile **Kokoda Trail** across the famous **Owen Stanley Ranges**. Used in the 1890s by gold prospectors, it follows a series of ridges and valleys, the steepest being the **Imita Ridge**. The trail takes 5–6 days, but there is no need to take a tent as there are rest houses in the larger villages, while in the smaller ones the villagers will offer rooms. Maps can be picked up from Murray Barracks in Port Moresby.

There is also a range of organized trips based on the lodges in the Highlands. One of the best of these is **Ambua Lodge** in the southern highlands. Perched on a hill at a height of 2100 m/7000 ft it commands superb views over the **Tari Basin**, a huge and mysterious valley where the mist rolls in like an ocean and the mountain peaks stand out like islands. From here there are tremendous opportunities to encounter the culture of the Huli people, to observe the spectacular birdlife and to explore the waterfalls and Alpine forest. There are also organized treks which include **Mt Wilhem**, Papua New Guinea's highest mountain at 4500 m/14 800 ft, and **Mt Giluwe**.

In the north of the country is the **Sepik river** which reaches over 1100 km/680 miles into the wild and remote interior near the northwest border. Exploring the river in a motorized, dugout canoe or a larger river boat, is an unforgettable experience. The Sepik river is a natural trade route: passing through tiny, isolated villages and creeper-entangled trees, you will also see a fantastic variety of plant and animal life, with birds, butterflies and orchids (as well as the odd crocodile), that you won't find anywhere else in the world. Two companies which offer 8-day to 21-day trips covering the highlands and rivers of Papua New Guinea are **The Natural World (52 Church Street, Twickenham TW1 3NR; tel: 0181 744 0474)** and the local operators, **Trans Niugini Tours (tel: 52 1490)**.

There are tremendous trekking opportunities on the unspoiled and relatively undiscovered island of **New Ireland**. **Grassroutes Ecotravel (tel: 675 921 755)** offers a 4-day trek through primaeval, tropical rainforest, along ridges with superb views of mountains and sea and around the cliffs and beaches of the coastline. You can also explore the beautiful villages and rolling hills of the island by bicycle on a four-day tour also organized by Grassroutes Ecotravel.

Those in search of adventure on or under the sea will find plenty of scope on the many smaller islands of Papua New Guinea. The **Duke of York Islands** are classically pretty coral atolls, fringed by reef on one side and lagoons on the other. These sheltered lagoons are ideal for canoeing, wind-surfing and water-skiing. On **Watom Island** there are beautiful beaches with excellent snorkelling, as well as some fascinating archaeological sites. **Grassroutes Ecotravel (tel: 675 921 755)** offers three-day trips to both these islands.

Madang, with its crystal-clear tropical waters and chain of coral reefs, is an excellent centre for snorkelling and scuba diving. Between **Kranket** and **Leper Island** is the beautiful 'magic passage', a dramatic coral passage dividing the reef, frequented by brilliantly coloured reef fish. In Madang Harbour, the intact wreckage of a Mitchell B25 Bomber offers a memorable dive. The **Melanesian Dive Centre (tel: 82 2655)** provides equipment hire as well as boat dives and snorkel trips around Madang.

There are also magnificent diving opportunities around the stunning volcanic caves and rocks of **Walindi** and **Rabaul**. **Trans**

Niugini Tours (tel: 52 1490) offers dive packages which include both sites.

FACTFILE

Climate: At sea level the climate is tropical and hot but the temperature is cooler in the highlands. The monsoon season is from December to March.

Health: All drinking water should be boiled. Malaria here is resistant to certain types of drugs. Consult your doctor about the best anti-malarial tablets to take.

PERU – INCA ENCHANTMENT

'He loved the broad spaces and the magnificent grandeur of the Andes . . . The Indian Rosendo attributed to them all the shapes and characters imaginable, and he spent long hours watching them. Deep within him, he believed that the Andes held the baffling secret of life.'

Ciro Alegría, Broad and Alien is the World

The third largest South American country, Peru is situated in the northwest bulge of the Continent, bordered by (from south to north) Chile, Bolivia, Brazil, Colombia and Ecuador. Some four times the size of the British Isles, the country boasts a great variety of landscapes, including tropical rainforests, a coastal desert 3200 km/2000 miles long, the river Amazon, the highest/largest lake in the world and the deepest gorge in the world. Its Inca history and culture have left a legacy of some extra-ordinarily fascinating remains and none more so than the legendary Machu-Picchu – 'Lost city of the Incas'.

There are three natural zones: the Pacific Ocean coast, the Andes and the Amazonian jungle. Along the **Pacific coast**, the ocean currents are cold, while the climate is dry and – for half of the year – misty. Peru's capital, Lima, is situated here, although this earthquake belt is not the best of places for cities in general. Of greater interest to adventure travellers are the Altiplano and **Andes**, with their deep canyons and grasslands, giving way to lofty and majestic peaks. The best time to visit the Highlands is during the May to September dry season. Although this is winter, days are normally bright and sunny, and this is the period when the coastal area is dull and misty. Situated at 3650 m/12 000 ft, **Lake Titicaca** is described as the highest navigable lake in the world. Living on floating reed islands on the lake, the local inhabitants are the Uru Indians, descendents of the original settlers here. The world's deepest canyon, 3400 m/11 160 ft, is found in the southern Peruvian highlands. Its rapids have been navigated, but only by seriously experienced kayakers.

The **Amazon Basin**, part of the much larger Amazonian region of the continent, covers more than half of Peru although it is mostly inaccessible for tourists. You can take a boat from Pucallpa to Iquitos, the largest city in the Peruvian jungle. Further on, you can take a trip deeper into the forest to areas inhabited by Amazonian Indian tribes (some 350 000 are thought to live in this region). Contrary to popular belief, swimming here is excellent.

For many travellers, however, it is the remains of the Inca civilization which lures them to this country. When Francisco Pizarro led his small band of Conquistadores into Peru in 1532 they did not seem to pose an immediate threat to the mighty Incas whose empire at that time extended over 2000 km/1200 miles. History proved otherwise, however, and within a relatively short time the whole Inca civilization was literally in ruins. Many of the Inca structures were hidden from Western travellers until relatively recently. It was not until 1911 that one Hiram Bingham chanced upon a previously unheard of Inca citadel which was to become the most famous ruin in all South America – **Machu-Picchu**. Although at the time this place was widely believed to have been the last Inca refuge from the invading Spaniards, the true site, **Espiritu Pampa**, beyond Quillabamba in the Amazonian jungle, was discovered as recently as the 1960s. But Machu-Picchu remains as the ultimate Inca symbol – one of the great sights of the world, dramatically situated in a terraced saddle between two lofty peaks, its precise white granite blocks standing proud over the Urubamba river, while beneath stretches the dark green forests and misty mountains.

For reasons given below (see Factfile), you do have to be confident to travel off-the-beaten-track as an independent traveller in Peru. If you do go independently, however, accommodation is patchy. There are 26 **Youth Hostels** in the country (for information contact **Youth Hostels, Lima, Casimiro Ulloa 328, San Antonio, Lima 18; tel: 14 465 488**), but there are no official camping sites here (as in most of the rest of South America). Camping out in the countryside is usually no problem, however. Very cheap hotels are present in many villages and these are clean, if somewhat spartan. Few roads in Peru are paved, landslides can occur and thus travel can be slow (and seriously interesting at times). Bus journeys are cheap, but are also long and gruelling, while trains are cheap but crowded and slow.

Itineraries for hiking the Inca Trail are offered by many adventure companies. **Explore** offers 'Heights of Machu-Picchu', a 15-day hotel/camping trip including Lake Titicaca and a 5-day Inca Trail Trek, for around £1300, all-inclusive. Their longer (22-day) trip includes the option of an Amazon lodge extension (£1500). **Exodus** has, among other tours, an 18-day 'Inca Llama Trek', which in addition to Lake Titicaca and Machu-Picchu, includes a high-altitude trek amidst 'some of the most dramatic scenery in the Andes.' Other operators include **Journey Latin America (14–16 Devonshire Road, Chiswick, London W4 2HD; tel: 0181 747 8315)**, who can advise clients on independent travel, and **Encounter Overland**.

A varied adventure holiday in Peru (and Bolivia) is offered by **World Expeditions** in their 'Andes and Altiplano' 25-day trip. After arriving in Lima, you fly to Cusco, former Inca capital, where you encounter a fascinating blend of Inca and Spanish cultures. On day 6 you are driven through the Sacred Valley of the Incas to Mollepata, for the start of an eight-day trek. This involves ascending jungle trails to reach the Alpine heights of the Cordillera Vilacamba, where camp is established on the flanks of Mt Salcantay (6402 m/21 000 ft). The trek itself takes from day 8 to day 16, the last day being spent joining the Inca Trail to Machu-Picchu. After returning to Cusco, you have a chance to unwind there on days 18 and 19. The following day you take a train to Lake Titicaca where you explore its shoreline, meeting small groups of Uros Indians who live on floating reed islands. A drive around the lake on day 22 takes you to Copacabana (the Bolivian one that is) and thence to La Paz on day 23. The trip concludes at La Paz on day 25. Trekking is graded moderate to strenuous, covering an average of 12–15 km/7–9 miles each day and demanding average fitness by participants. Camping equipment is provided by the company and porters and llamas accompany the group. Apart from the camping, accommodation is in good-quality hotels on the basis of twin-share bed and breakfast. Departures are from May to October and the cost for joining the group in Lima is about £1400 (the company can advise on low-cost airfares).

FACTFILE

Responsible tourism: Sendero Luminoso (Shining Path) guerillas operate in the remoter parts of Peru and it can sometimes be dangerous to stray too far from established tourist routes either alone or in small groups. Travelling with an adventure tour operator removes the risk. It should be stressed, however, that the vast majority of Peruvians are honest and friendly.

Communication: Try to learn as much Spanish as possible before you visit the country.

Addresses: A good source of detailed information is the **South American Explorers Club, 1510 York Street 214, Denver, CO 80206, USA**; or **Av. Portugal 146 (Brena), Casilla 3714 (Postal), Lima 100, Peru.**

RUSSIAN FEDERATION – IRON CURTAIN DRAWS ASIDE

It used to be called either the Soviet Union or the Union of Soviet Socialist Republics. Now it's called the Russian Federation – otherwise known to Europeans as the Commonwealth of Independent States, or to Americans as the Newly Independent States. Russia has undergone enormous political and social changes in recent years, the watershed occurring in 1991 when the Communist system – which had lasted for 74 years – finally disappeared. Today Russia is open for business with the rest of the world and, as such, is keen to develop its embryonic tourist industry. Its tourist authorities are also aware that, away from the main centres like Moscow and St Petersburg, Russia's tourist facilities are at best fairly basic, at worst non-existent. This is good news for adventure vacationers though, since it's these visitors who are able to enjoy the plethora of rich treasures that rural Russia has to offer – for the time being at least.

The Russian Federation (Russia for short) is vast – almost twice the size of the USA, or a sixth of the globe's total land mass. Stretching 10 000 km/6200 miles from east to west and 4500 km/2800 miles from north to south, it has three million rivers, is touched by twelve seas and possesses countless mountains. As you would expect in a country which spans ten time zones, the range of climatic and geographic conditions is extremely diverse, from the frozen tundra of Siberia to the Mediterranean climes of the Black Sea. Russia's population of 300 million is a polyglot conglomeration of over 100 European and Asiatic nations and nationalities, each with its own variation of language, culture, traditions and lifestyle.

Not long ago, when the Iron Curtain separated this region from the rest of the world, just getting past Russian immigration formalities was something of an adventure in itself. Only the very determined or the very privileged were able to see something of the country's special scenic secrets. But now, with small beginnings, the veil is slowly being lifted and groups of Western adventure travellers are being encouraged to venture into the interior. While packaged adventure opportunities are as yet fairly limited, the potential is virtually limitless. However, truly independent adventure travel is unlikely to become commonplace until early in the 21st century. At the moment, adventure holidays are confined to groups of between eight and sixteen. The current range of summer activities available includes mountaineering, mountain biking, river rafting and trekking, while Russia's legendary winters (Moscow has 164 days of snow a year!) enable plentiful skiing. The main areas for packaged adventure trips in Russia comprise the Caucasus, Siberia, Karelia and Central Asia.

Separating southwest Russia from neighbouring Georgia and Armenia, the **Caucasus** mountains stretch from the Black sea to the Caspian sea. Dominating the range is **Mount Elbrus**, at 5642 m/18 510 ft the highest peak in Europe. Its summit looks out onto a beautiful and diverse landscape: deciduous forest and meadows carpeted with flowers. The climb to Elbrus's summit is not technical, but it is demanding, fitness-wise. If you are happy to settle for less demanding trekking, the region around Elbrus is a mecca for hikers, with its six-day trekking circuits. Alternatively, you could extend the challenge of Elbrus by including three other summit climbs above the Adyl-Su valley system.

East of the Ural Mountains and covering an area of ten million square kilometres lies **Siberia**, an adventurer's paradise. The word 'Sibir' means 'sleeping land' and certainly this place epitomizes somnolent peace and quiet. It is a sleeping giant, with countless rivers, vast taiga forests, enormous steppes and innumerable mountains. But its principal attraction is **Lake Baikal**, the world's largest lake. It holds as much water as all the five great Lakes of North America put together: indeed, to fill this mighty chalice, all the rivers of the world would have to pour their waters into it for a whole year. **Intourist** offers what they call 'active rest' holidays in this area. In summer these holidays include hiking tours based on hunting huts, horse riding and sailing trips on the lake; while winter trips include ski touring and troika rides.

Another part of Russia opening up to adventure groups is **Karelia**, in the northwest. Situated close to Finland, this is a land of blue lakes, rivers running with swift, clear waters, picturesque waterfalls and forests. Finland itself is known as a country of lakes, but in Karelia there are twice as many lakes per square kilometre. The state preserve of Kivach is especially beautiful with its main river, the **Suna**, spilling over fifty waterfalls. All kayak and raft routes here start from Petrozavodsk, capital of Karelia, before setting out down the rivers Shuya, Suna, Vama and Vodla. These vary in Grade from a gentle I up to IV (see white-water rafting, p 79).

Russia's **Central Asia** region could be the subject of a book in itself. No adventure description of this region would be complete, however, without mention of **The Great Silk Road**. This centuries-old trading route linking China with Europe passes through ancient cities with evocative names like Samarkand and Tashkent. Using camel caravans, traders are recorded as using The Silk Road as early as the 2nd century BC and today it is still possible to travel along parts of it by camel. The best times of the year to travel this route are spring and autumn.

Explore runs a number of trips to Russia, such as '**Trekking in the Caucasus**', a 15-day hotel/camping trip including the Gondorai Valley, for around £1000. **Exodus**'s 22-day '**Footsteps of Genghis Khan**' journey to Mongolia and Siberia includes boat trips and camping, price £2200, all-inclusive. The country's largest internal tour Operator, **Intourist (Intourist House, 219 Marsh Wall, London E14 9FJ; tel: 0171 538 8600)** organizes special tours for groups of adventure holidaymakers, while an increasing number of external tour operators are including Russia within their portfolios. The **Association of Independent Russian Tour Operators (Moscow 101000, b/b 68)** has several subscribing operators which between them offer a wide range of adventure activities. These include cycle tours and hiking trips, river rafting, canoeing, caving, mountaineering, trekking and horse riding, and the main regions covered comprise Central Russia, Siberia, Lake Baikal and Sakhalin. You can even take a trip to visit the North Pole!

For an example of a moderate-to-demanding adventure holiday

in Russia, **Sherpa** offers an 18-day trip entitled 'The High Altai'. After arriving at Moscow on day 1, the group takes a flight to Barnaul, staying there overnight. On day 3, you fly to Ust-Koksa and drive to Katanda. The next 12 days are spent hiking in the High Altai, a mountainous region with dense forests – cedar, larch and birch – and diversity of wildlife. The trek starts at the settlement of Katanda, and while horses carry the loads, you trek into the surrounding mountains. Your route takes you from river valley to river valley, crossing several passes in the process (maximum altitude 3200 m/10 500 ft). Once over the Volzhski Pass you follow the Katun river up to its source, while up above you towers Mt Belukha; at 4506 m/14 789 ft the highest peak in Siberia. A crossing of the Verkhni Kapohalski Pass leads you down to Lake Kucherla where the trek itself ends. On day 16 you return to Barnaul, flying to Moscow on day 17 and leaving Russia on day 18. This trip is suited to experienced and fit walkers, accommodation is in hotels and camping, and baggage is carried by porters. The cost is approximately £900, all-inclusive.

FACTFILE

Health: Drinking the tapwater is not advisable.

Insurance: It is recommended that you take out medical insurance in advance of your journey.

Climate: Winter lasts from December to March, depending on how far north you are. Spring starts only in late April or May. While sub-zero winter temperatures are commonplace, summer temperatures can be quite hot, with temperatures rising to the mid-20s.

ST VINCENT AND THE GRENADINES – THE NEXT BEST PLACE TO HEAVEN

'There is no forgetting the islands, I said.
Where the sun has left no shadows.
They will fill your eyes with richness.'
Geoffrey Drayton

Forming the southern sweep of the Windward Islands and spanning some 35 miles of sea between St Vincent and Grenada, St Vincent and the Grenadines are often regarded as primarily a *luxury* holiday destination, an exclusive beach haven for the rich and glamorous. However, this small archipelago of rocky islands, sandy cays (pronounced keys) and exotic reefs holds in store for the more intrepid traveller a wealth of tropical adventure both on land and below the turquoise waves.

If you are willing to leave the beach, you will indeed be rewarded by a lush wilderness untouched in comparison with some of the Grenadines' rivals. Until very recently, few of the thirty-three islands and tiny cays that comprise St Vincent and the Grenadines had air contact with the outside world (though now several of the islands do have their own airports) and what lingers on is a profound sense of a seafaring society, a people very much in tune with the ocean that surrounds them. Most island-hopping remains in the hands of those who run dozens of short ferry trips from one tiny anchorage to another and you can still enjoy the feeling of idyllic isolation which sadly has been lost in other parts of the Caribbean.

St Vincent itself is a fertile volcanic island with prolific banana plantations, lush rainforests and coconut groves surrounding the craggy heights of the **Morne Garu** mountain range. Its highest peak is **La Souffriere**, an active volcano, which last erupted in 1979. But don't worry! It is rigorously monitored and, in any case, is unlikely to surprise the unwary traveller. This rocky terrain in turn sinks down to a coastline of beautiful beaches both of golden and black volcanic sand. St Vincent's main settlement, **Kingstown**, is a lively little port on the southern leeward coast, whose market on Saturday mornings is the perfect place to buy supplies of fresh fruit and vegetables for your island adventure. Like the tail of a kite, the islands of the Grenadines then trail south from St Vincent and remain gloriously off the beaten tourist track, whilst offering those not content with miles of white sand alone some of the most varied coral reefs and sailing waters in the Caribbean.

How you choose to spend your time in a part of the world where time seems to stand still is one of the dilemmas which inevitably faces travellers to this little corner of the Caribbean. For many who visit St Vincent and the Grenadines the real experience begins with a plunge beneath the waves of the **Caribbean Sea**. Whether you are an experienced diver or have never so much as put your face in the water, the riot of marine life which greets you there within the intricate system of coral reefs is guaranteed to inspire and addict. Just where you elect to explore this other world depends both on where you wish to be based and on whether you are a complete novice or a certified diver. There are several dive operators to choose from, who will either require of you an internationally recognized 'C' card diving qualification (PADI, BSAC, CMAS, or NAUI) or alternatively offer a variety of training courses. The latter vary from full-blown certification courses to fully supervised shallow water dives and include night dives, underwater photography courses and snorkelling tours. Just off St Vincent itself, there is the **New Guinea Reef**, a favourite with Vincentians, which offers myriad marine life amongst the distinctive black coral and which can be explored at any depth from just 7.5 m/24.5 ft to over 30 m/100 ft. **Bequia** is one of the largest of the Grenadines. Situated just south of St Vincent, Bequia offers several fine diving sites along its 11 km/7 miles of encircling reef. These remain comparatively unexplored especially on the leeward side of the island where a marine park prohibits spear fishing, netting, trapping and anchoring and where a vivid expanse of reef at different depths remains preserved.

Moving south some 64 km/40 miles from St Vincent, you find the five uninhabited islets which make up the **Tobago Cays**. Surrounding them lies **Horseshoe Reef** which offers perhaps some of the most exciting underwater vistas in the Caribbean. Excursions departing from St Vincent and from Union Island, just west of the Cays, visit daily and this can often mean that the solitude promised by the famous rum commercials shot here is difficult to come by! All the same, those who do drop anchor are rarely disappointed by what must surely be the cartoon prototype for all tropical islands. Above all, it is here that those visitors new to the underwater world are likely to fall in love with it forever, as it provides easy and excellent shallow diving and snorkelling, in crystal clear waters.

For the landlubber adventurer, there is much to delight ashore on St Vincent. For tourists prepared to swap flippers for hiking boots, a wealth of flora and fauna is waiting to be discovered. The most adventurous expedition is probably the four-hour trek to the lip of the smoking **Soufriere volcano**, which takes walkers through lush seasonal forest and original rainforest on the 1200 m/3900 ft climb. The best ways to approach this slumbering giant are either the easier climb from the Rabacca Dry River on the east coast, or the rougher but more scenic route from Richmond and Chateaubelair on the leeward coast. Above all, be sure to leave early in the morning, try to arrange a guide through your hotel or through the Tourist Bureau in Kingstown and always take plenty of drinking water (you inevitably need far more than you expect). More gentle walks are to be found in the immensely fertile **Buccament Valley** where bamboo forest meets rainforest. Here the Vermont Nature Trails allow you to wander through the natural habitat of the rare St Vincent parrot, most likely to be sighted between late afternoon and dusk. In the very north of the island the **Falls of Baleine** are to be found. These can really only be reached by boat after which a short walk up the river bed from the coast brings you to a cluster of natural swimming pools and the idyllic falls themselves. Incidentally, wherever you are walking on St Vincent try to avoid high noon when the sun is at its hottest, always wear a hat and ensure that you seek local advice as to which route to take before setting off.

St Vincent and the Grenadines' international reputation for outstanding sailing waters is more than just Tourist Board hype. In fact, they offer some of the least crowded stretches of sea and most idyllic selection of anchorages in the whole of the Caribbean. There are a number of yacht chartering companies to choose from, which can supply you with either bareboats or crewed vessels depending on your sailing knowledge and your inclination to work! From then on, it's just a matter of setting sail on your adventure and choosing where to drop anchor. Probably the best anchorage off St Vincent itself is at **Young Island** (a private resort island), opposite the aptly named Blue Lagoon. Here you can buy provisions for the rest of your cruise in Kingstown, though **Port Elizabeth** on Bequia's Admiralty Bay also provides a picturesque and well-equipped pit stop. Be sure that you take care only to drop anchor where it will not damage the reefs and, with that precaution in mind, many a deserted beach, sandy cay and palmy vista can be your own wilderness retreat.

Whether you decide to organize your own adventure in St Vincent and the Grenadines or whether you look for an inclusive package must ultimately depend on how much money you want to spend. Though it may well prove cheaper to cobble together your own arrangements, do bear in mind hidden costs that can be incurred this way. Lists of hotels and more reasonable guest houses are available from the Tourist Board. Dive operators offering a full range of instruction and facilities are **Dive St Vincent (tel: 809 457 4714)** around St Vincent itself and including the Falls of Baleine; **Grenadines Dive (tel: 809 458 8138)** around Union Island and The Tobago Cays; and **Dive Bequia (tel: 809 458 3504)**. **Caribbean Connection (Concorde House, Forest Street, Chester CH1 1QR; tel: 01244 329556)** offers seven nights for four people aboard a 44 foot yacht departing from Young Island at from around £700 in low season to over £1100 in high season. **Crestar (125 Sloane Street, London SW1X 9AU; tel: 0171 730 9962)** and **Camper and Nicholsons (31 Berkeley Street, London W1X 5FA; tel: 0171 491 2950)** also offer sailing packages to the Grenadines. Should you wish to charter a yacht off your own bat, among the 15 or so companies operating are **Trade Wind Yachts (tel: 809 825 7245)** who offer a certification package and other tailor-made deals; **Barefoot Yacht Charters (tel: 809 456 9324)**; and **Lagoon Marina Yacht Charters (tel: 809 458 4308)**. Walking tours can really only be organized *in situ*, but it is worth contacting **Paradise Tours (tel: 809 85417)** or the Tourist Bureau on arrival.

FACTFILE

When to go: The main advantage of a Caribbean holiday is that the difference between summer and winter is a mere 10 degrees (85°F–75°F) and there is no real wet season. The climate is definitely agreeable all year round.

Travel tips: The St Vincent and Grenadines **Department of Tourism** publishes a bi-annual brochure called *Escape* which is full of places to stay and other useful information. The London Office (see Appendix 1) will send you a copy upon request. It is worth finding out from the Department of Tourism when certain festivals and regattas are happening throughout the year, as coincidence with one of these could either be an added holiday bonus, or a time to avoid being there, depending on your inclination.

SOUTH AFRICA – A WORLD IN ONE COUNTRY

'The magnificent landscapes of Africa build up to a tremendous climax. Towering haze-blue mountain ranges – the Matroosberg, the Swarzbergen and the Hex – part like stage curtains to reveal the final epic image of Table Mountain and the wide Atlantic. It is a breathtaking display of natural beauty and one which raises all our tired spirits.'

Michael Palin, Pole to Pole

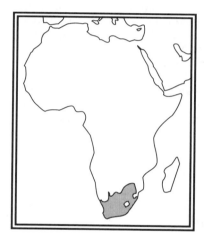

Nowhere else in the African continent can you find such a diversity of landscapes, such an enlightened approach to conservation and such an abundance of opportunities for adventure holidaymakers. With its reliable infrastructure, good communications, political relaxation and ever-sunny climate, little wonder, then, that South Africa is becoming one of the most popular long-haul destinations for Western visitors: in short, the ideal adventure introduction to Africa. In recent years, it has developed an extensive range of activity holidays from ballooning to diving, riding to hiking, white-water rafting to sailing, and many others besides. And for safari enthusiasts, South Africa has retained more animal species than any other African country. The wildlife figures are staggering: 10% of the world's total bird, fish, reptile and plant species, as well as 6% of its mammal species. In all, some twenty million acres of land have been given over to game reserves in the country.

Broadly speaking there are eight provincial areas – Orange Free State, Natal, Transvaal, Cape Province, Transkei, Bophuthatswana, Ciskei and Venda. To experience the plethora of South Africa's adventure possibilities fully would take a lifetime: lack of space here permits only a taste of what the country has to offer. But your first visit should carry a 'health warning': it is likely to lead to an addiction and is certain to create a desire to return.

Exploring the eastern highlands of the **Orange Free State** gives hikers a wealth of spectacular mountain scenery. If you've always fancied climbing Mount Everest but suffer from altitude sickness, then the small **Mount Everest Game Reserve** offers plenty of scope. And if you would rather not risk the chance of encountering rhino on foot, then horses or landrovers can be hired. The **Berg Marathon** held annually on 10 October, is strictly for fit enthusiasts: it originated when a British soldier, speaking to a local, referred to Platberg as 'that small hill of yours'. The local wagered that the soldier would not be able to run to the summit in less than 60 minutes. He did, and donated a floating trophy to all future winners. Further exploration on foot is well rewarded in the region of **Quaqua**: fairytale mountains covered in snow during winter and carpets of flowers in spring. At the hidden hideaway of Bergoord, a hiking trail leads via a famous chain ladder to the summit of Mont-aux-Sources in the lofty Drakensberg mountains. Superb hiking can also be experienced at the **Golden Gate Highlands National Park** in the foothills of the Maluti Mountains. A two-day Rhebuck Trail crosses streams, valleys and mountains picturesque at any time of the year. If watersports are more appealing, the 260 sq km/100 square mile **Vaal Reservoir**, surrounded by a Nature Reserve, offers plenty of scope. At the other extreme, the Karoo or 'place of the big drought' represents an interesting conservation exercise on a grand scale. Reintroduction of game to the 27 000 hectare/66 700 acre **Karoo National Park** started in 1977 (its animals were previously hunted to extinction). Today the area is a conservation success story: 180 species – including antelope and zebra – are well established in the Park. Armed with a permit from the Department of Environmental Affairs (see Factfile) you can enjoy the three-day Springbok trail through this often dry and dusty environment.

The north east of South Africa is the **Transvaal** region, characterized by wide open plains, majestic mountains and indigenous forests. This is a mecca for safari lovers. Its roll-call of game reserves, wildlife sanctuaries and National Parks is headed by the internationally renowned **Kruger Park**, without doubt a jewel in Africa's crown of National Parks. It supports the greatest variety of wildlife species to be found on the continent. You would have to be very unlucky (or in an an indecent hurry) to miss seeing elephants for example, while the chances of spotting large carnivores are very good. The best season for viewing game is winter, when the grass is scant and the animals congregate at waterholes: on the other hand ornithologists will find summer more rewarding. Although visiting this Park tends to fall into the 'softer' end of the adventure spectrum (most accommodation inclines towards the luxurious, for instance) you can get off the beaten track by taking one of the four wilderness trails recently established there. These are three-day walking safaris, made under the guidance of experienced rangers. There is a maximum of eight per group, and you have to be between 12 and 60. If time is limited, several companies offer short fly-in safaris to the airstrip at Skukuza rest camp.

Acting as a kind of buffer strip to Kruger, several private game reserves have been established on the western border of the Park. Some of these have become well known in their own right (for instance **Sabi-Sand** and **Timbavati**). Again, each reserve offers comfortable-to-luxurious accommodation, and game viewing is mostly by four-wheel drive vehicle, but more adventurous tastes can also be catered for in these areas.

Transvaal's adventure interest is by no means confined to safaris. Wonderful days can be spent taking in the so-called **Summit Route**, west of Kruger, with its spectacular waterfalls, variety of hiking trails, caves, potholes and nature reserves. Excellent walking can be found in the five-day **Blyde river** hiking trail which starts from the aptly named 'God's Window', a stupendous viewing point on the rim of the escarpment.

Adventure seekers to this part of South Africa should not overlook **Venda** – the area adjoining the northern section of Kruger – with its indigenous forests, mysterious lakes, tumbling waterfalls and hot springs. Venda's own **Nwanendi National Park** is worth including on your tour. Similarly, regions of **Bophutatswana** such as the **Borakalalo National Park** and **Botsalano Game Reserve** offer excellent game-viewing facilities.

Far away from dusty 'Jock of the Bushveld' country lies the **Eastern Cape**. Its **Romantic Coast** stretches northeast from Kayser's Beach, merging with Transkei's own **Wild Coast**. Broad beaches, placid lagoons and rocky promentaries abound, while swimming and surfing opportunities here are unrivalled elsewhere in South Africa. No adventurous visit to this area would be complete without experiencing the rugged and unspoilt five-day Wild Coast hiking trail between Port St Johns and Coffee Bay. Accommodation is in basic huts and you will need to find suitable crossings of the river mouths when the tides are up. At least nine shipwrecks add to the desolate atmosphere of this trail. Further west lies the Hogsback, a gravel road twisting through the spectacular Amatola mountain range. Its charm lies in its mountain scenery, yellowwood forests and country lanes – a perfect place to get away from it all.

Northeastern Cape has a distinct character of its own: stunning expanses of countryside with wide, sweeping foothills and beckoning mountains. Close to the Drakensbergs, the altitude here enables skiers to indulge their sport in the winter. On the ski lift slopes of **Ben Macdhui** (an African-style 'Munroe' at over 3000 m/ 9800 ft!) you could almost be in Scotland, except that the weather is warmer and the snow is usually much better.

Much of the Northern and Eastern Cape is Great Karoo country – a vast spacious upland expanse of dry sheep farms. High on the northern slopes of the Bankberg range, the **Mountain Zebra National Park** provides a sanctuary for survivors of the great herds of plains game which once roamed free over these lands. Its original population of 25 Burchell's Zebra has grown today to over 200. Of particular interest to adventure seekers is the **Karoo Valley of Desolation Nature Reserve**, with its network of hiking trails. The valley itself is more correctly a ravine comprising two parallel rock columns which rise precariously to over 100 m/300 ft. Only the adventurous should be prepared to negotiate the void between them.

The famous **Garden Route** is often considered more appropriate for the sedentary tourist, but its valleys, gorges, mountain passes and evergreen forests have plentiful appeal to adventurous holidaymakers as well. For exploration with a difference, the **Tsitsikamma Coastal National Park** is a rewarding destination. The first proclaimed coastal National Park in Africa, it contains several hut-to-hut hiking trails. Further west, **Knysna forest** offers a variety of forest hiking trails as well as watersports opportunities.

Wedged (but without artificial boundaries) between Namibia and Botswana lies the **Kalahari Gemsbok National Park**, which, taken together with its neighbouring Botswana National Park, is the largest nature conservation area in southern Africa and one of the largest unspoilt ecosystems in the world. Against a background of rust-coloured Kalahari duneland, game is usually very visible here. A network of windmills feeding dams and watering holes ensures the survival of animals in drier years. Apart from the Kalahari lion, carnivores include cheetah, wild dog, leopard and hyena. An astonishing variety and number of birds are also to be found here.

Not surprisingly many tour operators include South Africa in their listings, but because of the country's 'user-friendly' nature for independent adventurers, packaged adventure trips are not too plentiful. **Guerba** offers a number of trips which include safaris, hiking and options to go white-water rafting. Their trips vary from 22 days up to 8 weeks for the southern Africa multi-country circuit. Approximate prices vary from £1500 to £2100, including flights. **Exodus** offers a 23-day soft adventure '**South African Discoverer**' for about £1600. In common with a number of other operators, **Worldwide Journeys and Expeditions** will tailor independent itineraries for you, depending on your time and budget.

For a packaged adventure holiday to South Africa you could try **High Places**. Their 18-day packaged walking trip visits three contrasting highland areas: the Cedarberg Wilderness area of the Western Cape, the Oteniqua Trail on the Cape coast and the high

Drakensberg range bordering Lesotho. Your journey begins in Cape Town where you walk up the slopes of Table Mountain (day 2). You then drive north to the Cedarberg hills to hike over sculpted red sandstone ridges and across 'fynbos' bush, visiting bushman cave paintings en route (days 3 to 6). The next four days are spent on Cape Coast following the Oteniqua trail. Here the walking is up and down forested hills and valleys, with clear rivers and swimming holes. Wildlife is plentiful in this region. Five days are then spent among the Drakensberg, the highest mountain range in southern Africa, where you witness some of the area's dramatic ridges and summits. On day 17 you travel to Johannesberg for your return flight on day 18. Departures are in April and September and travel is by minibus. Accommodation consists of camping chalets and mountain huts (mostly on National Park sites) and hotels in towns. The all-inclusive cost is about £1600.

FACTFILE

When to go: March to May and September/October are good, but any time of the year is rewarding.

Travel tips: There is a very extensive network of hiking trails. Contact **National Hiking Way Board, Dept of Environment Affairs, Forestry Branch, Private Bag X447, Pretoria 0001.**

Other information: You can buy all goods which you would be able to buy at home.

SVALBARD – REALM OF THE POLAR BEAR

'Suffice it to say, that by dint of sailing north whenever the ice would permit us, and sailing west when we could not sail north, we found ourselves on the 2nd of August in the latitude of Spitzbergen . . . The whole heaven was overcast with a dark mantle of tempestuous clouds that stretched down in umbrella-like points towards the horizon, leaving a clear space between their edge and the sea, illuminated by the sinister brilliancy of the iceblink. In an easterly direction, this belt of unclouded atmosphere was etherealized to an indescribable transparency, and up into it there gradually grew – above the dingy line of starboard ice – a forest of thin lilac peaks, so faint, so pale, that had it not been for the gem-like distinctness of their outline, one would have deemed them as unsubstantial as the spires of fairy-land.'

Lord Dufferin, Letters from High Latitudes, 1856

Spitzbergen, or 'Pointed Mountains', is the largest of the group of High Arctic Islands called Svalbard (meaning 'cool coast'). Set within the storm-ridden Barents Sea, Svalbard lies midway between the north of Norway and the North Pole. It was thought to have been discovered in 1596 by Dutch explorer Willem Barents, but this has been subsequently disproved. Only 800 km/500 miles from the North Pole, it has been the jumping-off point for many a polar expedition, such as the ill-fated Italian airship expedition of 1928, and a more successful recent trip by Michael Palin. According to a 1920 treaty, Norway has full sovereignty over the area, but other parties to the treaty (including the UK) have certain rights (such as visitors not being obliged to show passports). Warmer than similar latitudes in Greenland or Canada, temperatures in summer (July and August) range from −5°C to a clement 15°C, while precipitation is generally low. Once it was only within reach of the really determined, but now Svalbard is rapidly becoming a mainstream Arctic destination for adventurers of all ages and abilities, thanks to good air and sea links. In fact this is about as close as you can get to the North Pole without mounting a major expedition. Adventurous visitors to the archipelago discover that Svalbard is supremely invigorating and refreshing, its fine weather and extraordinarily clear air giving rise to spectacular visibility.

Topographically, it is a wild and rugged land, carved through by massive glaciers and subsequently eroded by the power of water. Today, roughly half of Svalbard is covered with ice, although many glaciers are currently retreating. On some of the coastal areas, impressive sea cliffs drop down to wide fjords littered with ice floes and ice bergs. In other places, gentler deltas fan out onto shallow beaches, while further north, sharp nunataks can be seen poking out from glaciers and ice caps, remnants of the last ice age. Much of Central Spitsbergen is ice-free however, and this makes it eminently suitable for trekking and camping tours. Flowing rivers are the exception in Spitsbergen since any water remains frozen here for more than half of the year. Similarly, lakes and waterfalls are rare. Although Svalbard's permafrost reaches down nearly 500 m/1640 ft, the top layer melts during the short but intense Arctic summer. It is then that flowing water becomes the norm and these seasonally swollen rivers can present difficulties for hikers and backpackers wishing to cross.

In this frenetic summer period of continuous daylight, short Arctic vegetation – no more than a few centimetres high – puts on a growth spurt. In spite of its High Arctic latitude, Svalbard's tundra has a surprising variety of flora, including 48 kinds of flowering plants. Among these are found such species as Arctic willow, mountain avens, Arctic bell-heather, snow buttercup and Svalbard poppy. Particularly in the north, vegetation is extremely fragile and some areas here and elsewhere in the island have accordingly been given protection as nature reserves. The archipelago is warmed by the Gulf Stream and this gives rise to seas rich in plankton. In turn this brings crustaceans, fish and their predators; seals, walrus (once common but now sadly rare), beluga (or white) whale and killer whale.

The intense Arctic summer also brings in huge numbers of birds which come to breed here. Among the 70 or so species of migrating birds are found geese, eider ducks, phalaropes, snow buntings and the rare little auk and ivory seagull. Some fall prey to the Arctic foxes, one of the three resident species of land mammals in Svalbard. Reindeer – there are reckoned to be around 12 000 – live here, spending the summer building up body reserves for the long winter. King of the Arctic, the polar bear, also inhabits this land. Although they are found mainly in the northern ice pack area during the summer, you are never quite sure whether one will make an appearance even in the south, for Svalbard holds a fifth of the world's population of these magnificent beasts. Most of Spitsbergen's polar bear cubs are born in snow caves at Kong Karls Land, a polar bear sanctuary with forbidden access. Nine-tenths of Spitsbergen's visitors arrive in July or August. In contrast to other northern destinations, this place offers almost no infrastructure, so visiting parties have to be self-sufficient in food and equipment. Hiking tours require a good deal of fitness from participants and up-to-date equipment. The central area of Spitsbergen, good for hiking tours, is **Nordenskjold Land**, with wide valleys and plentiful peaks. Two of the highest peaks on Spitsbergen are **Newtowntoppen** and **Perriertoppen**, each 1717 m/ 5631 ft, situated in a very remote part of the island.

Several tour operators list Svalbard on their itineraries, including **Arctic Experience**. **Arcturus Expeditions (PO Box 850, Gartocharn, Alexandria, Dunbartonshire G83 8RL; tel: 01389 830204)** offers a number of sea voyages during the summer months on the ship *Professor Molchanov*, including a 9-day North Spitsbergen cruise (£2000 to £4000 depending on accommodation), an 11-day Northeast Spitsbergen cruise (£2400 to £5000) which includes a number of shore trips, and 13- or 14-day Round Spitzbergen trips (£2600 to £5600). A Norwegian-based adventure company which specializes in trips to this destination is **Svalbard Polar Travel A/S (SPOT), 9170 Longyearbyen, Norway; tel: 47 80 21 971; or Tveterveien 24 - 1344 Haslum, Norway; tel: 47 2 58 05 17)**. It has built up its own transport network using chartered boats. Among the several tours it operates are coastal cruises, strenuous trekking at the '**Rim of the North Pole**', ski and skidoo expeditions, the '**World's Northernmost Ski-Touring Holiday**' and '**Discover Spitsbergen in Winter**' (April).

Waymark (44 Windsor Road, Slough, SL1 2EJ; tel: 01753 516477) offers a 12-night trip to Svalbard, 'combining what is possibly the world's northernmost trekking with a short cruise in Arctic waters'. This **Spitsbergen** trip starts with a 2 am arrival in Longyearbyen. After a few hours sleep in a guesthouse, you board the little cruise ship and set out along Isfjord, briefly visiting the Russian-populated coal settlement of Barentsberg, before turning north through Forland Sound. Near the island of Moffen, whales and walrus may show themselves before the ship swings southwards into the Raudfjord to call at base camp. For the next four days you explore the surrounding valleys and peaks (there are several accessible 1000 m/3300 ft peaks here). The ship returns at midnight and by mid-morning sets you ashore at the second camp: Blomstrand on the Kongsfjord, where you can go glacier walking using the equipment provided. Three days later, the ship collects the group and takes you back to Longyearbyen for a final day of sightseeing and walking. Hiking is graded at 3 to 4, ie up to 7 hours walking a day, involving some scrambling, with ascents of 1500–2000 m/5000–6500 ft each day. Four nights are spent on board ship in four-bunk cabins; six nights are spent camping and two nights are spent at a guesthouse. Cost for the trip is around £1600, all-inclusive.

FACTFILE

Daylight: 24-hour daylight lasts from 20 April to 20 August.

Photography: Although daylight is constant in summer, fast film (200–400 ASA) and a UV filter are recommended, as are lenses of at least 300 mm focal length.

TANZANIA – GREATEST WILDLIFE SPECTACLE ON EARTH

'It was the kind of morning which always seems improbable even to the most calloused Africa hand . . . the sun had crawled up over the snow-capped round head of Kilimanjaro, chipping the first diamonds off the mountain, and causing the tall yellow thorn trees to glow waxily like enormous painted candles under their green visors of branch.'

Robert Ruark, Uhuru

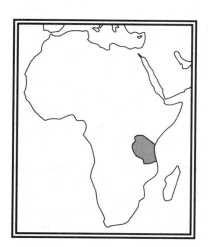

Tanzania is a game viewer's paradise, a country as old as time itself, in which nature still reigns. Its vast wilderness is home to the greatest and most spectacular concentration of game animals anywhere in the world – three million, give or take a few hundred thousand. Lake Tanganyika, on Tanzania's western border, is Africa's longest and deepest freshwater lake, and the second deepest in the world. Add to this the snowy equatorial challenge of Kilimanjaro – Africa's highest mountain – and you have the perfect recipe for an unforgettable African holiday adventure.

The scale of East Africa's largest nation is mind-boggling. Half the size of Western Europe, Tanzania's landscapes vary from a 800 km/500 mile tropical coastline (including the island of Zanzibar), to central plateau savanna, to the permanent snowy majesty of its famous mountain massif. But immensity is only one of the many extraordinary facets of this strangely haunting country. When Dr Mary Leakey unearthed the fossil skull of early man in the Olduvai Gorge in 1959, she revealed a history of our species dating back nearly two million years. That people have lived here in harmony with the land for a thousand times the span of *anno domini* defies the imagination. And yet the majesty of the Serengeti, the perfection of Ngorongoro Crater and the beauty of Arusha National Park remain little changed from the days of *Australopithecus boisei*, giving visitors to the country a humbling glimpse into the timelessness of African wilderness.

Part of the attraction of Tanzania to adventure travellers is the fact that it has never been as fashionable as neighbouring Kenya. It is thus more of a challenge with respect to getting about, communicating and finding accommodation. But while the supply of creature comforts can run a bit thin at times, Tanzania is not short of the creatures themselves. Its eleven National Parks cover a staggering quarter of the country's land surface, containing the greatest concentration of animals on the face of the earth.

Arusha, one of the most accessible National Parks, is a string of delightful lakes and hills concealed within the folds of a mahogany forest. To the southwest of Arusha lie the former hunting grounds of **Lake Manyara** and its surroundings, now one of Tanzania's most attractive wildlife sanctuaries. This National Park, with its shallow alkaline lake, nestles in the sides of the rift valley, not far from **Ngorongoro Crater**. One Professor Grzimeck, who spent years surveying this spectacular caldera, declared it to be a wonder of the natural world, and, indeed, to gaze from its intact rim over the 300 sq km/116 square mile floor is like watching a vast animal amphitheatre from a seat in the gods. Within the crater 'stage' itself is a mosaic of habitats, ideally suited to a wide range of wildlife 'players'. Though small in number, Black Rhino still cling on here, one of their last remaining sanctuaries in the whole of the continent.

But to the adventurer and wilderness lover it is the **Serengeti** which exerts a special kind of magnetism. Undoubtedly the world's most famous National Park, the Serengeti lies between the shores of Lake Victoria to the east and the Masai Mara to the north (Kenya's own answer to the Serengeti). Its super-abundance of plains game (there are reckoned to be over a million wildebeest and half a million gazelles alone), inspires a vision of Africa as it was in the days of the early explorers, when migrating columns of wildebeest sometimes took days to pass in front of the incredulous Western observer.

Tanzania's southern parks and sanctuaries are even less accessible and more likely to appeal to adventure holidaymakers, especially independent travellers. For a glimpse into unspoilt Africa, the **Selous Game Reserve** in southeastern Tanzania is without equal. Five times the size of the Serengeti, with dense forest, rolling savanna and a mighty river – the Rfiji – this reserve is one of the least-touched strongholds of the African elephant. Further east lies **Ruaha National Park**, with rocky gorges and deep pools, prime country for antelope. In the foothills of the Uluguru Mountains **Mikumi National Park** is also remote and rich in wildlife, particularly buffalo, lion and elephant.

No adventure trip to Tanzania would be complete without at least an attempt on **Mount Kilimanjaro** – in Swahili the 'pale mountain'. In 1848 when Johannes Rebmann announced that he had seen a vast snow-capped mountain at the equator he was ridiculed by the Royal Geographical Society. The local Chagga people always believed the mountain was the dwelling-place of an angry god who punished anyone who dared to climb it. But since the first recorded ascent in 1889 by Hans Meyer, many have taken a chance on incurring the god's wrath. Today several tour operators offer you the opportunity of tackling Africa's highest mountain and although it's not a technical climb, it is a tough trek, demanding fitness and hard physical effort, not to mention the possibility of altitude effects as you approach its 5895 m/19 341 ft summit.

For an all-round adventure trip to Tanzania, **Exodus** offers a 17-day 'Safari & Climb' package, taking in Ngorongoro Crater, the Serengeti and Lake Manyara followed by a five-day ascent of Kilimanjaro. Accommodation is a mixture of hotels, self-help camping and mountain huts. Group size is up to 16 and travel is by four-wheel drive vehicle. The trip is graded as 'expedition' status ie 'strictly for those who are confident about travelling in very remote and often difficult areas, where some discomforts are inevitable'. Price including flight and accommodation is around £1400.

Guerba offers a range of adventurous safaris in northern Tanzania, from 8 to 23 days. If you're short of time, their **'Serengeti Trail'** which includes the Ngorongoro Crater, Olduvai Gorge and Serengeti National Park, takes only 10 days and costs around £480 excluding flight. Travel is by four-wheel drive Bedford Truck and accommodation is mostly self-help camping. For another £240, you can bolt on a hot-air balloon safari in the Serengeti. **Worldwide Journeys and Expeditions** offers a choice of four safaris to Tanzania. Their 15-day **'Alternative Tanzania Safari'** takes you to the Selous and Ruaha National Parks and includes bush walks, boat excursions and four-wheel drive safaris. All-inclusive price is about £3000.

For an adventure holiday to remember, **Guerba** offers a 15-day **Serengeti and Kilimanjaro Camping** trip which costs around £1700 including airfare. Most of the travelling on this trip is in a purpose-built expedition truck (group size up to 21). Day 1 is spent travelling from Nairobi to Arusha, while day 2 is spent in Karatu. The next two days consist of a camping and game viewing safari in the Serengeti. A visit to the Olduvai Gorge is made on day 5 and you continue to Ngorongoro, spending a night on its rim. You descend its crater on day 6, travelling here by four-wheel drive vehicles. The next day is spent returning to Arusha for the start of the Kilimanjaro trip. On this trek you are accompanied by a local guide and porters. You spend 4 nights in mountain huts (Mandara hut, Horombo hut and Kibo hut). Day 13 is spent in Marangu and day 14 back in Arusha again. The tour ends in Arusha on the morning of day 15. As an optional extra you can take a Serengeti balloon safari for an additional £240.

FACTFILE

When to go: Best to avoid the rainy seasons (March–May and November–December).

Travel tips: Keep your currency declaration forms and bank receipts for when you exit the country. If you are on the coast, observe the strict Muslim codes of dress.

Other activities: Watersports on the coast.

THAILAND – TRIBES AND TREKS

For many years, the Kingdom of Thailand – previously known as Siam – was ruled by the Khmer Empire. Recently, formerly hostile relations with Thailand's Communist neighbours, Cambodia, Laos and Vietnam, have improved dramatically and, like Vietnam (see p 271), Thailand is now emphasizing and encouraging tourism in the wake of political stability in the region. Most Western visitors to the country see only the capital (Bangkok), the main tourist sights and the beaches in the south. Only a few discover the 'real' Thailand – the 'Golden Triangle' in the far north or the rural farmland in the central plains. This is a pity, since the remoter side of Thailand has a great deal of interest to visitors, especially those more adventurous travellers prepared to head away from the touristy hotspots and nightspots.

Stretching north of Bangkok, the **Central Plains** form Thailand's prosperous agricultural heartland. Here, great cities have risen, and fallen, during the course of history. **Phitsanulok** is one such place, a convenient location for trips into the surrounding area, such as the ancient city kingdoms of **Sukhothai** and **Kamphaeng Phet**. Thailand's western province of Kanchanaburi is perhaps best known as being the site of the famous 'Bridge Over the River Kwai', but it also boasts several beautiful waterfalls and limestone caves.

About three hours by road from Bangkok lies the **Khao Yai National Park and Wildlife Reserve**, in northern Thailand. This is the most popular of the country's Reserves, not only from the point of view of wildlife attractions, but also for its ancient and historical sites. Evidence of the ancient Khmer Empire abounds in the northeast, in such places as **Pimai**, **Lopburi** and **Phanom Rung**. The northeast also witnesses some special festivals, such as the elephant round-up at Surin which takes place every November. In the far north lies the country's second largest city, **Chiang Mai**, often described as 'the flower of the north'. You can make excursions into the surrounding region to see its ancient and beautiful temples, its teak forests with working elephants, its caves and waterfalls, and its northern tribespeoples with their unique cultures. Treks in the region usually take around four days, although some can last considerably longer. Before heading out on your trip it is worth visiting the **Hill Tribe Cultural Centre** at Chiang Mai University to get a feel for the variety of tribes and their cultural differences. There are three notable festivals in this region: Songkran in mid April, Loi Krathong in mid November and the Flower Carnival in the first week of February. In the **Mae Sa Valley** there's a training 'school' for elephants, while not far away you can visit an orchid farm. Longer trips can be made to see the **Doi Inthanon National Park**.

Northwest of Chiang Mai lies **Mae Hong Son**, a crossroads for Burmese opium traders and hill tribespeople and a good base for trekking trips. Not to be confused with Chiang Mai is the town of **Chiang Rai**, a good jumping off point from which to see the Mekong River and the Golden Triangle. Adventurous travellers will be drawn to the chance of river rafting in this region; not with rubber inflatables but on flimsy bamboo craft (don't forget to put your camera in a waterproof container). The trip from Tha Ton down the **Mae Kok River** is memorable: riverboats ply between Chiang Rai and Ban Tha daily. Many of the treks organized from towns like Chiang Mai, Chiang Rai or Fang include rafting options. There are day trips from Chiang Rai to Chiang Saen on the Mekong River and from there it's only a short distance to the Golden Triangle.

En route to southern Thailand is **Surat Thani**, a settlement located near to a national park with well preserved rainforests. The island of **Phuket**, in southwest Thailand, is becoming well-known as a busy tourist 'honeypot', but not far from here lies **Phang Nga Bay** (as seen in a James Bond film) which boasts one of the world's most stunning seascapes. Around 3500 'hongs' or islands are scattered in this region, forbidding and seemingly impenetrable from the outside. Until recently they were believed to be inaccessible from the surrounding sea but you can now take specialized canoe trips which enter through tunnels and cracks in the rock (when the tide is right) to reveal a fascinating hidden world rich in flora and fauna. Many coastal resorts offer adventure watersports, including Scuba diving (especially Pattaya and Phuket).

You can get around Thailand independently as an adventure traveller. There are Youth Hostels, YMCA and YWCA throughout the country and several camping areas situated mainly near the National Parks and usually under the management of the Department of Forestry. In general, however, camping is not popular in Thailand, since other forms of accommodation are relatively plentiful and cheap. Several tour operators offer adventurous Thailand group holidays, including **Guerba**, **World Expeditions** and **The Imaginative Traveller**. As an example of such a holiday, **Explore** offers a 22-day '**Northern Thai Adventure**' which comprises a varied and challenging trip. After flying to Bangkok, you board the overnight train to the northern hilltown of Chiang Mai, spending two days visiting the mountain region with its temple of Doi Suthep. On day 7 you head north and then southwest along the scenic Kok river to Fang and the large cave complex of Chiang Dao. On day 9 your seven-day hilltribe trek starts. You spend nights in different tribal villages learning about traditional ways of life of the different tribespeoples including the Lisu, Red and Black Lahu, Shan and Karen. Highlights include a short river rafting trip and riding working elephants to a Padung (long-necked) tribal village. Leaving Mae Hong Son, you drive directly south on a little-used route to Mae Samlap. From here (day 18) you travel down-stream by longtail boat on the Salween River and its tributaries (4 hours) and then continue by road to ancient Sukhothai. Finally you take the train back to Bangkok before departing on day 21. Accommodation on this trip consists mainly of bed & breakfast and guesthouses, as well as tribal bamboo huts and train sleepers. Trekking is graded as moderate with some strenuous patches (4–6 hours per day) at altitudes of around 3000–4000 m/9800–13 100 ft. Group size is from 12 to 16 and the cost is around £1000, including flights.

FACTFILE

Climate: It is generally hot, particularly between mid-February and June. The monsoon season runs from May to October and this period is still hot, with torrential rains. Best time for travelling is the cool season (November to February).

Culture: Thais seldom show emotion – only children are expected to show anger or frustration – and this behaviour in adults is culturally inappropriate. Keep a cool head in all situations, therefore, especially if things don't go to plan. Although unlikely to make a fuss about it, most Thais will be offended by provocative dress, particularly in the remoter villages of the north.

Trekking: If sweet, murky Thai coffee is too much for you, take a quantity of 'instant'.

TIBET – ROOF OF THE WORLD

'As we approached, the Potala towered ever higher before us. Our excitement was intense. We spoke no word, and to this day I can find no terms to express how overwhelming were our sensations.'

Heinrich Harrer

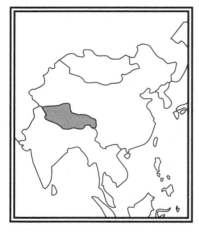

If the Greater Himalaya can be likened to a huge dam wall, Tibet is the vast reservoir of land behind it. With an average altitude of 4000 m/13 000 ft, much of the country is spectacular arid desert, stretching thousands of kilometres into Central Asia. South of this plain is an extensive area of mountainous grazing land inhabited by wild looking nomads living in yak hide tents, their livelihoods dependent on herding sheep, goats and yaks. Most Tibetans however, live in the southern region, a more hospitable area of gentle and protected valleys.

Tibet has always been a difficult country to penetrate. During their period of self rule Tibetans preferred isolation, shunning contact with the outside world. Reaching Lhasa was a major problem during the days of the British Empire. The year 1951 saw Chinese military occupation of Tibet followed by the Cultural Revolution and associated destruction of the country's shrines, monasteries and architectural heritage. Programmes of village resettlement, government ownership of livestock and prohibition of the Tibetan language were enforced in a systematic attempt to destroy Tibet's rich and fascinating culture. Fortunately this indoctrination largely failed and, since 1986, world opinion has gradually led Tibet to open its doors. The Dalai Lama, exiled spiritual leader of Tibet, now encourages Westerners to visit his nation and witness at first hand something of the discrimination shown against Tibetans in their own country.

Despite this relaxing of isolationism by Tibetans, the Chinese-administered **Tibetan Tourism Bureau** still encourages only 'official groups' of tourists. These groups are tightly controlled by the dozen or so appointed tour operators. Accommodation is restricted to a few expensive hotels and there are only a handful of recognized tour itineraries, largely revolving around city sightseeing. The majority of tourists start to unlock the door to Tibet's hidden secrets by taking 'the most scenic flight in the world' from **Kathmandu to Lhasa**. This passes over the great Himalayan range, giving (on a clear day) tremendous views of Everest and Kalu. Lhasa lies in the arid wilderness of the Tibetan plateau at an altitude of 3500 m/11 500 ft. Known as the 'forbidden city' Lhasa is dominated by the awe-inspiring Potala Palace, ancient seat of the Dalai Lama. Buddhism is omnipresent here, as evidenced by the thousands of religious pilgrims visiting what Heinrich Harrer called 'the holiest of cities'.

Serious adventurers will soon want to break out of Lhasa into the **Northern Nakchu** region referred to as Janthang or northern wilderness. This enormous treeless area covers nearly half of the country, but with its scanty 300 000 population is largely empty pastureland, home to yaks and sheep as well as wild antelope. Janthang's carpet of green grassland stretches out of sight for hundreds of miles with only the odd nomad yak tent here and there to break the empty horizon. At 4678 m/15 300 ft lies Antso, Tibet's largest lake. In August a sea of nomad tents appears around the area called Nahchi, where Tibetans gather to celebrate a centuries-old annual horse racing competition.

Returning overland from Lhasa to Kathmandu is as scenic as the view from the air. The route passes the beautiful turquoise blue waters of Yamdrok lake and heads over the **Kamba La Pass** with its phenomenal mountain views, before reaching Gyantse. Twisting and winding for day after spectacular day, the road heads over passes of up to 5220 m/17 100 ft giving breathtaking views of Makalu, Cho Oyu, Everest, Lhotse, and many other famous peaks.

Mount Kalish, the most holy mountain in all the Himalayas, has been the ultimate goal of religious pilgrims for centuries. Revered by Hindus and Buddists alike (it is home to the Hindu god Shiva as well as the Tibetan god Demchog), Mt Kalish is also the source of Asia's four most important rivers: the Indus, the Bramaputra, the Ganges and Sutlej. Most pilgrims attempt to perform Parkarama (circumnavigation) of both lake Mavasarvar (100 km/62 miles) and Mt Kalish (55 km/34 miles): those completing the circuit of Mt Kalish 108 times are assured entry into Nirvana. Westerners take about two to three days around the mountain, compared with the gruelling non-stop twelve to fourteen hours taken by many Tibetans. The most devout and ardent Buddhists circle the mountain by prostrating themselves head to toe, head to toe, all the way round!

Proper exploration of Tibet involves breaking away from officialdom and the restrictive sight-seeing insisted upon by the Chinese authorities, although this is easier said than done. Heinrich Harrer's exploits in this field are inspirational to many adventurers. In 1944, after escaping from a POW camp, he enjoyed many years climbing and adventuring in Tibet, travelling illegally and in disguise. It is important to be aware that independent travel is not allowed officially and offenders face fines or, at worst, deportation. Banning of tourist lift-giving by lorry drivers has made hitch-hiking difficult (though not impossible). The road from **Kashgar** to Lhasa is considered by many to be one of the roughest, most dangerous and most accident-prone in the world, and is not officially open to foreigners. A direct run from Lhasa to Kashgar takes nine days, but some hitch-hikers have taken between sixteen days and two months to achieve it and the risk of a vehicle accident is ever present.

Ngari – the western part of Tibet – is totally barren and sparsely populated by hardy nomadic Drokpas herders. This area is very bleak and uninhabited: anecdotes have it that the Indian government did not discover that the Chinese had built a road here until two years afterwards! This new highway passes Mazar, close to **K2** – the world's second highest peak. Trekking from Mazar to K2 base camp takes six days.

For adventurers wishing to follow in the footsteps of Alexandria David Neal, the famous French explorer who (aged 55) disguised herself as a Tibetan beggar and became the first European woman to enter Lhasa, one suggestion is to try and enter western Tibet through Nepal's remote **Himla valley**. This is real expeditionary stuff, requiring a trekking permit for Summikat in Nepal and then being totally self-sufficient in terms of food for the four-day trek to the border. After this you can continue to Mt Kalish (assuming officials don't turn you back).

Although still in its infancy, trekking is beginning to emerge in Tibet. Infrastructure is minimal and you have to be much more self-reliant if travelling independently (or even travelling in an organized group) than in, say, Nepal. Many treks approaching the north face of Mt Everest pass the **Rongbuk monastery**. One of the highest monasteries in the world at 5000 m/16 500 ft, it is the usual starting point for Everest expeditions. For adventurers who have done it all before, a trip by bicycle from Lhasa to Kathmandu is reckoned to be an experience not to miss.

Fewer operators offer trips to Tibet than to Nepal and the costs tend to be rather higher. **Classic Nepal (33 Metro Avenue, Newton, Alfreton, Derbyshire DE55 5UF; tel: 01773 873497)** lists a trip from Kathmandu to Lhasa followed by a trek to Everest base camp for around £3000 (22 days, all-inclusive). **World Expeditions** offers a

29-day Tibetan journey including a moderate-to-strenuous 12-day trek to the Kangshung face of Everest. All-inclusive cost is £2200 from Kathmandu or £2800 from London. Also on offer is a 29-day trip including a trek to Mount Kalish, cost on request. **The Imaginative Traveller** offers a 10-day soft adventure tour to Tibet, price £900 including domestic flights but excluding international flights.

One example of a Grade B trip (where A = easy and D = difficult) is a **Sherpa** holiday called '**Everest East Face**', an 18-day adventure which includes 9 days' trekking. On day 1 you arrive in Kathmandu for a pre-trek briefing session. The next day is spent acclimatizing in Kathmandu. On day 3 you are driven to Kodari and on day 4 you continue to Dingri, camping there overnight. Khartachu is the next destination and days 6 through 14 are spent trekking through the Karta and Karma valleys (maximum trekking altitude 5334 m). The Karta valley holds a fascinating collection of villages, while its wilder Karma counterpart supports huge rock cliffs, ice cliffs and glaciers. Below these are found pastures, home to mountain ash, blue poppies, gentian, rhododendron, birch and fir trees. At the far end of the valley you'll see Everest and the Kanshung glacier. On day 15 you are driven from Karta back to Dingri and thence to Zhangmu on day 16. The next day, it's back to Kathmandu again, the trip ending there on day 18. The total cost for this trip is around £2000 and departures are April and September.

FACTFILE

When to go: Avoid January to March, November and December.

Travel tips: Carry pictures of the Dalai Lama. These are much prized by Tibetans as gifts. If caught trekking illegally, always say you came from where you want to go!

UK – ACCESSIBLE ADVENTURE

'The champagne went straight to my head, and I came over all British and sentimental and began to spout about how these had been the best five weeks of my life, how Boogie and I had reunited ourselves with nature and developed a telepathic relationship in the process; how Britain had the richest and least understood countryside in the world and how it was daft taking a cruise round the Caribbean islands for your holidays when you could walk the coast paths of the South West.'

Mark Wallington, 500 Mile Walkies

With a population of 57 million and a population density of 238 people per square kilometre, you might be forgiven for thinking that the UK offers no adventure holiday prospects whatsoever. But you would be wrong on two counts. Not only are there corners of Scotland, England, Wales and Northern Ireland which are remote and inaccessible – wildernesses, even – there are also scores of accessible adventure centres scattered throughout the country which offer activity holidays to suit all tastes. In fact it is a great place for adventure holidays, whether you're 'cutting your teeth gently' or whether you're into more serious physical challenge. From a walking holiday along one of the long-distance footpaths of England or Wales, to a winter mountaineering holiday in the Highlands of Scotland, the UK has it all. You can try your hand at the full range of activities: water-based, wind-based, above-land and below-ground. And for independent adventurers, whether you're a 'wannabe wanderer' or an 'old-age traveller', the UK is as undemanding and user-friendly as you want it to be.

Another myth about the country – perpetuated mainly by the postcard industry – is that it's always raining. Nothing could be further from the truth. Although there is a saying that Britain does not have a climate – just weather – average rainfall is actually less than that of many African countries, for example. The difference is that, having no particularly dry season, the climate just *seems* to be wet. Despite being so far north (Newcastle lies on the same latitude as southern Alaska, for instance), the British climate is surprisingly mild, due to the benign effects of the Gulf Stream. What all this adds up to is a climate which is often variable and seldom predictable. Prepare for your adventures with this in mind, and all will be well.

A good way to experience the great outdoors in Great Britain is to visit one of the several **National Parks** which exist in England and Wales, or to visit the Highlands and Islands of Scotland. The Forest Enterprise, part of the **Forestry Commission** (see Factfile) – offers a variety of active outdoor opportunities within its many forests throughout England, Scotland and Wales. Northern Ireland also has its fair share of quieter haunts, in the form of forest parks, mountains and walking trails. To the independent adventurer in the UK, therefore, there are more remote places and adventure activities than you can shake a walking stick at. For information on local destinations and accommodation, you need look no further than the **Tourist Board** (see Factfile) which supplies a plethora of information both centrally and via its network of 800 local centres.

If you want to travel with a group of like-minded people, then a number of holiday companies can cater for your requirements. For example **The Imaginative Traveller** offers 'journeys of discovery' from as few as 3 days to as many as 22 days. You can experience mountain biking, river canoeing, windsurfing, sailing, pony trekking or hiking. Similarly, a range of both guided and independent walking holidays in Scotland, England, Ireland and Wales is offered by **Sherpa Expeditions**, while **Ramblers Holidays (Box 43, Welwyn Garden, Hertfordshire AL8 6PQ; tel: 01707 331133)** offers walking tours of the Lake District, graded at moderate to strenuous. With an emphasis on wildlife-viewing, **Discover the World** offers a collection of holidays in such places as the Isle of Skye in Scotland, Northumberland and Cumbria in England, and parts of Wales and Northern Ireland.

An example of the sort of small group holiday you can take is 'Historic Northumberland', an 11-day tour offered by **Sherpa Expeditions** within some of the country's most magnificent scenery: Northumberland's National Park and Heritage Coast. Day 1 involves travelling to the starting point. On the next day you walk from Bardon Mill to Wark via Hadrian's Wall. Day three involves a walk to Knowesgate via Sweethope Lough and day 4 takes you to Thropton via Simonside. You then continue to Uswayford via Clennel Street and on day 6 head for Skirlnaked via the Cheviot Hills. Day 7 involves walking to Bamburgh via Chillingham Castle and the next day you can either rest here or take a boat trip to the Farne Islands or visit Lindisfarne. On day 9 you walk from Bamburgh to Dunstan via Seahouses and Beadnall. Finally you head for Alnmouth via Alnwick on day 10, ending the holiday on day 11.

If you're looking to cram in maximum adventure into limited time, or if you would like to try an adventure activity which involves the use of expensive equipment, then one of the UK's many multi-activity centres is probably what you are looking for. There are whole lists of these centres (see Factfile – **Tourist Board**), so the examples below are only a fraction of what's on offer. **Acorn Activities (PO Box 120, Hereford HR4 8YB; tel: 01432 830083)** offers all-year-round activity holidays for small groups, both young and old, accompanied by instructors. Similarly, **Rock Lea Activity Centre (Peak Activities Ltd, Station Road, Hathersage, Peak National Park, S30 1DD; tel: 01433 650345)**; **Ardclinis Activity Centre** in Northern Ireland **(High Street, Cushendall, Co Antrim BJ44 0NB; tel: 012667 71340)**; **Open Door Outdoor Activities Centre** in Wales **(Penmaendovey Country Club, Pennal, Nr Machynlleth, Nr Aberdovey, Powys SY20 9LD; tel: 01654 791326)** and **Great Glen School of Adventure** in Scotland **(South Laggan, Nr Spean Bridge, Inverness-shire PH34 4EA; tel: 01809 501 381)** supply 'taster' to 'testing' multi-activity holidays for a range of ages, with on-site accommodation, trained supervisors and instructors.

More specialized centres exist to cater for particular demands. For instance, **The Castle Riding Centre (Brenfield, Ardrishaig, Argyll PA30 8ER; tel: 01546 603)** offers one-week trail riding holidays for confident riders in the beautiful scenery of Argyll. Or if airsports are more to your liking, **Active Edge Paragliding (Watershed Mill, Langcliffe Road, Setle, North Yorkshire BD24 9LY; tel: 01729 822311)** caters for hang-gliding and paragliding interests. The list of general and specialized centres is seemingly endless. For instance, the latter include catering for the needs of such special-interest groups as physically or mentally challenged individuals and their families (eg **The Calvert Trust, Kielder Water, Hexham, Northumberland NE48 1BS; tel: 01434 250232**). Describing itself as 'an adventure social club', **SPICE (13 Thorpe Street, Old Trafford, Manchester M16 9PR; tel: 0161 872 2213)** is an 'adventure group for ordinary people who want to do extra-ordinary things.' It has branches in Scotland and England which offer a wide range of activities lasting from a few hours to several weeks and there is an annual membership fee.

There are a number of larger-scale adventure holiday companies in the UK. For example, **PGL Adventure Ltd (Alton Court, Ponyard Lane, Ross-on-Wye, Herefordshire HR9 5NR; tel: 01989**

764211) offers a choice of over 75 different activities in 21 centres for individuals, groups, schools and families. The **Outward Bound Trust (PO Box 1219, Windsor, Berkshire SL4 1XR; tel: 01753 731005)** offers comprehensive confidence-building programmes for teenagers and young adults. The **Youth Hostels Association** offers group, individual and family multi-activity breaks at a number of centres in England and Wales (**Trevelyan House, 8 St Stephens Hill, St Albans, Herts AL1 2DY; tel: 01727 845047**) and Scotland (**Scottish YHA, 7 Glebe Crescent, Stirling FK8 2JA; tel: 01786 451181**).

Many UK companies are members of **BAHA** – the **British Activity Holidays Association**. Formed in 1986, BAHA aims to monitor safety standards, as well as improving instruction and quality within the activity holiday market throughout Wales, England and Scotland. It also runs a consumer advisory service (contact **British Activity Holidays Association, Orchard Cottage, 22 Green Lane, Hersham, Walton-on-Thames KT12 5HD; tel: 01932 252994**).

FACTFILE

Further information: The British Tourist Board issues a priced annual book entitled *Activity Holidays*, listing hundreds of adventure holiday centres throughout the British Isles. Contact **British Tourist Authority, British Travel Centre, 12 Regent Street, Piccadilly Circus, London SW1Y 4PQ; tel: 0181 846 9000**. The **Forestry Commission** is located at **231 Corstorphine Road, Edinburgh EH12 7AT**.

Safety: By their very nature, adventure activities carry an associated risk. If you are in any doubt about the safety of a particular centre, you should discuss this before going on your holiday. BAHA (see above) may also be able to advise. Some centres offer insurance: if not, take out personal insurance appropriate to your holiday.

USA: ALASKA – THE GREAT LAND

'The talk over the camp fire is entirely about Alaska. We are at the end of this trip now, and from the moment it began, no one has once mentioned anything that did not have to do with Alaska.'

John McPhee, Coming into the Country

The Aleut Native Indians called this land Alyeska – the 'Great Land'. Alaska is indeed great – far and away the largest of the states. Its huge, and for the most part untouched, area amounts to a staggering one-fifth of the continental US land surface. Alaska includes the northernmost (Point Barrow), westernmost (Semisoposchnoi Island in the Aleutians) and easternmost (Little Diomede island) points in the USA. Or putting it another way, the state has over a million acres for each day of the year. This vast size manifests itself in an impressive roll-call of wilderness superlatives: three million lakes, countless mountain peaks (nineteen above 4200 m/14 000 ft) over five thousand glaciers, and North America's highest mountain, Mount McKinley (6194 m/20 300 ft). But it is not the mind-boggling quantity which attracts adventure travellers to this Great Land, but rather the exceptional quality of the visit. Here you can gaze on sweeping Arctic tundra, glacier-draped mountains and lush forested islands; you can catch sight of cruising killer whales, or bears feeding on jumping salmon; you can watch the northern lights or the midnight sun; and you can indulge your every adventure whim. Of all Arctic regions, Alaska is both the most user-friendly and the best value for money. It is as much a destination for the independent traveller as the packaged adventure visitor. Plenty of local operators hire out equipment such as mountain bikes, skis, kayaks and canoes. Or you can opt to go on an accompanied adventure, be it backpacking, rafting, dog sledging, kayaking or hot-air ballooning.

Broadly speaking, the state divides into five regions – Southeast,

Southwest, South Central, Interior and Far North. Each has its own distinctive adventure opportunities. **Southeast Alaska**, the so-called 'Panhandle', is a 965 km/600 mile coastal ribbon of countless islands and fjords. The **'Inside Passage'** is the name given to the gloriously scenic route taken by ships threading their way northwards through these islands on their way up to and beyond Juneau, Alaska's tiny capital 'city' (population 25 000). This region supports a wealth of marine wildlife, including whales, porpoises, sea lions and sea otters. Panhandle Alaska is also home to the Haida, Tlingit and Tsimshian Indians, and glimpses of their cultural heritage – including abandoned clan houses and hauntingly evocative totem poles – can still be seen here and there. **Glacier Bay National Park and Preserve** encompasses numerous inlets within a bay 105 km/65 miles long into which no fewer than sixteen glaciers flow. The **Misty Fjiords National Monument** covers over two million acres of Scandinavian-like beauty, its 900 m/3000 ft high cliffs rising up sheer from blue-green waters below. At the **Bald Eagle Council Grounds** it is possible to see the world's greatest concentration of these eagles, with populations reaching as high as 3500 during the month of November. A wide range of adventure activities is available here including hiking, mountain biking, kayaking and rafting.

Southwest Alaska is home to the Kodiak brown bear, the world's largest carnivore, and nearly two million acres of wilderness have been put aside specifically for the bears in **Kodiac National Wildlife Refuge**. The **McNeill River State Game Sanctuary** is a particularly good place to see the smaller brown bears as they catch salmon in mid leap, from the plentiful rivers. You may spot up to sixty or so bears here, as they fish the falls together. This southwestern region of Alaska also exhibits some almost surreal landscapes, like the gentle grasslands of the Aleutian Chain archipelago, or the eerie volcanic formations in **Kitmai National Park**. Many of these volcanoes are still active, particularly in the Pacific 'Ring of Fire' islands. In general, this region is a haven for wildlife viewing and photography.

The region of **South Central Alaska** consists of mountain ranges, secluded coves, inlets and volcanoes. Only a few minutes from Anchorage, **Chugach National Forest** and **State Park** offers abundant wilderness and solitude, with eagles, bears, salmon and waterfowl. Other designated areas include **Kenai National Wildlife Refuge** and **Kenai Fjords National Park**, and **Wrangell–St Elias National Park and Preserve**. The latter has some superb mountain adventure opportunities, with such pursuits as riding, kayaking, canoeing, rafting, mountain biking and wildlife viewing.

Interior Alaska is a land of seemingly endless wilderness: tundra, forests, hills, mountains, wetlands and rivers, including the mighty Yukon. The transition to a more Arctic environment is reflected in the wildlife – caribou and wolf – as well as the moose and beaver found further south. The number of animals is staggering: there is a bunch of caribou so huge that it is called the Forty Mile herd. In the six-million acre **Denali National Park and Preserve** alone, there are more than 35 species of animals, 130 species of birds and 400 plant species. This is the major adventure attraction of the Interior. **Mount McKinley** (6194 m/20 306 ft) is the highest place in the North American continent and, if measured from base to summit, is the tallest mountain in the world. It is so massive that it creates its own weather. Not for nothing is it called 'Denali' (the 'great one'). The Park itself is very accessible and offers superb backpacking, hiking and mountaineering. There are few trails, but many natural hiking routes along gravel ridges, river bars or wildlife tracks. Back-country use permits are required for overnight trips but these are readily available on site. The range of adventure activities available in the Interior is comprehensive, but perhaps the most famous of all is the official state sport – dog mushing (sledging). Each March, hundreds of national and international visitors gather in Anchorage, Alaska's largest city, to see the Iditarod dog sled competitors off on the start of the 1688 km/1049 mile race to Nome in the 'Last Great Race on Earth'.

In winter, the **Far North** of Alaska is a bleak and inhospitable region. With its water supplies frozen and locked in the grip of ice and permafrost, and with low winter precipitation, the region is an Arctic desert. But in the short, intense Arctic summer here where the sun never sets, it's a wonderful adventure destination. Backpacking and hiking opportunities are plentiful and there is a lot of scope for mountaineering and rafting. The **Brooks Range** is an untrammelled and little-known secret, where people are few but wildlife is plentiful, especially the vast herds of caribou which migrate through the region each year. A completely different world can be encountered in the 19-million acre **Arctic National Wildlife Refuge**. Rafting the rivers here, you're alone with the caribou, wolf and bear.

Although user-friendly for independent adventurers, Alaska attracts a range of group tour companies, such as **Explore**, which offers a 17-day '**Outdoor Alaska**' soft adventure package including hiking, and the option to go rafting. Price, including flight from London, is around £1500. **Arctic Experience** has an '**Alaska Dossier**' with ideas for DIY trips and small-group adventure packages. **AmeriCan Adventures**' **(64 Mount Pleasant Avenue, Tonbridge Wells, Kent TN1 1QY; tel: 01892 512700)** 28-day 'Yukon to Alaska' includes a visit to Denali National Park (cost excluding flights, around £900). Five trips within Alaska are offered by **TrekAmerica**. Varying from 7 days to 26 days, these vary in price from £400 to £1000, excluding flights. An extensive range of Alaskan adventure trips, from soft through to hard, is also offered by **Super Natural Adventures**.

For a packaged adventure trek demanding a good level of fitness, you could try the 16-day 'Alaska – The Ruth Glacier' trip, offered by **Karakoram Experience (32 Lake Road, Keswick, Cumbria CA12 5DQ; tel: 017687 73966)**. After arriving at Anchorage on day 1, you are flown to Talkeetna on day 2 and the Ruth Glacier on day 3. Days 4 through 8 are spent trekking through the Ruth Gorge ('one of the world's most remote and dramatic natural wonders'), right up to the base of Mt McKinley's south face ('It's impossible to get any closer without climbing the mountain itself.'). Returning to Talkeetna on day 9, the following three days are spent on exciting rafting down the Nenana River along the eastern border of Denali National Park. This is followed by a short wildlife tour which will enable you to see some of the many species found here: grizzly bear, moose, dall sheep, wolf and countless birds. On day 14 you return to Anchorage for the return flight on days 15 and 16. The trek is graded blue in the company's brochure, meaning that it requires a fair degree of stamina and fitness, presenting a sustained physical challenge. Departures are in May and June and the price is approximately £2100 all-inclusive, or £1500 excluding international flights.

FACTFILE

Travel tips: Book your voyage up the inside passage early, since cruise ship tickets tend to be heavily subscribed.

US VIRGIN ISLANDS – SLICE OF AMERICAN PARADISE

'At the rinse station outside the dive shop, Fred, a strapping diver from New York, gingerly picks up a dime-sized frog that has wandered onto the rinse platform. He walks over to a tree and patiently waits for the frog to launch itself onto a branch. Feeling my curious gaze, he explains, "We amphibians have to watch out for each other." '

Steve Blount, Virgin Territory

In the Lesser Antilles, just west of their British Virgin sisters, lie the United States Virgin Islands, a collection of around fifty islands some big, some small, some merely rocks jutting out of the crystal-clear Caribbean water. When Christopher Columbus visited this place on his second voyage of discovery in 1493, he was enchanted by their unravished beauty and called them 'The Virgins', referring to the legend of St Ursula with her beautiful 11 000 virgins. In this legend, the son of a powerful pagan prince demands the hand in marriage of Ursula, beautiful daughter of the King of Britain. Although she has pledged herself to a life of saintliness, to save her father and his kingdom from the pagans, she consents on the condition that 11 000 of the most beautiful virgins in the two kingdoms must first be her companions for three years. Ursula trains the virgins into an army and sets off for Rome to pledge allegiance. But on their return in AD 238, the pagan prince fights them with his regular army and kills all 11 000.

After Columbus had left, the islands remained virtually forgotten for a century. Thereafter, variously fought over by the Spanish, the French, the Dutch and the English, this area was eventually purchased by the USA during the first world war (a snip at 25 million dollars!). Today, with its benign climate, its reputation for ecotourism, and its superb opportunities for watersports, the USVI offer a Caribbean adventure destination *par excellence*.

There are three principal islands within the archipelago – **St Croix**, **St John** and **St Thomas**. At 212 sq km/82 square miles, St

Croix is the largest of all the islands, and it was here, at Salt River Canyon, where Columbus first landed on his second voyage to the New World. He called the place Santa Cruz – hence its present-day name. The island has a small Botanical Garden and a remnant of rainforest, the latter privately owned but open to visitors. Of particular interest to underwater adventure-seekers is the 850 acre **Buck Island Reef**, the USA's only underwater National Park. Lying just off St Croix, this place is a sanctuary for endangered hawksbill turtles during their June to October nesting season. Thanks to the efforts of some 40 volunteer 'Hawksbill assistants' who help out with the island's turtle research project and who patrol the sandy beaches here, these turtles face a secure future. You can volunteer your own services to help this effort by contacting the **National Park Service Headquarters** on St Croix **(tel: 809 773 1460)**. One of the most important marine attractions in the entire Caribbean is **Buck Island's Underwater Trail**, located within the National Park. Although other Caribbean islands have picturesque snorkelling opportunities, this trail is generally re-garded as being the best of the lot. From a boat that takes you several hundred metres out to sea, you flop overboard to the start of the trail marked by metal arrows and signs fixed to the seabed. The stunning array of fish life, underwater vegetation and coral, in irridescent colours and fantastic formations, makes you forget all sense of time. Although only 4 m/12 ft deep, the water has a horizontal visibility of over 30 m/100 ft. This snorkelling experi-ence is regarded as the equal of many other Caribbean spots which are accessible only to scuba divers. For deep diving, the **Cane Bay dropoff**, accessible from a beach on St Croix, begins in 11 m/35 ft of water and plunges down 610 m/2000 ft. Or you could try the **Salt River dropoff** – 6 m/20 ft to over 300 m/1000 ft. All in all, there are thirty spectacular reefs to explore, all within 20 minutes reach of the island.

Although only 52 sq km/20 square miles small, **St John** is, according to many, the loveliest of all the US Virgin Islands. Surrounded by incredible coral reefs, some two-thirds of the island is in the protected **Virgin Islands National Park**, comprising tropical forest, wildlife and wildflowers. At **Trunk Bay** there is an underwater trail with weighted plaques interpreting the sub-sea sights. More serious diving is done two miles out. A 'must-see' dive for enthusiasts is an all-day dive to the wreck of the *Rhone* – a Royal Mail ship that went down off Salt Island and now rests 8–26 m/25–85 ft deep.

Some 85 sq km/33 square miles in size, **St Thomas** is the capital of the USVI. For a soft adventure experience, you could take the **Atlantis submarine** trip here for a 'hands-off' close encounter with the reefs and their wildlife. Also in the soft adventure line on St

Thomas is 'Coral World' – an underwater observation tower and marine park open to the sea – one of only three in the world. Other pursuits (here and on the other main islands) include windsurfing, kayaking, sailing and surfing. For landlubbers, horse riding is available on St Croix and St John. On St Croix, contact **Jill's Equestrian stable (tel: 809 772 2880)** or **Buccaneer Stables (tel: 809 778 8670)**. On St John, contact **Pony Express Riding Stables (tel: 809 776 6494)**. For airsport adventures you can get a birds-eye view of St Croix and St Thomas by parascending (parachute attached to a speeding boat). Boardsailing is very popular throughout the islands, thanks to calm waters, consistent winds and plentiful hire facilities. Beginners and experts alike will find lots of opportunities to 'catch the breeze' here. For an element of extra adventure during your stay, you could try night diving (for intermediate and expert divers only). Each trip takes around an hour and a half. Using powerful flashlights you move through an underwater world quite different from its daytime counterpart. Night or day, the water temperatures here average 82°C in summer and autumn; 78°C in winter and spring.

Humpback whales can be seen near the USVI throughout the winter months. From the high cliffs on the north side of St Thomas, humpbacks are often seen blowing out at sea. It is possible to take a boat out to the area where cows and calves go through their splashing and spouting antics. A 30 m/100 ft trimaran operates out of St Thomas to look for humpbacks, spinner and other dolphins. The cost for a half-day is around $US50. Contact **Wild Thing, Long Bay, St Thomas (tel: 809 774 8277)**. Other ecological holidays are offered by **Colony Cove (tel: 809 773 1965)** which provides sea ecology trips for divers, shore ecology for hikers and children's programmes as well. Accommodation is plentiful and there are camping facilities at St John (**Cinnamon Bay Camp; tel: 809 776 6330** or **Maho Bay Camp; tel: 809 776 6226**). UK visitors could try **Caribtours (161 Fulham Road, London SW3 6SN; tel: 0171 581 3517)**.

FACTFILE

Diving: Look for the international symbols NAUI, PADI, NASDS and SSI when seeking diving instruction. There are plenty of certified divers in the USVI. Spearfishing is strictly forbidden in the National Park. Every lobster taken must have at least a 5½ inch tail, be non egg-bearing and captured only by hand, snare, pot or trap.

Arrival: Visitors to St John fly into St Thomas and take a ferry from there.

VENEZUELA – WHERE AMAZON MEETS CARIBBEAN

'The ancient Dakota rumbled past the thatched terminal, along the jungle airstrip and lifted off, banking sharply to the left towards the distant hills. Fifteen minutes' flying time away was the Angel Falls, at 3200 ft the world's highest waterfall and, according to the tourist literature, Venezuela's Great Adventure in the Lost World of Bolivar State.'

Tim Austin, The Times, 8 May 1993

Located on the Tropic of Cancer, Venezuela is a country of countless landscapes, from tropical beaches to snow-capped mountains, from vast rivers to immense desert plains and from impenetrable jungles to urban jungles. Much of the land that Christopher Columbus described as 'a paradise' over 500 years ago is still as mysterious, enticing and enchanting to visitors today. But Venezuela has been slow to yield her secrets: it was only as late as 1937 that one Jimmy Angel, an American aviator, discovered his eponymous waterfall in Bolivar State's 'Lost World'. Today, much of Venezuela's wilderness still remains intact and for visitors the country offers a wealth of adventure possibilities. For ease of description, Venezuela can be divided into four major areas: the Caribbean, the Amazon Region, the Orinoco Delta and the Andes and Plains.

Virtually all of Venezuela's 4000 km/2500 miles of coastline borders the **Caribbean** sea. Its tropical sandy beach – known as the Litoral – runs like a golden ribbon, separating the warm waters of the sea from the chain of northern mountains, along the states of Carabobo, Aragua, Anzoategui, Miranda, Federal District and Nueva Esparta. Many of the coast's fine beaches and islands are inhabited only by flamingoes, scarlet ibis and other birds. Inland, the scenery varies greatly, with giant dunes at Coro, mangrove swamps in the **Morrocoy National Park**, and waterfalls of the **Cloud Forest** which plunge dramatically onto the beach at the Paria Peninsula. Off the Litoral lies a beautiful string of 72 islands, like a string of pearls, the most exquisite of which is **Margarita Island**, variously known as 'the pearl of the Caribbean' or 'Cherub's Teardrop'. A 45-minute flight north from Caracas, Venezuela's capital city, takes you to the 150 islands and cays which form the **National Park Archipelago Los Roques**. With its beaches of fine white sand and its warm and inviting waters, this area is one of the largest and best of all the marine parks in the Caribbean. It is a delight to snorkel or scuba dive here, camping, sailboarding or simply staying at a guesthouse. East of Les Roques lies the almost deserted **Blanquilla Island**, with its isolated beaches and cliffs. Adventurers will find much to explore here: rich and varied underwater fauna, spectacular coral formations and an abundance of birds. Closer to the Litoral is found **Mochima National Park**, its fish, shellfish and crustaceans protected by law. A catamaran tour can be taken through Mochima's many islands, cays and bays, or you can go undersea exploring amid the coral reefs in the transparent waters surrounding the National Park.

Completely different in character is the **Amazon** region: a dense and luxuriant habitat for such exotic species as macaws, monkeys and blue kingfishers. Within this vast area lies the 40 000 sq km/ 15 440 square mile **Orinoco Delta**, one of the largest unexplored adventure attractions in the country. Criss-crossed by a myriad of streams and covered by an intricate and diverse swath of forest, this area is best explored by water. You can take a flight from Maregarita to the port of San Jose de Bujas, where your river journey begins. Most trips start at **Tiger Island** base camp, where you can take boat trips up the Orinoco flow, or fish for piranhas or hike into the forest. In Bolivar State, south of Orinoco Delta is found one of the world's largest National Parks – **Canaima National Park**. This region is crossed by fast-flowing rivers, stained brown by the high tannin content. Sticking out amongst Canaima's jungle and savanna are the Park's **Tepuys** – strange, flat-topped mountains rising up vertically to heights of about 3000 m/9800 ft. Very few of these have been properly explored, although **Mount Roraima**, suggested as the site of Conan Doyle's 'Lost World', can be climbed on foot. Since this trip takes up to a fortnight, ample camping equipment and supplies should be taken. Within Canaima National Park is found the largest of all the Tepuys, **Auyantepuy**, site of the world's highest waterfall (the 964 m/3164 ft **Angel Falls**). The best way to get an overview of the falls is by air, en route to a stay at the Canaima National Park. Once there, you can go trekking or take a trip on a dug-out canoe. In the valley of Kamarata below the Auyantepuy mountain nestles **Kavac** camp, comprising traditional Indian dwellings called *wipas*. Accompanied by an Indian guide, you can make expeditions from here, wading the rivers and dodging the cascades of Kavac's canyon to gain an incredible close-up view of the waterfall and its abyss below. This is one of the country's great adventure trips.

Once you have tasted forest life in Amazon, you will want to return, but no adventure trip to Venezuela would be complete without experiencing life in the **Andes**. Here lies a forest of a different kind; peak after peak, with endless horizons and breathtaking views. Comprising the states of Tachira, Merida, Trujillo and part of Lara, this region includes five peaks over 4880 m/ 16 000 ft, the **Cordillera de Merida**, with a permanent covering of snow. The **Sierra Nevada National Park** offers opportunities for cross-country skiing between November and June, but at 4267 m/ 14 000 ft, this pursuit is for hardy adventurers only. As well as the mountains themselves, the Andes contain Alpine meadows, waterfalls galore, and historic settlements with ancient monasteries.

Between the Andes and the Amazon lie the vast, sweeping and sparsely populated plains of the **Llanos**, containing Venezuela's largest wildlife sanctuary. This area is relatively flat, varied here and there by slight upthrusts of land. Here, in these undisturbed habitats, you can find over 300 species of birds (including scarlet ibis, hoatain, screamers, soldier storks and spoonbills) as well as jaguars, ocelots, anteaters, honeybears and capybaras. In the slow-running rivers and swamps are found alligators, parrots, monkeys, egrets and many more species.

Camping in Venezuela can involve spending a weekend or longer at the beach, on the islands, in the Llanos or in the mountains. If you want to camp in the Amazon there are a number of adventure companies who organize such trips. As in much of South America, most camping facilities are rudimentary and specialized sites are absent, but there are many cheap hotels for travellers throughout the country.

Venezuela's international airline, Viasa, and Aereotuy, a leading tourist organization, offer flight deals and tours to adventurous destinations. In the UK, contact **Viasa** on **0171 830 0011** and **Aereotuy** on **0171 734 9354**. Other tour operators include **Ilkeston Co-Op Travel and Tours (12 South Street, Ilkeston, Derbyshire DE7 5SG; tel: 0115 9323546)**; and **Explore** (22 days, including ascent of Mt Roraima, for £1500, or 15 days, including Angel Falls and Orinoco for £1400, all inclusive).

As an illustration of a Venezuelan adventure holiday, **Journey Latin America (14–16 Devonshire Road, Chiswick, London W4 2HD; tel: 0181 747 8315)** offers 'Egret – The Lost World', an 18-day tour of the country's Gran Sabana. You need to be very fit for this trip. After arriving in Caracas from Heathrow, you fly on to Ciudad Bolivar on day 2, continuing to the Pemon Indian mission at Kamarata in the heart of the Gran Sabana. A three-hour walk takes you to a hidden waterfall at Kavac. Day 3 is the most arduous: a 7 hour trek along narrow tracks through savanna and rainforest, with knee-deep stream crossings to the plateau of Auyan Tepuy. On day 4 the group continues hiking upwards through rainforest to El Penon and on day 5 you reach the high plateau via a natural stairway. Up here in the Lost World, you sleep where you can – in rock shelters or under ledges. Day 6 is spent exploring the top before descending to El Penon. The following two days involve retracing your steps to the Indian settlement of Uruyen where you sleep in hammocks. Day 10 involves a walk of 4 to 5 hours to Kamarata and there then follows a river trip, with a motorized canoe voyage on days 11 and 12. You may find that you have to disembark and guide the craft around shallow stretches. On the afternoon of day 12 you reach the foot of the Angel Falls and overnight in hammocks. Day 13 involves an hour's early morning trek to observe the falls. On day 14 you leave the region with a flight to Caracas and an overland trip to Tacarigua where you can relax at a simple, isolated hotel for a couple of days. On day 17 you return to Caracas, arriving back at Heathrow on day 18. Departures take place in May, August, October and November, group size is from 6 to 10 and the all-inclusive price is approximately £1900.

FACTFILE

Climate: Varies greatly according to altitude. Lowland areas have a tropical climate, while Arctic conditions prevail on the high peaks. Dry season is December to April and the rainy season is May to December. Best time to visit is January to April.

Greetings: Handshakes, or the local *abrrazo* (a cross between a hug and a handshake) are the normal forms of greeting.

VIETNAM – LAND OF THE SLEEPING TIGER

'Every evening I would put on a loincloth and go to the wash-house where my ablutions were an object of great interest and mirth. One thing puzzled the monks. Why did I never relieve my bowels? Was I ill? Was I different in some curious respect? Since I had never had a moment of privacy from the time of my arrival, it was clear that something was wrong. On the third day, therefore, I announced that the time had come. Consternation! "No have kiss me," said a monk. This remark might have been disconcerting, had I not been aware that "Kiss Me" was a brand of toilet paper . . . I took my little can of water down the path, which led past a pleasant stream luxuriant with lotus blossom, beside which the secluded closets stood. A great wave of sympathy and pleasure spread through the monastery.'

James Fenton, Road To Cambodia

Vietnam is a fascinating country with a rich history stretching back 4000 years. Bordering China in the north (see p 154) and Laos and Cambodia in the west, mainland Vietnam, an S-shaped peninsula, covers an area of 330 000 sq km/127 000 square miles. The eastern side of the country, a tropical coastline 3300 km/2050 miles long, is dotted with thousands of islands. The country's unique landscapes include beautiful mantles of mountains and forests, and deltas containing some of the world's most interesting flora and fauna. Since Vietnam is located within the tropics and subtropics, it benefits from year-round sunshine and high temperatures (average 22–35°C). For many people, the country's name is synonymous with a bloody conflict, an image perpetuated by 'Nam war films. But despite the ravages of war, the country is steadily getting back on its feet, both politically and economically. Tourism is still in its infancy, but it is growing rapidly. Surprisingly perhaps, there is no animosity shown by the Vietnamese to Westerners. As a visitor you will be shown only genuine warmth, friendliness and open hospitality. The fact that Vietnam has, for the most part, a fairly rough and ready infrastructure, also makes it an ideal Asian destination for adventure travellers: not for nothing is it known as the 'last frontier in Asia'. Most tours start out from Ho Chi Minh City, still known by the locals as Saigon. Local tour companies are plentiful, offering a great variety of trips to the nearby **Mekong Delta**. Close to here lies **Da Lat**, set in the pine-covered Highlands of Vietnam, with a cool climate all year round. This area consists of lush green surroundings with lakes, colourful flower gardens and waterfalls. On the coast, to the north of Da Lat lies **Nha Trang** with its superb beaches and locally renowned Monkey Island, a good jumping-off point for those wanting to visit nearby coral islets. Still further north along the coast is **Da Nang**, home to some of Vietnam's most famous landmarks, including the Marble Mountain and Huyen Khong Cave, as well as one of the loveliest beaches in the country – China Beach. Northeast of Hanoi, close to the Chinese border, lies **Ha Long Bay** which houses around 3000 islands dotted with innumerable caves, grottoes and beaches.

Unless you are an intrepid independent traveller with time on your hands, it is recommended that you take advantage of one of the growing number of adventure companies offering trips to Vietnam. For example, **Guerba** offers a soft adventure **Vietnam Discoverer** trip lasting 18 days and costing around £1600 including flights. Similarly, **Exodus** offers a 21-day '**Vietnam Adventure**' which involves rail and boat trips, for around £1700. **Explore** offers either a 15-day or a 19-day '**Inside Vietnam**' trip on the Ho Chi Minh trail by coach, train and riverboat, price around £1500. Soft adventure tours are also available from **Westeast Travel (271 King Street, Hammersmith, London W6 9LZ; tel: 0181 741 1158)**.

For a Vietnam adventure trip with a difference, you could consider **World Expedition's 'Vietnam Bicycle Ride'**, first pioneered in 1993. Using specially imported mountain bikes, you average 80 km/50 miles per day, although there is a back-up vehicle should you get into difficulties. From Bangkok you fly to Ho Chi Minh City where heady pre-adventure evenings are scheduled at Madame Dai's and Maxims restaurants. Survivors then get on their bikes for what is essentially a flexible programme. By day you cycle through villages and beside rice paddies, stopping from time to time to partake of tea at a wayside stall, or to admire the view. Sometimes, villagers' invitations for you to visit their homes, or improvised games with local children, will necessitate packing your bike into the accompanying bus in order to reach the next town by evening. Nights are spent in old Palace Hotels or in Tourist Lodges and everywhere the Vietnamese cuisine is excellent – addictive, even. After nine days on the road, you pedal over the Hai Van Pass and freewheel down towards Hue. From here you board the overnight train to Hanoi, visiting the museums and markets, before celebrating with a final banquet. Each trip lasts 18 days, with departures from January to March and October to December. The cost for joining the group in Ho Chi Minh is around £1600, so you will need to find the airfare on top of that.

FACTFILE

Climate: Monsoon season is September to November, while the rainy/hot season is from May to October. The best time to visit is January to March.

Language: Although Vietnamese is the official language, English is commonly spoken.

Festivals: There are many traditional festivals, influenced by Buddhist and Christian holy days.

ZAMBIA – KINGDOM OF THE WILD

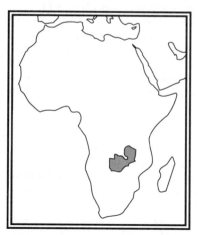

Zambia is a wild place, well deserving of its title – a huge, landlocked plateau set in the heart of central southern Africa. As old as time itself (some call it the oldest country in the world), Zambia qualifies as one of Africa's classic adventure destinations. With nineteen areas enjoying National Park status, almost a tenth of the country is protected in some way or another. Zambian safari trips are extremely rewarding, especially for those seeking a 'walk on the wild side' – that is, a safari on foot. These trips involve groups of no more than six people, accompanied by an armed guide. As well as its abundant game, the country is host to a multitude of birdlife. But it is not only the wildlife which attracts adventure-seekers to Zambia: magnificent scenery is also a major draw. In the south, the tranquillity of Lake Kariba is almost palpable, while further upstream the mighty Zambezi creates a thundering roar and cloud of spray as it forms Africa's greatest natural wonder – the Victoria Falls.

Luangwa Valley is regarded as one of the most exciting game reserves in the world. Part of the Great African Rift System, it contains five National Parks, each centred on the Luangwa River, a major tributary of the vast Zambezi. Zambia's strict policy of conservation is helping to maintain the extraordinary richness of wildlife interest within this area. The Luangwa Valley is home to a huge variety of animals, including elephant, hippo, lions, zebras, giraffes, antelopes, buffaloes, monkeys and wild dogs. North and South Luangwa and Kafue National Parks are among the largest and best known in all Africa; for sheer size unrivalled in the whole subcontinent. Dissected by the Luangwa River, **South Luangwa** holds one of the greatest concentrations of animals and birds of any National Park in the world. Its clear river lagoons support plentiful hippopotamus, while the plains are home to vast herds of elephant, antelope, giraffe and zebra. Leopards and other carnivores abound here, and countless numbers of birds can be seen. Walking safaris of up to eight days are available. As in the rest of Zambia, safaris in South Luangwa usually take place during the dry winter months, from June to November. **North Luangwa** is similarly impressive, its species list including some of the lesser known species such as puku, roan antelope and hartebeest.

Less than a one-hour flight from Zambia's capital – Lusaka – lies the vast National Park of **Kafue**, equal in area to the whole of Wales. All the well known plain-dwelling game congregates within the Park and you stand a good chance of seeing some of the 600 or so species of birds recorded here, especially along the flood plains and banks of the River Kafue. Notable among Kafue's wildlife is the black rhinoceros, although it tends to be solitary and secretive. The showpiece of this Park is the lechwe, a small antelope, all but exterminated by former poaching.

Despite its smallness, **Lochinvar National Park** boasts an extraordinary variety of bird life, and has the advantage of being readily accessible from Lusaka. Further north lies **Sumba National Park**, an undisturbed wilderness bounding Lake Tanganyika. Guided walks, night game-viewing drives and night boat rides are all available, while **Lake Tanganyika** is an angler's dream, supporting over 200 different species of fish. During the dry season (September to November), large herds of elephant congregate along the lake shore. You can fly to Sumbu from Lusaka, changing aircraft at Ndola.

The one sight not to be missed by visitors to Zambia is the famous **Victoria Falls**, on the border with Zimbabwe (see p 276), one of the great natural wonders of the world. From March to May, when the Zambezi is in full flood, more than five million litres of water surge over the falls each second, illustrating its centuries-old title 'smoke that thunders' (*mosi-oa-tunya*). There are several flights to Livingstone each week, departing from Lusaka International Airport. Alternatively you can hire a car in the capital and drive the five-hour journey to the Falls. Water-rat adventurers will want to experience rafting the river wild downstream from the Falls. A number of companies (such as **Adrift, Hyde Park House, Manfred Road, London SW15 2RS; tel: 0181 874 4969**) offer rafting safaris, between June and November. Lasting anything up to a week, these exhilarating trips take you from the base of Victoria Falls over some 200 rapids to Lake Kariba.

It is possible to travel within Zambia independently, but the logistics of organizing accommodation, travel and meals can be complicated. However, there are several tour operators which include Zambia within their portfolio. Having a common border with Zimbabwe (see p 276), plus easy access to Botswana (see p 124), Zambia is often combined with these countries to offer broader-based safari trips. Camping areas are available at most centres, including a number of the National Parks, but as these do become very busy, it is best to book up well in advance (some places will ask for a 50% deposit in advance).

Many adventure companies offer trips to this part of Africa, either as a single destination or combined with Zimbabwe. **Guerba** offers a 22-day safari which includes Zimbabwe and Malawi as well as Zambia for around £1000, excluding flight, while **Mountain Travel Sobek (6240 Fairmount Avenue, El Cerrito, CA 94530; tel: 510 527 8100)** offers rafting trips on the Zambezi. **Worldwide Journeys and Expeditions** specializes in Zambia, offering three safaris to the country. Its 13-day '**Shoebill Safari**' 'aims to recreate the adventure of David Livingstone's original expedition in search of the source of the Nile' (17 days, £2500), while its **Zambia Safari** (13 days, £2000) concentrates on the Luangwa Valley and southern reaches of the Great Rift Valley.

As an example of an original adventure holiday, **Worldwide Journeys and Expeditions' 'Classic Zambia'** is hard to beat. This walking safari is led by Robin Pope, an honorary ranger with the Wildlife Department who was raised in Zambia and has spent 18 years organizing safaris in the country. Arriving in Zambia from your international flight on day 2, you continue by chartered aircraft to the Luangwa Valley. Here you spend three days at Nkwali, wildlife viewing, going on night game drives and staying in a camp of six chalets set in ebony woodland overlooking the Luangwa plains. Days 5 through 9 are spent on a walking safari with Robin Pope along the Mupamadzi River, where you stay in pre-pitched camps. The safari ends at Tena Tena, an encampment on the banks of the Luangwa River, where you go wildlife viewing, bush walking and overnight game driving. Finally you fly back to Harare and the end of the adventure. Group size is limited to a maximum of only six and this means that the 13-day adventure is not cheap (about £2900), but for participants it is the trip of a lifetime. Departures are from June to September.

FACTFILE

Climate: Although situated in the tropics, Zambia's altitude keeps the climate from getting too hot. There are three seasons: cool dry winter from May to September; hot dry season in October and November; and the hot rainy season from December to April.

Clothing: Take tropical lightweight cotton clothes and rainwear for the wet season.

ZIMBABWE – A COUNTRY LIKE NO OTHER

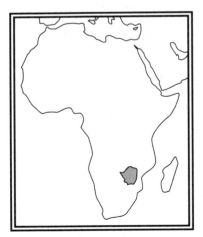

Zimbabwe is an old country but a young nation, home to amazing natural phenomena as well as landscapes which resemble early English watercolours; one of the last remaining areas of wild Africa – in short, a country like no other. Topographically varied, its mountainous Eastern Highlands contrast with the remote bush country of the Zambezi river valley. Although Zimbabwe lies within the tropics, its climate is moderated by altitude, so temperate conditions prevail all year round except in the Zambezi valley. With its unspoilt qualities, marvellous climate and abundant wildlife, Zimbabwe forms an African heart-land destination of beauty, excitement and space: this is the 'real' Africa, the ideal place for your off-the-beaten-track safari adventure.

Most famous of Zimbabwe's attractions, and one of the seven natural wonders of the world, is the **Victoria Falls**: twice as high as Niagara and half as wide again. Livingstone was the first white man to set eyes on this spectacle (see opening quotation). Lush tropical vegetation flourishes unexpectedly in the humid atmos-phere alongside the gorge. For water-orientated adventure seek-ers, exhilarating white-water rafting trips and kayaking expedi-tions can be taken below the Falls. This is one of the best places for rafting in the world: don't pass over the chance while you're here. **Mountain Travel Sobek (6240 Fairmount Avenue, El Cerrito, CA 94530; tel: 510 527 8100)** is one of the main rafting operators. Less energetic but equally memorable trips are the 15-minute 'Flight of the Angels' circling above the Falls by light aircraft, or a 'Sunset Cruise' (perhaps more accurately 'sundowner' cruise) in which you sip your 'croctails' and watch the wildlife slide by.

Downstream from its frenzied journey over the 'Vic Falls', the mighty Zambezi glides into **Lake Kariba** – at 13 000 sq km/5000 square miles one of the largest man-made watering holes in the world. In the late 1950s a massive operation rescued thousands of animals marooned on hilltops by the rising water level. These were released into surrounding **Matusadona** – one of Zimbabwe's ten National Parks – and what was then the largest man-made lake in the world gradually evolved its own surrounding ecosystem. A wide variety of bird species thrives here – mainly waterfowl, storks, herons and waders, not to mention the elusive lily-trotter. With its scattering of islands and fringe of forests, Lake Kariba is a paradise for game watchers and bird watchers alike. The relatively inaccessible **Bumi River** forms its eastern boundary, while the **Sanyati Gorge** borders the Park on its western side. Matusadona Park can be visited throughout the year, with accommodation in Bumi Hills, Tiger Bay, Fothergill Island or Spurwing Island.

Continuing through a series of gorges, the Zambezi flows into the **Mana Pools National Park** in northern Zimbabwe. With its grassy escarpments, lush mahogany woodlands and fertile flood-plains, Mana Pools has abundant birdlife, as well as being home to some of the world's last remaining black rhino. Accommodation here includes camps at Ruckomechi and Chickwenya.

In southwest Zimbabwe, near the border with Botswana and some two hours from Harare, lies **Hwange**. This is Zimbabwe's largest National Park, virtually a country in itself at over 23 300 sq km/9000 square miles (larger than Northern Ireland). Situated amongst its bush, forests and plains, is a network of numerous artificial water holes which supports plentiful herds of elephant (estimated at 20 000, as many as in the whole of Kenya), buffalo, sable, and of course, carnivorous predators. This is one of the few Parks in Africa where rhino exist in appreciable numbers. In all, over 100 animal species and over 400 bird species have been recorded.

Independent travel to Zimbabwe is worth considering if you are not short of time. The country's infrastructure is good (for Africa), with some excellent roads, and you can hire vehicles. There are a number of camping sites, except in the National Parks (but lodges are usually available in the Parks). A good starting point is the **Eastern Highlands** area, a high straggling range dividing Zimbabwe from Mozambique. Here lies the wild and remote **Nyanga National Park**, a place of moors, mists, waterfalls and pine-forested slopes where the clear champagne air produces its own brand of non-alcoholic intoxication. Its cliffs provide good opportunities for rock climbers, while hiking among the forest slopes below is an unforgettable experience. The highest point in Zimbabwe, **Mount Inyangani** (2700 m/9000 ft) is a place of reverence for the local people. Although the view from its summit is breathtaking, you climb it at your peril: legend has it that those who tread unwarily on its mist-shrouded slopes risk becoming invisible and disappearing forever. But the alert adventurer who does venture forth here may just be rewarded by the sight of leopard or rare forest antelope.

The jagged granite peaks of **Chimanimani Mountain Area** are a superb wilderness for hikers and climbers. An ancient trail – the traditional route from interior Africa to the east coast – provides sole access up the mountain, while a hut near the top is available to climbers. Chimanimani's hot springs are also a favourite stopping place for weary hikers. Access is by foot only, so all provisions must be carried in. One word of warning: you should treat these mountains with respect since sudden storms and cold mists can descend quickly, disorientating unsuspecting hikers.

Large numbers of tour operators offer trips to Zimbabwe, including **Abercrombie & Kent Travel (Sloane Square House, Holbein Place, London SW1W 8NS; tel: 0171 730 9600)** and **Guerba Expeditions**. Abercrombie & Kent offers a number of 10- to 17-day adventure safaris costing up to £3000 including full board, accommodation and flights. Active, month-long tours of Zimbabwe, Botswana and Zambia, or Zimbabwe, Malawi and Zambia with **Guerba** cost around £1600 including flights, while shorter trips are offered as well (22 days, £1500 and 15 days, £1300; all prices approximate). One of the leading local operators offering adventure trips is **Shearwater Adventures (PO Box 3961, Harare, Zimbabwe; tel: 2634 735712)** which offers canoeing, rafting, whitewater canoeing, walking safaris and horseriding trips.

A relative newcomer to the adventure holiday company scene, **Adrift (Hyde Park House, Manfred Road, London SW15 2RS; tel: 0181 874 4969)** offers a memorable rafting/safari trip in Zimbabwe via its '**River of the Gods**' trip. This lasts either 13 days (about £1200) or 15 days (about £1300, all-inclusive). The river-only element can be taken for approximately £600, excluding flights to and from the country. This adventure starts at Victoria Falls, where you receive a briefing on the ins and outs of rafting and camping. The rafting element itself takes from day 2 to day 9. Rafting in the gorges below the Vic' Falls is regarded as among the best in the world and there are dozens of adrenalin-pumping rapids (eg beneath the Batoka Gorge) interspersed with miles of calmer water (the Zambezi is rated 4.5). Each evening, a spacious beach is selected and camp is pitched. Cooking is over open fires and a camp fire is the social focus for evening 'raft-talk'. After the rafting element of the trip, days 10 to 13 (or 15 if you have more time) are spent on safari in Zimbabwe.

FACTFILE

When to go: February for birds and butterflies: mid-August to late October for game viewing. The rainy season usually lasts from November to March.

Travel tips: Anti-malarial precautions are not necessary in the mountains, though advisable in the rest of the country. Polygamy is legal and AIDS is widespread.

APPENDIX 1
Country data

ANTARCTICA
British Antarctic Survey
High Cross
Madingly Road
Cambridge CB3 0ET
Tel: 01223 61188

AUSTRALIA
Capital: Canberra
Population: 17 292 000
Currency: Australian Dollar
  (1A$ = 100 cents)
Languages: English
Time difference: 3 time zones,
  from GMT +8 to +10
Voltages: 240/250V
Entry requirements:
  UK – valid passport, visa, return
  ticket
  USA/Canada – valid passport, visa,
  return ticket
Vaccinations: none required
Tourist Board:
  Australian Tourist Commission
  Gemini House
  10–18 Putney Hill
  London SW15 6AA
  Tel: 0181 780 2227
  or
  Suite 1200
  2121 Ave of the Stars
  Los Angeles
  CA 90067
  Tel: 310 552 1988

BAHAMAS
Capital: Nassau
Population: 254 646
Currency: Bahamian Dollar
  (1Ba$ = 100 cents)
Languages: English
Time difference: GMT −5
Voltages: 120V
Entry requirements:
  UK – valid passport, return ticket
  USA/Canada – identification

documents, return ticket
Vaccinations: Typhoid, polio
Tourist Board:
  Bahamas Tourist Office
  10 Chesterfield St
  London W1X 8AH
  Tel: 0171 629 5238
  or
  Bahamas Tourist Office
  28th Floor North
  150 East 52nd St
  New York
  NY 10022
  Tel: 212 758 2777

BELIZE
Capital: Belmopan
Population: 190 792
Currency: Belizean Dollar
  (1 Bz$ = 100 cents)
Languages: English, Spanish
Time difference: GMT −6
Voltages: 110/220V
Entry requirements:
  UK – valid passport, return ticket
  USA/Canada – valid passport,
  return ticket
Vaccinations: Typhoid, polio, malaria
Tourist Board:
  Caribbean Tourism
  Vigilant House
  120 Wilton Rd
  London SW1V 1JZ
  Tel: 0171 233 8382

BHUTAN
Capital: Thimphu
Population: 1 375 400
Currency: Ngultrum
  (1 Nu = 100 chetrums)
Languages: Dzongkha
Time difference: GMT +6
Voltages: 220V
Entry requirements:
  UK – valid passport, visa, return
  ticket

USA/Canada – valid passport, visa, return ticket
Vaccinations: Yellow fever, cholera, typhoid, polio
Tourist Board:
Bhutan Tourism Corporation Ltd (BTCL)
PO Box 159
Thimpu, Bhutan
Tel: 22647

BORNEO (see MALAYSIA)

BOTSWANA
Capital: Gaborone
Population: 1 325 291
Currency: Pula (1P = 100 thebes)
Languages: English, Setswana
Time difference: GMT +2
Voltages: 220–240V
Entry requirements:
UK – valid passport, return ticket
USA/Canada – valid passport, return ticket
Vaccinations: Cholera, typhoid, polio, malaria
Tourist Board:
Tourism Development Unit
Ministry of Commerce & Industry
Private Bag 004
Gaborone, Botswana
Tel: 3 53024

BRAZIL
Capital: Brasilia
Population: 153 322 000
Currency: Cruzeiro
(1 Cr = 100 centavos)
Languages: Portuguese, French, German, Italian
Time difference: 4 time zones from GMT −2 to −5
Voltages: 110/126/220V
Entry requirements:
UK – valid passport, return ticket
USA/Canada – valid passport, visa, return ticket
Vaccinations: Typhoid, polio, malaria
Tourist Board:
Brazilian Information Office
32 Green Street
London W1Y 4AT
Tel: 0171 499 0877
or
3006 Massachusetts Ave NW
Washington, DC 20008
Tel: 202 745 2700

BRITISH VIRGIN ISLANDS
Capital: Road Town, Tortola
Population: 16 644
Currency: US Dollar
(US$1 = 100 cents)
Languages: English
Time difference: GMT −4
Voltages: 110/60V
Entry requirements:
UK – valid passport, return ticket
USA/Canada – valid ID card, return ticket
Vaccinations: Typhoid, polio
Tourist Board:
British Virgin Islands Tourist Board
110 St Martin's Lane
London WC2N 4DY
Tel: 0171 240 4259
or
Suite 511
370 Lexington Ave
New York
NY 10017
Tel: 212 696 0400

CAMEROON
Capital: Yaounde
Population: 11 540 000
Currency: CFA Franc
(CFA1 = 100 centimes)
Languages: French, English
Time difference: GMT +1
Voltages: 110/220V
Entry requirements:
UK – valid passport, visa, return ticket
USA/Canada – valid passport, visa, return ticket
Vaccinations: Yellow fever, cholera, typhoid, polio, malaria
Tourist Board:
Société Camerounaise de Tourisme (SOCATOUR)
BP 7138
Yaounde
Cameroon
Tel: 233 219

CANADA
Capital: Ottawa
Population: 27 408 900
Currency: Canadian Dollar
(1 Can$ = 100 cents)
Languages: English, French
Time difference: 6 time zones, from GMT −4 to GMT −8
Voltages: 110V

Entry requirements:
  UK – valid passport, return ticket
  USA/Canada – none
Vaccinations: none required
Tourist Board:
  Canada House
  Trafalgar Square
  London SW1 5BJ
  Tel: 0171 258 6346

CAYMAN ISLANDS
Capital: George Town
Population: 29 700
Currency: Cayman Islands Dollar
  (1 CI$ = 100 cents)
Languages: English
Time difference: GMT −5
Voltages: 110V
Entry requirements:
  UK – proof of nationality, return
  ticket
  USA/Canada – proof of nationality,
  return ticket
Vaccinations: Typhoid, polio
Tourist Board:
  Cayman Islands Department of
  Tourism
  Trevor House
  100 Brompton Rd
  London SW3 1EX
  Tel: 0171 581 9960
  or
  Suite 2733
  420 Lexington Ave
  New York, NY 10170
  Tel: 212 682 5582

CHILE
Capital: Santiago (de Chile)
Population: 13 599 441
Currency: Peso (1 Ch$ = 100 centavos)
Languages: Spanish, English
Time difference: 2 zones from
  GMT −3 to −6
Voltages: 220V
Entry requirements:
  UK – valid passport, return ticket
  USA/Canada – valid passport,
  return ticket
Vaccinations: Typhoid, polio
Tourist Board:
  Servicio Nacional de Turismo
  (SERNATUR)
  Casilla 14082
  Avenida Providencia 1550
  Santiago, Chile
  Tel: 2 236 0531

CHINA
Capital: Beijing
Population: 1 158 230 000
Currency: Yuan (Renminibi RMB) =
  10 chioa/jiao or 100 fen
Languages: Mandarin Chinese
Time difference: GMT +8
Voltages: 220/240V
Entry requirements:
  UK – valid passport, visa, return
  ticket
  USA/Canada – valid passport, visa,
  return ticket
Vaccinations: Yellow fever, typhoid,
  polio, malaria in some areas
Tourist Board:
  China Tourist Office
  4 Glentworth Street
  London NW1 5PG
  Tel: 0171 935 9787
  or
  China National Tourist Office
  60 East 42nd St
  New York
  NY 10165
  Tel: 212 867 0271

ECUADOR
Capital: Quito
Population: 11 078 400
Currency: Sucre (1 Su = 100 centavos)
Languages: Spanish with Quechua or
  Indian dialects
Time difference: GMT −5
  (Galapagos GMT −6)
Voltages: 110V
Entry requirements:
  UK – valid passport, return ticket
  USA/Canada – valid passport,
  return ticket
Vaccinations: Cholera, typhoid,
  polio, malaria
Tourist Board:
  Corporacion Equatoriana de
  Turismo
  Reina Victoriana 514 y Roca
  Quito
  Equador
  Tel: 2 527 002

FIJI
Capital: Suva
Population: 746 326
Currency: Fijian Dollar
  (1F$ = 100 cents)
Languages: Fijian, Hindu, English
Time difference: GMT +12

Voltages: 240V
Entry requirements:
UK – valid passport, return ticket
USA/Canada – valid passport,
return ticket
Vaccinations: Typhoid, polio
Tourist Board:
Fiji Visitors Bureau
Ministry of Tourism
GPO Box 1260
Suva
Fiji
Tel: 312 788
or
577 West Century Blvd
Los Angeles
CA 90045
Tel: 310 568 1616

FINLAND
Capital: Helsinki
Population: 4 998 478
Currency: Markka
(1FMk = 100 pennia)
Languages: Finnish
Time difference: GMT +2
Voltages: 220V
Entry requirements:
UK – valid passport
USA/Canada – valid passport
Vaccinations: none
Tourist Board:
Finnish Tourist Board
Greener House
66/68 Haymarket
London SW1Y 4RF
Tel: 0171 839 4048
or
655 Third Ave
New York
NY 10017
Tel: 212 949 2333

THE GAMBIA
Capital: Banjul
Population: 800 000
Currency: Gambian Dalasi
(1 Di = 100 bututs)
Languages: English
Time difference: GMT
Voltages: 220V
Entry requirements:
UK – valid passport, return ticket
USA – valid passport, visa, return
ticket
Canada – valid passport, return
ticket

Vaccinations: Yellow fever, cholera,
typhoid, polio, malaria
Tourist Board:
The Gambia National Tourism
Office
57 Kensington Court
London W8 5DG
Tel: 0171 937 6316

GREENLAND
Capital: Nuuk
Population: 55 533
Currency: Danish Krone
(1DK = 100 ore)
Languages: Greenlandic, Inuit, Danish
Time difference: GMT to GMT −4
Voltages: 220V
Entry requirements:
UK – valid passport, return ticket
USA/Canada – valid passport,
return ticket
Vaccinations: none
Tourist Board:
Danish Tourist Board
55 Sloane St
London SW1X 9SY
Tel: 0171 259 5959

ICELAND
Capital: Reykjavik
Population: 262 204
Currency: Iceland Krone
(1 IKr = 100 aurar)
Languages: Icelandic, English, Danish
Time difference: GMT
Voltages: 220V
Entry requirements:
UK – valid passport, return ticket
USA/Canada – valid passport,
return ticket
Vaccinations: none
Tourist Board:
Iceland Tourist Bureau/Iceland Air
172 Tottenham Court Road
London W1P 9LG
Tel: 0171 388 5346

INDIA
Capital: New Delhi
Population: 846 302 688
Currency: Rupee (1 RS = 100 paise)
Languages: English, Hindi, Urdu
Time difference: GMT +5.5
Voltages: 220V
Entry requirements:
UK – valid passport, visa
USA/Canada – valid passport, visa

Vaccinations: Yellow fever, cholera,
typhoid, polio, malaria
Tourist Board:
Government of India Tourist Office
7 Cork Street
London W1X 1PB
Tel: 0171 437 3677
or
Suite 15
30 Rockefeller Plaza
North Mezzanine
New York, NY 10112
Tel: 212 586 4901/2/3

INDONESIA
Capital: Jakarta
Population: 182 000 000
Currency: Rupiah (1 Rp = 100 sen)
Languages: Bahasa Indonesian
Time difference: GMT −9
Voltages: 110V, 220V
Entry requirements:
   UK − valid passport, return ticket
   USA/Canada − valid passport,
   return ticket
Vaccinations: Cholera, typhoid,
polio, malaria in some areas
Tourist Board:
Malaysian Tourism Promotion
Board
57 Trafalgar Square
London WC2 5DU
Tel: 0171 930 7932
or
Suite 804
818 West Seventh St
Los Angeles, CA 90017
Tel: 213 689 9702

JAMAICA
Capital: Kingstown
Population: 2 374 193
Currency: Jamaican Dollar
   (1J$ = 100 cents)
Languages: English
Time difference: GMT −5
Voltages: 110V (220V in some hotels)
Entry requirements:
   UK − valid passport, return ticket
   USA/Canada − valid national ID
   card, return ticket
Vaccinations: Typhoid, polio
Tourist Board:
Jamaica Tourist Board
1–2 Prince Consort Rd
London SW7 2BZ
Tel: 0171 224 0505

or
20th Floor
801 Second Ave
New York
NY 10017
Tel: 212 856 9727

KENYA
Capital: Nairobi
Population: 25 905 000
Currency: Kenyan Shilling
   (1KSh = 100 cents)
Languages: Kiswahili, English
Time difference: GMT +3
Voltages: 220V/240V
Entry requirements:
   UK/Canada − valid passport,
   return ticket
   USA − valid passport, visa, return
   ticket
Vaccinations: Yellow fever, cholera,
typhoid, polio, malaria
Tourist Board:
Kenya Tourist Office
25 Brook's Mews
London W1Y 1LG
Tel: 0171 355 3144
or
Kenya Tourism Office
424 Madison Ave
New York
NY 10017
Tel: 212 486 1300

LESOTHO
Capital: Maseru
Population: 1 700 000
Currency: Loti (1 Lo = 100 lisente)
Languages: Sesotho, English
Time difference: GMT +2
Voltages: 250V
Entry requirements:
   UK − valid passport, return ticket
   USA/Canada − valid passport, visa,
   return ticket
Vaccinations: Yellow fever, cholera,
typhoid, polio, malaria
Tourist Board:
Lesotho National Tourist Board
PO Box 1378
Maseru 100
Lesotho
Tel: 323 760

MALAWI
Capital: Lilongwe
Population: 8 556 000

Currency: Kwache
(1 Mk = 100 tambala)
Languages: English, Chichewa
Time difference: GMT +2
Voltages: 230/240V
Entry requirements:
  UK – valid passport, return ticket
  USA/Canada – valid passport,
  return ticket
Vaccinations: Cholera, typhoid,
  polio, malaria
Tourist Board:
  High Commission for the Republic
  of Malawi & Tourist Office
  33 Grosvenor Street
  London W1X 0DE
  Tel: 0171 491 4172/7

MALAYSIA
Capital: Kuala Lumpur
Population: 18 178 000
Currency: Rinngit (1R = 100 sen)
Languages: Bahasa Malaysian, English
Time difference: GMT +8
Voltages: 220V
Entry requirements:
  UK – valid passport, return ticket
  USA/Canada – valid passport,
  return ticket
Vaccinations: Cholera, typhoid, polio
Tourist Board:
  Malaysia Tourism Promotion
  Board
  57 Trafalgar Square
  London WC2N 5DU
  Tel: 0171 930 7932
  or
  Suite 804
  818 West Seventh Street
  Los Angeles
  CA 90017
  Tel: 213 689 9702

MOROCCO
Capital: Rabat
Population: 25 208 000
Currency: Moroccan Dirham
  (1DH = 100 centimes)
Languages: Arabic, French, Berber
Time difference: GMT
Voltages: 110–127V
Entry requirements:
  UK – valid passport, return ticket
  USA/Canada – valid passport,
  return ticket
Vaccinations: Typhoid, polio, malaria
  in some rural areas

Tourist Board:
  Moroccan National Tourist Office
  205 Regent St
  London WR1 7DE
  Tel: 0171 437 0073
  or
  20 East 46th St
  New York
  NY 10017
  Tel: 212 557 2520

NAMIBIA
Capital: Windhoek
Population: 1 426 700
Currency: South African Rand
  (1 R = 100 cents)
Languages: English, Africaans,
  German, Herero
Time difference: GMT +2
Voltages: 220/240V
Entry requirements:
  UK – valid passport, return ticket
  USA/Canada – valid passport,
  return ticket
Vaccinations: Yellow fever, typhoid,
  polio, malaria (rural areas)
Tourist Board:
  Namibia Tourism
  Private Bag 13346
  Windhoek
  Namibia
  Tel: 61 284 9111

NEPAL
Capital: Kathmandu
Population: 18 462 081
Currency: Nepalese Rupee
  (1 Rs = 100 piasa)
Languages: Nepali
Time difference: GMT +5½
Voltages: 220V
Entry requirements:
  UK – valid passport, visa
  USA/Canada – valid passport, visa
Vaccinations: Cholera, typhoid,
  polio, malaria (rural areas)
Tourist Board:
  Department of Tourism
  HM Government of Nepal
  Tripureshor
  Kathmandu
  Nepal
  Tel: 1 221 306

NEW ZEALAND
Capital: Wellington
Population: 3 434 900

Currency: New Zealand Dollar
(1NZ$ = 100 cents)
Languages: English, Maori
Time difference: GMT +12
Voltages: 230V
Entry requirements:
    UK – valid passport, return ticket
    USA/Canada – valid passport,
    return ticket
Vaccinations: none required
Tourist Board:
    New Zealand Tourism Board
    New Zealand House
    80 Haymarket
    London SW1Y 4TQ
    Tel: 0171 973 0360
    or
    501 Santa Monica Blvd
    Suite 300
    Santa Monica
    CA 90401
    Tel: 310 395 7480

NORWAY, SVALBARD/ SPITSBERGEN

Capital: Oslo
Population: 4 274 030
Currency: Norwegian Krone
    (1Nkr = 100 ore)
Languages: Norwegian, Lappish,
    English
Time difference: GMT +1
Voltages: 220V
Entry requirements:
    UK – valid passport
    USA/Canada – valid passport
Vaccinations: none
Tourist Board:
    Norwegian Tourist Board
    Charles House
    5–11 Lower Regent St
    London SW1Y 4LR
    Tel: 0171 839 6255
    or
    655 Third Ave
    New York
    NY 10017
    Tel: 212 949 2333

PAPUA NEW GUINEA

Capital: Port Moresby
Population: 3 772 000
Currency: Kina (1 Ka = 100 toea)
Languages: English, Pidgen English,
    Hiri Motu
Time difference: GMT +10
Voltages: 240V

Entry requirements:
    UK – valid passport, visa, return
    ticket
    USA/Canada – valid passport, visa,
    return ticket
Vaccinations: Cholera, typhoid,
    polio, malaria
Tourist Board:
    Tourist Development Corporation
    PO Box 7144
    Boroko
    Papua New Guinea
    Tel: 272 521
    or
    Papua New Guinea Tourism Office
    Suite 3000
    5000 Birch St
    Newport Beach
    CA 92660
    Tel: 714 752 5400

PERU

Capital: Lima
Population: 22 453 861
Currency: Nuevo Sol = 100 centimos
Languages: Spanish, Quechua
Time difference: GMT −5
Voltages: 220V
Entry requirements:
    UK – valid passport, return ticket
    USA/Canada – valid passport,
    return ticket
Vaccinations: Yellow fever, cholera,
    typhoid, polio, malaria
Tourist Board:
    Fondo de Promocion Turistica
    (FOPTUR)
    Calle Uno S/N Urb Corpac
    Piso 14
    Mitinci
    San Isidro
    Lima, Peru
    Tel: 14 408 333

RUSSIAN FEDERATION

Capital: Moscow
Population: 148 485 000
Currency: Rouble
    (1 Rub = 100 kopeks)
Languages: Russian
Time difference: varies
Voltages: 220V
Entry requirements:
    UK – valid passport, visa, return
    ticket
    USA/Canada – valid passport, visa,
    return ticket

Vaccinations: none
Tourist Board:
  Intourist Travel Ltd
  Intourist House
  219 Marsh Wall
  Meridian Gate 11
  London E14 9FJ
  Tel: 0171 538 8600
  or
  Suite 603
  610 Fifth Avenue
  New York
  NY 10111
  Tel: 212 757 3884

ST VINCENT & THE GRENADINES

Capital: Kingstown
Population: 106 499
Currency: Eastern Caribbean Dollar
  (1EC$ = 100 cents)
Languages: English
Time difference: GMT −4
Voltages: 220/240V
Entry requirements:
  UK – valid passport, return ticket
  USA/Canada – proof of identity,
  return ticket
Vaccinations: Typhoid, polio
Tourist Board:
  St Vincent & The Grenadines
  Tourist Office
  10 Kensington Court
  London W8 5DL
  Tel: 0171 937 6570
  or
  21st Floor
  801 Second Ave
  New York
  NY 10017
  Tel: 212 687 4981

SOUTH AFRICA

Capital: Pretoria
Population: 26 288 390
Currency: Rand (1R = 100 cents)
Languages: Africaans, English
Time difference: GMT +2
Voltages: 250V Pretoria, 220/230V
  elsewhere
Entry requirements:
  UK – valid passport, return ticket
  USA/Canada – valid passport,
  return ticket
Vaccinations: Cholera, typhoid,
  polio, malaria in some areas

Tourist Board:
  South African Tourist Board
  (SATOUR)
  5–6 Alt Grove
  London SW19 4DZ
  Tel: 0181 944 8080
  or
  SATOUR
  Suite 2040
  500 Fifth Avenue
  New York
  NY 10110
  Tel: 212 730 2929

SWEDEN

Capital: Stockholm
Population: 8 692 013
Currency: Swedish Krone
  (1SKr = 100 ore)
Languages: Swedish, Lapp,
  English
Time difference: GMT +1
Voltages: 220V
Entry requirements:
  UK – valid passport
  USA/Canada – valid passport
Vaccinations: none
Tourist Board:
  Swedish Travel & Tourism Council
  73 Welbeck St
  London W1M 8AN
  Tel: 01891 200 280
  or
  18th Floor
  655 Third Ave
  New York
  NY 10017
  Tel: 212 949 2333

SVALBARD – see NORWAY

TANZANIA

Capital: Dodoma
Population: 25 635 000
Currency: Tanzanian Shilling
  (1 TSh = 100 cents)
Languages: Swahili, English
Time difference: GMT +3
Voltages: 230V
Entry requirements:
  UK – valid passport, return ticket
  USA/Canada – valid passport, visa,
  return ticket
Vaccinations: Yellow fever, cholera,
  typhoid, polio, malaria

Tourist Board:
Tanzanian Trade Centre
78–80 Borough High St
London SE1 1LL
Tel: 0171 407 0566
or
Tanzanian Tourist Office
8th Floor
205 East 42nd St
New York
NY 10017
Tel: 212 545 0720

THAILAND
Capital: Bangkok
Population: 56 532 000
Currency: Baht (1 Bt = 100 satang)
Languages: Thai, English, Malay
Time difference: GMT +7
Voltages: 220V
Entry requirements:
UK – valid passport, return ticket
USA/Canada – valid passport,
return ticket
Vaccinations: Cholera, typhoid,
polio, malaria
Tourist Board:
Tourism Authority of Thailand
49 Albermarle St
London W1X 3FE
Tel: 0171 499 7679
or
Suite 2449
5 World Trade Centre
New York
NY 10048
Tel: 212 432 0433/5

TIBET – see **CHINA**

UK
Capital: London
Population: 57 649 200
Currency: Pound (£1 = 100 pence)
Languages: English, some Welsh and
Gaelic
Time difference: GMT (EST +5)
Voltages: 240V
Entry requirements:
USA/Canada – valid passport
Vaccinations: none
Tourist Board:
British Tourist Authority
Thames Tower
Black's Road
London W6 9EL
Tel: 0181 846 9000

or
7th Floor
551 Fifth Avenue
New York, NY 10176
Tel: 212 986 2200

USA
Capital: Washington, DC
Population: 255 082 000
Currency: US Dollar
(1 US$ = 100 cents)
Languages: English
Time difference: Various time zones
from GMT −5 to GMT −10
Voltages: 110/120V
Entry requirements:
UK – valid passport, visa, return
ticket
Canada – none
Vaccinations: none
Tourist Board:
United States Travel & Tourism
Administration
PO Box 1EN
London W1A 1EN
Tel: 0171 459 4466
or
14 Constitution Ave NW
Washington, DC 20230
Tel: 202 482 4904

VENEZUELA
Capital: Caracas
Population: 20 226 227
Currency: Bolivar
(1B = 100 centimos)
Languages: Spanish
Time difference: GMT −4
Voltages: 110V
Entry requirements:
UK – valid passport, return ticket
USA/Canada – valid passport,
return ticket
Vaccinations: Yellow fever, typhoid,
polio, malaria
Tourist Board:
Corpoturismo
Apartado 50200
Centro Capriles 7
Plaza Venezuela
Caracas
Venezuela
Tel: 2 781 8370

VIETNAM
Capital: Hanoi
Population: 66 200 000
Currency: New Dong
(1D = 10 hao = 100xu)
Languages: Vietnamese
Time difference: GMT +7
Voltages: 110/220V
Entry requirements:
UK – valid passport, visa, return ticket
USA/Canada – valid passport, visa, return ticket
Vaccinations: Cholera, typhoid, polio, malaria
Tourist Board:
West East Travel (UK handling agent)
39b Nicoll Road
London NW19 9EX
Tel: 0181 961 0117

ZAMBIA
Capital: Lusaka
Population: 8 023 000
Currency: Kwacha (1K = 100 ngwee)
Languages: English, tribal dialects
Time difference: GMT +2
Voltages: 220V
Entry requirements:
UK – valid passport, return ticket
USA/Canada – valid passport, visa, return ticket
Vaccinations: Yellow fever, cholera, typhoid, polio, malaria

Tourist Board:
Zambia National Tourist Board
2 Palace Gate
London W8 5NG
Tel: 0171 589 6655
or
237 East 52nd St
New York
NY 10022
Tel: 212 308 2155

ZIMBABWE
Capital: Harare
Population: 10 401 767
Currency: Zimbabwe Dollar
(1 Z$ = 100 cents)
Languages: English, Shona & Ndebele dialects
Time difference: GMT +2
Voltages: 220/240V
Entry requirements:
UK – valid passport, return ticket
USA/Canada – valid passport, return ticket
Vaccinations: Cholera, typhoid, polio, malaria
Tourist Board:
Zimbabwe Tourist Board
429 Strand
London WC2R 0QE
Tel: 0171 836 7755
or
Suite 412
1270 Avenue of the Americas
New York, NY 10020
Tel: 212 1090

APPENDIX 2
The Himalayan Tourist Code

Protect the natural environment.
Limit deforestation – make no open fires and discourage others from doing so on your behalf. Where water is heated by scarce firewood, use as little as possible. When possible, choose accommodation that uses kerosene, or fuel-efficient wood stoves.

Remove litter, burn or bury paper and carry out all non-degradable litter. Graffiti are permanent examples of environmental pollution.

Keep local water clean and avoid using pollutants such as detergents in streams or springs. If no toilet facilities are available, make sure you are at least 30 metres away from water sources, and bury or cover wastes.

Plants should be left to flourish in their natural environment. Taking cuttings, seeds and roots is illegal in many parts of the Himalayas.

Help your guides and porters to follow conservation measures.

As a guest, respect local traditions, protect local culture, maintain local pride.
When taking photographs, respect privacy. Ask permission and use restraint.

Respect holy places. Preserve what you have come to see and never touch or remove religious objects. Shoes should be removed when visiting temples.

Giving to children encourages begging. A donation to a project, health centre or school is a more constructive way to help.

You will be accepted and welcomed if you follow local customs. Use only your right hand for eating and greeting. Do not share cutlery or cups, etc. It is polite to use both hands when giving or receiving gifts.

Respect for local etiquette earns you respect. Loose, lightweight clothes are preferable to revealing shorts, skimpy tops and tight-fitting action wear. Hand holding or kissing in public are disliked by local people.

Observe standard food and bed charges but do not condone overcharging. Remember when you're shopping that the bargains you buy may only be possible because of low incomes to others.

Visitors who value local traditions encourage local pride and maintain local cultures. Please help local people to gain a realistic view of life in Western countries.

The above Code has been produced by the organization Tourism Concern. Although it refers specifically to the Himalayas, much of it is equally applicable in other wilderness areas in other parts of the world.

INDEX 1
Countries and what they offer

ANTARCTICA, 101–104
cruises; by light aircraft

AUSTRALIA, 104–108
bush-walking & outback tours; canoeing & kayaking; marine-life exploration; scuba diving & snorkelling; surfing; white-water rafting

BAHAMAS, 108–112
diving & snorkelling; safaris; swimming with dolphins

BELIZE, 113–116
diving; hiking; mountain biking; horse riding; safari tour

BHUTAN, 116–119
trekking

BORNEO, 120–124
expeditions & safaris; climbing & mountaineering; river rafting; wildlife

BOTSWANA, 124–126
safaris (mainly for wildlife – animals & birds)

BRAZIL, 127–129
exploration of Amazon & Andes; watersports & sailing; wildlife

BRITISH VIRGIN ISLANDS, 130–132
diving & snorkelling; horse riding; windsurfing

CAMEROON, 132–135
climbing & mountaineering; safaris; wildlife

CANADA: BRITISH COLUMBIA, 135–139
canoeing & kayaking; caving; climbing & mountaineering; hiking & trekking; mountain biking; horse riding; river rafting; scuba diving; skiing

CANADA: NORTHWEST TERRITORIES, 140–143
biking; camping & hiking; canoeing & kayaking; dog sledging; river rafting; scuba diving, ski touring

CANADA: THE YUKON, 143–146
climbing & mountaineering; cycle touring; dog sledging; hiking; river exploration (by canoe, kayak & raft); ski touring

CAYMAN ISLANDS, 147–150
diving & scuba diving; submarine trips; watersports (parasailing, waterskiing, windsurfing)

CHILE, 150–153
climbing; kayaking; horse riding; river rafting; skiing; trekking

CHINA, 154–157
cycling; guided packaged tours (esp along Silk Road); [cross-country skiing; mountaineering; hiking].

ECUADOR, 158–161
exploration of Andes, Amazon & Galapagos Islands; trekking with mules or horses

FAROE ISLANDS, 162–165
bird-watching; climbing; hiking/walking; sailing trips

FIJI, 165–167
hiking & trekking; rainforest excursions; caving; diving & snorkelling; watersports, especially windsurfing

FINLAND, 168–171
summer: camping & hiking; canoeing; cycling; sailing
winter: ski touring; reindeer safaris

THE GAMBIA, 172–174
'Soft' adventure: beach life, surfing & windsurfing; bird life; travel by bus or cycle

GREENLAND, 175–177
dog sledging, ski touring; trekking; birdlife, whale-watching

ICELAND, 178–181
hiking, back-packing in spectacular country; pony trekking; skiing

INDIA, 182–186
trekking at low or high altitude; white-water rafting; riding; skiing;

hang-gliding, paragliding, ballooning; scuba diving; wildlife; camel safaris
INDONESIA, 187–190
hiking & camping among rainforests and volcanoes; snorkelling & scuba diving; rafting; unique flora & fauna
JAMAICA, 191–194
watersports (windsurfing & waterskiing); scuba diving; sailing; river rafting; trekking to the interior (flora & fauna)
KENYA, 195–197
wildlife safaris – by vehicle, riding, on foot, by air, by balloon; mountaineering; watersports (windsurfing, snorkelling & scuba diving)
LESOTHO, 198–201
expeditions on foot or horseback, in vehicles or aircraft; pony trekking; Outward Bound Centre (for rock climbing, abseiling, canoeing, etc)
MALAWI, 201–204
safaris and treks for scenery and wildlife; rock climbing; scuba diving
MOROCCO, 205–208
Atlas Mountains for hiking, trekking and winter sports
NAMIBIA, 208–212
camping safaris in desert & mountain country; wildlife
NEPAL, 212–216
trekking and climbing expeditions in mountain terrain; jungle safari; river rafting; mountain biking
NEW ZEALAND, 217–220
hiking & walking treks; climbing; river rafting; canoeing; yachting; surfing and windsurfing; diving
NORWAY, 220–223
skiing and ski touring; canoeing; climbing; hiking; pony trekking; river rafting; scuba diving
PAPUA NEW GUINEA, 224–226
walking & trekking in mountainous hinterland; unique flora & fauna; snorkelling; scuba diving; windsurfing; waterskiing; canoeing
PERU, 226–229
trips in Andes Mountains and Amazon Basin; Inca trail
RUSSIAN FEDERATION, 229–232
packaged adventure, in summer (mountaineering, caving, mountain biking, trekking, riding, river rafting) and winter (skiing and troika rides)
ST VINCENT AND THE GRENADINES, 233–236
underwater exploration – diving and snorkelling; sailing; trekking in volcanic interior
SOUTH AFRICA, 237–241
almost unlimited activities: safaris (wildlife and flora); hiking; climbing; ballooning; diving; riding; sailing; river rafting; skiing
SVALBARD (SPITZBERGEN) 242–245
camping & trekking in 24-hour daylight summer; polar bears; birdlife
TANZANIA, 245–248
paradise for big-game viewing; climbing Kilimanjaro
THAILAND, 249–251
trekking to historical sites; wildlife; some river rafting; canoe trips; riding working elephants
TIBET, 252–255
officially approved parties only; mountainous terrain; Sherpa trekking holiday
UNITED KINGDOM, 256–259
many opportunities for outdoor activities (eg walking, hiking, climbing, canoeing, mountain biking, windsurfing, sailing, pony trekking; hang-gliding and paragliding) and in multi-activity centres run by trained instructors and supervisors
USA
ballooning; caving; diving; mountain biking; ski touring; tall-ship sailing; youth activities
USA: ALASKA, 260–263
user-friendly region of wilderness, mountain ranges, volcanoes, Arctic tundra, glaciers & forests: skiing; kayaking; canoeing; backpacking; rafting; dog sledging; ballooning; climbing; wildlife; flora & fauna
US VIRGIN ISLANDS, 264–266
underwater observation – snorkelling; scuba diving; board sailing
VENEZUELA, 267–270
exploration underwater and of Amazon region and the Andes; wildlife, especially birdlife

VIETNAM, 271–273
  tropical flora & fauna in scenic and
  colourful countryside; biking tours
ZAMBIA, 273–276
  camping safaris to observe abundant wildlife; Zambesi and Victoria
Falls; river rafting
ZIMBABWE, 276–279
  safaris to observe abundant wildlife
  including birdlife; Victoria Falls;
  river rafting and kayaking; hiking
  and climbing

INDEX 2
Activities and where to find them

Entries in capitals refer to activities profiled in Section 3

abseiling: Lesotho
back-packing: Iceland; USA (Alaska)
BALLOONING, 55–57: India; Kenya; South Africa; USA (Alaska)
biking, *also see* MOUNTAIN BIKING. Canada (NW Territories); China; Finland; The Gambia; Vietnam
birdlife: Botswana; Faroe Islands; The Gambia; Greenland; Spitzbergen; Venezuela; Zambia; Zimbabwe
board-sailing: US Virgin Islands
bush-walking: *also see* OVERLANDING. Australia; Kenya
camel safaris: India
camping: Canada (NW Territories); Finland; Indonesia; Namibia; Nepal; Spitzbergen; Zambia
CANOEING & KAYAKING, 57–59: Australia, Canada (British Columbia, NW Territories and The Yukon); Finland; Lesotho; New Zealand; Norway; Papua New Guinea; Thailand; UK; USA (Alaska)
CAVING, 59–61: Canada (British Columbia); Fiji; Russia; USA
CLIMBING & MOUNTAINEERING, 61–64: Borneo; Cameroon; Canada (British Columbia and The Yukon); Chile; China; Faroe Islands; Kenya; Lesotho; Nepal; New Zealand; Norway; Russia; South Africa; Tanzania (Kilimanjaro); Tibet; UK; USA (Alaska); Zimbabwe
cycle tours, *also see* biking and MOUNTAIN BIKING. Canada (The Yukon)
diving, *also see* SCUBA DIVING and

snorkelling: Bahamas; Belize; British Virgin Islands; Cayman Islands; Fiji; Kenya; New Zealand; St Vincent; South Africa; USA
DOG SLEDGING, 65–76: Canada (NW Territories and The Yukon); Greenland; USA (Alaska)
elephant riding: Thailand
EXPEDITIONS, 67–69: Borneo; Brazil; Lesotho; Peru; Venezuela
flora & fauna: Indonesia; Jamaica; Papua New Guinea; South Africa; Tanzania; USA (Alaska); Vietnam; Zambia; Zimbabwe
glaciers: USA (Alaska)
HANG-GLIDING, 70–71: India; UK
hiking: Belize; Canada (NW Territories and The Yukon); China; Faroe Islands; Fiji; Iceland; Indonesia; Lesotho; Morocco; New Zealand; Norway; South Africa; UK; Zimbabwe
horse riding: *see* RIDING & PONY TREKKING
Inca trail: Peru
kayaking: Canada (NW Territories); Chile; USA (Alaska); Zimbabwe
MOUNTAIN BIKING, 72–74: Belize; Canada (British Columbia); Nepal; Russia; UK; USA
multi-activity centres: UK
OVERLANDING, 74–76: Australia
PARAGLIDING, 77–79, and parasailing: Cayman Islands; India; UK
polar-bear watching: Spitzbergen
reindeer safaris: Finland
RIVER RAFTING, 79–81: Australia; Borneo; Canada (British Columbia, NW Territories and The Yukon); Chile; India; Indonesia; Jamaica; Nepal; New Zealand; Norway; Russia; South Africa;

Thailand; USA (including Alaska);
Zambia; Zimbabwe
RIDING & PONY TREKKING, 82–
84: British Virgin Islands; Canada
(British Columbia); Chile; Iceland;
India; Jamaica; Kenya; Lesotho;
Morocco; Norway; Russia; South
Africa; UK
rock climbing: see CLIMBING &
MOUNTAINEERING
SAFARIS, 84–86: Australia; Baha-
mas; Belize; Borneo; Botswana;
Cameroon; Kenya; Malawi; Nami-
bia; Nepal; South Africa; Tanzania
sailing: Brazil; Faroe Islands; Fin-
land; Jamaica; St Vincent; South
Africa; UK
SCUBA DIVING, 86–88: Australia;
Bahamas; Canada (British Col-
umbia and NW Territories); Cay-
man Islands; India; Indonesia;
Jamaica; Kenya; Malawi; Norway;
Papua New Guinea; US Virgin Islands
skiing: see SKI TOURING
SKI TOURING, 89–91: Canada
(British Columbia, NW Territories
and The Yukon); China; Finland;
Greenland; Iceland; Norway; Russia; South Africa; USA (Alaska)
snorkelling: Australia; Bahamas,
British Virgin Islands; Fiji; Indonesia; Kenya; Papua New Guinea; St
Vincent; US Virgin Islands
submarine trips: Cayman Islands
surfing: Australia; The Gambia; New
Zealand
swimming with dolphins: Bahamas

TALL-SHIP SAILING, 92–94: UK;
USA
TREKKING, 95–97; also see RID-
ING & PONY TREKKING: Bhu-
tan; Canada (British Columbia);
Chile; Ecuador; Fiji; Greenland;
Malawi; Morocco; Nepal; New
Zealand; Papua New Guinea; Rus-
sia; St Vincent; Spitzbergen; Thai-
land; Tibet
troika rides: Russia
underwater exploration: also see
SCUBA DIVING and snorkelling:
Australia; St Vincent; US Virgin
Islands; Venezuela
volcanoes: USA (Alaska)
waterskiing: Cayman Islands;
Jamaica; Papua New Guinea
watersports: also see SCUBA DIV-
ING, waterskiing and windsurfing:
Brazil; Jamaica; Kenya
whale-watching: Greenland
white-water rafting: see RIVER
RAFTING
wildlife: Borneo; Botswana; Brazil;
Cameroon; India; Kenya; Namibia; South Africa; Tanzania; Thai-
land; USA (Alaska); Venezuela;
Zambia: Zimbabwe
windsurfing: British Virgin Islands;
Cayman Islands; Fiji; The Gambia;
Jamaica; Kenya; New Zealand;
Papua New Guinea; UK
winter sports: Morocco, see also SKI
TOURING
yachting: New Zealand
YOUTH ACTIVITIES, 98–100: UK,
USA

INDEX 3
Tour operators

This index is confined to tour operators in the UK, the USA and Canada offering holiday activities worldwide. Details of local tour operators can be found in Section 3 (*Activities*) and Section 4 (*Countries*). Entries in bold type refer to companies described in Section 2 (*Companies*) on pages 36–52. Details of organizations specific to particular activities will be found under the appropriate heading in Section 3 (*Activities*) on pages 53–100.

Abercrombie & Kent 41, 56, 85, 103, 126, 278
Accessible Isolation Holidays 58, 59, 139
Acorn Activities 258
Action Holidays 99
Adrift 81, 275, 279
Adventure Center 38, 42, 43
Adventure Network International 103
Adventure Travel Centre 75,76
Adventure Travel Society 25, 34
Africa Exclusive 86
Africa Explorations 86
Alaska River Adventures 66
AmeriCan Adventures 262
Arctic Experience 36, 58, 69, 97, 143, 176, 180, 181, 244, 262
Arcturus Expeditions 66, 69, 103, 143, 176, 222, 244
Aurora Expeditions 177
Brathay Exploration Group 68
British Schools' Exploring Society 68
British Trust for Conservation Volunteers 68
British Virgin Island Holidays 131
Camper & Nicholsons 236
Caribbean Connection 193, 236
Caribtours 131, 266
China Adventures 156
Classic Nepal 64, 216, 255
Coral Cay Conservation 68

Crestar 236
David Oswin Expeditions 180
Dick Phillips 181
Discover the World 37, 86, 111, 257
Dive & Sail 149
Divers World 149
Dragoman 7, 38, 48, 75, 134
Earthwatch Europe 68
Encounter Overland 7, 39, 48, 75, 86, 123, 129, 134, 156, 228
Endeavour Training 68, 99
Exodus Expeditions 40, 48, 58, 59, 69, 73, 75, 86, 97, 119, 153, 156, 207, 211, 228, 231, 240, 247, 272
ExplorAsia 41, 64, 97
Explore Worldwide 42, 58, 59, 69, 86, 97, 119, 123, 153, 156, 160, 167, 190, 194, 203, 211, 228, 231, 251, 262, 269, 272
Frontier 68
Galapagos Adventure Tours 160
Gambia Experience, The 174
Glenmore Lodge 63
Guerba Expeditions 7, 43, 48, 69, 75, 86, 97, 123, 126, 134, 160, 197, 240, 247, 248, 251, 272, 275, 278
High Places 44, 73, 97, 153, 160, 185, 197, 203, 240
Himalayan Kingdoms 97, 160, 215
Himalayan Travel 40, 45, 46
Ilkeston Co-Op Travel & Tours 269
Imaginative Traveller, The 45, 48, 123, 189, 251, 255, 257
Inner Quest (USA) 100
Intourist 231
John Hunt Exploration Group 68, 99; *see* Endeavour Training
Journey Latin America 153, 160, 228, 269
Karakoram Experience 73, 119, 263
Kumuka 86
Marco Polo Travel Advisory Service 76
Mountain Travel Sobek 81, 86, 97, 153, 190, 219, 275, 277

Mysteries of India *see* Pleasureseekers
Natural World, The 166, 225
Norwegian Coastal Voyages 221
Okovango Tours & Safaris 58, 83
Outward Bound Trust (UK) 63, 99, 259
Outward Bound (USA) 66, 91
PGL Adventure 99, 259
Pleasureseekers 185
Raleigh International 68
Ramblers Holidays 97, 171, 257
Reef & Rainforest Tours 83, 88
Regal Diving 149
Safari Consultants 85
Sherpa Expeditions 46, 73, 97, 207, 255, 257
Simply Caribbean 131, 193
SPICE 54, 258
Super Natural Adventures 47, 58, 59, 81, 83, 139, 146, 263
Thin Air Expeditions 64, 215
Top Deck Travel 75
Trailfinders 16, 48
Trek America 49, 146, 263
Trekforce 68
Voyageurs J & C 83
Waymark Holidays 170, 222, 223, 244
Westeast Travel 272
Wexas International 25, 50, 86, 88, 197
World Challenge 68
World Expeditions 51, 64, 69, 156, 189, 215, 228, 251, 254, 272
Worldwide Journeys & Expeditions 7, 52, 63, 69, 85, 97, 119, 123, 207, 211, 240, 247, 275
Youth Hostel Association 60, 63, 79, 99, 259